Trans-Indigenous

Indigenous Americas

Robert Warrior, Series Editor

Chadwick Allen, *Trans-Indigenous: Methodologies for Global Native Literary Studies*

Raymond D. Austin, *Navajo Courts and Navajo Common Law: A Tradition of Tribal Self-Governance*

Lisa Brooks, *The Common Pot: The Recovery of Native Space in the Northeast*

Kevin Bruyneel, *The Third Space of Sovereignty: The Postcolonial Politics of U.S.–Indigenous Relations*

Daniel Heath Justice, *Our Fire Survives the Storm: A Cherokee Literary History*

Thomas King, *The Truth About Stories: A Native Narrative*

Scott Richard Lyons, *X-Marks: Native Signatures of Assent*

Jean M. O'Brien, *Firsting and Lasting: Writing Indians out of Existence in New England*

Paul Chaat Smith, *Everything You Know about Indians Is Wrong*

Gerald Vizenor, *Bear Island: The War at Sugar Point*

Robert Warrior, *The People and the Word: Reading Native Nonfiction*

Robert A. Williams Jr., *Like a Loaded Weapon: The Rehnquist Court, Indian Rights, and the Legal History of Racism in America*

Trans-Indigenous

Methodologies for Global Native Literary Studies

Chadwick Allen

Indigenous Americas

University of Minnesota Press
Minneapolis
London

A section of the Introduction originally appeared in "A Trans*national* Native American Studies? Why Not Studies That Are Trans-*Indigenous?*," *Journal of Transnational American Studies* 4, no. 1 (2012). An earlier version of chapter 1 originally appeared as "Unspeaking the Settler: 'The Indian Today' in International Perspective," *American Studies* 46, no. 3–4 (Fall–Winter 2005), and in *Indigenous Studies Today* 1 (Fall 2005–Spring 2006): 39–57. An earlier version of chapter 3 originally appeared as "Engaging the Politics and Pleasures of Indigenous Aesthetics," *Western American Literature* 41, no. 2 (Summer 2006): 146–75. An earlier version of chapter 4 originally appeared as "Rere Kē/Moving Differently: Indigenizing Methodologies for Comparative Indigenous Literary Studies," *Studies in American Indian Literatures* 19, no. 4 (Winter 2007): 1–26, and in *Journal of New Zealand Literature* 24, no. 2 (2007): 44–72. A section of chapter 5 originally appeared as "Serpentine Figures, Sinuous Relations: Thematic Geometry in Allison Hedge Coke's *Blood Run*," *American Literature* 82, no. 4 (December 2010): 807–34.

"Burial Mound" by Allison Hedge Coke is reproduced courtesy of the poet and Salt Publishing. "Sad Joke on a Marae" by Apirana Taylor is reproduced courtesy of the poet. "Blood Quantum" by Naomi Losch is reproduced courtesy of the poet. "Comparatively Speaking, There Is No Struggle" by Jacq Carter is reproduced courtesy of the poet. "Celebrators '88" by Kevin Gilbert is reproduced courtesy of his estate. "Carnegie, Oklahoma, 1919" by N. Scott Momaday is reproduced courtesy of the poet. "When I of Fish Eat" by Rowley Habib, with illustrations by Ralph Hotere, is reproduced courtesy of the Maori Purposes Fund Board. "Waka 29: waka taua," "51," and "53" by Robert Sullivan are reproduced courtesy of Auckland University Press. "The buffalo grass is still" from *Indians' Summer* by Nasnaga reprinted by permission of HarperCollins Publishers; copyright 1975 by Nasnaga.

Every effort was made to obtain permission to reproduce material in this book. If any proper acknowledgment has not been included here, we encourage copyright holders to notify the publisher.

Published by the University of Minnesota Press
111 Third Avenue South, Suite 290
Minneapolis, MN 55401-2520
http://www.upress.umn.edu

Library of Congress Cataloging-in-Publication Data

Allen, Chadwick.
   Trans-indigenous : methodologies for global native literary studies / Chadwick Allen.
(Indigenous Americas)
   Includes bibliographical references and index.
   ISBN 978-0-8166-7818-1 (hc : alk. paper) — ISBN 978-0-8166-7819-8 (pb : alk. paper)
1. American literature—Indian authors—History and criticism. 2. Indians in literature. 3. Indian aesthetics. 4. Indians, Treatment of—United States—History. 5. New Zealand literature—Maori authors—History and criticism. 6. Maori (New Zealand people) in literature. 7. Indigenous peoples. 8. Group Identity in literature. I. Title. II. Title: Methodologies for global native literary studies. III. Title: Native literary studies.
   PS153.I52A457   2012
   810.9'897—dc23

                                                                        2012023137

The University of Minnesota is an equal-opportunity educator and employer.

UMP LSI

For Marie Hubbard Holder, 1914–2009

Contents

Acknowledgments

Support for this project was generously provided by a grant-in-aid from the Division of Arts and Humanities at The Ohio State University; a Lannan Summer Institute in American Indian Studies at the Newberry Library in Chicago; an NEH Summer Seminar on "Reimagining Indigenous Cultures: The Pacific Islands" at the East-West Center at the University of Hawaii–Manoa; a CIES Senior Fulbright Research Scholarship to the Alexander Turnbull Library in Wellington, Aotearoa New Zealand; and the Moore Distinguished Visiting Professorship in ethnic literatures in the Department of English at the University of Oregon. While at Oregon I had the immense pleasure of hosting an event directly related to my research, Indigenous Literatures and Other Arts: A Symposium and Workshop, which received additional support from several departments and programs, the Many Nations Longhouse, and the Office of Institutional Equity and Diversity.

Individual chapters and the book as a whole have benefited greatly from the advice of colleagues and friends who read drafts; from the comments and questions of those who listened to early versions in the form of presentations; and to scholars, writers, and artists willing to engage in sustained conversation. I am especially grateful to Maria Bargh, Susan Bernardin, Lisa Brooks, Alex Calder, Jo Diamond, Allison Hedge Coke, Craig Howe, LeAnne Howe, Shari Huhndorf, Robert Jahnke, David Kukutai Jones, Hugh Karena, Brian Klopotek, Deborah Madsen, Sydney Moko Mead, Beth Piatote, Michelle Raheja, Nigel Reading, Te Ahukaramu Charles Royal, Paul Tapsell, Lisa Tatonetti, Alice Te Punga Somerville, Gail Tremblay, Robert Warrior, and Lydia Wevers. I am also grateful to the editors and anonymous readers at *American Literature*, *American Studies*, the *Journal of New Zealand Literature*, the *Journal of Transnational American Studies*, *Studies in American Indian Literatures*, and *Western American Literature* for their comments on essays that became parts of the manuscript, and to

Jason Weidemann at the University of Minnesota Press for making the book a reality.

Special gratitude is owed to my support team at The Ohio State University, Marti Chaatsmith, Shannon Gonzales-Miller, and Christine Ballengee-Morris; my family in Oklahoma; and Joel Tobin, whose unfailing support makes all of this possible.

Introduction

Ands turn *Comparative* turn *Trans-*

Indians, he said. They're pretty much like Maoris, aren't they?
More or less, I told him.
  ▶ Thomas King, *The Truth About Stories: A Native Narrative*

You seem to think things
are better off here
because you don't see us dying
  ▶ Jacq Carter, "Comparatively Speaking, There Is No Struggle"

Many of us are drawn to the comparative: to projects involving one
or more *ands*, to processes of thinking *between* or *among*, to conclusions that hinge on *like* and *unlike*. As students, we choose "compare
and contrast" over the singular focus. As instructors, we ask our own
students to set their chosen objects of study side by side with at least
one (beloved, tolerated, or despised) *other*, in the hope that through
an encounter with such situated configurations of voices, texts, and
contexts they will be enabled to see individual poems, stories, novels, plays, memoirs, essays, graphic texts, activist texts, videos, films,
music tracks, performances, or events in a light not simply "different"
or "new" but in some way both enlarged and more precise. In practice,
reading literary or other texts through comparative modes is more difficult to conceptualize—and more difficult to organize, perform, and
evaluate—than we imagine it should be. Within formal scholarship
that engages global Indigenous literatures written in English or primarily in English, comparative projects can seem especially fraught.

   While completing my graduate program in comparative cultural
and literary studies, when asked to describe my primary area of research in ten words or less, I chose these: American Indian and New
Zealand Māori literary and cultural studies. Spoken aloud, those ten

words became a staccato précis for an unwritten thesis—American Indian (pause) *and* New Zealand Māori (pause) literary (pause) *and* cultural (pause) studies—that was accurate as a general description but admittedly clumsy. The phrase implied an argument but lacked both relevant context and adequate precision. The *ands*, which I articulated as if in italics, were meant to signal a productive tension among the other terms: two (post)colonial settler nation-states, two large groupings of diverse Indigenous peoples, two expansive fields of study.[1] The order of the terms, too, was meant to signal, to indicate my position as a U.S.-based researcher, to privilege my primary interest in literature, broadly defined, but to attach to the literary the cachet of the cultural. (It was the 1990s; we have since embraced the literary with less embarrassment or sense of inadequacy.) The tension *between* terms, I would say, was the impetus for my pursuit of an interdisciplinary degree.

The problem with relying on coordinating conjunctions to do so much work is that their primary function is to connect words, phrases, or clauses performing grammatical functions that are the *same*. At a fundamental level, whatever the valence of the units of speech connected, the coordinating conjunctions emphasize sameness, not difference, and despite my own or others' best intentions, these *ands* are ill equipped to sustain anything in between.

Since graduate school, I have tried to turn away from a reliance on this function of *ands*, though often with little practical success. In an attempt to indicate scholarly interests beyond an exclusive focus on U.S. American Indian and New Zealand Māori texts (such as First Nations texts from Canada, Hawaiian texts from Hawai'i, and Aboriginal texts from Australia, among others), and in an attempt to admit more overtly the primacy of the literary in my research, I first turned to the simplified phrasing of *comparative* Indigenous literary studies in English. No overburdened *ands* in the general description. No fine distinctions between the literary and the cultural. Articulated this way, however, the principal adjective begins to look redundant. Is *comparative* meant to stand in for *global*? And what is a global Indigenous literary studies (with a capital *I*) if it is not, on some level, inherently comparative?

Such myopic attention to terms, their grammatical functions, and their definitions should not divert from issues of practice. What if we question, instead, the efficacy of comparison as an analytic framework for studies of global Indigenous literatures written (primarily) in English? The commonsense definition of literary comparison is a practice of reading that culminates in a statement of similarities and differences, a balanced list of *same* and its mirrored other, *not same*, the familiar "compare and contrast" ending in "like" and "unlike." While not bearing exactly the connotations of the coordinating conjunction *and*, in its Latin roots the verb *compare* unites "together" (*com-*) with "equal" (*par*). In the abstract, "together equal" sounds like a noble goal; in the actual practice of literary scholarship, it is often impracticable—or simply uninteresting. It is certainly a strange objective for anticolonial or Indigenous-centered readings of a body of distinct literatures emanating from distinct cultures, brought together by the historical accident of having been written in the shared language of those who colonized the communities of their authors. Within a context of ongoing (post) colonial relations, shouldn't the objective of a global Indigenous literary studies in English run more along the lines of "together (yet) *distinct*"?

Many Indigenous intellectuals, inside and outside the dominant academy, are understandably wary of global comparative frameworks for Indigenous studies—literary, cultural, or otherwise—when there is so much work still to be done within specific, distinct traditions and communities. (Projects arranged by settler nation-state, by geographical or geopolitical region, or by hemisphere, while often advocated for their progressive potential, can be viewed as problematic within Indigenous-focused paradigms for similar reasons.) The local, having finally won a place at the academic table, becomes engulfed (once again) in the name of the global. Perhaps more so than their non-Native colleagues, some Indigenous intellectuals wonder how a single scholar or even a small group of scholars can possibly know enough to bring together multiple Indigenous literatures emanating from multiple distinct cultures and histories on a truly equal basis. If *together equal* is the primary goal, they ask, what kind and what quality of scholarship can be produced? Whose interests can it serve?[2]

The latter question, of course, evokes a frustrating history of settler-driven, colonial comparisons. For all the potential of comparative paradigms to displace settler interests from the center of intellectual activity and to produce new knowledge, especially those that stage comparison as Indigenous-to-Indigenous, Native peoples know too well that the abstract concept of *together equal* is easily turned against the political interests of specific individuals, communities, and nations and various forms of coalition. The American Indian writer Thomas King (Cherokee) and the Māori poet Jacq Carter capture aspects of this problematic in the chapter epigraphs. In *The Truth About Stories,* King relates personal narratives of traveling as an American Indian in the 1960s in New Zealand and Australia, where settlers casually equate him with Māori based on "positive" generalizations about inherent similarities ("compare" resulting in "like") and just as casually distance him from Aboriginal peoples based on "negative" generalizations about inherent differences ("contrast" resulting in "unlike"). After recording the "damp, sweltering campaign of discrimination that you could feel on your skin and smell in your hair" conducted by settlers against Indigenous Australians, King writes: "The curious thing about these stories was I had heard them all before, knew them, in fact, by heart" (50, 51). In Carter's dramatic monologue "Comparatively Speaking, There Is No Struggle," the Māori speaker is forced to respond, yet again, to the uninformed, blunt commentary of white Australians visiting Aotearoa, who find the "Mahrees," like King's "Indians," relatively "lucky" compared with the "Abos" back home (41).[3] Rather than producing an enlarged view of evolving cultures or their (post)colonial histories, or a more precise analysis of self-representation, this form of Indigenous-to-Indigenous comparison recenters the (uninformed) dominant settler culture and produces hierarchies of Indigenous oppression—or legitimacy or authenticity—that serve only the interests of the settler, his culture, his power, his nation-state.[4]

In response to these and other complications, more recently I have begun to turn from both *ands* and *comparative* to the prefix *trans-,* experimenting with the idea of global literary studies (primarily) in English that are *trans*-Indigenous. The point is not to displace the necessary, invigorating study of specific traditions and contexts but rather to complement these by augmenting and expanding broader, globally Indigenous fields of inquiry. The point is to invite specific studies into different kinds of conversations, and to acknowledge the mobility and multiple interactions of Indigenous peoples, cultures, histories, and texts. Similar to terms like *trans*lation, *trans*national, and *trans*form, *trans*-Indigenous may be able to bear the complex, contingent asymmetry and the potential risks of unequal encounters borne by the preposition *across.* It may be able to indicate the specific agency and situated momentum carried by the preposition *through.* It may be able to harbor the potential of *change* as both transitive and intransitive verb, and as both noun and adjective. Is it possible to load a single, five-letter prefix and its hyphen with so much meaning? At this moment in the development of global Indigenous literary studies (primarily) in English, *trans-* seems the best choice.

Trans- could be the next *post-*. It could launch a thousand symposia, essays, and books, enlist sympathetic responses, provoke bitter critiques. It could propel the growth of a still-emerging field toward still-unexplored possibilities.

Turning from *ands* to *comparative* to *trans-* acknowledges that a global Indigenous literary studies (primarily) in English must move beyond scenarios in which Great Book from Tradition A is introduced to Great Book from Tradition B so that they can exchange vital statistics, fashion tips, and recipes under the watchful eye of the Objective Scholar. Other projects—less foreordained, less forcibly balanced—are more intellectually stimulating, more aesthetically adventuresome, more politically pressing. Scholarship outside established formulas embraces difficulty and assumes risk, but these projects will be more productive within an academic field that increasingly defines itself as sovereign from the obsessions of orthodox studies of literatures in English.

Indigenous Juxtapositions

Two large, related projects drive the critical study of contemporary Indigenous literatures written (primarily) in English around the globe. These can be named by broad terms: on the one hand, *recovery,* on the other, *interpretation.* Additional terms, in English and Indigenous languages, can serve equally as well; it is not the terms per se but the ongoing projects that are worth articulating, investigating, interrogating. In my effort to demonstrate the potential for literary reading through the mode of the trans-Indigenous, each of the five chapters in this book intersects both projects, and each attempts to make manifest the productive relationships and tensions between them.

The two chapters in part 1, "Recovery/Interpretation," foreground the development of methodologies for reclaiming diverse Indigenous texts. As we enter the fourth decade of organized study of contemporary Indigenous literatures, we continue to locate our full archive and to recognize its possibilities; as important, we continue to legitimize our expanding archive for inclusion within formal scholarship. The chapters in part I, therefore, demonstrate how the recovery of texts, discursive and representational practices, and contexts largely excluded from the scholarly conversation thus far necessarily refocus and redirect methods of literary interpretation. These chapters happen to center on recovering texts, practices, and contexts from the 1960s and 1970s, the early decades of the so-called Indigenous literary renaissance of the mid- to late twentieth century, a period that continues to be historicized and interpreted through investigations of a relatively narrow range of published texts, primarily longer works of prose fiction, especially when such studies center on writing by American Indians published in the United States.[5] Similar to reclamations of Indigenous texts from the nineteenth and early twentieth centuries, the projects of mid-twentieth-century recovery in chapters 1 and 2 highlight not only unknown, lesser-known, or forgotten works in those genres that dominate orthodox literary studies—the novel, certain forms of memoir, certain forms of poetry, and, increasingly, narrative film—but also works of nonfiction, works engaging multiple genres and media, and other forms of Indigenous writing and artistic self-representation.[6] More precisely, these chapters take up the challenge of recovering Indigenous texts and practices from *within* dominant discourses produced in the 1960s and 1970s that claimed either to adequately represent Indigenous identities and experiences through the limited archive of their sanctioned documents, as in the case of what I call the "settler survey," or to fully subsume Indigenous identities and experiences through the limited repertoire of their sanctioned performances, as in the case of what I call the "settler celebration."[7] Reclamations of such texts, practices, and contexts from multiple traditions offer avenues for reassessing Native agency and self-representation that are trans-Indigenous. And they suggest the likely existence of additional archives within and outside dominant discourses that have yet to influence our work.

The three chapters in part 2, "Interpretation/Recovery," then foreground the development of methodologies for the productive interpretation of a continually expanding body of contemporary literatures that place Indigenous histories and politics, cultures and worldviews, and multiple realities at their vital center. More precisely, chapters 3, 4, and 5 demonstrate methodologies for engaging Indigenous *aesthetic systems* and *technologies* in the interpretation of twentieth- and twenty-first-century Indigenous literary texts.[8] What can literary scholars learn from highly developed aesthetic systems for various "textual" arts, such as painting, weaving, and carving? And what can we learn from highly developed technologies that intersect with the particular practices of painting, weaving, and carving, as well as with a range of other "making," "building," and "moving" practices, such as architecture, engineering, mathematics, astronomy, mapping, and navigation? These related projects of critical engagement with Indigenous aesthetics and technologies aim neither to unduly reject nor to unduly rebuke orthodox methods for English-language literary interpretation. Rather, they aim to augment and significantly refocus those methods, not by simply centering the cultures immediately relevant to particular texts but by fully prioritizing the *global Indigenous*—including but not limited to the designations Native North American, New Zealand Māori, Hawaiian, Indigenous Australian, or other typical large-scale groupings—within Indigenous literary studies in English.[9]

The broad categories of literary *recovery* and *interpretation* are brought together in these chapters in order to engage the multiple connotations of each concept on its own and, simultaneously, their multiple interactions as a yoked set. All acts of literary recovery—the recognition, selection, and classification of texts as appropriate for the archive so that they can be presented for formal analysis—involve multiple (prior and simultaneous) acts of interpretation. Similarly, all acts of literary interpretation—explanation through extratextual resources, elucidation through textual analysis, assessment of significance through context or theory, evaluation through aesthetic system, cultural valence, or political efficacy—involve multiple (prior and simultaneous) recoveries (recognitions, selections, classifications) and, indeed, recoverings (when familiar texts are seen anew).

Across the two parts of the book, the chapters demonstrate concretely rather than describe abstractly what recovery and interpretation through Indigenous-focused methodologies might look like for trans-Indigenous literary studies in English. These chapters enact, in other words, a series of distinct but related experiments. What holds the book together, beyond an attention to formal innovations and several recurrent themes, is a methodology of focused *juxtapositions* of distinct Indigenous texts, performances, and contexts. Where *compare* unites "together" (*com-*) with "equal" (*par*), *juxtapose* unites "close together"

(Lat. *juxta-*) with "to place" (Fr. *poser*). Indigenous juxtapositions place diverse texts close together across genre and media, aesthetic systems and worldviews, technologies and practices, tribes and nations, the Indigenous–settler binary, and historical periods and geographical regions. This book asks: Which specific formats for *purposeful* Indigenous juxtapositions are productive within scholarship in the field of literary studies? How might the potential of specific juxtapositions to provoke readings *across* various categories enable interpretations of a broad range of texts and practices? And how might such juxtapositions contribute to calls not only for the intellectual and artistic sovereignty of specific nations but also for an Indigenous intellectual and artistic sovereignty global in its scope?[10]

Rather than attempt to balance recoveries and interpretations *equally* across settler nation-states, Indigenous groupings, historical periods, genres, or other categories, this book grounds its work, foremost, in mid-twentieth- through early twenty-first-century U.S. American Indian literatures. Although not always acknowledged, all scholarship is historically situated and, to some degree, influenced by the biography of the scholar. The series of purposeful Indigenous juxtapositions performed in the following chapters thus radiate outward from my intellectual home in American Indian literatures and cultures— where I have personal and genealogical connections, have received the most formal training, and have the most professional experience—to other Indigenous literary and cultural traditions represented (primarily) in English.[11] I turn most readily to Māori literature and culture, since these are areas to which I have devoted considerable study and in which I received relevant formal training—and, consequently, to which I now feel personally as well as professionally connected—and then to Hawaiian, Aboriginal Canadian, and Indigenous Australian literatures and cultures, areas in which I hold considerable interest but with which I have had more limited opportunities to develop high levels of expertise. Māori scholar Alice Te Punga Somerville articulates a similar approach to trans-Indigenous literary studies from her own subject position:

> It is worth being very clear about this: comparative work does not (and indeed, given the attention Indigenous Studies pays to specific land and specific place, it must not) insist that a

"fair" comparison needs to focus on the objects of comparison in exactly the same ways or to the same degree. When
comparative methodologies insist that engagement must be
"equal" they privilege the idea of an objective view in which
the scholar's job is to step back and survey things from afar.
My comparative work with Indigenous texts from a number
of contexts is conducted by myself as a Maori scholar (and indeed conducted here on Maori land) and this both guides and
underpins my comparisons. So, I am doing Maori-centered
comparative work. (25)

Through purposeful juxtapositions I work from my position in what
is now the United States to develop a trans-Indigenous literary studies grounded in—but not confined to or by—American Indian literatures, cultures, and scholarship.

Scholarship *Across*

So much of the work of orthodox literary studies has been to limit the
possibilities for reading and interpretation to a single track among the
many parallel, perpendicular, and intersecting tracks of movement and
engagement possible among written literatures and other representational arts. My goal in staging purposeful Indigenous juxtapositions
is to develop a version of Indigenous literary studies that locates itself
firmly in the specificity of the Indigenous local while remaining always
cognizant of the complexity of the relevant Indigenous global. Over
the course of this book, through an explicit process of experimentation
with different forms of juxtaposition, the chapters return to a central
question: What can we see or understand differently by juxtaposing
distinct and diverse Indigenous texts, contexts, and traditions?

It is fair to state that this project began within contexts of both ex-
citement and frustration. About the time I completed primary research
and began revisions for my first book, *Blood Narrative: Indigenous Identity in American Indian and Maori Literary and Activist Texts* (notice the
work of the *ands*), two texts were published in the emerging international and interdisciplinary field of Indigenous studies that continue to
influence and challenge its practitioners: Māori scholar Linda Tuhiwai
Smith's *Decolonizing Methodologies: Research and Indigenous Peoples*

(1999) and Creek and Cherokee scholar Craig Womack's *Red on Red: Native American Literary Separatism* (1999). In the conclusion to *Blood Narrative*, published in 2002, I cite Smith and Womack to emphasize what appeared, at the turn of the new century, a blueprint for the primary work of Indigenous studies in the foreseeable future: centering Indigenous concerns and perspectives within academic research paradigms and localizing Indigenous theories and analytic methodologies.

A decade after the initial publication of these paradigm-shifting works, the realization of Smith's and Womack's calls for new forms of Indigenous scholarship remains largely at the level of potential rather than standard practice. This situation seems especially true within studies of literature and representation. Moreover, as time has passed and Smith, Womack, and scholars who embrace their ideals have been read in multiple contexts, a number of questions have been raised about the details of implementation for their suggested programs. How, for example, should scholars working within the text-based humanities and arts disciplines, including literary studies, appropriate Smith's ideal "decolonizing" methodological practices, which were developed within the context of education and other sociologically based research, typically conducted on individual human subjects and in human communities? Although interviewing authors, their associates, their descendants, or their broader communities can be essential to biographical scholarship and to literary history, it is not always possible or practical, and it is not always a productive strategy for literary interpretation. Related issues apply to the idea of actively collaborating with authors, their associates, or their communities, who may or may not be interested in the kinds of work literary scholars undertake. Soliciting authors or their communities to set the research agenda for their own works—while potentially provocative—will not always produce the most useful or innovative scholarship. How do we harness the potential for the kind of collaborative and community-based research Smith advocates without limiting the possibilities of our field? Similarly, how should literary scholars who may or may not be enrolled citizens of Indigenous nations (terminology specific to the United States) emphasize the local in the form of the tribally specific, as Womack's "working from within the nation" paradigm promotes, without sacrificing the interpretive power of intertribal, regional, national, international, and global contexts and approaches (12)? What might, say, a Māori-grounded or Indigenous Australian–grounded reading of American Indian works bring to the community-based critical conversation? Can we conceive a "politicized" discussion of aesthetics not exclusive to the "autonomy, self-determination, and sovereignty" of specific nations but expanded to the global Indigenous (11)?

This is not to dismiss the increasing number of articles, special issues of journals, monographs, collections, and academic events organized toward the ideals articulated by Smith, Womack, and other Native and non-Native scholars interested in issues of critical practice and scholarly methodology for Indigenous studies. The collective decision to form the Native American and Indigenous Studies Association (NAISA) at a preliminary conference in 2008 and, in 2009, NAISA's successful inaugural meeting are but two examples of promising large-scale engagements with these and related issues.[12] That said, it is important to articulate that the coordinating conjunction at the center of the new association's name—absent from its acronym—records historical and ongoing tensions over the attempt to bring a U.S.-based paradigm of Native American studies into productive dialogue with other situated paradigms for Native studies (such as Hawaiian studies, New Zealand Māori studies, or Australian Aboriginal studies) and with a more globally based paradigm of Indigenous studies. From a U.S. perspective, the name of the organization and its outreach to include Indigenous others through this coordinating *and* can appear progressive, suggesting outward-looking and expansive approaches to members' objects of study and scholarly methods. From other positions on the globe, the same name can look more like business as usual, with U.S. power and the idea of a U.S. exceptionalism assuming an unmarked, primary position and the rest of the Indigenous world lumped together to be put in its secondary place. *Trans-Indigenous* locates its project within the very tension captured by the present-but-absent coordinating *and* in NAISA, one of several productive tensions likely to define trans-Indigenous literary studies for the near future.

Because the number of book-length works devoted to "comparative," Indigenous-to-Indigenous literary studies is small, national and, especially, international scholarly events have been primary influences on the development of a practice of Indigenous juxtapositions and a still-emerging field of trans-Indigenous literary studies. Presentations, workshops, conferences, staged dialogues, and symposia—even collaborative projects in writing and editing, conducted in person or across vast distances over the Internet—demonstrate in immediate and concrete terms the situated nature of knowledge and the active role of context in all forms of communication. Not simply who participates but the venue of conversation matters, and in ways both practical and profound.[13] A challenge, then, for U.S.-based organizations like NAISA, and for all scholarly journals based in particular nation-states, is to be as inclusive as possible when deciding who gets invited into relevant conversations, where they are staged, and which of the many possible forms of collaboration they are allowed or encouraged to enact. Both explicit and implicit collaborations promote approaches to scholarship embracing multiple perspectives rather than a singular focus.[14] Such multiperspectivism must be a hallmark of trans-Indigenous literary studies, even when particular works are singly rather than collaboratively authored.

Making *Across*

One of the multiperspectivist strategies of *Trans-Indigenous* is to place contemporary Indigenous literature in dialogue with other Indigenous arts and aesthetics. Scholars have long looked to oral traditions as significant contexts and possible antecedents for written works. Few have considered, however, the potential relevance of other arts practices to the analysis of literature or how literary studies might benefit from explicit conversation with scholarship on arts and media. Strikingly, this is not true of Indigenous writers and artists, who often work in multiple media and who often juxtapose genres and forms, such as a written poem and a drawing, painting, sculpture, carving, textile, basket, photograph, moving image, or live performance. In the United States, the writer-artists N. Scott Momaday (Kiowa/Cherokee), Wendy Rose (Hopi/Miwok), Peter Blue Cloud (Mohawk), Gail Tremblay (Onondaga/Micmac), Nora Naranjo-Morse (Santa Clara), and Eric Gansworth (Onondaga) come immediately to mind, as does the writer-musician Joy Harjo (Creek) and the writer-filmmakers Sherman Alexie (Spokane/Coeur d'Alene) and Diane Glancy (Cherokee).[15] Other writers collaborate with visual or media artists on particular projects. When we conceive written literatures within a more expansive, inclusive context of Indigenous arts, the alphabetic text becomes simply one option within a larger field of self-representation. Literary scholars, I argue, ought to join writers, artists, and arts scholars to engage in Indigenous-centered conversations across the boundaries of traditional disciplines.[16]

Particularly instructive for the development of methods for Indigenous juxtapositions has been the analysis of overtly trans-Indigenous works of art. Consider, for instance, the mixed-media sculpture *Whaka-mutunga (Metamorphosis)* by the Māori artist Fred Graham, part of the trans-Indigenous exhibit *Manawa—Pacific Heartbeat: A Celebration of Contemporary Maori and Northwest Coast Art* staged at the Spirit Wrestler Gallery in Vancouver, British Columbia, Canada, in 2006. (I return to this exhibit in chapter 3.) Graham's sculpture is composed of a three-dimensional figure of a diving whale, carved from New Zealand swamp kauri and inlaid with pāua shell, set against a two-dimensional background of an ocean horizon fashioned from stainless steel.[17] The upper end of the diving whale (the tail and fins) is carved and decorated in a distinctly American Indian style from the Northwest Coast known as formline, while the lower end of the whale (the head) is carved and decorated in a distinctly Māori style of interlocking koru (spirals). As is typical of classic Northwest Coast design, the primary color of the sculpture is black, with red used as a secondary color to emphasize details carved in shallow relief. In Graham's piece, red emphasizes carving primarily on the whale's tail and fins, which might be expected in Northwest Coast style, but also emphasizes the whale's tongue, an important feature of Māori carving, among the interlocking spirals of the whale's head. Luminescent pāua is inlaid between these interlocking spirals, emphasizing their three-dimensional and dynamic qualities.[18]

The stainless steel background behind the diving whale is decorated with a repeating triangle design in variations of black and white accented with red, colors that evoke Māori artistic traditions, such as the kowhaiwhai scroll painting often seen on the interior rafters of wharenui (meeting houses). Moreover, the use of subtle and progressive color variation within the background's regular geometric patterning is evocative of the Māori tradition of taniko weaving. More overtly, this variation of color creates an explicit, permeable horizon and equator for Graham's sculpture, a zone of contact between sky and sea and between north and south that coincides with the zone of transformation in the figure of the whale, where its Northwest Coast body intersects its Māori head. The horizon line/equator suggests, too, in the single plane, a demarcation between (bright) daylight in the upper, northern half of the stainless steel background and (darker) evening or night in the lower, southern half. This effect is accentuated with additional details of a red circle situated in the upper half that suggests the midday sun and a red band spread across the lower half that suggests the setting sun reflected in the sea.

Graham explains this symbolism in an artist's statement in the exhibit catalog:

> The whale is a frequent traveler between the Northern and Southern Hemispheres. In my sculpture, as the whale crosses the equator it changes both in shape and in body design, from Northwest Coast Indian to Maori. Day changes to night. The visits of the whales "down under" remind me of the visits of Northwest Coast Indian artists to Aotearoa, where they become one of us: *tangata whenua*—people of the land. In 1992, [the Northwest Coast artist] George David stayed with my wife, Norma, and me. Earlier this year, his brother [the artist] Joe David stayed with us for a few days. He drew the Northwest Coast design for me, and I hope my sculpture does his drawing justice. (105)

Multiple trans-Indigenous connections and collaborations are evident here, as are multiple kinds of trans-Indigenous travel.

At first glance, Graham's bilingual title for his mixed-media sculpture appears to contain an error, possibly a misspelling or transposition of letters. *Whakamutunga* is not a Māori translation for the English word *metamorphosis*. Depending on context, *whakamutunga* typically is translated into English as either "conclusion" or "youngest child" (*mutu* = "brought to an end"; *mutunga* = "end," "conclusion," "terminus"; "youngest"). The English word *metamorphosis* typically is translated into Māori as "whakaumutanga" (*whakaumu* = "to transform"). On the page, *whakamutunga* and *whakaumutanga* look similar enough to suggest a misprint, especially to the untrained eye. Closer examination, however, combined with contemplation of the specifically Māori orientation of the sculpture, suggests other possibilities. Graham's dynamic figure depicts an artistic transformation in a particular direction, *from* Northwest Coast Indian *to* Māori styles of carving and decoration; similarly, his artist's statement indicates an intention for the figure to function as a directional symbol for First Nations artists who journey *from* the West Coast of North America southwest *to* Aotearoa, for the diving whale to function, that is, as a sign literally *in transit* between northern and southern hemispheres of an Indigenous Pacific. It is notable that the stainless steel background projects a distinctly Māori style in its chromatic similarity to kowhaiwhai painting traditions and in its geometric similarity to taniko weaving designs. And it is notable that the bilingual title places the Māori term, *whakamutunga*, in the primary and unmarked position and the English term, *metamorphosis*, in the secondary and marked position. The English term is not simply set apart but contained by the mirrored arcs of parentheses. Rather than a direct translation, the English sign *(metamorphosis)* can be read as a commentary on the Māori sign *whakamutunga*—or vise versa.

How, then, might we understand these terms, *whakamutunga* and *(metamorphosis)*, as neither substitutable "equivalents" across languages nor markers of asymmetrical status within a (colonial) hierarchy, but rather as complementary components within a more complex, Indigenous-to-Indigenous idea? In what way or ways might the stylistic *transformation* of the figure of the diving whale and the symbolic shift from day to night be understood as the *conclusion* to a process of trans-Indigenous travel? How might we understand a diving, transforming whale framed by a diving, transforming sun? Is the whale not demonstrative of a mobile syntax for becoming tangata whenua, for becoming "people of the land," set outside a settler–Indigenous binary opposition? Is the central, permeable line of the horizon and equator—the least visually distinct element of the sculpture's background and yet the most conceptually important element in the demonstration of Indigenous-to-Indigenous artistic connection—not evocative of a cyclical, ongoing process of cross-cultural exchange (set) free of the colonial and transnational relations of center and margin?

Is Graham's sculpture not an inscription of Indigenous-to-Indigenous survivals and renewals? In the exhibit titled *Manawa* (which can be translated from Māori into English as "heart," "breath," "mind," and related concepts), such resurgence occurs neither in an idealized Indigenous past nor in a hoped-for Indigenous future, but in our own contemporary and, indeed, ordinary era. Gallery space and exhibit catalog become a different kind of "border" or "contact" zone. Not the frontier site of "cultures in conflict," not the colonial site of assimilation or conversion, not the postcolonial site of reaction or rejection, but rather a site of travel, exchange, and collaborative production explicitly marked trans-Indigenous.

Readings *Across*

Inspired by the possibilities of such trans-Indigenous figures, the chapters that follow experiment with reclamations, connections, and analyses across media, genre, and form. Chapter 1, " 'Being' Indigenous 'Now': Resettling 'The Indian Today' within and beyond the U.S. 1960s," begins the process of recovery/interpretation by situating the 1965 special issue of the *Midcontinent American Studies Journal (MASJ)*, "The Indian Today," within multiple configurations of relevant companion texts. All of these works relate to the special issue through a similarity of (ambiguous) title, descriptive focus, and predominantly nonfiction genre. Chapter 1 organizes its multiple sets of juxtapositions first synchronically and globally (related texts from similar times but different places) and then nationally and diachronically (related texts from similar places but different times) in order to demonstrate the degree to which distinct contexts and analytical situations affect literary reading, analysis, and interpretation. The 1965 special issue produces distinct types of meaning and raises distinct types of questions depending on its proximity to other texts. Although it was promoted and largely read in its original context of a continental-focused U.S. American studies as an unorthodox, "hip" assessment of the lives of contemporary Native Americans, the special issue reads differently when placed in critical conversation with similar overview texts of contemporary Indigenous status and aspirations also produced in English in the mid-1960s but in the recently incorporated extracontinental U.S. state of Hawai'i and in the (primarily) Anglophone settler nation-states of Canada, Australia, and Aotearoa New Zealand. The special issue reads differently, as well, when placed in critical conversation with similar surveys produced across the twentieth century within the continental United States by a diverse group of Native and non-Native public intellectuals, academic scholars, and government employees.

The juxtapositions staged in chapter 1 help defamiliarize and refocus the all-too-familiar story of non-Indigenous researchers, writers, scholars, and editors dominating the production of "authoritative" nonfiction discourses about the contemporary status and aspirations of American Indians, whether in the mid-1960s or across the century. Although a large number of Native intellectuals produced nonfiction texts in the 1960s, these Indigenous voices too often went unheard outside their local contexts.[19] They were all but overwhelmed by the settler survey—a vast sea of non-Native voices offering "comprehensive" coverage and "expert" opinions—and they often remain unremembered, unacknowledged, and unstudied within contemporary scholarship. By displacing U.S. isolation and its implicit discourse of exception, Indigenous juxtapositions reveal the context of ongoing colonialism operative in the production of the 1965 special issue. And they reveal that there were, in fact, other options for representing "The Indian Today," not only outside but also within the conventions of the settler survey.

Chapter 2 then works to recover the largely forgotten history of American Indian responses to the 1976 American Revolution bicentennial observance. Titled "Unsettling the Spirit of '76: American Indians Anticipate the U.S. Bicentennial," chapter 2 juxtaposes this set of surprisingly diverse Indigenous texts and performances with the set of better-known responses of Aboriginal and Torres Strait Islander intellectuals, writers, and activists to Australia's bicentennial observance in 1988. The relatively visible and well-documented responses of Indigenous Australians to the settler celebration down under, which were both event centered and discursive, provide an interpretive framework for focusing an initial study of how American Indians responded to the so-called Spirit of '76. This Indigenous Australian framing helps to make more visible and more legible the diffusive and anticipatory nature of American Indian responses to the U.S. bicentennial, features that have rendered those responses invisible and illegible within contemporary scholarship. The majority of chapter 2 is devoted to reading reports of proceedings, journalism, essays, poems, and—most surprising—novels published in the early to mid-1970s that anticipate the 1976 U.S. settler celebration and that imagine possible Indigenous responses. In the case of the 1975 novel *Indians' Summer* by Nasnaga (Remnant Band Shawnee), those responses include formal secession from the United States during the Independence Day holiday and the formation of a new, intertribal Indian Nation. The chapter's juxtaposed readings thus resituate the better-known anticipatory fiction of Gerald Vizenor (Anishinaabe) in his comic novel *The Heirs of Columbus*, published in 1991 but set during the Columbus quincentenary in 1992, as following in a particular tradition of American Indian activist writing. The chapter ends with a brief consideration of the different legacies of Indigenous Australian and American Indian responses to the spirits of '88 and '76.

Part 2, "Interpretation/Recovery," is organized as a three-part meditation on the development of interpretive methodologies for trans-Indigenous literary studies that are radically "comparative" in practice (reading *across* and *through* texts "close together placed" rather than "together equal") and that are situated in dialogue with scholarship on Indigenous arts and technologies. This meditation is conducted through concrete engagements with literary texts rather than through more abstract discussions of theory, and it enacts multiple formats of Indigenous juxtapositions.

The format of chapter 3, "Pictographic, Woven, Carved: Engaging N. Scott Momaday's 'Carnegie, Oklahoma, 1919' through *Multiple Indigenous Aesthetics*" relates to that of chapter 1 in its performance of multiple analyses of a central text. Chapter 3 stages three readings of Momaday's brief poem "Carnegie, Oklahoma, 1919," originally published in 1992, the year of the Columbus quincentenary. Each reading is grounded in a distinct worldview and system of aesthetics: Kiowa, with which Momaday identifies personally and genealogically and with which the specific content and overt themes of the poem can be aligned; Navajo, with which Momaday has extensive personal and professional experience and about which he has expressed a high regard;[20] and Māori, with which, as far as I am aware, Momaday has no personal or professional experience and in which he has no particular stake. More precisely, the first reading engages the conventions and highly developed aesthetics of Kiowa and other Plains Indian pictographic discourses, most often associated with "winter counts," "ledger art," and other mnemonic devices designed to aid in multimedia events of storytelling. The second reading engages the conventions and highly developed aesthetics of Navajo textile designs, which are based in a complex semiotic geometry, and connects this geometry back to Plains Indian traditions through the graphic forms of parfleche designs. And the third reading engages the conventions and highly developed aesthetics of Māori whakairo (carving in wood, stone, and bone), especially those forms meant to serve as conduits for contemporary contact with ancestors. The three readings thus move outward from a tribally specific approach to Indigenous literary reading and interpretation toward an intertribal or international approach and toward the possibility of a more global, trans-Indigenous approach. The chapter ends with a meta-analysis of the multiple sites and configurations of contemporary Indigenous literary studies, and it raises specific, ongoing challenges for the further development of such studies given the typical limitations of graduate training in departments of English.

Similarly, the format of chapter 4, "Indigenous Languaging: Empathy and Translation across Alphabetic, Aural, and Visual Texts," relates to that of chapter 2, where multiple juxtapositions of texts related by content and theme provoke new questions, readings, and interpretations. Chapter 4 thus shifts from a format of juxtaposing three Indigenous-centered interpretive engagements with a single poem (one text, multiple approaches) to one of staging a series of juxtapositions of diverse Indigenous texts composed in a range of genre and media (multiple texts, multiple approaches related by a singular focus). The series begins with "Carnegie, Oklahoma, 1919," the focus of chapter 3, but now situates Momaday's poem among four similarly evocative texts: "Sad Joke on a Marae" by Māori poet Apirana Taylor, "Tangata Whenua" by Māori hip-hop group Upper Hutt Posse, "Blood Quantum" by Hawaiian poet Naomi Losch, and "When I of Fish Eat" by Māori poet Rowley Habib (Rore Hapipi) and illustrated by Māori visual artist Ralph Hotere. In the course of these juxtapositions, several additional texts are engaged as well, including the mixed-media basket *Strawberry and Chocolate* by American Indian poet and weaver Gail Tremblay, the music video produced to augment Upper Hutt Posse's rap composition "Tangata Whenua," a single sentence from the novel *Potiki* by Māori author Patricia Grace, and bilingual Māori–English signage produced for the National Library of New Zealand/ Te Puna Mātauranga o Aotearoa and for an exhibit on display at the Museum of New Zealand Te Papa Tongarewa. Linking these diverse texts is the absence or presence of Indigenous language and the mobilization of literary and artistic strategies that spotlight the power of Indigenous "bilingual punning" and "bilanguaging." The literary and cultural theorist Walter Mignolo defines the latter concept as not simply the grammatical act of translating from one distinct language to another but rather the political act of operating *between* two or more languages and cultural systems, actively engaging the politics of their asymmetry within (post)colonial relations.[21] Also linking these texts is an engagement with the theory of "trans-customary" art proposed by Māori artist and art scholar Robert Jahnke, which he defines as contemporary Indigenous art that demonstrates "empathy" with customary arts practice.[22] The chapter concludes by juxtaposing the several published versions of the 1987 novel *The Whale Rider* by acclaimed Māori author Witi Ihimaera, which was adapted as the international feature film *Whale Rider* in 2003. The multiple versions of Ihimaera's story demonstrate one possible outcome of a process of translating an Indigenous literary text from the "local" to the self-consciously "global"; their trajectory offers a productive counter and something of a caution to chapter 3's celebration of Momaday's multiple literary returns to a single event of personal, familial, and communal significance.

Finally, chapter 5, "Siting Earthworks, Navigating Waka: Patterns of Indigenous Settlement in Allison Hedge Coke's *Blood Run* and Robert Sullivan's *Star Waka*," enacts a third format of sustained juxtaposition of Indigenous literary works connected by genre and theme, each published near the turn of the twenty-first century and the new millennium: the book-length sequence of poems *Blood Run* by the American Indian poet Allison Hedge Coke (Cherokee/Huron/Creek) and the book-length sequence of poems *Star Waka* by the Māori poet Robert Sullivan. *Blood Run* explores the art, engineering, culture, and history associated with the Native American earthworks—often described as "mounds"—of the Blood Run site on what is now the South Dakota–Iowa border. *Star Waka* explores the multiple meanings of Polynesian *waka*, a term that indicates any kind of "vessel" but signifies, especially, large, ocean-voyaging "canoes." The sustained juxtaposition of these book-length poetic works illuminates how each sequence of poems engages a specific, highly emblematic Indigenous technology not simply as a primary theme but also as a primary logic for its elaborate formal structures and multiple structural patterns. Each poet works to disrupt the dominant discourses that typically code Indigenous technologies as inferior to those of settlers, in part by actively demonstrating the efficacy of ancient, historical, and ongoing Indigenous technologies through her or his contemporary poetics. (Such demonstrations represent other instances of contemporary empathy with customary practice.) In a brief coda, the chapter concludes by resituating Hedge Coke's and Sullivan's sequences of poems within a broader framework of prior attempts, by the early to mid-twentieth-century intellectuals D'Arcy McNickle (Cree/Salish) and Te Rangi Hiroa (Sir Peter Buck, Māori), to reveal and celebrate the complex patterns of Indigenous technologies for exploration, migration, trade, and settlement.

Across the chapters, as in *Blood Narrative*, I engage English and Indigenous languages on equal terms, outside the binaries familiar/ exotic or domestic/foreign. I do not italicize words and phrases from Māori, Hawaiian, Navajo, or other Indigenous languages except where italics are part of a quotation or will aid clarity or effect.

Identities *Across*

The juxtapositions of Hedge Coke and Sullivan with McNickle and Te Rangi Hiroa at the end of chapter 5 emphasize what is implicit in the preceding chapters: the wide range of Indigenous locations, allegiances, knowledges, and authorities extant and changing across the twentieth century and into the twenty-first, within North America and around the globe. In different ways, each of these individuals contradicts and complicates any reductive assumption that "authentic" Indigenous writers worthy of scholarly attention are (only) those who are born into and then maintain unbroken affiliations with the Indigenous communities, languages, and cultures from which they are genealogically descended, or that, over the course of their lives and careers, "authentic" Indigenous writers represent and advocate on behalf of (only) those specific communities, languages, and cultures. Hedge Coke, Sullivan, McNickle, and Te Rangi Hiroa, like other writers and artists engaged in this study, embody in their persons and evoke in their works different kinds of access to and personal involvements with Indigenous communities, languages, and cultures—their own and others'. All four describe themselves as being of "mixed" descent, inheritance, and experience; all four led or lead lives of physical, intellectual, and artistic travel; all four have produced diverse and complex bodies of work. Similar to Graham's three-dimensional sculpture, which documents metamorphosis as the end result of Indigenous movements and connections across fluid space and time, their multidimensional works in multiple genres evoke the transformative power of lived experience and imagined exploration across multiple categories of the local and global Indigenous.

Taken together, the lives and published works of the writers, artists, scholars, activists, and intellectuals engaged in *Trans-Indigenous* represent much of the "authentic" diversity of twentieth- and twenty-first-century Indigenous identities. Assessing the complexity of this diversity, in all its personal and political nuance—with all its potential for both affirmation and controversy—is beyond the scope of the present project, which is devoted to expanding the archive and exploring new methodologies for a global Indigenous literary studies in English. That said, it is important to state that, in the contemporary period, the vast majority—if not literally all—of the writers, artists, scholars, activists, and intellectuals who self-identify as Indigenous and/or who are claimed by Indigenous communities are similarly situated. Whether mourned as loss or celebrated as survivance, the realities of contemporary Indigenous identities describe multiple kinds of diversity and complexity; often, they describe seeming paradoxes of simultaneity, contradiction, coexistence.[23] These qualities are the contemporary Indigenous norm rather than its tragic exception.

In the chapters that follow, I employ conventional vocabulary for large-scale Indigenous groupings, and I mark specific Indigenous affiliations with the convenient shorthand of parenthetical notations of nations and tribes, fully aware of the limitations of these terms. They cannot situate individuals or communities within relevant history; nor can they convey degrees of active involvement, residency in traditional or relocated homelands, cultural or linguistic expertise, and so forth. Where it seems necessary for my analysis, I expand on these brief designations either in the text or in notes.

Given the diversity and complexity of Indigenous identities in the twentieth and early twenty-first centuries, the immediate question is not how to define clear criteria for which writers and works can be legitimated for Indigenous scholarship—that is, how to newly articulate old regimes for the regulation of "authenticity"—but rather how to recognize, acknowledge, confront, and critically engage the effects of *differential* experiences and performances of Indigenous identities. The more important question, then, becomes not which writers and texts are (absolutely) in or out but rather how to train ourselves—and how to train the generation behind us—for the Indigenous scholarship of the future, when Indigenous identities will be only more and not less diverse and complex, and in ways we have yet to imagine. How do we harness this diversity for our own rather than others' intellectual and political purposes? How do we control the discourses of an Indigenous-centered scholarship rather than allow rigid or fundamentalist versions of those discourses to control us? And how do we include in such scholarship the realities and representations of our own and others' movements, connections, identities, and representations that are not simply tribal, intertribal, and inter- or transnational but significantly and increasingly trans-Indigenous?

Patterning *Across*

The five chapters of this book develop processes for recovery and interpretation rather than fixed criteria for inclusion in the archive, and none asserts the inevitability of specific readings. As Thomas King comments in *The Truth About Stories*, "It's lucky for [us] that literary analysis is not about proof, only persuasion" (115). I hope to persuade readers of the efficacy and productive potential of methodologies for literary reading marked as trans-Indigenous.

To conclude this introduction, then, I offer a final juxtaposition. In her essay "Speaking in a Language of Vital Signs" for the 2008 exhibition catalog *Joe Feddersen: Vital Signs*, Gail Tremblay describes how, through an innovative use of patterning, Okanagan print, textile, basket, and glass artist Joe Feddersen purposefully creates pieces that can be interpreted in different ways by different audiences. By employing multiple designs and multiple artistic processes within single pieces, Tremblay writes, Feddersen is able "to create visual relationships that sometimes cause the eye to read designs in multiple ways, shifting negative and positive space as the viewer focuses on shifts in value and color that reveal different ways of understanding their geometry based on traditional approaches to reading meaning in pattern" (43). Moreover, Tremblay writes that Feddersen often has chosen "not to copy traditional designs but to combine the mnemonic signs used by basket makers and layer them so that viewers [can] organize abstract visual patterns and shift the way they see designs when reading them" (43). She concludes, "Feddersen's ability to innovate allows viewers with different levels of cultural knowledge to experience these works in relation to either tradition or modernity" (44). In the 2007 novel *Miko Kings: An Indian Baseball Story* by LeAnne Howe (Choctaw), the contemporary protagonist, an international journalist, describes an encounter with the ghost of a Choctaw ancestor from the turn of the twentieth century, Ezol Day, a theoretician of the interactions among language, time, and reality. The terms of Ezol's theories of language resonate with Feddersen's practice of pattern:

> [Ezol] smiles. "Choctaw words are tools. They form equations, much the same as geometry," she says confidently. "Geometry may be guided by facts, but those facts are ultimately the choice, or consent, of a specific group. Language, rules of grammar, and meaning are the agreement of a particular group based on their practiced experience. I theorized that Choctaws didn't have the same experiences with time as those of Europeans because we speak differently. This is revealed in our vast differences in verb usage. What the Choctaws spoke of, they saw. Experienced."
> (37)

Reading through Indigenous juxtapositions reveals the potential for these levels of complex patterning and theory within trans-Indigenous scholarship. There is much exciting work to be done.

PART I

Recovery / Interpretation

recovery. n. **1.** An act, instance, process, or duration of recovering. **2.** A return to a normal condition. **3.** Something gained or restored in recovering. **4.** The act of obtaining usable substances from unusable sources, as waste material.

interpretation. n. **1.** The act, process, or result of interpreting; explanation. **2.** A representation of the meaning of a work of art as expressed esp. in representation or performance.

▸ *American Heritage Dictionary*, Second College Edition

"Being" Indigenous "Now"

Resettling "The Indian Today" within and beyond the U.S. 1960s

> The Fall 1965 issue of the Mid-Continent American Studies Journal, published at the University of Kansas, deserves special mention here because its collection of articles *does attempt* to let the Indian stand forth as a person and a group member in our contemporary industrialized society—to give some meaning to values that operate in Indian life.
>
> ▶ D'Arcy McNickle, "The Indian Tests the Mainstream"
> (emphasis added)

Autumn 2005 marked the fortieth anniversary of "The Indian Today," the Fall 1965 special issue of the *Midcontinent American Studies Journal (MASJ)*. Over the intervening four decades, while much changed for Indigenous peoples in what is now the United States, too much remained the same. For the interdisciplinary field of American Indian studies (AIS), though, advancement was substantial and dramatic. As the genealogies, backgrounds, and professional training of AIS practitioners broadened across two generations of graduate students and scholars, the field's areas of study expanded from the social sciences and law into the arts and humanities and emerging interdisciplines. Drawing on the energy of 1960s and 1970s political activism and critical methodologies developed in the 1980s and 1990s in the adjacent fields of U.S. ethnic and postcolonial studies, by the new century AIS had begun to develop its own theories and practices, increasingly celebrated as "Native," "Red," or "Indigenous." In 2005, the *MASJ* no longer existed, but the editors of its successor, *American Studies*, turned the occasion of the fortieth anniversary of "The Indian Today" into a call to assess these innovations and continuities across Indian country and within Native American and Indigenous studies. The result was a special double issue, *Indigeneity at the Crossroads of American Studies,* which included an earlier version of this chapter.[1]

"The Indian Today" was conceived, in part, as a response to the 1961 American Indian Chicago Conference (AICC) and to the document produced by delegates to that signal event, *The Voice of the American Indian: Declaration of Indian Purpose.*[2] In the wake of the AICC, Stuart Levine, regular editor of the *MASJ* and a professor of American studies at the University of Kansas, began a correspondence with Sol Tax, an anthropologist at the University of Chicago and one of the AICC's principal non-Native organizers. When Levine expressed interest in creating an "Indian" issue for the journal, Tax recommended he collaborate with Nancy O. Lurie, a non-Native professor of anthropology at the University of Wisconsin–Milwaukee who had helped Tax organize the AICC. With Lurie on board as field liaison and guest coeditor, Levine solicited "Indian" essays from a range of anthropologists. These were ready for final editing in 1964–1965. Following the special issue's positive reception in 1965–1966, including favorable notice in the *Nation* by prominent American Indian intellectual D'Arcy McNickle (Cree/Salish), who, along with Tax and Lurie, had been instrumental to the success of the AICC, "The Indian Today" was expanded into *The American Indian Today,* a substantial scholarly collection with popular appeal, published in 1968 by the commercial press Everett Edwards. Penguin Books released a paperback edition in 1970 and a reprint in 1972.[3]

Four decades after their initial publication, what is immediately striking about both titles is their seeming transparency. Each version unselfconsciously deploys an authoritative definite article and a universalizing singular noun, suggesting that the collections offer comprehensive overviews of their subject and that comprehensiveness is possible in a single volume. Moreover, the combination of definite article and singular noun tends to gender these terms (exclusively, primarily, or ideally) male. In addition, each title foregrounds the relative time marker "today," declaring a spotlight on the contemporary moment. This use of the time marker is well established. Conventionally, its appeal lies not only in the immediacy it conveys, its connotation of "now," but also in its situated flexibility within a simplified, three-part system: its capacity as noun and adverb to specify a time just beyond "yesterday" quickly becoming "tomorrow." At first glance, its meaning appears straightforward. But the relative time marker is notoriously ambiguous, temporally and spatially. Exactly when—and where—is this "today" meant to signify? On the cover of the Fall 1965 issue of the *MASJ*, does it stand for the still-unfinished 1960s and the (mid) continental United States? Or does it evoke the entire post–World War II era and all U.S. states and territories? (Alaska and Hawai'i had been brought into the union as recently as 1959.) Or does it mean something else: a broader expanse of time and space, a briefer moment more precisely immediate and geographically specific?

The time marker "today," which typically evokes the "modern," gains particular force in its juxtaposition with "The Indian" and "The American Indian," unmarked terms that tend to be read as narrowly gendered male and as heavily freighted with temporal and spatial misconceptions (and with negative or romantic stereotypes) in popular, governmental, and scholarly discourses. The relativity of the marker thus indexes a comparison with an implied past (an imagined "long ago") and an implied isolation (an imagined "far away") that are, within dominant discourses, inevitably more "primitive" and "pure" and therefore more authentically "Indigenous" than any time or place marked "today" (let alone "tomorrow"). Most non-Native Americans in the mid-1960s, including probably many of the Americanist scholars who were the primary audience for the special issue, were confident that "real" Indians lived in a "yesterday" safely distant from the turbulent social and political concerns of the contemporary United States; certainly these "real" Indians had succumbed to the pressures of a superior civilization, if not by the end of the nineteenth century then surely by the end of World War II, long before "today."[4] Juxtaposed, then, with "The Indian" or "The American Indian," the relative time marker effects an extreme temporal compression: all Indigenous history preceding "today"—the ten, twenty, thirty, one hundred, one thousand, or ten thousand years—flattens into a single past that can be recognized by dominant culture as "classic" and "real." (Typically, these are the moments immediately before first European or U.S. "contact.") In this way "today" functions not only as an ambiguous, ambivalent marker of compressed time and shifting space but also as the primary modifier for the monolithic terms "The Indian" and "The American Indian." Within a context of imperialist nostalgia—the public, ritualized mourning for that which the settler nation itself attempted to

destroy—"today" becomes synonymous with *degraded*, marking contemporary descendants of North American nations as inherently dis-
possessed, inauthentic, unreal.[5]

Admittedly, this analysis may apply undue critical pressure to—and
imply undue criticism of—these versions of the special issue's title. The
purpose of these remarks is not to condemn "The Indian Today" for being
a product of its era or for employing undeniably conventional phrasing;[6]
and I leave it to others more qualified than I to judge whether or not the
scholars brought together in the 1965 special issue were fair, accurate, or
reasonably inclusive in their assessments of the status, challenges, and
aspirations of Indigenous peoples living in the U.S. lower forty-eight
in the early 1960s (the general parameters for the essays). Instead, I am
interested in how the special issue engages the seemingly transparent
phrasing of its title as code for the more complicated and, especially for
non-Native readers, more disturbing idea of *ongoing Indigenous–settler
relations in the United States in the 1960s,* which more accurately describes
the issue's (potential) subject matter and more overtly implies the journal's and its contributors' relationships to power. As we shall see, this
phrase can be extended to indicate *by whom* these ongoing relations were
being assessed, as well as *for whom* and *in whose interests.* Exactly whose
"Indian Today" is this?

Indigenous juxtapositions help us see in more precise terms how
a particular idea of "the" (American) Indian "today" was conceptual-
ized, authenticated, distributed, and interpreted through the special
issue of the *MASJ* and that other options were available, even in 1965.
Rather than read this text in isolation, or situate it within typical contexts of Indianist discourses about "vanishing" or "returning" Natives
or Americanist discourses about the status of U.S. "minorities," we can
analyze "The Indian Today" from within a matrix of historically situated international discourses that explicitly describe—and implicitly
thematize—similar ongoing Indigenous–settler relations "today." In
other words, we can read the special issue *beside, across,* and *through*
other overview texts about the contemporary status and aspirations of
Indigenous peoples produced in English in the mid-1960s but outside the continental United States: in the new off-shore settler state of
Hawai'i, across the northern border in the neighboring settler nation-
state of Canada, and on the other side of the globe in the geographically
distant settler nation-states of Australia and Aotearoa New Zealand.

What might be gained from such juxtapositions? Situated internationally, the special issue more obviously reveals itself as a locus of primarily settler—not exclusively or exceptionally U.S.—interests, obsessions, limitations, and contingencies. It also more obviously reveals itself as a site of self-erasure by settler culture and dominant power. In particular, it now can be understood as a site in which the very term "settler," as conceived within the Indigenous–settler binary, is *unspoken* by predominantly non-Native academic researchers, scholars, writers, and editors. Nonetheless, or perhaps more so because of this erasure, both the term and its colonial power continue to govern not only the focus but also the structure and tone of this authoritative nonfiction discourse on the contemporary status of peoples indigenous to the world's most powerful settler nation-state.

It may be the mid-1960s; the special issue may be "hip" and progressive by academic standards of its time and place; but within the global settler–Indigenous dynamic, in too many ways it is simply business as usual.

Indigenous and Settler "Today"?

How does the special issue look set beside similar 1960s survey texts from other settler states or nations? What questions do such juxtapositions provoke?

To begin, consider brief overviews of the publication and distribution histories of relevant international texts. In 1962, prior to the publication of the special issue, the Indian Affairs Branch of Canada's Department of Citizenship and Immigration published a brief promotional booklet titled *The Indian in Transition: The Indian Today*.[7] Addressed to "other," non-Native Canadians, the illustrated booklet highlights mid-twentieth-century Indian "progress" toward integration in a number of key areas and promotes the branch's several programs for Indian advancement. The booklet's rhetorical strategies also work to engender goodwill toward First Nations peoples among the general public. The following year, the Indian Affairs Branch appears to have updated and repackaged its booklet into a more concise, essay-length version less obviously a promotional vehicle for government policies. Titled "Canadian Indians Today" and attributed to the non-Native writer William Dunstan, the illustrated essay was the lead article in the

December 1963 issue of the *Canadian Geographical Journal,* a monthly publication of the Royal Canadian Geographical Society, based in Ottawa. Dunstan was a former journalist and public relations counsel, as well as a former Information Officer for the Department of Citizenship and Immigration; in 1963 he worked for the Indian Affairs Branch as an administrative officer in public relations and information services.[8] It is possible he either wrote or helped produce *The Indian in Transition* in 1962. Similar to its more official-looking predecessor, Dunstan's essay is addressed to non-Native "fellow Canadians" who have recently "rediscovered" Indians living in their midst. Following journalistic rather than governmental discourse conventions, the essay supports its arguments for Indian "progress" and builds its case for promoting goodwill by profiling the considerable accomplishments of contemporary First Nations individuals and communities. In 1964, as part of its ongoing efforts, the Indian Affairs Branch released a slightly updated but otherwise identical edition of *The Indian in Transition.*[9]

Also in 1964, a year before publication of the special issue, when it would have been in copyediting and early production, the Hawaiian writer John Dominis Holt saw his short book and photo essay *On Being Hawaiian* published with the Star-Bulletin Printing Company, an arm of Honolulu's major newspaper.[10] Holt's project, intended primarily for an audience of Hawaiian state citizens, residents, and tourists, was a response to the kinds of questions repeatedly posed by non-Hawaiians about the distinctiveness and value of Hawaiian identities "today." (A second printing, with a new introduction offering an account of the book's origins, was issued a decade later by Honolulu-based Topgallant Publishing.)[11]

In Australia, the Sydney-based commercial press Angus and Robertson released a collection of scholarly essays, *Aborigines Now: New Perspective in the Study of Aboriginal Communities,* edited by the non-Native anthropologist Marie Reay.[12] Like the 1965 special issue, *Aborigines Now* had been inspired by an unprecedented event in 1961, the Conference on Aboriginal Studies sponsored by the Australian Social Science Research Council and convened by the renowned non-Native anthropologist W. E. H. Stanner of the Australian National University. According to Reay and to reports she cites from the *Sydney Morning Herald,* the conference featured the work of older, eminent anthropologists but ignored contributions by their junior colleagues. In her introduction Reay promises a surprisingly singular "new perspective" on "aboriginal questions" [sic] by presenting, instead, essays by a range of "younger" anthropologists, non-Native researchers whose fieldwork had begun no earlier than 1950 (xv). Their research reveals how contemporary policies promoting "assimilation" and "integration" affect "aboriginal life today" [sic].¹³

Meanwhile, across the Tasman in Aotearoa New Zealand, in 1964 the Department of Maori Affairs, based in Wellington, released an updated and expanded third edition of its illustrated promotional booklet *The Maori Today*. Emphasizing a narrative of ongoing Māori "progress" alongside the maintenance of Indigenous cultural traditions, this publication was aimed at both a national audience and at educated international visitors. Previous editions had been produced under the same title in 1949 and 1956. Between the release of the second and third editions, in 1960, the New Zealand National Film Unit, working in conjunction with Maori Affairs and the Departments of Information Services and Tourist and Publicity, completed a sixteen-minute documentary film version of the booklet, also titled *The Maori Today*. The short film was screened at locations throughout Aotearoa New Zealand in 1961. As with its print publications, the government hoped its film would not only highlight a record of achievement in race relations but also inspire Māori to work toward the "progress" it desired. Over the remainder of the decade, the film circulated among New Zealand's international diplomatic postings, in its original English version and in several versions dubbed into European and Asian languages, for the purposes of building a positive image abroad and promoting tourism.

Finally, in 1968, the year the revised special issue appeared in book form, the New Zealand commercial press Blackwood and Janet Paul, based in Auckland, published a substantial collection of essays, *The Maori People in the Nineteen-Sixties: A Symposium*, edited by Erik Schwimmer, who was a Pakeha (New Zealander of European descent), a former officer in Maori Affairs, and a former editor of the department-sponsored journal *Te Ao Hou/The New World*.¹⁴ The press editors had conceived this project in 1964 as an updated version of the 1940 collection *The Maori People Today: A General Survey*, edited by the Pakeha scholar I. L. G. Sutherland and published by the Auckland branch of Oxford University Press. Although this text remained popular two decades after its initial release, its focus and much of its content were no longer current, and it was long out of print. *The Maori People in the Nineteen-Sixties* was expected to appeal, similar to its 1940 predecessor, both to scholars and students and to educated lay people interested in Māori culture. Although published commercially, cost of production was defrayed by a literary grant from the Maori Purposes Fund Board of the Department of Maori Affairs.

One immediate effect of setting the special issue within this broader context is to further highlight its editors' choice of the relative time marker. Levine and Lurie were not alone in giving prominent place to ambiguous language, but they clearly had other options. It seems appropriate to ask: Is their "today" the same as that asserted for First Nations peoples in Canada or Māori in Aotearoa New Zealand? Does it coincide with the "being" of Hawaiians or the "now" of Indigenous Australians? And given Levine's and Lurie's non-Native identities and secure locations within the U.S. academy, what is the political and ethical valence of their ambiguous "today"? Is it a recognition of survivals and transformations, a celebration of people continuing to "be" Indigenous "now" "in the Nineteen-Sixties" despite change, or is it a sad accounting of communities and individuals judged "today" to be inevitably less Native than their ancestors? We might highlight, as well, the varying use of the authoritative definite article and universalizing singular noun. The titles by Dunstan and Reay stand out for their lack of any article and for their explicit use of the plural nouns "Indians" and "Aborigines." A more significant effect of placing the special issue beside similar surveys is that it raises questions about which individuals and institutions possess the material power to have their "accurate" and "up-to-date" assessments of Indigenous peoples published in the dominant media and circulated widely within a given historical period. In the 1960s, following the success of the AICC—which had brought together some 460 delegates representing ninety Indigenous nations and which had incited the formation of the National Indian Youth Council—whose voices were invited to speak within the expressive field of the provocative phrase "The Indian Today"?[15] And who ultimately controlled their selection, arrangement, tenor, and volume?

Consider basic comparisons of the eight print texts I list, including subject positions and status of their authors and editors, their relative sizes, their organizing structures and methodologies, and their inclusion of illustrations or supplementary materials:

1. "The Indian Today" (United States, 1965)
   + It is coedited by two non-Native scholars, one man and one woman.
   + It comprises eleven pieces (one of which is cowritten) by twelve contributors, six men and six women, all but one of whom has an academic affiliation.
   + Two contributors are American Indian, one man and one woman, though they are not identified as such; both have academic affiliations.
   + Eleven contributors, including the two Indians, work within anthropological or sociological methodologies; one, the regular editor, works in the interdiscipline of American studies.
   + A small cartoon heads each essay; two essays include as illustrations a total of thirteen black-and-white photographs of older Indian individuals, Indian artifacts, and reservation buildings.
   + The front cover includes a color photograph of a "Sioux dance and give-away" on the Rosebud Reservation in South Dakota, taken by the regular editor.

2. *The American Indian Today* (United States, 1968)
   + It is coedited by the same non-Native scholars.
   + It comprises thirteen pieces (one of which is cowritten) by thirteen contributors, six men and seven women.
   + The essays are now arranged into five titled sections, including an overview section on American Indian history.
   + It includes a section titled "About the Authors," which identifies two contributors as American Indians, one man and one woman.
   + It includes a brief bibliography and, as an insert, a fold-out map of the North American Indian population distribution in 1950.[16]
   + It includes nine black-and-white photographs as illustrations for only one essay.
   + The same photograph is on the front cover.

3. *The Indian in Transition: The Indian Today* (Canada, 1962, 1964)
   + It is an anonymous government publication.
   + It is divided into eight titled sections.
   + It is primarily written from a sociological perspective.
   + It is illustrated with sixteen black-and-white photographs of mostly contemporary Indian men, women, and children in a variety of relevant scenes: labor, housing, education, government, and health.
   + The front cover uses stark black-and-white contrasts and incorporates a subtle graphic design of arrows and tipi.

4. "Canadian Indians Today" (Canada, 1963)
   + It has a single male non-Native author with no academic affiliation, employed by the government.
   + It is an essay-length text with a primarily sociological perspective, presented in a journalistic style.
   + It is illustrated by seventeen black-and-white photographs of contemporary men, women, and children in various occupations, plus a map of the Indian population distribution in 1961, a chart of the Indian population by linguistic families in 1962, and a chart of the Indian population distribution by province in 1963.

5. *On Being Hawaiian* (Hawai'i, 1964)
   + It has a single male author of Hawaiian descent, with no academic or government affiliation.
   + It is an essay-length text followed by fifty-three illustrations, historical and contemporary black-and-white photographs of Hawaiian landscapes, artifacts, and men, women, and children in a variety of scenes.
   + It is written from an insider's perspective and has a primarily literary rather than a primarily anthropological or sociological voice.
   + The front and back covers feature a thousand-year time line of Hawaiian history, illustrated by a contemporary mural of relevant Hawaiian scenes.

6. *Aborigines Now: New Perspective in the Study of Aboriginal Communities* (Australia, 1964)
   + It is edited by a single female non-Native anthropologist.
   + It comprises a foreword by an established, male non-Native anthropologist and an introduction by the female editor, followed by thirteen pieces written by younger contributors, seven men and six women, all non-Native. Seven of the contributors are identified as holding PhDs, four master's degrees, and two bachelor's degrees; eight are identified as currently having academic affiliations, one as holding a government position, and one as working as a journalist.
   + Nine of the contributors work within the field of anthropology; the other four work within the fields of history, human geography, demography, and literary studies.
   + The essays are loosely arranged by geographical location of researcher's fieldwork.
   + It includes ten black-and-white photographs of contemporary Indigenous men, women, and children as general illustrations and three reproductions of contemporary drawings as figures for a specific essay. It also includes a brief note on terminology and a list of contributors.
   + The cover features four of the black-and-white photographs included as illustrations.

7. *The Maori Today*, third edition (New Zealand, 1964)
   + It is a mostly "anonymous" government publication.
   + It comprises a foreword by the minister of Māori affairs, a male Pakeha, followed by thirteen titled chapters. Only one chapter is attributed to a specific author, who is male with an academic affiliation and who is identified as being of Māori descent.
   + It is illustrated with ninety-five black-and-white photographs of contemporary Māori men, women, and children in a variety of scenes and includes three maps, lists of relevant statistics, and a table of Māori population figures from the 1961 census.

* It is written with a predominantly sociological approach but includes a chapter on Māori language written by a linguist.
* The front cover features detail of a Māori feather cloak, and the back cover features the same cloak with a green-stone hei tiki (jade carving).

8. *The Maori People in the Nineteen-Sixties: A Symposium* (New Zealand, 1968)
   * The male academic Pakeha editor is supported by an editorial board, two male Pakeha scholars and one male Māori consultant who works in broadcasting and continuing education.
   * It comprises sixteen pieces (one of which is cowritten) by fifteen contributors, twelve men and three women, nine of which are identified as having academic affiliations in New Zealand (the editor moved to Canada during production).
   * Five contributors are of Māori descent, three men and two women; two of the men have academic affiliations.
   * Approaches are dominated by anthropological and sociological methodologies but include linguistics, literature and arts criticism, Indigenous history, and creative writing. Pieces are arranged alphabetically by author rather than by subject matter or approach.
   * Fifty-four contemporary black-and-white photographs of Māori men, women, and children are organized into four groups interspersed among the chapters. The book includes a glossary of Māori words, an extensive general bibliography, and a separate comprehensive bibliography of literary representations of Māori.
   * The front cover features a photograph of a contemporary Māori wood carving; the back cover lists contributors and affiliations.

None of these surveys develops sustained international comparisons. Each equally focuses on its national situation; if contributors glance outward, typically it is to engage examples of better-known "minorities," such as African Americans, or "immigrants," primarily from Europe.[17] Juxtaposed, however, their outlines demonstrate significant differences and draw attention to what is either minimal in the special issue of the *MASJ* or absent from its pages: an individual and personal Indigenous perspective on contemporary identity, status, challenges, or aspirations; a diversity of methodological approaches; maps, statistical data, and comprehensive bibliographies made available for readers' study; photographs of Indigenous men, women, and children in a variety of contemporary scenes; and a keen interest in language, literature, and the arts as vital aspects of indigeneity. What are the implications of these differences?

On Being an Indigenous Citizen

Although it lists authors' academic affiliation at the end of each article, the special issue includes no contributor biographies and gives no indication of the twelve authors' ethnic or tribal identities. Two contributors, Shirley Hill Witt (Mohawk) and Robert K. Thomas (Cherokee), identified personally and professionally as American Indians, but since their names do not mark them as Native, it is likely that many original readers were unaware of their Indigenous status or links to specific Indian nations.[18] The placement of Witt's and Thomas's work is thus of particular interest, as is the tenor of their published voices and how they are framed by their own prefatory remarks or those of the non-Native editors.

Witt's and Thomas's essays are positioned directly after those of coeditors Levine and Lurie, giving them some prominence. Titled "Nationalistic Trends among American Indians" and "Pan-Indianism," respectively, the essays appear related to each other but, at first glance, stand out as distinct from the seven essays that follow. All but one of these are based on localized anthropological or sociological fieldwork in primarily reservation or rural settings, and all offer accounts of how a set of issues affects a specific (often isolated) Indian community. In fact, Witt's and Thomas's essays are more similar to the others than they first appear: both work comfortably within anthropological or sociological methodologies. In the 1960s, this means their authors take a more or less "objective" stance toward their subject and do not emphasize their perspectives, experiences, or feelings as individuals or members of specific groups. It appears, however, that the editors worried about this aspect of the essay by Witt. Hers is one of only two preceded by a headnote written by the regular editor.[19] Levine draws attention to the potentially polemical nature of Witt's position and voice, confirming that anthropological "objectivity" is the expected norm. The headnote also subtly hints at but does not disclose Witt's Indigenous identity: "The paper which follows is not only a review of the historical antecedents of Indian nationalism, but also a *characteristic statement* of the point of view of the highly vocal National Indian Youth Council.—SGL" (51; emphasis added). Witt is not identified as a member of this activist organization, and the tone and actual content of her work are professional. There is no *personal* or *political* voice active in this scholarly essay, marked or unmarked. If anything, a distinctly Indigenous voice is carefully avoided.

The inclusion of an Indigenous personal voice, whether primary or one mode among several, profoundly affects *On Being Hawaiian* and *The Maori People in the Nineteen-Sixties.* Holt's rumination on the early 1960s experience of "being" Hawaiian was originally intended for newspaper publication, and his words fill only twenty of the book's ninety-five pages, the others being devoted to fifty-three illustrations. This brief meditation is powerful as a personal statement on contemporary Indigenous identity and an ethical statement on human dignity and the rights of colonized peoples to be subjects as well as objects of study. Early on, Holt states, "They tell us we are all kinds of things, but what do we think of ourselves?" (7). Though well educated, Holt was not a professional scholar; he confronts the complexity of his own and others' identities as Hawaiians from an unapologetically insider's perspective and in a decidedly literary voice. He begins with two related but distinct questions: "What is a Hawaiian?" and "Who is a Hawaiian in the modern state of Hawaii?" (7). In his answer, it becomes clear that Holt's intended audience includes not only non-Native state citizens, residents, and tourists but other Hawaiians, especially those, like himself, in a position to influence the sentiments of the dominant culture. Holt's arguments are not those of a nationalist; he concedes the loss of a sovereign Hawaiian nation (11). Instead, he positions himself as a patriotic citizen both of the state of Hawai'i and of the United States of America who is "statistically, as well as ethnically, a keiki hanau o ka aina—a child born of the land—and a part-Hawaiian" (9). Similar to other Indigenous intellectuals in the post–World War II era, part of his project is to respond to "exaggerations, misrepresentations, half-truths, and sentimental images" of his ancestors and contemporary community produced by outsiders (23).

In his effort to more accurately conceptualize and better articulate 1960s Hawaiian experience, Holt develops two main paradigms. The first, "sentiment," "aesthetics," and "consciousness," can be grouped together under the rubric of epistemology, particularly epistemology of the self, by which I mean ways of organizing knowledge and self-knowledge. Holt writes, "I am a Hawaiian in sentiment, perhaps in a sense aesthetically, for I am governed in my feelings as a Hawaiian by an ideal, an image, a collection of feelings fused by the connecting links of elements that go deep into the past, and which play in my consciousness with the same result produced by great music, painting, or literature" (11). His analogy with the effects of experiencing the arts—psychological, emotional, and embodied—evokes the affective aspects of culture and inheritance. These are perhaps the most difficult to describe in anthropological or sociological terms, but they are often considered the most important aspects of culture by community members. Moreover, in Holt's formulation these important "felt" aspects of culture are transhistorical and intergenerational: "To think as a Hawaiian of the fantastic navigational feats of our ancestors [. . .] inspires awe . . . respect! I gain a *vicarious sense* of courage" (13; emphasis added).[20] It is this difficult-to-describe "thinking as a Hawaiian" and connecting to the Indigenous past that Holt is most interested in expressing for his mixed audience. In his second paradigm, Holt concentrates on the land itself and, inseparably, the fact of Hawaiians' relatively long tenure in the islands. In this way, Holt explicitly relates land to epistemology: "The land quivers," he writes, "from the southern tip of Hawaii Island to Kauai's far western shores, with living elements of the ancient past" (22). Everyone in Hawai'i is "in one degree or another, affected by the impact of the abstract force of past events"; for Indigenous Hawaiians, however, this impact is a particular "burden": "We are, to some extent, the walking repositories of island antiquity; living symbols of a way of life long dead, but which strangely persists in shaping the character of life in the fiftieth state" (22, 23). Relationship to the vital force of the land and sensitivity to local history distinguish Indigenous experience. In Holt's terms, this "burden" has been compromised by outsiders' representations of Hawai'i and Hawaiian culture, which have become dominant to the point that many Hawaiians are "confused" and "do not know how to think about the past, even if we have some glint of knowledge of what happened then" (21, 22).

Having claimed inextricable links between Hawaiians, land, and history, Holt concludes his rumination with possibilities for the future.[21] "All around me," he writes, "I see evidence among Hawaiians of a renewed interest in themselves, and the future, and their community." Yet despite this evidence of enabling self-interest with which to fight "confusion," Holt resists both certainty and ambiguity, offering instead a vision pragmatic and complex: "I see scores of handsome children who will grow up to *be less* the victims of their heritage than I and my generation were; and who will *be somewhat less* able to enjoy the aesthetic lift we enjoyed for being Hawaiians; but who will *be less* hampered, *less* bound to the fragmented, but imposingly powerful, image of the past" (26; emphasis added). In each iteration, repetition of a phrase linking "being" with "less" enacts a shift in tone, optimism to melancholy, liberation to loss; Holt strains two semicolons and two conjunctions to coordinate the four phrases of his vision across Hawaiian heritage, aesthetics, and history. From his vantage in 1964, he sees inevitable loss of cultural feeling as the next generation achieves material and social gains. In the juxtaposition with the special issue of the *MASJ*, we note the connection made in these statements between the rhetorical and affective complexity of Holt's Indigenous personal voice and his ultimate focus on contemporary children and the coming generations.

An Indigenous personal voice informs *The Maori People in the Nineteen-Sixties*, as well, and here it is conspicuously focused on the perceptions of Indigenous children. "One Two Three Four Five" by Arapera Blank dramatizes the experience of a five-year-old Māori child entering the New Zealand school system. Engaging the conventions of the short story rather than the academic essay, Blank writes in the first-person perspective of the child and in the colloquial Māori English of rural Aotearoa New Zealand. Fictional discourse allows her to present the psychological and emotional effects of dominant (colonial) institutions on Māori children—both positive and negative—in a highly expressive manner. Blank concludes with a postscript titled "*O nga ao e toru*," which can be translated into English as "Of Three Worlds." This section is set when the child has grown into a young man and is better able to reflect upon the complexities of leaving his Māori-speaking home for school, where only English is allowed: "I am older now. I have finished school. And now I like everything. That's what's wrong with me. I am a three-legged creature. I can't put my three legs down at once either. The world isn't ready for such a creature. But this is what education in a European world has given me. Three legs" (94). He explains the significance of these three "legs": one Māori, one Pakeha, and a third leg "fashioned from *looking at* the other two" (95; emphasis added). In the mid-1960s, the bifurcated optics that create this third leg—the double consciousness demanded by contemporary Aotearoa New Zealand—is "too much of a nuisance" and brings mostly confusion and pain for the educated young man who no longer feels fully at home among Māori but is not fully Pakeha, either (95). Blank refuses easy resolution, ending with the conundrum of the protagonist's situated anguish: "No one wants to see two sides of the question. Only liars can see two things at once. [. . .] And now nobody wants me. All three legs are a curse. I wish I could have had only one as I would have had if I had never turned five" (96).

Like Holt, Blank valorizes the affective, deeply personal, conflicting aspects of Indigenous experience that standard anthropological accounts either exclude or unduly pathologize. This can have an obvious appeal for Indigenous audiences. In addition, the Indigenous personal voice takes non-Native readers especially—and perhaps uncomfortably—out of the familiar terrain of the third-person ethnographic present, abstract statistics, generalized "types," and highly managed informants, insisting that Indigenous peoples be understood as complex, contemporary individuals as well as members of Indigenous communities and descendants of Indigenous ancestors. If this personal voice is successful, it offers all readers the potential for a different kind of experience of intellectual engagement and, possibly, a different kind of psychological and emotional empathy.

Demonstrating the Indigenous Modern

Works by Holt and, especially, Blank highlight the potential for analytical methods and discursive practices other than the typical anthropological or sociological survey approaches of their day to evoke important aspects of Indigenous experience. Their works demonstrate, moreover, how individuals and communities who identified as Indigenous in the 1960s in Hawai'i and Aotearoa New Zealand lived in multiple forms of relationship with non-Native peoples, dominant settler culture, and its public and private institutions. Complex and diverse, such relationships defy simple binaries of gain and loss, or positive and negative effects. These and other 1960s works thus point, as well, to the limitations of Levine's attempts to frame the special issue of the *MASJ* as an analysis of "the" Indian in isolation or in a one-sided exchange rather than as an analysis of ongoing interactions among Indigenous peoples and settlers.

Similar to its 1949 and 1956 predecessors, the 1964 edition of *The Maori Today* showcased the recent history of New Zealand race *relations* as a story of Māori "progress" for which Māori and Pakeha could both take credit and be proud.[22] Such stories were meant to meet two distinct aims of the government: to "inspire" Māori to better themselves by participating fully in mainstream society and to promote an international image of New Zealand as a progressive nation with a superlative record of interracial harmony. (Both the Canadian government's promotional publication and Dunstan's essay had similar goals and used similar strategies, if on a more limited scale.) The booklet's chapters highlight Māori "progress" in a range of areas: government administration; farming and land development; housing, health, and education; apprenticeship, occupational, and career opportunities; welfare programs and community building; participation in men's and women's sports; language revival and instruction; and, especially, a record of exemplary military and civil defense service during two world wars, the Korean conflict, and the Malayan emergency.[23] Each chapter is generously illustrated with black-and-white photographs of Māori men, women, and children participating in all aspects of New Zealand society. The booklet includes maps of the North Island showing historical iwi (tribal) areas and contemporary Māori demographics, as well as Māori population tables from the 1961 census. It ends with "The Future," a section that acknowledges, albeit briefly, that New Zealand's record on race relations is not "without blemish" but focuses mainly on the rich promise of the future Māori and Pakeha will share together. Māori cultural heritage is described as "fine and noble"; the expectation expressed is that Māori culture will not lose its specificity or distinctiveness but will continue to be "adapted to the conditions of the times."

The Maori People in the Nineteen-Sixties, published in 1968 and ed-ited by Erik Schwimmer with the assistance of John Forster, a Pakeha lecturer in Education at Victoria University; William (Wiremu) Park-er, a Māori broadcaster and educator; and James Ritchie, a Pakeha so-ciologist, focuses similarly on ongoing Māori–Pakeha *relations*. The project was conceived in 1964 as a study of "Aspirations and Stresses of a Minority," and the editor imagined commissioning essays on nine-teen relevant topics by "some eighteen of the best qualified people in New Zealand," including professional scholars, community-based researchers and educators, and seven writers of Māori descent: John Rangihau, Jacqueline Baxter (J. C. Sturm), Hugh Kawharu, Hei Rog-ers, William (Wiremu) Parker, Katarina Mataira, and Pei te Hurinui Jones.[24] During their first meeting, the editorial board revised the table of contents from nineteen to an even twenty essays, now arranged into five sections: (1) "General Survey," (2) "What Do the Statistics Mean?," (3) "Personality," (4) "Community," and (5) "Forms of Expression."[25] Two Māori authors were dropped from the list of invited contributors, but two others, Arapera Blank and Bruce Biggs, were added, maintain-ing a total of seven.

A number of factors kept several invited authors, Pakeha and Māori, from completing their essays before the publisher's deadline. Including Schwimmer's lengthy introduction, "The Aspirations of the Contemporary Maori," and a brief postscript written in 1957 by the Pakeha anthropologist Ernest Beaglehole, the published volume comprises sixteen pieces by fifteen contributors (Schwimmer wrote an essay, as well as his introduction).[26] The sections have been removed, and the essays, covering a wide range of topics—language, education, social conditions, intermarriage, the King Movement, urbanization, art, literature, development, health, labor and employment, children, and government institutions—are arranged alphabetically by author's surname. Five authors are of Māori descent: Biggs, who writes about language; Blank, who writes about education; Jones, who writes about the Māori King Movement; Kawharu, who writes about urban im-migration; and Mataira, who writes about art. Four groups of pho-tographs are interspersed among the chapters under the headings "Family Life and Education," "Maori Leaders," "Artists in the Commu-nity," and "The Maori in the Community." The book concludes with a three-page glossary of Māori words, an extensive general bibliography, and a separate bibliography to "The Maori and Literature 1938–65" by the Pakeha scholar Bill Pearson. Pearson's bibliography is divided into three sections, "Writing by Pakeha," "Writing by Maori," and "Other References," with the first two subdivided by genre.

While the five essays written by Māori draw particular interest for their range of subject matter, discursive style, and political tone, *The Maori People in the Nineteen-Sixties* as a whole is remarkable, juxtaposed with the special issue of the *MASJ*, for its variety of methodological approaches. The non-Native editor of each collection had definite ideas about what he saw as the contemporary status of Indigenous peoples in his settler nation-state and what he thought should be the proper course of future Indigenous development. A striking difference in their editorial projects, then, is that Schwimmer—who had considerably more experience working with Indigenous colleagues and who was arguably better informed about the diversity of contemporary Indigenous lives—either encouraged or allowed competing voices and alternative visions into the collection under his charge. A number of these potentially challenge or shift emphasis away from the arguments of his introduction, which promotes a model for national "inclusion." In contrast to Schwimmer's endorsement of Māori integration into the Pakeha mainstream, Blank details the potential negative effects of the dominant school system on Māori children; Jones deploys Māori epistemological traditions to record an Indigenous history that does not end with the coming of Europeans but extends into contemporary times; and Kawharu reveals the complexities of ongoing relations *among different groups of Māori* living in urban centers, where new immigrants to the city find themselves in potential conflict with not only Pakeha, Pacific Islanders, or other non-Māori residents but established *tangata whenua* (people of the land, or hosts; those Māori indigenous to the specific area). These contrasts result in a wide-ranging collection that aspires to the ideals of a symposium. The lack of agreement offers a vision of a modern Indigenous people living in a settler nation-state in the 1960s that, while not exhaustive, is more diverse and complex than the singular vision of "The Indian Today."

At this point it is instructive to consider the counterexample of *Aborigines Now*, published in 1964 in Australia. This collection of thirteen essays by younger scholars is similar to *The Maori People in the Nineteen-Sixties* in its range of methodological approaches, which includes literary studies, history, human geography, and demography along with conventional anthropology. It is more closely aligned with "The Indian Today," however, in the way it promotes itself as "progressive" yet often assumes a paternalistic tone. Moreover, *Aborigines Now* exceeds the colonial implications of "The Indian Today" in its inclusion of only non-Native contributors and the tendency of these authors to overgeneralize from limited studies and to represent the Indigenous sources of their research as anonymous voices rather than as specific individuals. The editor, Marie Reay, a fellow in the Department of Anthropology and Sociology at the Australian National University in Canberra and a member of the Advisory Panel on Anthropology of the Australian Institute of Aboriginal Studies, illustrates these alignments and deviations in her opening and closing remarks. In the introduction Reay characterizes the collection's diverse essays in terms of their break with orthodox research and policy:

> Two themes recur in these essays. Firstly, the authors stress that the aborigines' [*sic*] own wishes and choices are important in planning successfully for the future; secondly, they draw attention to the presence of aboriginal [*sic*] communities and urge that the method of administering native policy in Australia should change from a preoccupation with individual assimilation to an emphasis on community development. (xvi)

At the same time, her discourse moves effortlessly from seemingly progressive language ("all [contributors] are sympathetic and try to see the aborigines' [*sic*] point of view and what is behind it" [xvii]) to language that is overtly racist ("despite their dark skins and savage ancestry" [xviii]) to language that is more subtle but equally prejudicial (for instance, when she repeatedly refers to the so-called Aboriginal problem [xix]). Throughout the introduction, Reay exercises her power as editor to correct or rebut the more liberal conclusions of her contributors, typically in the first-person voice: "I would not like to see . . ." (xvi), "I myself think that . . ." (xvii), "It may be wiser, in my view . . ." (xviii).

At the end of the volume, in a brief "Note on 'Aborigines' and 'aborigines,'" Reay remobilizes this voice to defend her personal preference—and her editorial insistence across the essays, no matter the wishes of the authors—to write the general term "aborigine" without an initial capital letter. In response to a contributor who petitioned for the capital, Reay states:

> I would argue that if I, an Australian, lay claim to Scottish descent I am not claiming Scottish nationality but simply an ancestral association with a geographical region and a tradition. That is all any name of our aboriginal people needs to imply. To use a general term with world-wide applicability as a distinctive name for a tiny segment of a particular nation seems to me parochial in the extreme. These people will doubtless find a name if they ever develop the kind of social, cultural, or political unity that might inspire a need for one.[27] (168)

Followed only by the list of contributors and the index, Reay's remarks conclude the volume with the dismissive phrasing "these people" and an exposed chauvinism. As we shall see, Reay's assertive and at times acerbic voice, her personal beliefs, and her editorial stance help bring into sharper focus the voices, beliefs, and editorial stance of coeditors Levine and Lurie in the 1965 special issue of the *MASJ*.[28]

Picturing Possible Indigenous Futures

The 1960 documentary *The Maori Today* was produced to fulfill similar promotional goals as the publications of the same title, and its content is similar to that of the 1964 booklet.[29] The New Zealand government is less effective in its presentation of Māori "progress," however, in the visual and aural medium. The film's narration is generally too vague or simplistic to convey the complexities of contemporary life, and the absence of a central storyline makes the film appear a random collection of scenes. Unlike in the print texts, many images feel dated or less than representative. In fact, in 1968 New Zealand's ambassador to Germany sent a detailed memo to the secretary of external affairs in Wellington complaining that the film was of little use as a promotional tool, since it is too misleading for foreign viewers. In particular, he notes the lack of a specific theme; the film's episodic nature; the use of both too obviously posed shots and shots that were fortuitous but will be seen by foreign viewers as typical; that Māori are on display but never seen speaking to each other or speaking the Māori language; and that the film focuses on the positive role of government but fails to show Māori helping themselves. The ambassador strongly suggests the film "be re-made in the near future."[30] Despite such cogent critique, it never was. Even as we acknowledge its significant limitations, it is important to point out what the film does well, which is to provide viewers with actively present images of younger Māori men and women participating in multiple aspects of society, including "traditional" cultural practices as well as contemporary occupations and leisure pursuits, and to provide viewers with actively present images of thriving children, the future generation of Māori. These are, in the main, not the kinds of photographic still or moving images of Indigenous peoples produced at the end of the nineteenth and beginning of the twentieth centuries, in which individuals, communities, and cultures understood or desired to be "vanishing" were captured on film—and typically posed in a limited range of contrived scenes—for the dominant culture's pleasure and self-edification.[31] On the contrary, although these images inevitably participate in the ethnographic mode of that earlier "salvage" photography, they are oriented to the present and future. This power of photographic representation to emphasize the possibilities of the near and more distant future, and to imagine specifically Indigenous futures, is also evident in many of the print texts described in the previous sections.[32]

The fifty-three illustrations in *On Being Hawaiian* are exemplary in this respect. Holt arranges his diverse photographs to disrupt the strict time line on the front and back covers of his book.[33] Supporting his primary theme of Hawaiian epistemological continuity despite material changes, grounded in Hawaiian relationships to the land, Holt mixes contemporary and historical images, including photographs of his own ancestors, among representations of early contact with Europeans and photographs of Hawaiian artifacts and landscapes. He relates the distant past, the recent past, the present, and possible futures—in the form of contemporary children—by principles other than strict chronology or a narrative of cause and effect. Importantly, he captions the final photographs in the book "Keikis—A Trio of Hawaiian boys" (91) and "Crew of an outrigger canoe. This is still a popular Hawaiian sport" (92). *On Being Hawaiian* ends with images of smiling children at play and robust young men participating in an innovated "traditional" sport, suggesting a "new" Hawaiian future still linked to the Hawaiian past.[34] Other print texts include almost exclusively photographs from the late 1950s and early 1960s to illustrate their analyses of Indigenous "progress." *The Indian in Transition: The Indian Today* includes a photographic juxtaposition to demonstrate this central thesis. Positioned on facing pages, the photographs are captioned "Yesterday . . ." and "Today"; the former depicts a staged camp scene of staked tents and drying meat (it could be a cropped photograph of an old museum diorama), whereas the latter depicts modern houses of wood (12, 13). Other photographs in the booklet prominently feature children and young people participating in contemporary activities at school, play, work, and home. The twelve-page article "Canadian Indians Today" includes seventeen black-and-white photographs; moreover, four are a half-page size and others are a quarter page. All support Dunstan's claim that "progress of Indians is evident everywhere" (190). While most depict adult men (and one woman) successful in a range of rural and urban occupations—trapping, politics, fishing, nursing, ranching, mining, construction, steelwork, engineering, and traditional and contemporary arts—several depict children at school or on family outings; one depicts an Indian child in happy conversation with a child who is non-Native.[35] Māori children and young adults are similarly prominent in a range of scenes in *The Maori Today*, third edition, and *The Maori People in the Nineteen-Sixties*.

In contrast, the special issue of the *MASJ* employs a limited range of photographs that emphasize not the vibrant present or possible future but a waning, stereotypical past. Each version features the same color photograph on its cover, taken by Levine on the Rosebud Reservation in South Dakota, of a "Sioux dance and give-away honoring a boy leaving for Haskell Indian Institute [in Lawrence, Kansas]."[36] Although vivid and attractive, the image contributes to the problematic of juxtaposing the monolithic term "The Indian" with the relative time marker "Today" in that it fulfills U.S. and international stereotypes of "authentic" Indians as exclusively or ideally Sioux.[37] Moreover, its caption rehearses a colonial scene in which Indigenous children are removed to boarding schools, typically associated with the nineteenth and early twentieth centuries, and its most prominent figures are young men sporting feathered dance regalia in an outdoor setting. And although the caption potentially reveals the close proximity of the Haskell Indian Institute to the University of Kansas, where Levine worked and produced the special issue, a photograph of students actually attending

Haskell in the 1960s, appropriately captioned, would have made this connection more clear and more vital.[38]

Only two essays in the special issue, and one in the expanded book version, include photographs as illustrations. Set beside those in the texts from Hawai'i, Canada, and Aotearoa New Zealand, these black-and-white images stand out for their almost exclusive depiction of elders and artifacts. Younger adults and children are visible in but one of the thirteen photographs in the special issue, and they are part of the background, obscured by the central figure of an elder described in the caption as deceased. The book features nine photographs; including that previously described, only two include younger adults or children. The second resembles the first in that its central figure is also an elder, now dressed in regalia; its extended caption reads: *"Polyethylene Indianism. When Pow Wow day comes around, representatives of the assimilated, off-reservation faction appear in costumes which bear little resemblance to authentic, traditional Potawatomi wearing apparel. Conservative Potawatomi refer to these plastic and nylon outfits as 'Santa Claus' suits"* (n.p., inserted between 122 and 123). "Polyethylene" suggests "synthetic" or, less euphemistically, "fake." Whatever the intentions of the authors or editors, the effect is to reinforce stereotypes of Indian "authenticity" as existing only in the past or outside contemporary society, on the brink of extinction.

Here, it is instructive to return to *Aborigines Now*. Its ten black-and-white photographs are divided into two sets. The first contains four photographs, two on each side of the leaf inserted between pages 28 and 29, three-quarters of the way through "The Self-conscious People of Melbourne" by the anthropologist Diane Barwick. The two photographs facing page 28 are each captioned "Pintubi women, June 1962." In the upper image, five women and three children sit on bare ground among scrub grass, several holding wooden bowls, all unclothed. In the lower image, what appear to be the same five women now stand on similar bare ground, each carrying a billy can in her hand, three also supporting cans or boxes on their heads, all clothed in ill-fitting shirts or dresses that suggest government or mission handouts.[39] The two photographs facing page 29 are captioned "Pintubi men, June 1962" and "Pintubi family, July 1962." Similar to the first set, in the upper image four men sit on bare ground among scrub, apparently unclothed. In the lower image, a man, a woman, and two children sit on bare ground before a small fire, the children naked, the man and woman dressed in ill-fitting clothes that again suggest handouts.

None of these "ethnographic" images, presumably taken in the Pintubi's desert homelands in Western Australia and the Northern Territory, directly illustrates the essay by Barwick, which describes "the Kuris" or so-called dark people of Melbourne—that is, urban Indigenous Australians in the southern state of Victoria.[40] Barwick's statements at these points in the essay, however, create jarring captions for the photographs of the Pintubi. In the middle paragraph on page 28, facing the women sitting or standing together on bare ground, Barwick states: "Apparently an assimilated aborigine must live in standard urban housing, keep off the relief rolls, and must avoid large and conspicuous groups of relatives and friends." And farther down, Barwick states: "The dark people of Melbourne do not as yet form one community." On page 29, facing the men and family, Barwick states, "Some new forms of interaction help to reassure the Kuris that they can achieve standards of dress, behaviour, and organizing ability equal to those of the white," and, "Family celebrations such as weddings, anniversary dances, and twenty-first birthday parties are highly valued forms of conspicuous consumption." The juxtapositions disturb because the statements appear to belittle the individuals captured in the photographs; in turn, the apparent realism of the ethnographic images alongside this authoritative anthropological discourse reinforces stereotypes of Indigenous Australians as backward and degraded.

The second set, inserted between pages 44 and 45, toward the end of "Aborigines, Alcohol, and Assimilation" by the anthropologist Jeremy Beckett, contains six photographs, three "ethnographic" head shots and one "fashion" head shot of Indigenous individuals on one side of the inserted leaf and two journalistic shots of indoor urban scenes on the other. The three ethnographic head shots were all taken outdoors, and their captions indicate they were produced in New South Wales, the far west of which was the setting for Beckett's fieldwork in 1957. In addition, the captions read: "Resident of an aboriginal station" (an older woman), "Part-aboriginal man" (also older), and "Part-aboriginal lad" (pictured with his bicycle). In contrast, the fashion head shot was taken indoors; while its caption does not designate location, it both names and describes its subject: "Aboriginal model, pretty Lois

Briggs."[41] The two images of contemporary urban scenes are captioned "Robert Tudawali, bearded film star, with friends in Melbourne" and "Aboriginal night life in an Australian city." Both shots focus on three individuals, and both appear posed, as for a newspaper photographer. In the first a smiling Tudawali, wearing a tuxedo, stands between two well-dressed Indigenous women, who also smile for the camera.[42] In the second an attractive, well-dressed Indigenous woman is flanked by two Indigenous men who wear tuxedos and hold boomerangs. Juxtaposed with Beckett's essay about Indigenous alcohol consumption in small towns in western New South Wales, these evidently positive images, especially the fashion shot of Briggs and the group scenes of urban success, leisure, and sophistication, are subtly undermined. On page 45, facing Tudawali and his female friends, Beckett states: "Worse, drunken men are liable to assault their wives." And facing the well-dressed woman and the men holding boomerangs in a restaurant or club, the text reads, "This does not imply a sense of guilt or a resolve not to drink in future; drunkenness seems to provide him with a moral alibi. The whole affair is viewed with a wry amoral cynicism which is characteristic of aboriginal attitudes on many matters."[43] Stereotypical views are once again reinforced through the juxtaposition of realistic image and authoritative discourse. As with her voice and editorial vision, Reay's selection and placement of photographs in *Aborigines Now* better situate choices made by Levine and Lurie in "The Indian Today."

Arts and Indigenous Communities "Today"

Read alongside similar 1960s survey texts from other settler states and nations, perhaps the most glaring absence of the special issue of the *MASJ* is its lack of sustained interest in contemporary Indigenous languages, literatures, and arts. *The Maori People in the Nineteen-Sixties* provides an obvious contrast. Scattered among the symposium's anthropological, sociological, and historical pieces are Biggs's essay on Māori linguistics and language revival, Mataira's essay on new developments in Māori arts practice, and Pearson's essay on Māori and literature, which considers work by both non-Māori and Māori writers.[44] Also included are photographs of contemporary Māori poets, singers, carvers, painters, and sculptors and examples of recent Māori artwork.[45] The latter, especially, concretely demonstrate how Māori artists innovate both Indigenous and settler aesthetic traditions.

The inclusion of these essays and photographs may reflect Schwimmer's personal interest in language, literature, and the arts or his knowledge of these fields from his experience as editor of the Māori affairs journal *Te Ao Hou/The New World* from 1952 through 1961. They may also reflect a general awareness in New Zealand of the high quality of Māori artistic and performance traditions or a greater degree of comfort with depictions of a "modern" Indigenous people, at least within academic and government circles. But whatever the specific reasons, the effect is similar to that of the inclusion of personal voices and photographs of young people in this collection and in Holt's *On Being Hawaiian*, a greater sense of contemporary—and future— Indigenous vitality. As I have argued, an Indigenous personal voice and realistic, contemporary depictions of Indigenous young adults and children offer greater potential for developing a more nuanced understanding and empathy among Native and non-Native readers than do orthodox anthropological and sociological approaches on their own. Sustained attention to language, literature, and the arts engages more fully the complex and at times contradictory realities of Indigenous experiences and aspirations. This is true for any historical period, but certainly for twentieth-century periods marked "today." These elements potentially do more, as well. They help challenge outmoded, stereotypical ideas about Indigenous peoples, their representation, and their agency developed and calcified over the course of many "yesterdays." Surely this should be a primary aim of any project in the field of Indigenous studies that claims among its goals comprehensiveness and greater cross-cultural understanding.

An international approach to analyzing the 1965 special issue within its discursive and representational contexts suggests that such inclusion is, in fact, not too much to ask of settler surveys of Indigenous status produced in the mid-1960s. Forty years on, it seems even less to ask of our own decade—or of the many decades ahead. These first, global juxtapositions raise questions, however, about the conventions of U.S. survey texts. Was the special issue of the *MASJ* actually typical of U.S. practices in the twentieth-century representation of American Indians "today"?

Isolated "Today" in the Continental U.S.A.?

Survey texts with titles similar to that of the 1965 special issue were published in the United States across the twentieth century. Keyword searches in Internet databases, walks through the stacks of a university library, and visits to used bookstores reveal a wealth of material for juxtaposition and analysis. Among such texts published in the mid-1960s, several offer, similar to the special issue, general overviews of American Indian status; others focus more narrowly on specific geographical regions, states, or tribal groups. In 1964, for instance, the Tourist Division of the New Mexico Department of Development, based in Santa Fe, published the booklet *New Mexico's Indians of Today* by the anthropologist Bertha Pauline Dutton, head of the Division of Research at the Museum of New Mexico. In 1965, Hildegard Thompson, a former chief of education in the federal Bureau of Indian Affairs (BIA) and the author of books used in BIA schools, published the illustrated juvenile title *Getting to Know American Indians Today* through the New York–based commercial press Coward-McCann.[46] Also in 1965, the Mormon writer Dean L. Larsen published the booklet *American Indians Today* through the Division of Continuing Education at Brigham Young University in Provo, Utah.[47] In 1966, Dorothy F. Robinson, an Arizona-based author of popular books for young adults, published *Navajo Indians Today* through the San Antonio, Texas–based commercial press the Naylor Company ("Book Publishers of the Southwest"). Although introduced by an associate professor of education at Arizona State University, Dr. Bruce S. Meador, *Navajo Indians Today* is directed primarily at adolescent readers. Similar to the special issue, which was revised and expanded into a book, Robinson's book was released in a "revised and enlarged" edition in 1969.[48] At least one survey in this period limited its focus to a specific individual. In 1967, Ruth Kirk, an accomplished photographer and a prolific author of travel, natural history, and juvenile titles, published *David, Young Chief of the Quileutes: An American Indian Today* with Harcourt, Brace and World, a major commercial press based in New York.[49] Through an engaging story and sixty black-and-white photographs, Kirk introduces readers to four generations of Quileute living on Washington's dramatic Olympic Peninsula by staging a visit with the family of eleven-year-old

David Rock Hudson (Hoheeshata)—"Chief of an ancient people in a modern world" (8).

Though these mid-1960s surveys all include an ambiguous "today" in their titles, all but Kirk's, which is focused on an individual rather than a collective, render the term "Indian" explicitly plural, whether referring to a national category, a state-specific category, or a specific Indigenous nation category. This minor distinction suggests the possibility of a less monolithic approach to describing Indigenous peoples living in what is now the United States. Similarly, none of the titles employs an authoritative definite article. Their target audiences are diverse, however, including scholars and educated general readers but also tourists, juvenile readers, and readers from a particular religious denomination, making it perhaps less meaningful to juxtapose their methodological approaches with those of the special issue. Instead, given this diversity, it seems more productive to analyze *how* each text asserts or implies its primary audience.

Similar to their international counterparts, these mid-1960s U.S. surveys are directed primarily and often explicitly to non-Native readers. Robinson's *Navajo Indians Today* is of particular interest because there is a disjuncture between the description of the book's target audience in the foreword and that in the preface. In the foreword Meador asserts the text is aimed not at general readers (that is, non-Natives) but rather at Navajo, especially young adults. He writes, "The Navajo have asked, in private conversations and in public meetings, for books such as this one. There is widespread interest among the Navajos in education, and it is only natural that they would want books included which teach their youth about their traditions" (viii). Meador bases his claims on personal experiences at Arizona State: "I have observed many Indian college students, and I have noticed a keen interest on the part of many of them—not all—in learning about Indians. This book will help fill a void that exists among the Navajos, a readable account of their past and present" (ix–x). In contrast, Robinson, whom Meador describes as having "an interest in, and an admiration for, the Navajo and a professional background in writing and research," is much less assertive that the book is intended for or likely to appeal to Navajo. She begins her preface, which immediately follows Meador's foreword, "This book is written so that non-Navajos will become aware of this important tribe which has lived in the Southwest for hundreds of years, and appreciate their struggles in the past as well as the efforts they are making to build a good future." She then states, somewhat tentatively in the passive voice, "It is also hoped that this book will help the Navajos themselves to realize that they can not only be proud of their history but also have real contributions to make to others" (xi). While Robinson's statement is less confident and rhetorically less dramatic than Meador's assertion that the book will help "the Navajo retain his Navajoness" (viii), it describes a more realistic ambition for this book.

From the first page of the first chapter, the focus of Robinson's descriptions and the highly generalized nature of the information she presents—as well as her overall tone, specific word choices, and phonetic pronunciation guide for many Navajo and Spanish words—make clear that this work is intended primarily if not exclusively for non-Navajo (and non-Native) readers and that it is unlikely to appeal to many Navajo (or other Native) young people. Robinson opens chapter 1, "Navajoland Today," with a brief description of "Bennie Begay [. . .] a Navajo pupil at the Phoenix Indian School." Almost immediately, she refers to this child as "the small redskin," using language that many readers in the period—and certainly "today"—would recognize as offensive, especially if directed toward a Native audience (1). The chapter, marked as focused on contemporary life, consists of less than five pages. The book quickly moves to the brief chapter "Early Navajo Life" (that is, before the 1860s); it then moves to the more developed chapters "Resettlement" (an oblique reference to the Navajo Long Walk, which is the title of a subsection, followed by a second subsection titled "Back Home"), "Changing Patterns of Life" (with subsections devoted to education, economy, government, industry, farming, arts, and health), and "Religion and Tribal Customs" (with subsections on religious beliefs and tribal ceremonies). The trauma of the 1864 Long Walk, while discussed in some detail, is introduced in surprisingly positive terms: "The idea [of resettling the Navajo at Fort Sumner, New Mexico,] was excellent, but many things went wrong" (30). Pressing contemporary issues, such as federal relocation programs, are mentioned only in passing and, similar to the Long Walk, described positively: "Another answer to overcrowding would be to have families learn skills, leave the reservation and get jobs in cities. At present more than 3,000 men, women and children have done that.

However, they keep close ties with the life at home" (53). In her discussion of "religion," Robinson demonstrates her desire to create goodwill and understanding among non-Indian readers by comparing Navajo conceptions of "gods" to those of "Greek and Norse myths" (67) and Navajo conceptions of "ghosts and witchcraft" to the "similar beliefs" of "the Puritans" (70). The Navajo "today," in other words, are made to represent distant "yesterdays" of the dominant culture.

Robinson provides no separate conclusion; following a space break at the end of chapter 5, "Religion and Tribal Customs," she sums up her settler survey in two brief paragraphs:

> The Navajo are a tough people—tough in the sense of being strong and durable. They had to be, to overcome their years of hardship and adjust to the Atomic Age. In less than a hundred years they have changed from a hunting civilization to a complex culture that requires many highly intellectual skills. Knowing their history, non-Indians agree to the justice of their proud boast, "I am a Navajo!"
>
> In the future it is expected that the Navajos will take their places beside other Americans in industry, arts and sciences as the world of the future develops. (80)

In these few lines Robinson confirms her primary appeal to a non-Native audience. Though proffered as a compliment, her description of Navajo as "durable" is especially telling.[50] And rather than grapple with the implications of current problems or government policies for the future of the Navajo nation—or admit her inability to adequately describe their complexity—Robinson ends with an odd repetition of the word *future* and a number of well-worn clichés.

It is difficult to share Meador's confidence that *Navajo Indians Today* will speak to Navajo readers and meet their specific needs. Following the earlier juxtapositions of international texts, however, we can identify at least two aspects of Robinson's book that may have appealed to readers who identified as Navajo, American Indian, or Indigenous. First, although the image on the book's cover is a "timeless" representation of a Navajo hogan and brush arbor set against an empty southwestern landscape, the endpapers comprise a detailed map of the contemporary Navajo reservation that indicates the presence of towns and roads, as well as the proximity of several cities. And second, sixteen black-and-white photographs are situated between the preface and first chapter, preceded by a list of detailed captions. The photographs depict contemporary men, women, and children in a variety of scenes, including individuals and groups weaving, dancing, showing livestock at a 4-H competition, traveling, going to school, and working, as well as several reservation landscapes and communities. One photograph depicts a group of contemporary tribal leaders, who are all named in the caption; another depicts a performance by the Los Angeles Navajo Club, which, Robinson reports in chapter 4, "won top honors in the tribal dance contest" held on the reservation in 1965 (53). While nine of the photographs were provided by the BIA, the Arizona Development Board, commercial studios, and Arizona newspapers, seven were taken by Dr. Robert Roessel, the celebrated non-Navajo educator and Indian advocate who founded the innovative Rough Rock Demonstration School (now Rough Rock Community School) in 1966. In 1968, along with Ruth Roessel, his Navajo wife, Robert Roessel helped found Navajo Community College (now Diné College), the first tribal college opened in the United States; he also served as the college's first president.[51]

This reading of *Navajo Indians Today* suggests it may be productive to consider how the special issue described its own target audience. An academic periodical, the *MASJ* had an established readership of dues-paying members of the Midcontinent American Studies Association (MASA), but the editors hoped that their special issue, devoted to a specific topic, would attract an audience beyond its regular readers and be adopted for university courses. A year prior to its publication, as the special issue was being developed, the Fall 1964 issue announced that the editor and his special coeditor were in the process of collecting essays "devoted to briefing specialists in American studies on the current state of research in anthropological studies of the American Indian." Explicitly designed for nonanthropologists, the essays are meant to serve "as a primer of current *live* issues in the field of American Indian Studies" (n.p.; emphasis added). The announcement ends with instructions for ordering "extra copies." The following issue, published in spring 1965, announced that the "Indian Issue" would be devoted "to a series of papers on the current status of Indians in—and on the borders of—our society." Why were these nonspecialist anthropological studies of American Indians being gathered for American studies scholars in 1965? "Because," the announcement asserts, "although anthropologists are not agreed on a name for it, something important is happening in the Indian world." The announcement then quotes from a letter Levine wrote to Tax, in which he repeats his interest in "live issues": "One can't be an interdisciplinarian without knowing the *live* generalizations in the different disciplines" (n.p.; emphasis added). Like the earlier announcement, this one ends with instructions for ordering additional copies. Moreover, it boasts that the unpublished special issue "has already been adopted as a text in three different courses" and invites readers to "please spread the word."[52]

The special issue was specifically targeted, in other words, to American studies scholars, nonanthropologists, and university students and expressly designed to update these readers on the current state of scholarship in American Indian studies. Given the mission of MASA and its journal, these goals make sense. What is notable, though, is the strong assumption that, while American studies is by definition an interdisciplinary field, the complexities of American Indian studies— its "live issues" and "live generalizations"—can be grasped through an exclusive focus on anthropology. No other fields need be consulted. Less overtly, the announcements indicate a target audience not only of American studies scholars and their students but also of non-Indians. Levine does not share Meador's confidence, however misplaced in relation to Robinson's book, in the possibility of an Indigenous readership—nor does he consider what these readers might expect from a general survey of "The Indian Today."

At this point in the analysis, the casual phrasing of the second announcement's title and its simple illustration draw attention. Set in all caps, the title reads, "NOW, ABOUT THIS INDIAN ISSUE . . . ." The black-and-white line drawing, running along the length of the page's right margin, presents a stylized image of a male powwow dancer in full regalia (prominent bustle, knee-high moccasins, upright feather headdress) produced by the hand of Levine himself. Especially when viewed in conjunction with the pun on the word "issue"—suggesting that the title can be read "Now, about This Indian *Problem* . . ."—the illustration previews the problematic of the special issue's cover. The image appears based on the same photograph or a similar scene of the "Sioux dance and give-away" Levine attended on the Rosebud Reservation.

In the special issue itself, Levine foregoes the language of "live" issues and generalizations. Instead, in his introduction, "The Indian as American: Some Observations from the Editor's Notebook," he emphasizes his interest in interdisciplinarity:

> In scholarship, good fences do not make good neighbors. This set of essays is intended to break down as many fences as possible, not only to expose those of us who are not Indianists to what Indianists are up to, but also to expose the specialists to the attitudes and experience of those who deal with other areas of American Studies.[53] (3)

"Indianists"—that is, American Indian studies scholars—are equated with non-Native anthropologists (the inclusion of essays by Witt and Thomas notwithstanding). In the remainder of the introduction, Levine details his desire to create intersections among disciplines and reveals his and his field's anxieties about the role of American studies scholarship within the larger academy and the larger world. Written by "specialists" as a "general briefing" for nonspecialists, "The Indian Today" is to serve as a model of and a catalyst for reciprocal scholarly exchange. "There are things we can learn from our 'Indian problem,'" Levine tells his non-Native readers, "which we need to know in areas as diverse as cultural history and foreign policy, as well as things which we already know, from fields as diverse, which might help us to deal with Indians more successfully in the future than we have in the past" (3). The ambiguity of Levine's pronouns potentially implicates Americanists in a wide range of scholarly and extrascholarly pursuits. Levine repeats his point that, "outside of his own specialty, every specialist is a generalist" (4), and he emphasizes his concern that for Americanist scholars, in particular, "whose field is so broad and whose specialties and angles of attack [are] so various [. . .] there is always danger of their getting out of touch with developments in specialties other than their own" (4). He then states what many readers may have begun to suspect: "A second purpose of this collection, then, is to promote scholarly cross-fertilization, in the hope that the thinking it produces will show hybrid vitality" (4). It is not the future of American Indians that is at stake in this work; it is the health of American studies scholarship, the "hybrid vitality" of its interdisciplinary research. These concerns are taken up again in the "MASA Bulletin" section of the issue, also written by Levine.[54]

The aspirations expressed by Levine are admirable, and his concerns about potential pitfalls for the field's practitioners are legitimate. As the editor of a prominent journal in a relatively young and still marginalized interdiscipline, he writes in an enthusiastic, even maverick style that must have been invigorating for colleagues and graduate students in the mid-1960s. Reviewing his introduction four decades later and through the lens of contemporary Indigenous studies, one is struck by how much emphasis Levine places on the figure of the (non-Native) American studies scholar and by how little emphasis he places on American Indians as members of sovereign nations. With the exception of a single, oblique reference to "old treaties," Levine fails to explore the significance of the nation-to-nation relationship between American Indian nations and the United States confirmed in nearly four hundred treaties and other binding agreements (6). Levine focuses on Indians exclusively as individuals; deploying the rhetorical device of second-person address, he ostensibly offers such individuals this advice: "If *you* want to deal successfully with the dominant culture, *you* have to learn to think its way. In doing so, *you* of course become less Indian" (16; emphasis added). A substitution of pronouns reveals the statement as a conventional projection of the dominant culture, which can imagine only one future for Indigenous peoples—namely, assimilation into the mainstream. "If *they* want to deal successfully with the dominant culture, *they* have to learn to think its way. In doing so, *they* of course become less Indian." From the dominant perspective, everyone wins. In a similar vein, Levine sets out to debunk any notion that American Indians remain distinctive from other U.S. "minorities." Under the subheading "How Different Is an Indian?," he concludes, "Thus the Indians, though certainly unique, are no more unique than many other groups" (17). "Besides," he adds, "for what it is worth, even Indian diversity is not really unique" (18). "It is just as easy to list things which Indians have in common with other American minorities as it is to list ways in which they are different. [...] This list will not prove anything, but it does suggest that there is more potential for understanding and fellow-feeling than we may suspect" (19). Levine's final sentence reiterates his sense of the inevitability of Indian assimilation: "All of this is probably for the best, not because our culture is 'better' than any of theirs, but because it is better for living in this country right now" (21).

For the revised and expanded book version, a better-informed and less overtly assimilationist Levine titles his foreword "The Survival of Indian Identity," the final section heading in the introduction to the special issue. Early in the new foreword, he points to the "special mention" given the special issue by D'Arcy McNickle in the *Nation*. What Levine fails to mention is the context for McNickle's discussion. Titled "The Indian Tests the Mainstream," McNickle's article is a response not to the 1965 special issue but to Philleo Nash being ousted from his position as commissioner of the BIA. McNickle contextualizes Nash's forced resignation, in part, by discussing the lack of understanding of Indian issues among U.S. politicians and among U.S. citizens more generally. While he does single out the special issue for "special mention [...] because its collection of articles does attempt to let the Indian stand forth as a person and a group member in our contemporary industrialized society" (275), he emphasizes the *attempt* over the accomplishment, and he devotes no space to Levine or his introduction. Instead, McNickle singles out coeditor Lurie, whom he inaccurately describes as "the guest editor for this special issue," as "set[ting] the theme for the several essays by asking: Is there an Indian renaissance?" (275). He singles out as well the articles on Indian education by Murray and Rosalie Wax, on pan-Indianism by Robert Thomas, and on tribal self-government by Henry Dobyns as attempts to look at contemporary Indian issues from Indian perspectives (275–76).

Distinctly unlike Levine, McNickle supports his assertions about the contemporary Indian situation with quotations from a large number of U.S. and Canadian Indians. He ends his article in the *Nation* with a critique of government programs and a call for self-determination that counters Levine's expressed opinions about the inevitability of assimilation:

The Indians are ready [to make their own decisions], as their own statements suggest—statements, as we have tried to show here, which grow out of consensus thinking, in the way of the Indian tradition. [...]

When decision making is restored to the Indian people (they were making decisions as living societies long before

Columbus blundered into his first landfall), they can be expected to become involved in their own fate. It will be appropriate after that, and in due course, for them to become concerned with the fate of the larger society and with their place in it. (279)

Although Levine does not describe the process through which his thinking evolved in the period between writing his introduction to the special issue and writing his foreword to the book, he appears to have read McNickle closely and to have adjusted his language accordingly. He states in his foreword: "It would be presumptuous for this writer, a newcomer to Indian affairs, to offer any sort of general program or proposal for dealing with the problems and aspirations of this intriguing people. I don't know enough to make recommendations; indeed, I am not sure that anyone does" (7–8). Like many newcomers before him, Levine makes suggestions nonetheless.

When and Where Is "Today" in the U.S.A.?

Beyond the mid-1960s, a surprisingly large number of twentieth-century texts were published with titles either anticipating or echoing "The Indian Today" and its variants. To conclude, we might ask how the 1965 special issue stands up among this catalog of surveys by non-Native and Native individuals, organizations, and institutions, equipped with diverse knowledge and training, different biases and purposes, and distinct investments in Indigenous futures. Some, of course, are more appropriate for juxtaposition with a special issue of an academic journal than others. Before the mid-1960s, relevant titles include George Bird Grinnell's 1911 *The Indians of Today*; Charles A. Eastman's (Dakota) 1915 *The Indian To-day: The Past and Future of the First American* (reprinted in 1975); Flora Warren Seymour's 1926 *The Indians Today*; Robert Gessner's 1931 *Massacre: A Survey of Today's American Indian*; Mario and Mabel Sacheri's 1936 *Indians Today*; the Indian Council Fire's 1936 *Indians of Today*; the Indian Rights Association's *Indians Today, 1940* and *Indians Today, 1944*; the Indian Council Fire's 1947 *Indians of Today*, second edition; the U.S. Department of Interior, Office of Indian Affairs's 1950 pamphlet *Indians Yesterday and Today*; Carolissa Levi's 1956 *Chippewa Indians of Yesterday and Today*; Edith Dorian and W. N.

Wilson's 1957 *Hokahey! American Indians Then and Now*; Encyclopedia Britannica's 1957 short film *American Indians of Today*; the Minnesota Governor's Human Rights Commission's 1958 *Minnesota Indians (Yesterday and Today)*; the Indian Council Fire's 1960 *Indians of Today*, third edition; Gabe S. Paxton and Ann Nolan Clark's 1960 *We Are the Pima: The Pima Indians of Southern Arizona, Yesterday and Today*, published by the Pima Indian Agency; Kathleen R. Kepner's 1961 *The Wisconsin Indians of Yesterday and Today*, published by the Wisconsin Legislative Reference Library; Bertha P. Dutton's 1961 *Navajo Weaving Today*, published by the Museum of New Mexico Press (with a revised edition published in 1975); and Kathryn Hitte's 1961 children's book *I'm an Indian Today*, published in the Little Golden Book series.[55]

After the mid-1960s, relevant titles include the Portland (Oregon) American Indian Center's 1970 *American Indians of Today*; the Indian Council Fire's 1971 *Indians of Today*, fourth edition; the Society for Visual Education's 1971 *Indians of the Southwest Today*; John I. Griffin's 1972 *Today with the Havasupai Indians*; Howard M. Bahr, Bruce A. Chadwick, and Robert C. Day's 1972 textbook *Native Americans Today: Sociological Perspectives*; Olga Hoyt's 1972 *American Indians Today*, published for a juvenile audience; the proceedings of the 1971 Second Convocation of Indian Scholars, published in 1974 by the Indian Historian Press as *Indian Voices: The Native American Today*; Ervin Stuntz's 1975 self-published work *Our First Americans: The Indians of Today*; BFA Educational Media's 1976 film *Native Americans— Yesterday and Today*, produced for elementary and junior high schools; Annals of the American Academy of Political and Social Sciences's 1978 volume "American Indians Today"; Elaine Jahner's 1981 scholarly work *American Indians Today: Their Thought, Their Literature, Their Art*; Alvin M. Josephy's popular 1982 work *Now That the Buffalo's Gone: A Study of Today's Indians*; Finn Madsen's 1983 *American Indian Today: The Native American in Text and Poems*; Frank W. Porter's 1983 *Maryland Indians, Yesterday and Today*, published by the Museum and Library of Maryland History; Brent Ashabranner's 1984 *To Live in Two Worlds: American Indian Youth Today*, published for a juvenile audience; William L. Bryon's 1985 *Montana's Indians: Yesterday and Today*, published by *Montana Magazine*; Arlene B. Hirschfelder's 1986 *Happily May I Walk: American Indians and Alaska Natives Today*; Judith Harlan's 1987 *American Indians Today: Issues and Conflicts*; Floy C.

Pepper and Pat Badnin-Yoes's 1990 *Indians in Oregon Today*, published by the Oregon Department of Education; the BIA's 1991 *American Indians Today: Answers to Your Questions*; Eleanor West Hertz's 1991 *The Chickahominy Indians of Virginia: Yesterday and Today*; Roberta L. Hall's 1991 *The Coquille Indians: Yesterday, Today, and Tomorrow*; Arlene B. Hirschfelder and Martha Kreipe De Mantano's 1993 *The Native American Almanac: A Portrait of Native America Today*; renowned Laguna writer Leslie Marmon Silko's 1996 *Yellow Woman and the Beauty of the Spirit: Essays on Native American Life Today*; and William Moreau Goins's 1998 *South Carolina Indians Today: An Educational Resource Guide*.[56] If we add the first years of the new century, we can include Jack Utter's 2001 scholarly work *American Indians: Answers to Today's Questions* and the 2004 book series North American Indians Today, written by various authors and developed for use in public elementary and junior high schools, with separate titles for specific Indian nations, including Navajo, Iroquois, Cheyenne, Apache, Ojibwe, Sioux, Cherokee, Potawatomi, Seminole, Crow, Osage, Pueblo, Creek, Huron, and Comanche.[57]

The catalog of twentieth- and early twenty-first-century variations on "The Indian Today" is actually more extensive than this list suggests. If we include not only books and films but also essays, articles, government and organizational reports, and published speeches, it grows exponentially. These titles and the histories of their publication and distribution indicate that the 1965 special issue is but one attempt to satisfy a perennial desire by non-Native and Native individuals and organizations, public institutions, and government agencies to understand, define, and proclaim how American Indians do and, more often, do not fit into a "contemporary" world. The long list of twentieth-century surveys indicates, as well, the kinds of choices the editors of the special issue made with the conventional and flexible but ultimately ambiguous language of "the" Indian juxtaposed with "today." What is the effect of this limited phrasing compared with the effect of the more expansive juxtaposition of "the" Indian and its variants with the coupled relative time markers "yesterday and today"? And what can it mean that only two titles—one from 1915—refer to the promise of Indigenous lives beyond the present, either by adding a third relative time marker, "tomorrow," or explicitly stating the "future"?[58]

Within this diachronic approach to juxtaposition, of particular interest are those texts authored by American Indians or sponsored by Native organizations. In 1939, for instance, D'Arcy McNickle delivered "The American Indian Today" at the Fifth Annual Spring Conference of the Missouri Archaeology Society; the speech was then published in the society's journal, *The Missouri Archaeologist*, in September of that year. A prominent employee of the Office of Indian Affairs (OIA; now the Bureau of Indian Affairs), McNickle was a strong advocate for the 1934 Indian Reorganization Act and other OIA policies developed under the administration of John Collier. In the early parts of the speech, McNickle addresses his audience of archaeologists as "students of the past" and, accordingly, recounts salient episodes from the "yesterday" of nineteenth-century U.S. and American Indian history (1). He focuses the majority of his remarks, though, on the contemporary "right of Indian culture to survive" and "to build a future world" (9, 10). McNickle makes his case for relating the Indian past to an Indian present moving into the future through brief but specific examples of cultural continuity. "The Hopi are a living people," he states, "yet they are an archaic people. And throughout the Indian world this same symbiosis exists—the past functioning in the present. Sometimes that past is hard to discover; it may be fragmentary and distorted, yet inevitably it crops out" (4). He concludes by narrowing his focus to the defining relationship Indian people continue to have, he argues, with their land and by appealing to his audience's sense of a common, land-based humanity: "The Indian has the quality of belonging to the earth which, I suppose, at one time all peoples of the earth had and enjoyed. He belongs to the earth because he has never divorced himself from it." In the past, McNickle argues, misguided federal policies attempted "to break the Indian" from this sense of belonging in order to force assimilation. In contrast, with new OIA policies "we have decided that an Indian, like an Anglo-Saxon, is entitled to believe in himself, in the strength of his past, and in the glory of his future" (10). Addressed to a non-Native audience, and specifically to non-Native "students" of the Indian "past," McNickle's 1939 "Indian Today" concerns itself with ongoing Indigenous–settler *relations* and expresses explicit interest in creating a climate for Indian *futurity*. Set beside the 1965 special issue of the *MASJ*—addressed to scholars of the American past and present actively engaged in imagining its possible futures—McNickle's speech in Missouri makes the "progressive" collection guided by Levine and Lurie look oddly narrow and old-fashioned.

Of particular interest, too, are the four editions of *Indians of Today* sponsored by the Indian Council Fire organization based in Chicago and published by small Chicago presses in 1936, 1947, 1960, and 1971. Compiled and edited by the prolific non-Native writer and Indian advocate Marion E. Gridley, these collections of brief biographies spotlight "modern" and "living" American Indian educators, artists, physicians, judges, business people, athletes, and tribal, civic, and religious leaders. In his foreword to the 1936 edition, the noted politician of American Indian descent Charles Curtis writes, "The purpose of 'Indians of Today' is to indicate the progress of the American Indian race through the achievements of some of its outstanding individuals" (5).[59] This first edition contains ninety-six entries, most of which include a current black-and-white photograph of the notable man or woman. Several had achieved national and even international renown, such as Gertrude Bonnin (Zit-ka-la-sa), Henry Roe Cloud, Henry Chee Dodge, Charles A. Eastman (Ohiyesa), Mourning Dove (Mrs. Fred Galler), Arthur C. Parker, Mollie Spotted Elk, and James F. Thorpe.[60] The majority of entries, however, profile men and women whose achievements were largely unknown outside their local, tribal, regional, or professional circles. In her foreword to the 1947 edition, the Cherokee educator and activist Ruth Muskrat Bronson, then executive secretary of the National Congress of American Indians (NCAI), describes the subjects of these biographies more specifically as "Indians who have made successful adjustments in the White World" (4). The intended audience, Bronson writes, is "Indian youth" and "Indian boys and girls" who may be "insecure and doubting" of their ability "to hold their own in this alien, oftentimes hostile, White world" (3). These "examples of Indian accomplishments" will provide Indian children and young adults with "the incitement to endeavor" through "examples out of their own blood and cultural backgrounds against which to measure their own potentialities" (4, 3). In her focus on the urgent needs of Indigenous young people, Bronson's sense of purpose in representing Indians "today" echoes McNickle.

The third and fourth editions continue to highlight the Indian present for the purpose of building Indian futures. In her foreword to the 1960 edition, Indian Council Fire president Ethel Frazier Walker (Santee Dakota) restates Bronson's reasoning: "We therefore need encouragement, constructive criticism, and above all the inspiration specially provided by those of our own people who have accomplished and realized their ambitions in every profession and walk of life. These individuals serve as a beacon, as it were, to all who will heed and follow" (n.p.). The introduction to the 1971 edition notes that Gridley made a point to include biographies not only of adults but also of "young people . . . who, though just starting out in life, have already demonstrated ability and shown promise of potential greatness" (v). This final edition profiles 372 notable living American Indians and includes twenty pages of photographs of art produced by living American Indians, featuring paintings and print works alongside sculpture, pottery, and baskets. Of the hundreds of accomplished individuals profiled in the four editions of *Indians of Today*, almost none gains mention in either version of the 1965 special issue.

The most compelling survey to juxtapose with the special issue of the *MASJ* is the March 1978 issue of the bimonthly *Annals of the American Academy of Political and Social Science*. Titled "American Indians Today," the volume was coedited by J. Milton Yinger, a professor of sociology and anthropology, and George Eaton Simpson, a professor emeritus of sociology and anthropology at Oberlin College in Ohio. Composed of a brief foreword by the editors and twelve essays by sixteen contributors, twelve men and four women (including Yinger and Simpson, who cowrote an essay, as well as their foreword), the volume ranges across issues of economics, education, health care, government policy, culture and identity, law and litigation, the Indian Claims Commission, demographics, urbanization, and integration. Among the contributors are Lurie, Thomas, and the Waxes from the two versions of the special issue. In addition to Thomas, the *Annals* includes two other American Indian authors: Raymond V. Butler (Blackfeet), a BIA official appointed acting commissioner of Indian affairs in 1977, and Vine Deloria Jr. (Standing Rock Sioux), former executive director of the NCAI and former chairman of the Institute for the Development of Indian Law, as well as a prolific writer and social commentator. As Yinger and Simpson point out in their foreword, the March 1978 issue of the *Annals* was produced as a twenty-year follow-up to the May 1957 issue, "American Indians and American Life," which

Simpson and Yinger also coedited. Similar to its 1978 counterpart, the 1957 volume is composed of a brief foreword by the editors and sixteen essays by twenty-three contributors, sixteen men and five women (including Simpson and Yinger, who cowrote an essay with a third male author). In the 1957 volume, essays are arranged into four categories: "The Background," "The Administration of Indian Affairs," "Institutional Aspects of Contemporary Indian Life," and "The Integration of American Indians." The only contributor to the special issue also included here is Lurie. Like the 1978 volume, the 1957 volume includes essays by three American Indians: McNickle (listed as Flathead), then director of American Indian Development, a privately financed project devoted to Indian leadership training; Helen L. Peterson (Oglala Sioux), executive director of the NCAI; and Edward P. Dozier (Santa Clara Pueblo), an assistant professor of anthropology at Northwestern University.[61]

These "Indian" volumes of the *Annals*, published twenty years apart, neatly bookend the 1965 special issue of the *MASJ*, and a juxtaposition of Simpson and Yinger's editorial framings with those of Levine suggests what may now seem an obvious conclusion to this chapter. Part of Simpson and Yinger's 1957 foreword reads as extreme understatement "today": "White Americans seem continually to be rediscovering the Indians" (vii). Indeed, my lists of publications make this observation abundantly clear. The coeditors note, however, an important mid-twentieth-century context never mentioned in either Levine's introduction to the special issue or foreword to the revised book version: "World-wide attention to questions of *colonialism* and minorities have been among the forces renewing America's interest in her Indian citizens" (vii; emphasis added). Two decades later, Yinger and Simpson open their 1978 foreword: "A great many changes have occurred in American society and among Native Americans since the appearance of an earlier issue of The Annals (May 1957)." Yet despite these "significant changes," they comment, "We are struck also by the continuity" (vii).

What transpired during the decades between the two "Indian" volumes of the *Annals*? Indigenous peoples in the United States survived and protested the disastrous effects of Termination legislation passed in the early 1950s, finally seeing that legislation overturned in 1972. They survived (and sometimes benefited from) federal urban relocation programs begun in the same era, as well as a host of new economic, social, and education programs developed for (and occasionally by) American Indians across the 1960s and 1970s. A large number of Indian leaders, including a growing cohort of younger activists, attended the 1961 AICC; later that year, some of the younger activists founded the National Indian Youth Council. American Indian artists and writers began to attend the newly founded Institute of American Indian Arts in Santa Fe in 1962; Navajo and other college students began to attend an Indigenous institution of higher learning, Navajo Community College, which the Navajo nation founded at the end of 1968. American Indian intellectuals gathered for the First Convocation of American Indian Scholars in 1970 and for the second convocation in 1971. A wide range of American Indians, of all ages, founded local, regional, and national activist organizations and instigated vibrant political activism: from major events that included the "fish-ins" begun in the Pacific Northwest in 1964, the occupation of Alcatraz Island in San Francisco Bay by Indians of All Tribes from 1969 to 1971, the Trail of Broken Treaties caravan and occupation of BIA headquarters in Washington, DC, supported by the American Indian Movement in 1972, the armed occupation at Wounded Knee, South Dakota, in 1973, and the International Indian Treaty Council held in 1974 to an ongoing series of smaller sit-ins, occupations, protests, and councils organized throughout the settler nation. They anticipated and responded to the amnesia of the U.S. bicentennial celebrations in 1976. And they published an astonishing amount of writing in all genres, including journalism and social critique; history, anthropology, and linguistics; legal and political studies; memoir and drama; poetry and short fiction; and the novel, including N. Scott Momaday's *House Made of Dawn* in 1968, which won the Pulitzer Prize in 1969, and Leslie Marmon Silko's *Ceremony* in 1977, which became the most discussed Indigenous literary text in the United States for several decades.

Moreover, between 1957 and 1978, Indigenous peoples in other settler nation-states fought similar political and social battles, often using similar tactics, and they made similar gains in access to education, political power, and publishing. The Federal Council for the Advancement of Aboriginals and Torres Strait Islanders was founded in Australia in 1959. Canada's National Indian Council formed in 1961, regrouping as the National Indian Brotherhood and the Native Council of Canada in 1967–1970. In Aotearoa New Zealand, the Maori Organization on

Human Rights was founded in 1967; the activist group Nga Tama-
toa (The Young Warriors) emerged in 1970; and the first Maori Artists and Writers Conference was held in 1973. Indigenous Australians
erected a Tent Embassy on the Parliament grounds in Canberra in
1972, and they formed the National Aboriginal Forum in 1974. Māori
activists organized a National Land March in 1975, culminating in
their own Tent Embassy erected on the Parliament grounds in Wellington. The World Council of Indigenous Peoples held a preparatory
meeting in Guyana in 1974, followed by a first General Assembly in
Canada in 1975 and a second in Sweden in 1977. The first Inuit Circum-
polar Conference was held in 1977 in Alaska. Non-Indigenous organizations, too, took significant action on behalf of Indigenous peoples
during these years, including the International Labour Organization,
the United Nations, the International Work Group on Indigenous Affairs, Survival International, and Cultural Survival.[62]

As Yinger and Simpson emphasized in 1978, these were "significant
changes." But the coeditors were so struck by how much things had
not changed for American Indians over those twenty years they were
prompted to simply reprint in full their foreword from the 1957 volume: "For it may suggest the distance we have yet to go before the
country has truly redefined its racial and ethnic practices. It may also
emphasize the importance of the study of those practices for an understanding of American society" (vii). Among the things that had
not changed during the years of research, publication, revision, and
republication of the 1965 special issue of the *MASJ*, of course, was the
ongoing but evolving context of colonialism—and the ongoing lack
of understanding of how the settler colonialism practiced within the
borders of the United States might relate to off-shore U.S. imperialism
and to various manifestations of colonialism around the globe.

Whose "Indian" is this? Whose "today"?

And what might be possible—if the term *settler* were openly
articulated—"tomorrow"?

2

Unsettling the Spirit of '76

American Indians Anticipate the U.S. Bicentennial

> I guess we're saying that we have the right to read the Declaration of Independence.
>> ► Vernon Bellecourt in an interview by Richard Ballard, July 1973

> We need to examine the state of the modern Indian social movement and try to anticipate some of the things that can be done to make 1976 a celebration of independence for American Indians as well as other Americans.
>> ► Vine Deloria Jr., "1976: The Desperate Need for Understanding"

Graffiti on the footpath declared, "FIRST FEET WERE ABORIGINAL," and farther along, "YOU ARE STANDING ON ABORIGINAL LAND." The concrete path meandered through grass and gum trees and then up a steep rise, eventually leading visitors to a scenic overlook where outcroppings of red rock framed postcard views of the famous Sydney Harbor. There, less than ten feet above the bold graffiti, another tourist readied his camera—not to record the legible evidence of a historic protest but rather to snap the expected souvenir of his wife on holiday. The woman positioned herself near the viewpoint's protective railing, clutched her handbag, and smiled. Behind her the expanse of blue sky dotted with clouds and the expanse of blue sea dotted with sailboats and tall ships sparkled brilliantly.

The year was 1988. Several days prior to the tourists' visit, Australia had observed a bicentennial anniversary considered crucial by its settler government and a majority of its settler citizens, both to understanding the young nation-state's past and to securing its future. In a dramatic reenactment, the First Fleet—those eighteenth-century tall ships that carried the original British settlers to the shores of Port

FIGURE 1. Indigenous graffiti at a scenic overlook above Sydney Harbor during the 1988 Australian bicentennial celebrations. Activist slogans included "You Are Standing on Aboriginal Land" and "First Feet Were Aboriginal." Photograph by author.

Jackson, now Sydney—had arrived in the harbor yet again. Although Captain James Cook landed on the east coast of Australia and claimed its soil for Britain on August 22, 1770, and although his accomplishments were recognized during the first Australian bicentenary of 1970, the Great Explorer and his men had not settled. The so-called First Fleet, captained by Arthur Phillip, landed in the harbor on January 26, 1788, with a crew of naval officers and convicts. Under authority of the crown, it was Phillip who founded the city of Sydney and the colony of New South Wales, becoming its first governor.

Celebrations of January 26—as birth date for Australian settler identity and point of origin for a coherent narrative of Australian settler history—have occurred at least since 1808, the twentieth anniversary of Phillip's landing and momentous proclamation, although the first official observance of Foundation Day, as it was then called, was not held until the thirtieth anniversary in 1818. For the fiftieth anniversary in 1838, January 26 was declared a public holiday by the colonial government of New South Wales and officially designated Australia

Day. In 1888, the centennial was distinguished by national celebrations of Anniversary Day, as was the 1938 sesquicentennial, when, in addition to formal dinners, parades, a sailing regatta, and other sporting events, the anniversary featured a "living history" reenactment of Phillip's landing on shore and formal declaration of colonial possession. After World War II, not only New South Wales but all Australian states and territories (which had sometimes observed the anniversary and sometimes not) marked January 26 as Australia Day on an annual basis. The bicentennial celebrations in 1988, however, marked the first observance of January 26 as a fully synchronized public holiday across the continental expanse of the Australian settler nation.[1]

Indigenous Australians renamed January 26 as Day of Mourning at least as early as 1938. That year, activists seized the sesquicentennial as a national platform from which to launch the "first major expression of Indigenous [Australian] sovereignty" in the contemporary era (Foley, 121).[2] While settlers enjoyed their festivities, the newly founded Aborigines Progressive Association met in Sydney's Australian Hall for a conference, "Our Historic Day of Mourning and Protest," and produced a number of documents meant for broad distribution.[3] In *Aborigines Claim Citizenship Rights!*, for instance, the association declares to the settler nation: "We do not ask for your charity; we do not ask you to study us as scientific freaks. Above all, we do not ask for your 'protection.' No thanks! We have had 150 years of that! We ask only for justice, decency and fair play" (Attwood, 83). The Aboriginal activist Gary Foley describes how "from that day in 1938 to the present day, Indigenous people know January 26 as 'Invasion Day' [...]. This simple but symbolically powerful appropriation by Indigenous people of white Australia's most important national day is in itself both an assertion of Aboriginal sovereignty and the most enduring legacy of the 1938 'Day of Mourning' protest" (122).

During the buildup to 1988, as the settler nation prepared for its two hundredth birthday, Indigenous activists threatened to disrupt the festivities with a countercelebration of their remarkable survival despite two hundred years of colonialism. Australia Day 1988 was "officially dubbed 'the Celebration of the Nation' and irreverently called the 'Masturbation of the Nation' by Indigenous activists" (Foley, 130). Writing in the *Melbourne Age* on August 26, 1987, the Aboriginal activist Galarrwuy Yunupingu stated the Indigenous perspective in these terms:

Next year's celebration of 200 years of European occupation
of Australia, as it stands, spits in the face of every Aboriginal
and Islander person. You are asking us to stand by while you
congratulate yourselves of having stolen our land. You want us
to keep quiet while you celebrate the raising of the first British
flag in 1788. For us, this was an act of war which led to genocide. (Attwood, 315)

Similar to the sesquicentennial, the 1988 festivities included, once
again, a "living history" reenactment of the eighteenth-century First
Fleet arriving in a twentieth-century Sydney Harbor. In an attempt
at conciliation with the Indigenous community, though, the costume
drama of Phillip's landing on shore and formal claiming of the colony
were not performed. Nonetheless, despite this preemptive gesture of
"goodwill," an estimated 15,000 Indigenous Australians from around
the continent gathered in Sydney on January 26 to stand in unity
against the tall ships, to demonstrate that, indeed, "First *Feet* Were
Aboriginal." From Redfern Oval to Hyde Park, they marched through
the thick of the colonial celebration under the banners "Freedom, Justice and Hope" and "We Have Survived." Non-Indigenous allies were
invited to join the march at its halfway point, swelling the protest to an
estimated 40,000. The largest event of Indigenous activism ever staged
in Australia, the unprecedented march was also a celebration of active
Indigenous presence.[4] Images of Indigenous and non-Indigenous Australians marching together, the defiant slogans of their banners, and
the striking black, red, and yellow colors of the Aboriginal flag were
disseminated across the country and around the globe through newspaper photographs, television news footage, and the documentary film
Australia Daze.[5] The following day, Foley, who had been instrumental in organizing the march, was quoted in the *Melbourne Sun*: "It's so
magnificent to see black and white Australians together in harmony.
It's what we always said could happen. This is what Australia could and
should be like" (Attwood, 315).[6]

The graffiti the tourist couple walked upon several days later had
no doubt been produced by those gathered for the march. If Foley
was correct, the bold block print of the painted slogans, which
seemed to shout from the footpath, was not simply an angry affront
to settler citizens or international visitors. More important, it was yet

another attempt at education, a gesture toward a genuine reassessment of history—truth telling as an unsettling and ultimately decolonizing strategy—a necessary prerequisite for any form of reconciliation and any possibility of future progress.[7]

That no actor was scheduled to play Phillip landing on shore and proclaiming ownership over Australian soil did not deter Indigenous activists from planning colonial dramas of their own. While 15,000 marched in unprecedented protest and celebration, a smaller group, led by Michael Mansell, staged its own, revised reenactment. In the activist version of "living history" and Phillip's now mere *attempt* at arrival, Aboriginal defenders successfully repelled the invaders, playfully dumping the British captain into the surf. Moreover, as the tall ships had sailed from Portsmouth in England to Sydney in Australia, the Aboriginal ecologist, actor, and political activist Burnum Burnum had traveled by air in the opposite direction. Having successfully landed on English soil, on January 26 he planted the bold colors of the Aboriginal flag on the beach below the White Cliffs of Dover, those iconic guards against invasion from an all-too-close-by continental Europe. In a parody of Phillip's 1788 proclamation, from this strategic vantage Burnum assumed possession of the whole of England on behalf of Indigenous Australia. "In claiming this colonial outpost," he declared, "we wish no harm to you natives, but assure you that we are here to bring you good manners, refinement and an opportunity to make a Koompartoo—'a fresh start.'" Burnum's declaration is appropriately ironic in its overview of how Indigenous colonizers will treat the "Caucasian race" of England, and the details of his several "assurances" to the natives provide a compressed summary of the trauma inflicted by the colonizing English and other settlers over the previous two hundred years. These include Burnum's "pledge not to sterilize your women, nor to separate your children from their families," his "intention" not to "souvenir, pickle and preserve the heads of 2000 of your people, nor to publicly display the skeletal remains of your Royal Highness," and his "solemn promise not to make a quarry of England and export your valuable minerals back to the old country Australia."[8] In this respect the dark humor of Burnum's declaration echoes the parodic "Alcatraz Proclamation to the Great White Father and His People" delivered by the activist group Indians of All Tribes near the beginning of their nineteen-month occupation of Alcatraz Island in San Francisco Bay from 1969 to 1971.[9]

Throughout 1988, Indigenous Australians honored their activist forebears by marking the settler bicentennial as the Year of Mourning while celebrating their survival and actively building toward their future. Activists demanded the negotiation of a treaty acknowledging Aboriginal rights, while the Bicentennial National Aboriginal and Torres Strait Islander Program helped fund a number of Aboriginal Keeping Places (museums), as well as oral history, art, and literary projects.[10] The poet and activist Kath Walker, who in 1964 had become the first Aboriginal woman to publish a book of poems, *We Are Going*, readopted her tribal name, Oodgeroo Noonuccal, to protest the bicentennial.[11] The Aboriginal political writer and poet Kevin Gilbert saw the landmark collection he edited, *Inside Black Australia: An Anthology of Aboriginal Poetry*, published by Penguin Books. In his introduction, Gilbert asks, "How many will remember *Aboriginal* history as Australia marches to the 1988 Bicentenary to celebrate the *terra nullius* fiction—the lie of peaceful settlement [...]?" (xxiv). In one of his own contributions to the anthology, "Celebrators '88," Gilbert imagines this disturbing answer:

The legislators move their pen in poise
like thieves a'crouch above the pilfered purse
how many thousand million shall they give
to celebrate the Bicentenary
and cloak the murders in hilarity
and sing above the rumble of the hearse.
 (198)

Against such "cloaking" of theft and violence, Indigenous individuals, communities, and activist groups worked to refocus the settler celebration and the media attention it garnered to promote truth telling and to further their agenda of recognition and justice.

Standing on the footpath above Sydney Harbor, I could not resist taking my own photograph of the tourist couple snapping the expected souvenir of their holiday. When they proudly displayed the photo to family and friends, I wondered, would they remark upon their unexpected insertion into the (post)colonial ironies of Indigenous–settler history, politics, and public discourse? Would they describe how, in order to capture the full spectacle of the eighteenth-century First

Fleet moored in a twentieth-century Sydney Harbor, they had literally walked across and stood upon the insistence that "First *Feet* Were Aboriginal"? But I also wondered something else: Had Indigenous peoples responded similarly to the bicentennial celebrations in the United States more than a decade earlier? In 1976, were there large-scale protests and unprecedented gatherings to disrupt the official birthday of the world's most powerful settler nation? Had American Indians across the continent—or, for that matter, Inuit and Alaska Natives in Alaska, Hawaiians in Hawai'i, Chamorro in the U.S. territory of Guam, or Samoans in the U.S. territory of American Samoa—declared Independence Day a Day of Mourning or staged countercelebrations for two hundred years of survival? Had activists seized the settler anniversary to assert the long histories of tribal nations, which far outstretched a mere two centuries, or to assert prior and ongoing relationships to the land? Had they inscribed protest graffiti—shouted memory—on the land itself? Invited non-Native allies to march in unity? Attempted an ironic counterclaim to Europe?

In 1988, I had no idea. Although aware of the major events of American Indian activism of the late 1960s and early 1970s, including not only the occupation of Alcatraz from 1969 to 1971 but also the Trail of Broken Treaties cross-country caravan and occupation of the BIA in Washington, DC, in late 1972 and the armed struggle at Wounded Knee, South Dakota, in early 1973, both of which involved the American Indian Movement (AIM), up to that point I had not heard of any protest action or activist discourse associated specifically with the U.S. bicentennial—and had never thought to ask.

The discrepancy between highly visible Indigenous responses to the Australian bicentennial and a seeming absence of Indigenous responses to its U.S. predecessor came into sharper focus as additional commemorations of settler colonialisms were planned, staged, and actively protested in the years following. These included the sesquicentennial of the signing of the Treaty of Waitangi in Aotearoa New Zealand in 1990, the Columbus quincentenary observations in Europe and the Americas in 1992, the centennial of the U.S. overthrow of the Hawaiian kingdom in 1993, and the related centennial of the U.S. annexation of the Hawaiian Islands in 1998. In graduate school I learned that the Pulitzer Prize–winning Kiowa and Cherokee writer N. Scott Momaday published not one but two book-length works of literature in 1976:

a collection of dynamic and precise poems illustrated by the author, *The Gourd Dancer*, and a provocative memoir and family chronicle, complete with photographs, *The Names*. Once I began to look, I found book-length American Indian works published during the bicentennial in nearly every genre, including the compilation of journalism and other writings *Tribal Scenes and Ceremonies* by Gerald Vizenor (Anishinaabe); the collection of speeches *Contemporary Native American Address* edited by John R. Maestas; the novel *The Reservation* by Ted C. Williams (Tuscarora); the poetry collections *Turtle, Bear, and Wolf* by Peter Blue Cloud (Mohawk), *To Frighten a Storm* by Gladys Cardiff (Cherokee), *Naming the Dark: Poems for the Cheyenne* by Lance Henson (Cheyenne), *Going for the Rain* by Simon Ortiz (Acoma), and *Long Division: A Tribal History* by Wendy Rose (Hopi/Miwok); and the anthologies *Carriers of the Dream Wheel* edited by Duane Niatum (Klallam) and *The First Skin around Me: Contemporary American Tribal Poetry* edited by James L. White. All of these works, however, had been outsold and overshadowed by the purported Cherokee autobiography *The Education of Little Tree*, also first published in 1976, written under the name Forrest Carter by Asa Earl Carter, a non-Native writer and a known racist who assumed an Indian identity.[12] Was the seeming absence of Indigenous responses to 1976 more accurately an erasure? It was hard to tell. None of the works I initially cataloged appeared to respond overtly to the U.S. settler celebration. Where was the bold graffiti, the swelling throngs of activists, the planting of Native flags, and the mock Declarations of Independence?

Between 1988 and 2008, inspired by Indigenous responses to the Australian bicentennial, I slowly located the kinds of texts I first thought to look for while approaching the scenic viewpoint above Sydney Harbor. Over those two decades, I accumulated an archive of newspaper and magazine articles, government and academic reports, museum and gallery exhibition catalogs, editorials, speeches, essays, poems, and—most surprising—novels that explicitly document the responses of Indigenous peoples to the U.S. bicentennial. As the archive increased, I developed a more nuanced understanding of why these written texts and the many protest events they report, plan, or imagine have not been featured in typical accounts of American Indian activism. The results of my protracted inquiry were other than I could have anticipated while photographing tourists standing on Aboriginal graffiti in early 1988. *Anticipation,* however, turned out to be a key heuristic for interpreting American Indian responses to the Spirit of '76.

Anticipating Settler Celebration

At first glance, Indigenous responses to the 1976 U.S. bicentennial (officially designated the Bicentennial Celebration of American Independence and the American Revolution Bicentennial Observance) appear much less dramatic than the unprecedented march, rally, and counter-reenactment organized by activists in Sydney or Burnum's flag planting and colonial counterclaim in Dover. There was no single event of mourning protest or survival celebration, nor any single proclamation, serious or satiric, that coalesced into a national statement or slogan. The response to 1976 was more diffuse and more muted, and understandably, it has received far less attention than other aspects of 1970s activism and writing. Paul Chaat Smith (Comanche) and Robert Warrior (Osage), for instance, see no reason to mention the U.S. bicentennial in their seminal account of the era, *Like a Hurricane: The Indian Movement from Alcatraz to Wounded Knee* (1996). My own research confirms Smith and Warrior's conclusions about the "unraveling" of the national Indian movement in the wake of the siege at Wounded Knee: the government's extended legal assault on AIM exhausted both material and human resources for ongoing, large-scale opposition to federal policies—or, for that matter, settler celebrations (270). It is thus not surprising that American Indian responses to the U.S. bicentennial cluster in the several years prior to 1976, rather than during the year itself, and that much of their energy focuses on *anticipating* the importance of the bicentennial as an icon of an enduring colonial ideology rather than on marking a single day, such as the Fourth of July, as an important anniversary around which to rally.[13] Despite these constraints, however, similar to Indigenous responses to the bicentennial in Australia, American Indian responses in the United States were nonetheless both event centered and discursive, and they were far more extensive than our current scholarship would suggest.

A full account of Indigenous responses to the U.S. bicentennial is a task better suited to a historian than to a literary scholar, and I do not attempt to produce such an account here. Rather, in the early sections of the chapter I analyze the discourse produced during what appears to have been the largest event of American Indian anticipation of the bicentennial observances, the American Indian Bicentennial Conference held in Arizona in early 1973. In later sections, I analyze American Indian discursive anticipations of 1976, including a number of literary texts. In addition to essays and poems, I draw attention to the mostly forgotten anticipatory fiction of *Indians' Summer,* a novel by Nasnaga (Remnant Band Shawnee) published in 1975, as well as to the mostly forgotten alternative historical fiction of *The Indians Won,* a novel by Martin Cruz Smith (Seneca del Sur/Yaqui) published in 1970. I conclude with brief analyses of a range of Indigenous discourses published during the bicentennial year itself, including works by well-known American Indian intellectuals Vine Deloria Jr. (Dakota) and N. Scott Momaday. As an epilogue, I return to the explicit juxtaposition with Indigenous Australia to consider possible legacies of these unsettled Spirits of '88 and '76.

Looking toward the Settler Century III

A full decade before the bicentennial anniversary of the U.S. Declaration of Independence from Britain, on July 4, 1966, the U.S. Congress chartered the American Revolution Bicentennial Commission (ARBC), a small committee of part-time volunteers charged to "plan, encourage, develop, and coordinate the commemoration of the American Revolution Bicentennial" (ARBA, 1:n.p.). Six years later, on July 4, 1972, President Nixon issued the "Invitation to the World," a call to join the United States in its upcoming celebrations. By the beginning of 1973, however, it was clear that the volunteer and part-time commission was less than ideally suited for its monumental task, and it faced a series of criticisms in the national media and in government inquiries. By the end of the year, at the public urging of the president, Congress restructured the ARBC as the American Revolution Bicentennial Administration (ARBA), granting it broader organizational and fiscal powers; in early 1974, John W. Warner was appointed as administrator.[14] The ARBA remained active throughout 1976. In early 1977, as required by its charter, the administration completed a five-volume final report of its activities; the ARBA was then abolished on September 30.

Part of the administration's challenge, and one of Warner's explicit goals, was to involve the full range of the U.S. population—young and old, women and men, urban and rural, demographic majority and racial, ethnic, and religious minority—in the bicentennial festivities. These diverse events and community projects were to be organized around three broad themes. Under the banner of the first theme, Heritage '76, citizens were encouraged "to remember our form of government, our Founding Fathers, our forgotten people, the places and things of our past, the events of our past and, most important, our freedoms." The second theme, Festival U.S.A., was meant to help citizens celebrate "the richness of our diversity, the vitality of our culture, our hospitality, the American scene and the traditions of our people." And within the scope of the third theme, Horizons '76, the American people were asked to actively plan "to shape a better tomorrow by beginning with individual initiative, by drawing inspiration from the innovations of today, by seeking the blessing of liberty for ourselves and others and by setting our Century III goals" (ARBA 1:n.p.). The final report emphasizes the ARBA's confidence in its themes to focus citizens on the settler nation's rich history, present diversity, and hopes for the future by playing on the visual pun between the pronoun *us* and the abbreviation *U.S.*: Heritage '76, "Let Us Remember!"; Festival U.S.A., "Let Us Celebrate!"; and Horizons '76, "Let Us Shape a Better Tomorrow!" (ARBA 1:251). Organizing this national remembering, celebrating, and planning was no small endeavor. Early in its own planning, the ARBA decided to forego scheduling a single national event in the style of the 1876 Centennial Exhibition in the colonial city of Philadelphia and, instead, to encourage large and small communities around the nation and among its several off-shore territories (no matter their lack of connection to the original colonies) to create local events of national significance. Involving racial, ethnic, religious, and immigrant minorities, including Indigenous communities on reservations and in rural and urban areas around the country, proved especially challenging. As noted in the final report, among other so-called minority groups, "many Native Americans and Blacks were seriously questioning whether they had anything to celebrate" (1:191).

The final report devotes a surprising amount of space to Native questioning of the bicentennial and to Native participation in—or protest of—specific events. Early in volume one, for instance, the report acknowledges that 1976 marked a second anniversary of particular significance for American Indians: "Another historical footnote. Just one hundred years ago our Western frontier was still open. While the world participated in the Centennial exhibition in Philadelphia, General George A. Custer and his troops were wiped out by Indians led by Sitting Bull at the Battle of the Little Big Horn" (1:14). Despite its stereotypical language and seeming lack of self-awareness in its use of pronouns, the report nonetheless records Indigenous perspectives. Later in the volume, in the section titled "The States and the Communities Celebrate," the report includes the subheading "Native American Communities," remarking:

> The Bicentennial was providing a new insight into the status and problems of Native Americans. As the nation celebrated its 200th year, they hoped the Bicentennial would be instrumental in drawing attention to such problems as treaties, water and natural resources and the need for a better standard of living, better health facilities and better housing and education. (1:99)

In its account of a bicentennial reenactment of the Boston Tea Party, where colonists dressed as Indians to protest unfair treatment by Britain, the report mentions that the Boston Indian Council staged a protest of its own, "claiming defamation of character" (1:107). One of the several subheadings under the section "Commemorating Our Heritage" is "The Earliest Americans." The report states:

> Many people believe the treatment of Native Americans as the nation spread west is an embarrassing blot on our national history. It came as no surprise, then, that Native Americans approached the Bicentennial observance with caution, coolness and, at times, bitterness. Why, after all, should the American Indian celebrate the founding of the nation which treated his ancestors to massacre and plunder, forcing them off the land occupied by his people for centuries? Charles Johnson, director of the Portland Urban Indian Program, declined an invitation to join a Bicentennial Wagon Train passing through Oregon. "We felt the invitation was like the Germans inviting the Jews to celebrate Hitler's rise to power," he said. (1:130)

In the subsection that follows, "Here Come the Beads and Trinkets," the report describes part of the consultation process the ARBA conducted with Indigenous peoples and notes that Native Americans eventually "did take part in the Bicentennial observance, mounting impressive programs highlighting their traditions and culture, often with the assistance of funds provided by the ARBA" (1:130). The next subsection, "Indians Favor Tangible Projects," describes several projects that received federal funding: the building of a tribal museum, an urban Indian Center, and a community house. Clearly, the ARBA was invested in highlighting its theme of building for the future while commemorating the past.

Further into the volume, under the heading "People, People, People," the report reveals specific details about the ARBA consultation process and how so many Native communities came to actually propose programs and "tangible projects." Under the subheading "The Nation Ought to Know," the report states, "Many Native Americans approached the Bicentennial with little enthusiasm. The American Indian Movement and other activist groups even suggested a counter-commemoration to celebrate the 100th anniversary of the Indian victory over General George A. Custer at the Battle of the Little Bighorn on June 25, 1876, or a boycott of the whole Bicentennial" (1:191). The report then states, "At the prodding of Thomasine Hill, a Crow Indian and one of the newest and youngest members of the ARBC, a three day conference was held in Tucson, Arizona in January 1973 to explore the problem" (1:193). The "problem" explored by the conference held in Tucson was, of course, how American Indians ought to respond to the settler nation's call to participate in its bicentennial. Thomasine Hill served as one of the part-time volunteer members of the ARBC between 1972 and 1974. Of Crow and Pawnee descent and raised on the Crow Reservation in Montana, where her father was a member of the tribal council, Hill had gained national exposure when named Miss Indian America in 1968. From 1972 to 1974, she was the youngest member of the ARBC and the sole American Indian on the commission. She happened to be an undergraduate at the University of Arizona, located in Tucson, where she was majoring in American history with a minor in the new interdisciplinary field of American Indian studies.[15]

The final report states that the so-called Tucson conference involved "150 representatives of more than 30 Indian tribes in 20 states"

(1:193). Though accurate, this account does not acknowledge that the event was held at the University of Arizona or that it was organized by neither government officials nor tribal leaders but by the Amerind Club, the university's Native student organization, of which Hill was an active member. At the end of their four-day National Bicentennial Conference, which ran from January 7 to 10, the students and their faculty adviser wrote, edited, and published a detailed report of the proceedings, *Indians and 1976: Native Americans Look at the American Revolution Bicentennial Observance*. In their own report, the students state that "Indians representing the more than 200 tribes in the United States were asked to attend, along with over 300 Indian and non-Indian representatives of the government, business, education, the Bicentennial Commission, and private parties. Those in attendance at the conference made up the body called the Native American Indian Council" (n.p.). It was the first event in which American Indians anticipated, on a national scale and as a self-described collective body, their potential responses to the settler celebration.

A Permanent Process of Renewal

University of Arizona president John P. Schaefer concludes his foreword to the Native students' 1973 conference report: "At a time when Indian problems—and many other problems—are resulting in turmoil and bloodshed, the American Indian Bicentennial Conference, by its very success, becomes a lesson of national significance" (ii). The ARBA final report echoes these sentiments in an early section titled "Tension Everywhere," acknowledging that the determining contexts for planning the bicentennial included the 1963 assassination of John F. Kennedy, large-scale U.S. military involvement in Vietnam beginning in 1965, President Johnson's 1968 decision not to run for reelection, the assassinations of Martin Luther King Jr. and Robert F. Kennedy that same year, and President Nixon's resignation in 1974 (4–8). What the ARBA report does not acknowledge, but the university president suggests, is the additional context of large-scale American Indian activism in the late 1960s and early 1970s. In particular, the Trail of Broken Treaties caravan and occupation of the BIA had occurred on the eve of Nixon's reelection in late 1972, when the Native students and their guests would have been preparing for the conference in Tucson; the so-called Siege at Wounded Knee had begun in late February 1973, a little over a month following the conference, when the students and their adviser would have been preparing their report for publication. In other words, the American Indian Bicentennial Conference was immediately preceded and followed by national events of Indigenous political protest and confrontations with U.S. state and federal forces. The events of the early 1970s were looking awfully similar to their counterparts from the century before.

The Amerind Club organized its conference around the three themes proposed by the ARBC: Heritage '76, Festival U.S.A., and Horizons '76. Prominent Native and non-Native individuals were invited to address each theme; speeches were followed by caucus meetings during which participants debated specific topics and worked to build consensus toward the final resolutions that were to be delivered to President Nixon and the ARBC on behalf of the Native American Indian Council. In their report, the students provide the texts of all but one of the keynotes, as well as summaries of the caucus deliberations and the concluding discussion, recommendations, and resolutions. The Heritage '76 section featured speeches by Ed McGaa (Oglala Sioux), cochairman of Minnesota's Bicentennial Commission, and Helen Byrd, who spoke on behalf of James Biddle, chairman of the Heritage Committee of the national ARBC, who was unable to travel to Tucson. The Festival U.S.A. section featured speeches by George E. Lang, chairman of the Festival Committee of the ARBC (whose speech is briefly summarized but not reported in full); David Warren, cultural director of the Institute of American Indian Arts in Santa Fe, New Mexico; and Emory Sekaquaptewa (Hopi), professor of anthropology and director of the Indian Studies Program at the University of Arizona. Finally, the Horizons '76 section featured speeches by Frank Angel, who is described as "a Chicano member of the Commission"; Wendell Chino (Mescalero Apache), who had held leadership positions in his tribe and in the National Congress of American Indians (NCAI); Harvey Little Elk Wells, who is not identified by tribal affiliation but is described as "associated with the American Indian Culture Center at UCLA" and as a leader in AIM; and Charles Trimble, who also is not identified by tribal affiliation but is described as former executive director of the NCAI and current director of the American Indian Press Association.

Speeches range widely in content and tone, as do caucus discussions. In the opening set of speeches, McGaa and Byrd seem oddly in sync with each other but out of sync with the spirit of the conference. In "The Dilemma of the Non-Indian World," McGaa generalizes a vague Native "respect" for "Mother Earth" and urges the United States to relearn this respect to be "more successful as a nation" (4). In "The Meaning of Heritage '76," Byrd explains the ARBC's philosophy as a recognition that "the American Revolution is a permanent process of renewal, change and improvement" and, thus, "a continuing revolution" (6). How might American Indians participate in this ongoing renewal? In offering specific suggestions, Byrd echoes McGaa. She notes there is a "need for a comprehensive history of the tribes of the American Indian [. . .] an encyclopedia of the Native American—that could be a lasting contribution for the Bicentennial, not only for all Americans, but for the entire world" (9). In addition, "We need to recreate that sense of community life in America that has always been a part of the American heritage. And the American Indian can help the nation do so" (9). More precisely:

> We have a great deal to learn from the American Indian. It is more apparent now when our country becomes increasingly concerned over the protection of the natural environment. The American Indian symbolizes the human love of nature and, I believe, has preserved a better sense of man's deep-seated dependence on nature than his fellow Americans. (10)

In a final suggestion, Byrd notes, "The tribes could play an important role as hosts to people from the cities in bringing them closer to nature for at least the vacation part of the year" (10). In brief, Byrd suggests American Indians can participate in the "continuing revolution" by producing a comprehensive written history of their tribal past, helping the settler nation to re-create its lost sense of community, serving as a symbol of the settlers' lost respect for Mother Earth (this is also McGaa's recommendation), and hosting urban non-Natives on their rural reservations for back-to-nature holidays. She concludes, "To sum it all up, history is an interpretation of the past" (10). Or stated plainly, for the bicentennial Indians were asked to serve as icons of an idealized past that was distinctly of the settlers' making and for the settlers' benefit.

The summary of the first caucus discussion focuses on neither McGaa nor Byrd. Instead, conference participants pose the larger questions these speakers failed to raise:

> How do we participate in the American Revolution Bicentennial? What do we want to accomplish? What goals and objectives shall we attain? How well can Indian History benefit us in the future? Also, the question: "Shall we participate?" has to be considered. Will we be celebrating the defeat of our people? (12)

Moreover, participants wanted basic questions answered about federal funding: "How much money will be available?" (12). By the end of discussion, they reached consensus that "the American Indians want[ed] to make known that their history and culture exceed[ed] the established 200-year anniversary" and that they "should have veto power over the Indian's part in the celebration" (13). But there was no clear agreement about *how* or even *if* Indians should participate:

> Some suggested that we ask for a separate Indian Bicentennial and ask for funding from the American Revolution Bicentennial Commission. Others pointed out the alternative of whether we should participate at all. We could hold a counter-celebration, celebrating the Little Big Horn on June 25, 1976, or the Pueblo revolt [of 1680], or even boycott the celebration, expressing our discontent with the exploitation and oppression that has continued since July 4, 1776. (14)

The caucus summary ends with an activist sentiment directed at Byrd and the ARBC committee she represented: "In any case, whether we participate or not *our needs* should be met according to *our standards* instead of those of the whiteman" (14; emphasis added).

The second and third sets of keynotes were more diverse. Of particular interest are the speeches by Sekaquaptewa, "Strengthening Indian Traditions"; Wells, "Bicentennial No! Counter-celebration Yes!"; and Trimble, "Indian Horizons: A Contemporary Look." All three raise political implications of the bicentennial in the context of the difficult realities that Indian communities had faced for decades and were likely to continue to face in the near future. Reworking Byrd's slogan of a "permanent process of [U.S.] renewal," Sekaquaptewa emphasizes how "the Indian, with the help of the white man in some cases, is revitalizing his Indianness." He notes, however, that "once again the Indian faces the question of whether his survival is a political matter or whether it is a cultural matter" (21). The dominant society defines survival in terms of cultural traits linked to the past, ignoring political issues set in the present and limiting conceptions of the future: "Under these pressures, the Indian seems more concerned about convincing the whiteman about his Indianness—rather than to strengthen his own feelings about being an Indian." "But is the Indian enhanced through better understanding of him by non-Indians?" Sekaquaptewa asks. "Who is the real beneficiary?" (22). Wells, in keeping with the activist slogans of his title, takes a position directly opposed to Byrd's and advances arguments for commemorating the 1876 Indian victory at the Little Bighorn rather than the U.S. bicentennial. Wells continues Sekaquaptewa's distinction between political and cultural revitalization: "The American Revolution's victorious conclusion was in fact the death knell for the sovereignty, independence, and freedom of our people. The victory of the American government cannot be interpreted as a victory for us" (36). Finally, Trimble invokes the "crisis situation in Indian affairs today." He is the only speaker to refer directly to the recent Trail of Broken Treaties in Washington, D.C., noting that although these events did not create the current situation, "We can safely say that those disruptions provided the catalyst to escalate the crisis" (38). In Trimble's account the problem is Indian leadership that is neither unified nor adequately independent of the U.S. government: "Where are the Indian voices of protest? Where is the Indian leadership? Indian *leaders* have emerged in abundance. Indian leadership is nearly totally absent" (40).

While the caucus discussions covered equally diverse ground, they often returned to practical issues, such as "the present conditions in reservation and off-reservation housing and the urbanization of Indian life" (26). The students report the sentiments of participants this way: "America is free for 200 years, but the Indians are not free on their own reservations. How can anyone be proud in such a situation?" (26). Similar concerns were raised about education: "It was obvious to most participants that the whole educational system for the Indian students must be to interrelate and fuse traditional contexts and methods with current knowledge and educational innovations. This challenge must be taken up by Indians and concerned non-Indians" (47). Inevitably, discussions returned to the question of whether Indians should participate in the bicentennial, create a countercelebration, or boycott. The students report, "[The] rationale offered by boycott advocators failed in the end when participants voted in favor of participation as opposed to non-participation (complete boycott) on the one hand and tokenism on the other" (49). All participants agreed that "communication was […] a basic problem for Indian groups in all subject areas dealing with the bicentennial observance" and highly recommended the creation of a "Central Indian Information Center" as a vehicle that would "disseminate bicentennial information to all tribal and urban groups" (50). The report ends its summary of discussions, "The greatest unity existed regarding the importance of not allowing Indians to be taken for granted in the bicentennial plans and operations." In what appears another direct response to Byrd's speech on behalf of the Heritage Committee, the students state, "The days of performing Indians seems to be over" (52).

After listing the caucus recommendations under each theme and the three resolutions passed by a majority vote of participants, the students conclude their report with the two-page letter Thomasine Hill sent to President Nixon on January 19, 1973. Hill briefly overviews the purpose of the American Indian Bicentennial Conference, notes the active participation "of over 150 individuals from 20 states and over 30 tribes," and lists a sampling of the "represented organizations." She also announces that the proceedings will be published by the University of Arizona Press. Enclosed with her letter are the conference program and the three formal resolutions, which ask that (1) the ARBC actively seek Indian staff members, (2) states with significant Indian populations include Indian representation on their state-level bicentennial commissions, and (3) the president and the ARBC consider the formation of a separate National American Indian Bicentennial Committee "to insure proper representation of Native Americans in all aspects of planning" (63–64). Hill states that, in addition to President Nixon, she is sending copies of her letter "to the National and State American Revolution Bicentennial Commissions, Arizona Senators and Congressmen, and over 500 urban [and] reservation Indians and organizations." To conclude, she situates the immanent near future of 1976 within broader understandings of the significant distant future and the significant past: "The American Indian involvement in the American Revolution Bicentennial Observances is an act of faith and hope that the *next* 100 years will be more promising than the *last* 200 years" (emphasis added). Hill signs her name under the suggestive closing "In the Spirit of '76" (66).

The letter and the three resolutions Hill sent to President Nixon appear to have been received within that spirit of revolution. A number of changes were made to how bicentennial planning was conducted at the federal level after 1973. On July 1, 1974, not long after Warner's appointment, the newly commissioned ARBA established a Native American Programs Office in Denver, Colorado, "in recognition of the special relationships existing between the Federal Government and the American Indian and of the desirability of encouraging Native Americans to become an integral part of the Bicentennial commemoration."[16] The following year, on August 4, 1975, Warner established the Racial, Ethnic, and Native American Advisory Committee; four of its twenty-five members are identified as American Indians and one as a Pacific Islander (ARBA, 2:34). Warner met with American Indian representatives in Washington, DC, during 1975, and by 1976 he had "visited 111 different tribes" around the country, "encouraging them to take part in the Bicentennial however they saw fit, but in any event to participate" (ARBA, 1:193). The Native American Programs Office reported in September 1975 that, as a result of these and other efforts at consultation and encouragement:

> 25 Indian tribes and reservations have been designated as Bicentennial Communities by ARBA thus far, 42 projects have been funded from non-appropriated funds for a total of $661,340, and 62 projects have been funded from appropriated funds for a total of $1,326,469, and 56 native projects have been funded from Title X of the Public Works and Economic Development Act of 1965 in the amount of $6,122,700. (foreword, n.p.)

By the end of 1976, according to the ARBA final report, the number of tribes designated as Bicentennial Communities had risen to thirty-eight (1:193). The Native American Programs Office describes the wide range of funded projects as "perpetuating Indian culture and tradition, the improvement of communications among the tribes, the establishment of museums and handicraft centers, and the promotion of tourism to Indian areas, among others" (n.p). Whether these projects would result in a "permanent process of renewal" for Indigenous individuals and communities, of course, could not be known at the time. The official reports suggest there was considerable enthusiasm for the high level of direct funding and for the high level of local input and control.

Beyond Tucson: Other Indigenous Voices

Several prominent intellectuals were absent from the American Indian Bicentennial Conference, including D'Arcy McNickle and Vine Deloria Jr. McNickle would have been completing his influential study *Native American Tribalism: Indian Survivals and Renewals*, published toward the end of 1973. He was likely also already updating *They Came Here First: The Epic of the American Indian*, his work of history and anthropology originally published in 1949; the revised edition was released in 1975. Deloria, too, was busy with timely projects. His widely read polemic on American Indian spirituality, *God Is Red*, appeared in 1973, followed in 1974 by his historical and legal contextualization of recent American Indian activism, *Behind the Trail of Broken Treaties: An Indian Declaration of Independence*.

Although their titles seem pointed at the bicentennial, none of these books overtly anticipates the coming festivities of 1976. Each does, however, assess the impact of contemporary activism on the Indigenous near future. "It now seems likely, after Washington and Wounded Knee," McNickle writes in the preface to *Native American Tribalism*, "that anger will hang in the air, like a combustible vapor, for some time to come" (xii). In the conclusion, he attributes the potential for volatile anger to effect positive change not to Indigenous action per se but rather to Indigenous writing and publication: "All through North America, from the Arctic to the Florida peninsula, the long submerged Indian minority has been discovering the value of the published word, and this may prove to be the decisive force in bringing into being an enduring policy of self-determined cultural pluralism" (169). Like the students at the University of Arizona who organized conference participants into a collective body, McNickle envisions the power of activist voices in terms of collective agency:

Finally, it can be noted in closing that the spokesmen of earlier years who tried to accept what an alien world offered their people, seeing no other choice open, are now silent. If the Indian race is to be destroyed, the new voices avow, the destroying agent will have to contend with an integrating tribal people, not with isolated individuals lost in anonymity. (170)

In the wake of the multi- and intertribal activism of the Trail of Broken Treaties and the Siege at Wounded Knee, and in the tidal surge of new Native writing in all genres, McNickle anticipates a future of "integrating tribal people." As we shall see, McNickle was not alone in envisioning the power of collective action to create a distinctly Indigenous near future.[17]

Other commentators were more direct in either contemplating or performing Indigenous responses to the upcoming U.S. bicentennial. In its Fall 1974 issue, for instance, *The Indian Historian*, the journal of the American Indian Historical Society, based in California, published "The Bi-Centennial Celebration and the Native American" by Helen L. Harris (Choctaw/Creek), who is described as having earned a PhD in English. Harris is particularly concerned about the kinds of representations that will inevitably circulate—and the kinds of representations that will most likely not circulate—during 1976. She writes:

The crux of the ever-current disparagement of the Indian, and especially now, as the bi-centennial date approaches, has always been the same: it was his country and he somehow escaped complete extermination. He is also the most damaging witness against the image that the conservatives want to reaffirm in 1976. The Indian "problem" must be settled once and for all.

To serve that purpose, the tattered old arguments of the past have re-surfaced in popular rallying cries. (5)

As a concrete example of these "tattered old arguments" in action, Harris analyzes *Tom Sawyer*, a "family" film produced by the popular periodical the *Reader's Digest*, based on the novel *The Adventures of Tom Sawyer* by Mark Twain, first published during the U.S. centennial in 1876.[18] Harris argues that the popular film adapts Twain's novel, "a parable of frontier America [that shows] why it should rid itself of the

Indian," to accentuate the already negative portrayal of the character Injun Joe, especially through its "visual effects" and its creation of highly stereotypical scenes that emphasize "Joe's presence as a malevolent threat to the town" (6):

> This exploitation of Mark Twain's literary reputation and augmentation of his portrayal of the Indian's malevolence in order to glorify the past and justify killing the Indian is only one example of an indirect method of disparaging the Indian. Rather than risk being recognized as a "racist"—bad for one's image—the defender of manifest destiny selects and publicizes disparagement from a revered source. (7)

She concludes by situating *Tom Sawyer* within the context of Twain's later works, in which he critiqued the excesses of U.S. colonialism. Harris implies that, in its pursuit of a popular view of the U.S. nineteenth century, the film not only maligns Indians as savages but also mischaracterizes Twain, one of the period's more complex thinkers about race and colonialism and an example of the dominant culture's ability for self-critique and change.

The same issue published a letter from Charles Tate (Chickasaw), who wrote in response to a call "for comments from leading Indian people about the role of the Indian in celebration of the bicentennial" (35). Tate writes, "As a member of the Chickasaw Nation, I see no reason to celebrate the 200th anniversary of the United States." He goes on, however, to place the colonial anniversary within a broader analysis of the history of democracy and justice:

> The political theorists who gave birth to the nation, of "a government of laws, not of men," are still searching for a home. The history of this nation's treatment of the aboriginal peoples also serves as a summary of the attitudes and the political posture which this country has assumed towards all its citizens, Indians and non-Indians alike. (35)

Anticipating 1976, Tate remarks further, "It is a truly amazing phenomenon that so many tribes have survived and today maintain a strong sense of 'Indianness,' which is difficult to define but exists nonetheless" (35).

Not surprisingly, the two national American Indian newspapers published during the mid-1970s, *Akwesasne Notes*, produced by the Mohawk nation in upstate New York, and *Wassaja*, produced by the American Indian Historical Society in California, printed articles, letters, advertisements, and occasionally poems that anticipate the bicentennial. In its January/February 1975 issue, for instance, *Wassaja* published "Indians and the U.S. Bicentennial," an overview that rehearses issues similar to those debated during the 1973 conference and details a number of Native community projects that had already received federal funding (18). In the April 1975 issue, Ken Powlas, author of the regular column "The Beat of Dissent," published "The Bicentennial Celebration of Independence Day: Another Beat" (11). He describes his column as a transcript of an invited speech he gave, on a "Topic of Controversy of the Day," to "a group of white business men, whom I can best describe almost to the man as 'Red, White and Blue Patriots.'"[19] For his white audience, Powlas lists the many reasons why Indians might choose not to celebrate the bicentennial—a history of genocide, land loss, broken treaties—and then asks, "What Indian pride can be engendered for your American Heritage?" He concludes by anticipating a possible, better, distant future: "Perhaps, by your 400th Anniversary of the Declaration of Independence, if there are any of us left, the Great Spirit will have seen fit for the surviving tribes to have an Independence of their own to celebrate, daily, not once a year or every century in the hereafter." The June 1975 issue includes a letter from Wilson W. Wolf Jr. that echoes the sentiment of AIM and other activists: "Why not stage our own Indian celebration to coincide with the 4th of July festivity! When a glorious victory of June 28, 1876 [*sic*] was scored at the Little Big Horn. It will be the centennial of that important date" (13). In the August 1975 issue, *Wassaja* reports that AIM is establishing "truth squads" to "protest bicentennial celebrations across the nation." While the newspaper cannot confirm the story, the anonymous columnist notes, "There seems to be no doubt that the Indian people are divided on the issue of the Bicentennial, and that most individual Indians have expressed disapproval of the various events being planned for the celebrations" (6).

At least one poem published in *Wassaja* anticipates the settler celebration of 1976 and seems to embrace the ideal of AIM's rumored truth squads. "Bicentennial" by the novelist and scholar Michael Dorris

(Modoc) appears in the issue dated September 20, 1975. Divided into side-by-side columns, the poem is organized as a settler call and Indigenous response. The first part presents an Indian view of how the dominant culture, designated "You," attempts to set the terms for how Indigenous peoples are allowed to respond to the bicentennial:

> You say: It's your bicentennial too.
> No party-poopers allowed.
> Where else such presents?
> Union Pacific cards and
> Hand-forged iron(s).
> A niche in history and
> Boy Scout shadows,
> Taco tias in every town.
> Don't forget:
> You have no dates!
> Your calendars
> Are in our museums
> Unflipped in crumbly stone.
> This is your only anniversary:
> Would you make a noise
> In the forest,
> If you fell unheard by us?

In Dorris's vision of bicentennial "truth," the dominant culture attempts to erase Indigenous peoples and their counterclaims to histories outside the U.S. nation-state not through exclusion but through a forceful *inclusion*. Settler discourses deny the possibility of ongoing American Indian distinctiveness or, ironically—given the reverence for a revolutionary Spirit of '76—American Indian independence. The second part of the poem imagines a collective Indigenous response to the demand for inclusion and compliance. Echoing AIM and other activists, the collective speaker responds to the dominant "You":

> Stay cool: we'll blow out
> Your candles, one by one.
> Of course we celebrate:
> Two hundred years is

Two hundred years less.
Your Centennial was marked
At the Little Big Horn, and
We may even commemorate 1776
After you've long gone.
Better not to forget
In order to remember.
Let's join hands
In looking back.
While Hopi prophets ghost dance
All night, till dawn.
        (10)

Similar to participants at the 1973 conference, Dorris embraces the bicentennial theme of celebrating the past while building toward the future, but with an Indigenous focus and articulation that the dominant culture appears unable to imagine and never to have anticipated.

Dorris was not the only Native author to engage the upcoming bicentennial in poetry published in 1975. That year saw the publication of the anthology *Voices of the Rainbow: Contemporary Poetry by American Indians*, edited by Kenneth Rosen, which includes "Discovery of the New World" by Carter Revard (Osage) (99–101).[20] Revard's celebrated poem deploys the futuristic discourse of science fiction and an Indigenous dark humor: his speakers are space aliens reporting back to their leader as they systematically colonize the Earth, consume its resources, and destroy its inhabitants. The poem has been read as a general meditation on European conquest, as well as a critique of Manifest Destiny. Since the 1990s, it has been viewed, as well, as a predecessor to Gerald Vizenor's 1991 comic novel, *The Heirs of Columbus*, which anticipates the events of 1992, and other works that respond to the quincentenary.[21] A number of details suggest Revard's poem also anticipates 1976.

When the aliens report, "Their history bled from one [human] this morning / while we were tasting his brain / in holographic rainbows / which we assembled into quite an interesting / set of legends," the specific references are not to Columbus or Cortez or other European colonizers but rather to "a certain General Sherman." The ironically named William Tecumseh Sherman served as a general in the Union army during the Civil War and as commanding general of the army from

1869 to 1883, during the height of the U.S. assault on Plains Indian nations. Those years included the U.S. centennial and the Battle of the Little Bighorn in 1876. As he had in the Civil War, in the wars against Indian nations Sherman sought to destroy not only armed combatants but entire communities and their resources—it is this history that is evoked in the aliens' report to the mothership. Moreover, the concluding lines echo the language of "Life, Liberty, and the pursuit of Happiness" enshrined in the Declaration of Independence. Looking ahead to their own near future, the aliens anticipate: "We'll soon have it [the Earth] cleared / as in fact it is already, at the poles, / Then we will be safe, and rich, and happy here forever." Manifest Destiny, an ideal of 1876, will finally reach its ultimate conclusion.

A surprising number of American Indians from diverse backgrounds expressed their anticipations of the bicentennial in print.[22] Three more will suffice to set the stage for the novel-length anticipations of Nasnaga and Smith discussed later. On the eve of the bicentennial year, in its November/December 1975 issue, *Wassaja* published "Bicentennial Perspectives" by Dorothy Davids (Stockbridge-Munsee), "an Indian specialist" at the University of Wisconsin Extension Center for Community Leadership Development and chairperson of the Stockbridge-Munsee Museum Commission.[23] Davids responds to the bicentennial as a member of an Indigenous nation that "fought in the American Revolution" in 1776 and lost lives in that conflict. She asks, "What liberty and justice did the Stockbridge people enjoy [for their sacrifice]?" Her answer is a brief history of how the Stockbridge-Munsee "lost most of [their] language and culture" and "lost [their] land." What the Stockbridge-Munsee do have to celebrate in 1976, Davids argues, is that in 1972, by an act of Congress, the tribe finally realized a stable land base, and in the few years since, they have "established a research library and museum." "In this way," she writes, "we Stockbridge are celebrating our survival, our self-determination and a growing awareness of our identity as a People." She concludes with a promising anticipation, an Indigenous revision of Byrd's idea of a "continuing American revolution": "The *Native American* Revolution, bringing liberty and justice, may just be beginning" (5; emphasis added).[24]

Other commentators felt similarly that their nations' specific histories of interaction, struggle, and ongoing engagement with the United States uniquely qualified them to reflect on the ideal of a "continuing

American revolution." On January 7, 1975, Peter MacDonald, governor of the Navajo Nation, stated a version of his people's understanding of American ideals during his inaugural address:

> As the United States moves forward to celebrate its Bicenten-
> nial, we find that too many Americans have forgotten both the
> importance and the price of freedom. We find they have forgot-
> ten the days when America itself was an emerging nation. To
> the Navajo, however, the struggle for freedom goes on. [. . .]
> For many Americans, the struggle for freedom is only his-
> tory. For us, however, it is a continuing part, not only of our
> heritage, but of our daily lives. We, like our parents and grand-
> parents before us, have battled for our survival against extermi-
> nation—termination—and assimilation.
> Because our struggles are so recent and, in fact, because
> they continue, we alone, perhaps among all Americans[,] ap-
> preciate how truly precious and truly rare freedom is. (214)

MacDonald's refusal to embrace the easy slogans of dominant forms of U.S. nationalism and his insistence, instead, on characterizing "the struggle for freedom" as an ongoing process relevant to all peoples and not simply as a completed chapter in a heroic U.S. history resonate across Indigenous anticipations of 1976.

Although such responses do not appear in the book-length works published by Deloria in 1973 or 1974, his essays and presentations in 1975 offer some of the most intellectually savvy engagements with the upcoming bicentennial from the period. In February 1975, for example, Deloria delivered "The American Revolution and the American Indi-an: Problems in the Recovery of a Usable Past" at a two-day confer-ence on "The American Indian and the American Revolution" held at the Newberry Library in Chicago.[25] In November 1975, he published "Why Indians Aren't Celebrating the Bicentennial" in the education journal *Learning*. In the Newberry presentation, Deloria introduces his analysis of relevant colonial history:

> The frightening thing about the celebrations of the bicenten-
> nial is that we are tempted to simply increase the velocity with
> which we manipulate the familiar symbols of our past without

coming to grips with a more profound understanding of our history. Things have probably been much better and much worse than we can imagine, and it is only when we enter the arena of discussion of American Indians and the American Revolution that we can determine just how polarized the events of American history have been. (206)

He concludes his cogent analysis:

The American Indian has an intimate relationship to the American Revolution because, of all the peoples in the world, the American Indians have had to bear the impact of the criminality of the United States and to attempt to soften its impact on the rest of the world. In biblical terms, American Indians have had to be the suffering servant for the planet; their role has been to change the American conception of a society from that of a complex of laws designed to protect property to one in which liberty is not a matter of laws, coercive power, or a shadow of government but is characterized by manners and a moral sense of right and wrong. (221)

Rather than accept the assigned role of either "noble" or "savage" victim, Deloria reclaims Indigenous agency on both the national and the global stage.

In his essay, Deloria stresses the contemporary context for the bicentennial, in which, on the one hand, Indian activists "consider themselves to be at war" with the United States and, on the other, "most Indians do not presently know what their relationship to the United States really is" (200). He explores, too, the dysfunctional nature of ongoing Indigenous–settler relations, in which well-meaning non-Indians seek out and invite Indians to celebrate the past and, inadvertently, "simply reinforce the cycle of emotional hurt" (205). In response, Deloria argues, "We should be celebrating the goals of the next hundred years instead of the failures and successes of the past two hundred." To move beyond these cycles of dysfunction, moreover, "we should be making a determined effort to move forward in the creation of a *continental* culture that understands itself as a totality and a novelty whose only concern is developing forms of existence that provide everyone involved with a sense of integrity and identity" (205; emphasis added). As we shall see, however, in contrast to this ecumenical vision, the novelists who envisioned a future 1976 in which Indigenous peoples either maintain or regain "a sense of integrity and dignity" had very different ideas about who should determine the culture(s) of the North American continent.

Native to the Future: *Indians' Summer* and *The Indians Won*

At least one book-length work of Native fiction explicitly anticipates the U.S. bicentennial. Published in 1975, *Indians' Summer* by Nasnaga (Roger Russell) was the fourth selection in Harper and Row's short-lived Native American Publishing Program.[26] Long out of print, this novel of militant activism has fallen out of most studies of Native American literature. Moreover, little is known about its author. According to the novel's dust jacket:

> Nasnaga was born April 13, 1941, in Dayton, Ohio. He is a member of the Shawnee Nation, United Remnant Band. The Remnant Band is composed of predominantly mixed-blood Shawnees who are actively working to restore and reinvigorate the traditional way of life of their people.[27] Nasnaga grew up in Ohio, and then moved to Texas in 1968 after serving a hitch in the United States Navy. An artist, he has supported himself both from his paintings and by working as a draftsman. This is his first novel.

In the author's photo a serious-looking Nasnaga is dressed in "traditional" Shawnee regalia.[28]

Although published in 1975, *Indians' Summer* is set during 1976 in the period between June 27—the centennial of the immediate aftermath of the 1876 Indian victory at the Little Bighorn—and September 5—the anniversary of both the assembly of the First Continental Congress in 1775 and the death of the Lakota visionary and war chief Crazy Horse in 1887—with action concentrated on the Fourth of July and the days immediately following. The importance of the bicentennial and the idea of armed revolution are emphasized immediately in the artwork created by Nasnaga for the dust jacket. Against a black background, the Declaration of Independence dominates the cover. The parchment-colored document, with "In Congress" and "July 4, 1776" inked prominently across the top, has been pierced through its "heart" by a painted and feathered arrow. Blood pools around the fresh wound and streams through the document's discourse of liberation and the signature of John Hancock. The novel's title appears in all caps above the declaration in a bold block print the same color as the blood, with "a novel by Nasnaga" placed immediately below the title in a smaller typeface the same color as the parchment. This color symbolism is repeated in the hardback edition's construction: front and back boards are the color of parchment; front and back endpapers are a bright blood red.

Before the narrative begins, Nasnaga sets the tone for his story and indicates a primary source of inspiration with an epigraph from the activist Vernon Bellecourt (Ojibwe), who is identified as "International Field Director, American Indian Movement." Originally published in *Penthouse Magazine* in July 1973, Bellecourt's statement predates the reorganization of the ARBC as the ARBA and Warner's work to actively consult with Indigenous communities:

> A bicentennial celebration is going to take place in 1976. We, the hosts, haven't been asked about our involvement. We feel that if this government is expecting to celebrate its two hundredth birthday in our country, they'd better involve us. . . . Unless the conditions change one hundred eighty degrees, it will be our duty and our responsibility to blow out the candles on the two hundredth birthday cake.[29]

Bellecourt's identity as Ojibwe (also known as Chippewa and Anishinaabe) will turn out to be significant to Nasnaga's conception of Indian activism and unity. The title and copyright pages contain more artwork by Nasnaga, with additional examples placed throughout: line drawings of feathered roaches and headdresses, decorated shields, coup sticks, tomahawks, knives, and, at the end of the novel, a pipe. Nasnaga dedicates his work to "the Indian People" and to his daughter, acknowledges those who helped make its publication possible, and provides a glossary of sixteen "words in this book that probably won't be familiar to many readers" (n.p.).

Finally, on the last unnumbered page before the narrative, Nasnaga prints an untitled poem that picks up on Bellecourt's Anishinaabe identity and foreshadows the novel's theme of collective action. Similar to McNickle's 1973 anticipation of "integrating tribal people," Nasnaga reconciles the complexity of tribal diversity with a vision of Indian unity. In the brief poem reconciliation is accomplished through the evocative imagery of "dust devils":

The buffalo grass is still.
Dust devils die from neglect.
    I know how they feel.
I am Indian.

Like unborn dust devils
    I wait for a fresh breeze.
It comes. Dust devils are born.
    I listen. I learn. I grow strong.
I am Indian.

A body of many parts
    Scattered to the four winds.
My mouth speaks in many tongues.
    Like dust devils, all are the whole.
I am Anishinabe!

Part of the poem's activist energy arises from the term "dust devils," which charges natural phenomena with the colonialist Christian binary that marked Indigenous peoples as "red devils." The speaker's description of "scattered" parts functioning as a "whole" anticipates a major plot element of the novel, as does the movement from an exclusively English declaration, "I am Indian," to an emphatic bilingual declaration, "I am Anishinabe!" In his glossary Nasnaga defines "Anishinabe" as "an Algonkian word meaning The People."[30] Following McNickle's lead, the speaker declares his movement from isolated individual to powerfully collective voice.

Nasnaga divides the 195 pages of his narrative into part 1, "What Indians?," and part 2, "'Hail to the Chief' Sounds Like Hell on Drums!" Each part is preceded by an epigraph from a nineteenth-century Sioux leader, and each is further divided into a total of forty-one unnumbered chapters. Rather than a title, each brief chapter is headed by a designation of a specific place, date, and time. The fragmented structure and the emphasis on location in space and time, combined with the concise, unembellished style of Nasnaga's prose, create a journalistic quality and a sense of on-the-spot news reports or immediate updates as the action unfolds.[31] The novel's plot can be summarized briefly. After a period of planning, on July 4, 1976, the Navajo, Sioux, Mohawk, Apache, and Pueblo nations unite as the Anishinabe-waki Democracy, which Nasnaga defines as "Algonkian for Land of the People, or simply, Indian country," and declare their independence from the United States. This new, multitribal, geographically dispersed Indigenous nation is led by Joel Turning Hawk, great-grandson of John Captures Many Horses, the last living Sioux war chief with genealogical ties to the 1876 Battle of the Little Bighorn (through his father) and the 1866 Battle of the Hundred Slain (through his grandfather).[32] Turning Hawk thus represents a sixth-generation war chief who will prepare the way for the seventh generation's freedom from U.S. oppression. The Anishinabe, as members of the new nation refer to themselves, are enabled in their coordinated military maneuvers in the Southwest, on the northern plains, and on the U.S.–Canadian border in the northeast by the fact that so many of their men are either active in the National Guard or ex-servicemen from the war in Vietnam, including paratroopers and special forces veterans, as well as by the fact that the United States has posted the abundance of its troops in West Germany to oppose mounting Soviet forces. Focused on the Cold War abroad, the United States is taken completely by surprise at home. The Anishinabe easily control large sections of Arizona and New Mexico, the Dakotas, and northern New York.

The Anishinabe also attack the United States along the diplomatic front. Their emissary Roy Bear Walks Backward has spent two years working with the consulate of India—in an obvious play on the (mis) naming of peoples in the Americas—to prepare the way for formally declaring both independence and war from within the forum of the United Nations. India presents the Anishinabe manifesto to the UN General Assembly, which is received, to the dismay of the U.S. president, with less-than-subtle glee by the USSR and others eager to challenge U.S. power. The United States is placed in an embarrassing public relations position and in a situation of almost impossible diplomacy. Faced with similar problems, the Canadian prime minister takes his own life. The president does not resort to self-violence but moves steadily toward alignment with his principal military adviser, who argues that the Indians must be destroyed and quickly. They contemplate the use of limited nuclear weapons—and the possibility of a third world war—rather than recognize Indigenous sovereignty. Led by Edward Small Wolf, Turning Hawk's cousin and a U.S. congressman who rediscovers his Indian loyalty during the crisis, the Anishinabe offer a last-minute diplomatic solution that recognizes the sovereignty of Anishinabe-waki while allowing the United States to save face internationally. The United States responds with a demand for full surrender and the threat of immediate military action, and Small Wolf is forced to play the Anishinabe trump card: he informs the president that the Minuteman missiles siloed deep in the Dakota plains have been reprogrammed to fire on Washington, DC. U.S. antimissile technology, designed to intercept foreign missiles only, will not respond; the capital will be destroyed. When the president finally relents, readers learn what they may already have suspected: Small Wolf bluffed, and unlike the United States, the Anishinabe never entertained a doomsday scenario. The bicentennial festivities resume, but they resume with the celebration, as well, of "the birth of a new nation" (193).

The handful of reviews *Indians' Summer* received in 1975 are decidedly mixed. The reviewer for *Booklist* assumes Nasnaga's "seriocomic" and "provocative" novel is intended only for "older teenagers" rather than a broad audience.[33] The reviewer for *Virginia Quarterly Review* is openly hostile to the "ludicrously contrived fantasy" of a plot about "American Indians supposedly getting even for their history"; he argues that Nasnaga "never transcends the level of mere ethnocentric propaganda."[34] In a brief review for *Library Journal*, Anne Freling of the Mt. Pleasant Public Library in Michigan describes Nasnaga's premise as "interesting" but argues that *Indians' Summer* is "essentially a one-concept novel."[35] Writing for the newly created *American Indian Quarterly*, Lawrence Evers offers a more balanced review, stating that the novel is "simple and timely" and that Nasnaga "gives us synoptic commentaries on contemporary militant American Indian politics and endless homilies on American Indian world view."[36] The most sympathetic reviews were published in the *Christian Science Monitor* and the

New Republic. Although Robert M. Press begins his review like the former ones, "Of course it is not likely to happen," he later confesses, "You put [the novel] down for awhile, saying it could not happen, but you sneak back to see how it turns out." Press is the only reviewer to note that 1976 is "the 100th anniversary of the United States cavalry's annihilation at the battle of the Little Bighorn," suggesting that this is a relevant context.[37] The *New Republic* offers the most extensive review as well as the most positive. Its writer is identified only as "a fiction-reading correspondent, CH"—suggesting the initials of the nineteenth-century Lakota war chief Crazy Horse, whom Nasnaga quotes in his epigraph to part 1 and whom this reviewer quotes at the very end of his piece. CH is the only reviewer who places Nasnaga's plot within a broader bicentennial perspective. He (or she) writes, "Those who find the idea of Indians attempting to regain part of the US far-fetched should remember what led the American colonies' revolt against George III." Farther into the review, CH writes, "But now, in this fiction, we see [American Indians] as they are once again[,] dignified, seeking to correct past injustices. *Indians' Summer* is not written in anger, but as a warning, a prophecy perhaps."[38]

In his 1978 study *American Indian Fiction,* Charles R. Larson engages *Indians' Summer* in a brief "Coda" to chapter 6, "Survivors of the Relocation," in which he analyzes "the most recently published novels" by American Indians.[39] Unlike the early reviewers, who either miss or downplay the novel's elements of satire (especially in its portrayal of the president and his advisers, who bear historically significant names such as General Sherman and Colonel Jackson), Larson initially describes *Indians' Summer* as a "satirical spoof" as well as a "fantasy" (161, 162). Rather than develop this genre criticism, though, he quickly turns to how the narrative operates as "rhetoric—written, it appears, as a reaction to the 1973 Wounded Knee confrontation (which is referred to several times)" (162). Larson argues that "the potential force known as Pan-Indianism" is a "major theme" of the novel and that Nasnaga "proclaims the need for inter-tribal cohesion if Native Americans are ever to regain control over their collective destiny" (163, 164). It is true that *Indians' Summer* refers to the events in South Dakota in spring 1973 at least six times. Early in the novel, for example, "the Wounded Knee affair in 1973" is used by Native characters to mark when "the longstanding undercurrent of racism [against Indians] began rising to the surface" (10) and, in a symmetrical contrast, by the U.S. president to mark recent Indian protest (30). In the second half of the novel, readers learn that Turning Hawk "did not particularly care for the way the [American Indian] Movement had handled itself in 1973. He felt Wounded Knee had been a waste of lives, especially since the American people hadn't given a damn about a few dead Indians" (128). Most significantly, Turning Hawk asserts, "The idea of an Indian nation had not been born at Wounded Knee that long spring in 1973"; rather, "the 1973 incident *had* made some people start thinking in the right direction" (129). Although never mentioned explicitly, however, the autumn 1972 Trail of Broken Treaties caravan, which culminated in an occupation of the Bureau of Indian Affairs in Washington, DC, is equally as important a context for understanding how Nasnaga anticipates the bicentennial. Moreover, attention to the novel's consistent engagement with the broader discourse of treaties helps explicate Nasnaga's vision of an Indigenous future marked by intertribal solidarity rather than by what Larson calls the "potential force" of "Pan-Indianism."[40]

A number of Native publications followed the Trail of Broken Treaties. Best known is Deloria's 1974 *Behind the Trail of Broken Treaties: An Indian Declaration of Independence*. A year earlier, Akwesasne Notes published *Trail of Broken Treaties: B.I.A. I'm Not Your Indian Anymore*.[41] Both help contextualize the premise of Nasnaga's novel, as well as its narrative tactics and symbolism. In its introduction, for instance, Akwesasne Notes describes the cross-country caravan and occupation of the BIA headquarters as "one of the most serious attacks upon the United States Government on its own turf since the British sacked Washington during the war of 1812." Similarly, Nasnaga imagines Indians uniting across the continent to attack the United States "on its own turf" in Washington, DC, and on turf the United States sometimes considers its own, the United Nations in New York City. In addition, Akwesasne Notes highlights its decision to present the events of 1972 "in day-by-day reports as [they] happened, rather than as a past-tense report"; Nasnaga also divides his novel into "day-by-day reports." Akwesasne Notes concludes its introduction, "Thus this book contains history—and future" (iv). Nasnaga juxtaposes his plot set in the near future with highly charged epigraphs from nineteenth-century Sioux leaders Crazy Horse and Sitting Bull, while several of his characters consider a history of resistance to U.S. and European forces that begins not in 1976 or 1876 or even 1776 but in 1676 with the war waged against invading colonists by the leader of the Wampanoag Confederacy known to the English as King Philip (130). In a significant anticipatory scene, Small Wolf, the Sioux diplomat, awakens from a dream set "somewhere on the High Plains—Land of the Lakota Nation . . . Circa 1870" that prefigures the nuclear showdown with the United States as a conflict between the cavalry armed with repeating rifles and a lone Lakota armed with *metal-pointed arrows* (153–54).

Following its introduction, as an epigraph to *Trail of Broken Treaties*, Akwesasne Notes quotes Eddie Benton, who paraphrases "a prophecy in our Ojibway religion, that one day we would all stand together. All tribes would hook arms in brotherhood and unite." Benton remarks, "I am elated because I lived to see this happen. Brothers and sisters from all over the continent were united in a single cause. That is the greatest significance to Indian people—not what happened or what yet may happen as a result of our actions" (1). Nasnaga's anticipatory plot is based on a similar fulfillment of the Ojibwe—Anishinaabe—prophecy. Akwesasne Notes also alludes to historical attempts to create Indian unity that may have had particular resonance for Nasnaga as Shawnee. *Trail of Broken Treaties* is framed by a quotation attributed to Tecumseh (1768–1813), the martyred Shawnee leader from what is now Ohio who lived through the American Revolution in 1776 and who, with the help of his younger brother, the prophet Tenskwatawa, attempted to unite Indians into a confederation from which to resist the encroaching United States.[42] The repeated quotation from Tecumseh includes this statement: "Unless each tribe unanimously combines to give check to the avarice and oppressions of the whites, we will become conquered and disunited and we will be driven from our Native Lands and scattered like Autumn leaves before the wind" (2). Although Nasnaga never refers directly to Tecumseh, the "dust devil" imagery of his untitled poem—"A body of many parts / Scattered to the four winds"—reworks the above quotation. In addition, Nasnaga creates a minor but significant character who identifies as Shawnee. As the narrative builds toward its climax, Turning Hawk is interrupted in his thinking by "a light-skinned young man" whose "eyes were gray" and whose "shoulder-length hair was brown." When the young man says that he has "come from my [vision] quest," Turning Hawk asks, "Are you Lakota? I do not know your face though you appear as they say our Strange One did" (165). The young man replies, "No, my Chief, though I do know of Crazy Horse. I am Shawnee." The young man identifies himself as "Maka Meen-de-gah," which Nasnaga translates as "Shawnee for Black Owl," and says that he has brought Turning Hawk news from his quest: "He [the spirit being] said he had seen the People. They were many . . . as many as before. They would follow and soon to this land would come peace. We would be as we were. We would be the *People*" (166). Thus, Nasnaga not only aligns his apparently mixed-blood Shawnee character with the historical Lakota visionary and warrior Crazy Horse but with a vision of the future similar to that proposed by the Shawnee warrior Tecumseh and his prophet brother. In this way Nasnaga inserts his subject position as mixed-blood Shawnee into the narrative and into an anticipated Indigenous future.

This scene is of interest, as well, for the specific terms of its prophecy. "We would be as we were" suggests "the *People*" will be diverse and multitribal rather than homogenous and "pan-Indian." Indeed, the novel consistently balances its "rhetoric" of unity with an emphasis on multitribal diversity. Scenes are set among Indians in New Mexico, Oklahoma, South Dakota, New York, and Canada, and characters identify as Navajo, Sioux, Mohawk, Apache, Acoma, Osage, Hopi, Cheyenne, Sac-Fox, and Shawnee. The Anishinabe-waki Democracy is not a single entity but a federation of three "new states": Cabolclo (located in New Mexico and defined by Nasnaga as "a Tupi-Guarani word meaning copper colored"), Lakota ("the name of the western, or Teton division of the Sioux nation"), and Akwesasne ("the Mohawk name for their reservation, officially known as St. Regis, which spans the St. Lawrence River in the United States and Canada") (49).[43] The American Indians' connection to the Asian nation of India, which offers Anishinabe-waki diplomatic support, is explained not only in terms of their common bond of oppression "at the hands of the white man who brought his so-called civilization to the poor, backward natives" but, more significantly, in these terms: "Both nations were characterized by cultures within cultures, many racial types within one people, and by languages and dialects which differed completely within only a few miles of each other" (126). In other words, similar to historical India, Nasnaga's imagined future Anishinabe-waki remains diversely multitribal.

Throughout the narrative, moreover, characters refer to treaties between Indian nations and settler governments in the United States and Canada. When the consul for India delivers his speech before the UN, he describes how "the trust [the Indians] placed in the government of the United States has been rewarded with over four hundred broken treaties" (77). He invokes this history again during an emergency meeting of the UN Security Council (121). During one of the president's tense meetings with his military and civilian advisers, between "large belt[s] of scotch," a senator evokes both the stereotypes and the political force of the discourse of treaties:

"'As long as the grass grows and the river flows . . . etc., etc., etc.!' Mr. President, how do you 'deal' with a people you've lied to and murdered for five hundred years? I think they'd rather have smallpox than our promises. We gave them both and it's hard to say which was more deadly!" [. . .]

"If we get cornered into trying to make all those old treaties good, we'll end up with Plymouth Rock, and damn lucky to hold that!" (94)

As the novel moves toward conclusion the Indian nation asserts its sovereignty, in part, by negotiating treaties with the Canadian province of Quebec and with the nation-states of France and Mexico (170). These are negotiated at Akwesasne, in the heart of the Iroquois confederacy, a model of intertribal organization and unity without loss of tribal distinctiveness or autonomy.

Five years before Nasnaga published *Indians' Summer,* another mixed-blood novelist anticipated a future 1976 in which American Indians retain a substantial land base and wield substantial political as well as cultural sovereignty, including the specific power to negotiate treaties. Martin Cruz Smith has since become a celebrated author of political thrillers and mysteries; in 1970, he was a young journalist and struggling writer of fiction. *The Indians Won,* which he wrote in 1969, when Indian activists were beginning to make their voices heard on a national scale, was his first published novel.[44] Similar to *Indians' Summer* in its anticipation of 1976, *The Indians Won* explores the possibilities of a unity among diverse American Indian individuals, communities, and nations that is both expansive and effective. Unlike Nasnaga, however, who sets his novel entirely in an imagined near future with only occasional references to the past, Smith imagines a highly detailed, alternative history that begins with the major battles fought between Plains Indian nations and the U.S. cavalry in the nineteenth century. In Smith's alternative version, the 1876 defeat of Custer at the Little Bighorn no longer represents the Indians' final military victory, nor the beginning of the end of independent Indian nations. Rather, that battle represents the beginning of a movement among the Sioux and their historical allies toward a stronger unity among themselves and, as they gain power, between themselves and other, more distant Indigenous nations. The defeat of Custer is also the beginning of the Indians' full realization of their sovereignty. Defying expectations of both the United States, against whom they fight, and the European powers, from whom they receive assistance, Smith's nineteenth-century Indians develop an Indigenous nation-state.

The bulk of the novel details this alternative history in a faux-documentary style. Smith's protagonist in these sections is John Setter (also known as Where the Sun Goes), a well-educated, well-traveled, and well-connected Mandan who enlists the Ghost Dance prophet Wovoka in his efforts to persuade Indians to unite as a single force to resist the cavalry on the plains and the broader U.S. settler encroachment onto Indian lands. Following a brief prologue set in 1875, prior to the central action of 1876 and its aftermath, Smith divides each of his six chapters between his alternative history centered on Setter and on his alternative present of the 1970s. In these less developed sections, Smith's protagonist is Holds Eagles, a prominent diplomat for the now century-old Indian Nation. The diplomat's contemporary mission is to negotiate with the president of the United States—a nation no longer contiguous across the continent but straddling the sovereign Indian Nation in eastern and western branches—in order to avert a looming war over national borders. As in the past, the United States desires more Indian land. Similar to *Indians' Summer*, the drama of these sections of *The Indians Won* revolves around the possibility of a nuclear conflict between the United States and the smaller but equally armed Indian Nation.

Although Smith never specifies the date, details suggest the present of *The Indians Won* is the "now" of its first readers. Cover art for the paperback edition indicates that this "now" is more precisely the near future of 1976. Positioned above and below the title, the artwork depicts two sides of a commemorative medal. On one side, the bust of a Sioux warrior is flanked by the years 1876 and 1976, with the caption "Red Shirt Indian Nation."[45] Emblazoned on the other, above two crossed Indian staffs, are the words "Commemorating Victory At Little Big Horn, Which Led To The Founding Of The Indian Nation." The medal counterbalances the U.S. bicentennial with an imagined Indian Nation centennial. The synopsis on the back cover emphasizes the relationship between the multiply significant 1876 and this "now":

> THE YEAR IS 1876. The United States has just suffered its third successive Indian defeat at the Custer massacre. The Presidency has been stolen in the country's worst political scandal. In the midst of economic depression, violence erupts and mobs control the cities. All this is in your history book. Now, what if the Indians won?
>
> THE TIME IS NOW. The United States straddles a vast unconquered Red Nation. For the first time in a hundred years the long unguarded borders are threatened. The Indians have the bomb. Indian sympathizers in the United States are called Pinkos. The President is terrified. The CIA is in stalemate.

It is unclear whether Smith was aware of the activist invasion of Alcatraz Island in late 1969 when he wrote his anticipatory novel, and *The Indians Won* was published before the subsequent large-scale activist events of 1972 and 1973.[46] Nonetheless, similar to Nasnaga, Smith honors a pre-1876 history of attempts to create Indian unity through a minor character identified as Shawnee (174). His most arresting plot innovation, however, is that he imagines a coming 1976 in which the political and racial violence of the 1960s culminates in the assassination of the leader of the American Indian nation. In his faux-documentary style, Smith delivers the recent history of this near future in the voice of a U.S. reporter for the "education network":

> The waves of violence that began growing in the Sixties seem about to engulf us. The assassination of a President and of a candidate for President, the war in Vietnam, student protests and, this year, the assassination of the Indian Chief of Nations, Buffalo Rider, by an American, all of these events seem to be accelerating to some sort of terrible crescendo. (63–64)

The Indian diplomat Holds Eagles turns out to be the newly elected Chief of Nations to replace Buffalo Rider, and despite attempts by corrupt U.S. officials to divert him from high-level talks and to frame him for murder, he successfully begins the negotiation of a new treaty with the U.S. president, averting the imminent threat of a nuclear exchange. In the novel's final scene, Smith has the president anticipate his nation's relationship with the Indians in the coming Century III: "The next hundred years will see vast changes on the continent we share. We must meet the challenges of those changes together. We must change, too" (218). Offering tobacco, the Indian Chief of Nations anticipates his own nation's Century II and agrees.

The anticipatory plots of Nasnaga's and Smith's fictions share an emphasis on the recurrent nature of crises in Indigenous–settler relations rather than on any linear progression, as well as on the ongoing difficulties in creating effective channels for Indigenous–settler negotiation. In this way, Nasnaga and Smith expand McNickle's and Deloria's nonfiction anticipations of a complex but increasingly sovereign Indigenous near future. In all four visions McNickle's "integrated" tribes continually work and rework their relations of power among themselves and with the United States. And both novelists, similar to participants in the American Indian Bicentennial Conference, assert the sovereign right of American Indians to prioritize their own needs and their own standards as they negotiate political authority and shared responsibilities. Rather than fantasy utopias of Indigenous isolation from the settler nation, they anticipate far more pragmatic—and far more likely—futures of Indigenous–settler interdependence.

In the Year of '76

During the bicentennial year itself, the national American Indian newspapers published articles, editorials, letters, and poems that further detail the multiple Indigenous responses to the Spirit of '76. In its July issue, for example, *Wassaja* published the brief article "Bicentennial" by Thomas Dion (Houma). Taking a hard line against the ideology undergirding the U.S. festivities, Dion asks, "What does this [celebration] mean to an Indian?" He answers, "What it does is remind us of the lands that we lost; of the schools we never had; and the hatred, bigotry and animosity felt for us for so many years!" (3). In the same issue, *Wassaja* published "'Be Thankful': The Bicentennial," focused on the views of Charles Trimble, executive director of the NCAI and a keynote speaker at the Bicentennial Conference. The anonymous reporter describes Trimble as promoting the idea that "the Indian should join the bicentennial celebration, but be thankful for survival." Repeating views he expressed in Tucson in 1973, Trimble emphasizes the need for effective tribal leadership in order to produce a more successful Indian future:

> American Indians have a long way to go to achieve their independence, but they must move toward this goal by participating in tribal government and by learning leadership, Trimble said. "With it the next 200 years will certainly be better for the Indian than the last 200 years [...]." (6)

Similar ideas were expressed by John C. Rainer, chairman of the board of regents for the Institute of American Indian Arts in the commencement address he delivered to the IAIA graduating class on May 21. Rainer describes himself and the students as "Natives of this country, with a rich and proud background." Aware of that history, he asks his audience to consider their place in a contemporary United States. "For the non-Indian graduates of 1976," he states, "there are many challenges to question, correct and make improvement on the establishment." In contrast, he argues, "For the Indian graduates, the burden of challenges to retain, maintain, correct and improve the whole question of Indian Affairs appears difficult and almost insurmountable" (220). Part of the context for Indigenous peoples is the demographic fact that "over half of the entire national Indian population is composed of Indians 27 years and younger." Thus, Rainer tells the IAIA graduates, "you are the vanguard" (221). His conclusion echoes Trimble in its emphasis on "the dire need for well trained Indian men and women who can and will be the future leaders in tribal and community affairs" (224).

Wassaja also published poetry voicing Native intellectual, psychological, and emotional responses to the bicentennial.[47] The June 1976 issue features a poem by R. Houle, "200 Years," that rehearses the violence of Indian–settler contact but ends with a focus on the future:

Some day I hope we all can be free.
Right now, Ward of the Gov., that's me.
For sure, my spirit, they'll never own or claim,
Not even after the Owl calls my name.
    (2)

In addition to the articles discussed above, the July 1976 issue features a poem by Patricia Eagle Elk, also titled "Bicentennial." Similar to the article by Dion, Eagle Elk's poem is written in the voice of critical satire:

For your genocidal heroes,
For the treaties you never honored,
For your freedom and democracy,
Happy Birthday, America.

In the final stanza, Eagle Elk evokes possibilities similar to those explored in the anticipatory novels by Nasnaga and Smith:

Ring your bell of liberty
And proclaim freedom and democracy.
We have heard you for hundreds of years.
Are you indivisible . . .
And are we the Native people so invisible?
    (3)

Two of the era's most celebrated Native intellectuals and writers, Deloria and Momaday, were each invited to offer "the" American Indian response to the bicentennial in the pages of major periodicals. Deloria was asked to write for a special Fourth of July issue of the *New York Times Magazine* titled "America at 200." His is one of fifteen articles that offer perspectives on the present and future of the settler nation.[48] Published under the ironic heading "The Ex-Majority," Deloria's article bears the evocative title "A Last Word from the First Americans." In the center of the full-page article, an artist for the magazine has altered a photograph of the National Mall in Washington, DC, replacing the iconic Washington Monument with a massive flint arrowhead.[49] With characteristic humor, Deloria deflates the importance of the young nation-state's two hundred years by noting, first, "Most traditional medicine men have sacred drums, pipes and wampum that are nearly twice that age, so the white man's concept of longevity is not really bowling people over on the reservations," and, second, "Perhaps the chief puzzlement among Indians about the nationwide celebration is their amazement at the white man's idea of progress" (80). Developing the latter point, Deloria reports:

> Indians wonder how the white man could have achieved such startling moral and economic bankruptcy in only 200 years. The evolution of American statesmen from Washington and Jefferson to Nixon and Kissinger seems to defy the theory of progress, and in view of modern taxing policies, the celebration of a revolution against unjust taxation appears the height of folly.

Deloria ends his discussion of how "little has changed in two centuries that would bring the several tribes into the celebration with enthusiasm" by focusing on the promise of the future. "Looking toward the next hundred years," Deloria notes, "Indians are depressed but still optimistic." One area of hope is the dominant culture's apparent changing attitudes toward the environment: "We have brought the white man a long way in nearly 500 years—from a childish search for mythical cities of gold and fountains of youth to the simple recognition that lands are essential for human existence."

The potential for the settler nation to learn a more positive environmental ethic from American Indians appears in a number of Indigenous responses to 1976. Like Deloria, Momaday was asked to write for a special issue of a major publication, *National Geographic*. Their July 1976 issue is titled "This Land of Ours," and as explained by the editor, "We at the Geographic decided that The Land was at the heart of the matter in this July of 1976—the land and how our people have used, often abused, often cherished, often exploited, and often fought over it" (1). Momaday's title for his contribution, "A First American Views His Land," is playful: while his audience may assume that this "First American" is the contemporary author, he evokes the perspective of the mythic "First Man" and imagines how the earliest ancestors might have viewed the land "one hundred centuries ago" to suggest how neither the idea of the sacred nor the concept of conservation is static but rather evolves (13).

Threaded through this meditation are passages from the poem "New World" from *The Gourd Dancer*, also published in 1976.[50] In his magisterial style, Momaday, who was then a professor at Stanford, never actually mentions the bicentennial by name. Instead, he states matter-of-factly:

> I tell my students that the American Indian has a unique investment in the American landscape. It is an investment that represents perhaps thirty thousand years of habitation. That tenure has to be worth something in itself—a great deal, in fact. The Indian has been here a long time; he is at home here. That simple and obvious truth is one of the most important realities of the Indian world, and it is integral in the Indian mind and spirit. (14)

Momaday responds to the settler conception of land "in terms of ownership and use" by stating, "This way of thinking of the land is alien to the Indian. His cultural intelligence is opposed to these concepts" (18). Momaday concedes nothing to dominant culture in its *National Geographic*. The conception he offers of the best future for the United States—for the entire planet—is presented wholly in Indigenous terms: "It is this ancient ethic of the Native American that must shape our efforts to preserve the earth and the life upon and within it" (18).[51]

Epilogue: Bicentennials Past, Indigenous Futures

Reports of Australia Day 2008 focused on the announcement made by Kevin Rudd, the new prime minister, that his first act upon opening Parliament would be to apologize to Indigenous Australians on behalf of the settler government. Not only Indigenous and non-Indigenous Australia but also much of the colonizing, colonized, and formerly colonized world watched on television or over the Internet as Rudd kept his promise on February 13. In the apology, presented before the Australian House of Representatives, Rudd declares, "The time has now come for the nation to turn a new page in Australia's history by righting the wrongs of the past and so moving forward with confidence to the future. [...] We today take this first step by acknowledging the past and laying claim to a future that embraces all Australians." Rudd amplifies his points with details of the history of Indigenous–settler relations and their possible, better future. Although speaking two decades after the last reenactment of the arrival of the First Fleet in Sydney Harbor, Rudd concludes with language reminiscent of the 1988 bicentennial: "First Australians, *First Fleeters*, and those who first took the Oath of Allegiance just a few weeks ago. Let's grasp the opportunity to craft a new future for this great land: Australia" (emphasis added). A speech that should have been made twenty years earlier had finally been delivered. And although Indigenous Australians praised the symbolism and truth telling of Rudd's long-overdue statement, they were understandably skeptical of its real-world effects.

Commentators around the globe noted that the United States has a colonial legacy similar to that of Australia's—and to that of Canada, which made its own overdue statement to Indigenous peoples a few months later—but had yet to offer a formal apology.[52] Apology bills have been introduced in both the U.S. House and Senate but have yet to pass. Senator Brownback, Republican of Kansas and principal sponsor of the Senate bill, has noted, "The resolution of apology does not authorize or serve as a settlement of any claim against the United States and does not resolve many of the challenges still facing Native peoples."[53] Indeed, while many would welcome a formal apology, others understandably wonder, similar to their Australian counterparts, about real-world effects. The issues raised in anticipation of the U.S. bicentennial observances—broken treaties, water and resources rights, low standards of living, needs for better health facilities, housing, and education—remain inadequately addressed. And new issues have arisen in the intervening years, including the mismanagement of federal trust funds and new assaults on sovereignty in the era of tribal gaming. Much has changed since American Indians anticipated the U.S. bicentennial, but much remains the same.

If the settler Spirit of '76 endures in the United States, does the Indigenous? Does the vision of integrated voices and collective action articulated by the Amerind Club at the University of Arizona, D'Arcy McNickle, and others in the 1970s also endure?

The answer appears to be emphatically yes. Native writers, artists, social commentators, and activists continue to anticipate collective futures alternative to those assumed and celebrated by the settler nation. To take one provocative example, in 2007 the award-winning Choctaw filmmaker Ian Skorodin and his Barcid Productions company released

Crazy Ind'n The Movie, a twenty-minute stop-motion feature that stars plastic action figures in an alternative reality set in the near future. Carrying the visions of 1970s writers like Smith and Nasnaga forward into the Internet age, Skorodin imagines beyond armed resistance to the U.S. nation-state and physical reclamation of the North American continent to a multifront Indigenous uprising to retake the entire planet. The elaborate website built to support the *Crazy Ind'n* project offers this synopsis of relevant backstory:

> The year is 2008, the Indigenous people have taken control. A small group of Aotearoans have seized New Zealand and invaded Australia, the Cook Islands, and Hawaii. South American Indian holy men hear of this and lead massive uprisings. Canada is quickly overrun by a coordinated and massive Aboriginal assault. The United States is surrounded by Indigenous forces. The U.S. loses California, Utah, and eventually the Midwest. Texas becomes a U.S. stronghold and the eastern seaboard is protected from an Indigenous takeover. A treaty is signed on the Tarahumara Nation-Texas border. . . .[54]

In *Crazy Ind'n The Movie* the hero's specific quest is to repatriate the skull of the Apache freedom fighter Geronimo, stolen from the cemetery at Fort Sill, Oklahoma, in 1921, which involves hand-to-hand combat with George Armstrong Custer the Tenth—"every Indian's dream"—and a showdown with U.S. special forces led by none other than President George W. Bush. For the 2009 sequel, *Crazy Ind'n The Feature*, on behalf of the World Indigenous Council, based in La Paz, Bolivia, the hero leads "our brave soldiers of the Indigenous Preservation Forces (IPF) to Europe in search of stolen holy relics and the remains of our leaders"; significant actions in the ongoing campaign are reported as they happen by an "unbiased and trustworthy" Indigenous Television Network. These details echo and update the anticipatory techniques of Smith's faux-documentary style and Nasnaga's day-by-day reports. The world map featured on the *Crazy Ind'n* website, titled "Fear of a Red Planet . . . ," gestures toward Nasnaga's anticipatory vision, as well: parts of Europe have already been renamed, including a United Saami Federation in the north and, less expectedly, in central Europe, a New Anishinabe.[55] Skorodin's project in stop-motion animation and real-time virtual reporting continues projects of truth telling begun in the American Indian anticipation of the U.S. bicentennial, and it highlights the power of anticipatory fiction to imagine alternative futures, even during periods of crisis and assault. *Crazy Ind'n* anticipates a future of active Native presence not merely national, transnational, or global in its reach but profoundly trans-Indigenous.

PART II

Interpretation / Recovery

interpretation. n. **1.** The act, process, or result of interpreting; explanation. **2.** A representation of the meaning of a work of art as expressed esp. in representation or performance.

recovery. n. **1.** An act, instance, process, or duration of recovering. **2.** A return to a normal condition. **3.** Something gained or restored in recovering. **4.** The act of obtaining usable substances from unusable sources, as waste material.

▸ *American Heritage Dictionary,* Second College Edition

3

Pictographic, Woven, Carved

Engaging N. Scott Momaday's "Carnegie, Oklahoma, 1919" through
Multiple Indigenous Aesthetics

He toi whakairo   Where there is artistic excellence
He mana tangata   There is human dignity

► Māori proverb

The juxtapositions of the 2006 exhibit *Manawa—Pacific Heartbeat: A Celebration of Contemporary Maori and Northwest Coast Art* may have struck some viewers as unprecedented, perhaps as exotic or "unique." In fact, they were built on a foundation of at least twenty-five years of active exchange among Māori and Northwest Coast First Nations artists, as well as on a series of collaborative exhibitions staged on both sides of the Pacific since the 1980s (Reading and Wyatt, 28). The catalog for *Manawa* (which can be translated from Māori into English as "heart," "breath," "mind," and related concepts) includes a coauthored essay by the non-Native curators Nigel Reading and Gary Wyatt of the Spirit Wrestler Gallery in Vancouver, British Columbia, the site of the exhibit; an introduction by the acclaimed Māori painter and curator Darcy Nicholas; and color photographs of over sixty contemporary works—carvings, weavings, paintings, sculptures—produced by Māori and Northwest Coast artists. Reading and Wyatt observe, "Thematically [the work in *Manawa*] speaks of ancient connections, marriages, parallel customs and powerful friendships that can exist between individuals who share a similar passion and responsibility toward maintaining cultural traditions" (49). Statements by the individual artists describe histories of physical and intellectual travel that cross and recross borders of tribe and nation-state. Reading ends his separate preface to *Manawa* by emphasizing the significance of these Indigenous-to-Indigenous connections, quoting a whakataukī (saying, proverb) he learned from a Māori artist: "*He toi whakairo, he mana tangata.* Where there is artistic excellence, there is human dignity" (5). What Reading does not mention (and may not have known) is that, twenty years earlier, this same whakataukī was voiced to commemorate a specifically Māori achievement, one that opened the way for future exhibits like *Manawa.* The whakataukī was composed as a response to the 1984–1986 traveling exhibition *Te Maori,* a groundbreaking showcase of 174 objects from the Māori classic period (about 900 to 1850 CE), including architectural sculptures, carvings in wood, stone, and bone, weapons, tools, musical instruments, and personal adornments.[1] *Te Maori* was the first international exhibit devoted exclusively to Māori art; more important, a group of Māori accompanied the objects on their long journey overseas, ensuring the observance of proper protocol for taonga (treasures, prized possessions) and providing a living, actively present context for historic Indigenous artworks. The overwhelming success of *Te Maori* fostered pride in the Māori artistic heritage for both Māori and Pakeha (New Zealanders of European descent) and generated interest in subsequent exhibitions of classic and contemporary Māori art at home and abroad.

The compact, grammatically parallel structure of the whakataukī captures this sense of pride and, in particular, its Māori resonance. The Māori-language version is a balanced juxtaposition that bonds aesthetic achievement (toi whakairo) to the mana (power, prestige) of the individual or the people (tangata). By extension, and especially through its expression in the Māori language, aesthetic achievement is linked to the mana of the Māori nation. In the mid-1980s, the whakataukī highlighted the role of customary arts in the Māori political and literary "renaissance" that had begun about 1970, asserting a moral victory—human dignity—within a contemporary Aotearoa New Zealand where the tangata whenua (people of the land) were relegated to ongoing demographic substatus and political, economic, and social subordination. The whakataukī asserts, as well, a significant challenge to dominant, European-derived standards of human value that historically had denigrated Māori people and their artistic traditions and that continued, in the 1980s and beyond, to marginalize contemporary Māori arts, including not only carving but also weaving, painting, and tattooing, oral and performance traditions, and the extension of these into other media, including alphabetic writing in

Māori and English languages. Bolstered by the success of *Te Maori*, the whakataukī asserts the manifest power of Māori to represent themselves (whakairo [carving or, more broadly, to ornament with a pattern]) as an index of their intrinsic value (mana [power, prestige]). In this way, the whakataukī functions as an activist statement of the enduring distinctiveness of the Māori community despite a history of settler colonialism, missionary and government attempts to impose systematic acculturation, and both coerced and voluntary change.

I begin with the celebratory repetition of this whakataukī in order to make the general point that one of the aims of Indigenous arts production and presentation, within the contexts of resistance to multiple forms of ongoing colonialism, is the defiant assertion of enduring cultural and communal distinctiveness. A corollary to this general point is that Indigenous arts historically have been either relegated to the field of anthropology rather than engaged by the fields of arts criticism and art history or, when addressed specifically as arts rather than as ethnographic data, marginalized or denigrated by European-derived systems of aesthetics. As Darcy Nicholas remarks, "Until 'Te Maori,' New Zealand art galleries had labeled Maori art as '*marae* decoration.' *Marae* are traditional Maori gathering places" (19). There was little room for Māori "art" in non-Māori art spaces.

First Nations scholar Kateri Akiwenzie-Damm raises similar issues about the marginalization of Indigenous literatures. In the preface to the international anthology *Skins: Contemporary Indigenous Writing* (2000), she remarks, "For the most part, there is a form of what [Laguna writer and scholar] Paula Gunn Allen terms 'intellectual apartheid' as well as what I would call 'aesthetic apartheid' operating around the world. Our creative work, and there is a lot of it, going back thousands and thousands of years and forward to this day, continues to be segregated, denied, oppressed, ignored, silenced" (vi). It is important to grapple with the complexity of these statements. Since the periods of early European contact and throughout the nineteenth and twentieth centuries, various non-Native commentators have shown interest in Indigenous artistic customs and have praised specific Indigenous artistic achievements. In the main, however, such commentary did not have a positive impact on the relative status of Indigenous arts within dominant modes of arts criticism or within the academic field of art history. This account holds true for Aotearoa New Zealand, Australia, Hawai'i, and North

America. The well-respected non-Native art historians Janet C. Berlo and Ruth B. Phillips, for instance, describe the North American context for Indigenous arts scholarship in these terms:

> As we would expect, the early ethnologists shared the theories of art in general circulation at the end of the nineteenth century. Among these was the notion, formulated in the aesthetic theory of Immanuel Kant, that functionality limited the "highest" capacity of a work of art to achieve formal beauty and to express ideas. For this reason they assigned most Native American arts, which often adorned "useful" forms such as pots, clothing or weapons, to the inferior category of "applied art" or craft. (15)

The whakataukī quoted above is suggestive, then, of the need for artists, writers, critics, and scholars to develop alternative systems of contemporary Indigenous arts criticism and aesthetics—that is, alternative systems for describing how contemporary Indigenous arts (in all their evolving, [post]colonial complexity) not only convey culturally inflected *meaning* but also produce culturally coded aesthetic *pleasure*, what producers and audiences recognize as "beauty," "power," and "excellence."

This work is already under way, conducted along lines that are tribally specific (e.g., Lakota arts, Hopi arts), multitribal (e.g., Plains Indian arts, Southwestern Indian arts), and intertribal (e.g., powwow arts).[2] In Aotearoa New Zealand, to look at one notable example, Māori artist, scholar, and activist Ngahuia Te Awekotuku has focused attention on the roles of *innovation* and *improvisation* in Māori women's artistic practices in the nineteenth and twentieth centuries—particularly those of women in her own iwi (tribal group) of Te Arawa—in her efforts to reassert a specifically Māori critical discourse on arts and performance traditions. Te Awekotuku argues for an awareness that despite the presence of colonizers and settlers, Māori arts changed and shifted emphases "on our own terms, for our own reasons" and that Māori coped "with an immediate situation creatively, and with style" (111). She argues, moreover, that even within Māori performance for tourists, "innovation and change were more likely to take place for

Maori pleasure, than [for] simple touristic spectacle and gratification. [. . .] All the innovations occurred before a Maori audience first—a critical, knowing audience, not a busload of uninformed, anonymous consumers" (130, 132).

The idea of a "critical, knowing audience" is key to developing new modes of inquiry, appreciation, and interpretation for Indigenous arts in all media, including written literatures. The non-Native art historian Gaylord Torrence, writing about customary artistic practice among Plains Indian women from the eighteenth through the twentieth centuries, emphasizes that "in tribal groups, where everyone's creative efforts were well known and compared, the people formed a critical audience that valued exceptional ability. Industry, virtuosity, and innovation were highly esteemed" (24–25). Those traditions and others, across North America and around the globe, continue, although until recently they have not often been recorded in texts accessible to—or influential among—critics and scholars, especially from the dominant culture. A notable exception occurred in 1975 when, as part of an exhibition of Indian art from the Northwest Coast, the Institute for the Arts at Rice University in Houston, Texas, invited the non-Native art historian Bill Holm, author of the seminal study *Northwest Coast Indian Art* (1965) and himself an accomplished artist, and the acclaimed Haida carver Bill Reid to examine the pieces in the collection and to engage in a critical dialogue about the quality of their artistry. The transcript of those conversations conducted over a period of three days and concerning some 102 decorated objects—pipes, daggers, hair combs, spindle whorls, spoons, ladles, bowls, boxes, baskets, blankets, shirts, hats, rattles, masks, painted screens—resulted in the 1975 publication *Form and Freedom: A Dialogue on Northwest Coast Indian Art*, reprinted and made more widely available in 1976 as *Indian Art of the Northwest Coast: A Dialogue on Craftsmanship and Aesthetics*. Holm and Reid's discussion is wide ranging, detailed, and precise; it is serious but often playful; above all, it is exceptionally *knowing*. As they initiate conversation, the two artists set parameters for their discourse on Northwest Coast aesthetics:

HOLM: Well, one thing I'm wondering—do we limit the kind of thing we talk about?

REID: I think we should talk about the things we're interested in, as opposed to what we imagine the general public would be interested in.

HOLM: I think that's the best thing. (29)

It is precisely this critical, knowing dialogue that often has been lacking in discussions of Indigenous arts intended (or assumed to be intended) for a more "general" public.[3]

Artists and art scholars such as Te Awekotuku and Holm and Reid demonstrate the possibilities of appreciation, critique, and scholarship based in particular Indigenous aesthetic systems. Perhaps the most pressing challenge posed by these and other artist-scholars is how to develop methodologies that enable analysis at appropriate levels of complexity. How might we take seriously the roles of knowledge and imagination not only in Indigenous arts production but also in Indigenous arts reception? How might we engage, that is, with the reality of multiple audiences for Indigenous arts, performances, and texts, including highly knowledgeable, well-traveled, and intellectually savvy audiences of Indigenous peoples themselves, both "local" and "extralocal"? In the following sections and in the next two chapters, I build on this ongoing work in Indigenous arts scholarship to suggest the possibility for appreciation and interpretation of Indigenous literatures informed by multiple, distinct systems of Indigenous aesthetics across tribal, national, geographic, and cultural borders. In other words, I suggest the possibility of trans-Indigenous literary analysis based in multiple understandings of aesthetics. Let me be clear: I do not argue for an understanding of aesthetics that is *pan*-Indigenous, which would suggest a single aesthetic system applicable to all Indigenous cultures in all historical periods. On the contrary, I argue for the possibility of engaging distinct and specific Indigenous aesthetic systems in the appreciation and interpretation of diverse works of Indigenous art, including written literature.

This chapter is the initial component in a three-part proposal for a new methodology, and it performs three readings of the same text, each informed by a distinct Indigenous worldview and aesthetic system: Kiowa, Navajo, and Māori. Through these juxtaposed experiments in close reading, contextualization, and interpretation, chapter 3 thus explores how multiple Indigenous perspectives on aesthetics can be applied to contemporary Indigenous texts. It demonstrates, as well, how multiple perspectives might enrich the production of literary meaning and pleasure rather than produce balanced lists of similarities and differences. My purpose is neither to offer definitive accounts of specific cultures or aesthetics nor to offer exhaustive readings from these perspectives. My understandings of Kiowa, Navajo, and Māori cultures and arts, while greater than when I began this project, remain necessarily limited. Nonetheless, I contend that scholarship on Indigenous literatures must move in this direction in order to advance in ways that will be meaningful not only for Native and non-Native scholars but also for Indigenous individuals and communities outside the academy. It is my hope that such experiments will spur others, knowledgeable about specific Indigenous worldviews and aesthetic systems, to take up this challenge and push it further. He toi whakairo, he mana tangata.

A Provocative Strangeness

For my primary text I have chosen the poem "Carnegie, Oklahoma, 1919" by the acclaimed, sometimes controversial Kiowa and Cherokee author N. Scott Momaday. I find myself repeatedly drawn to these twelve lines.[4] In terms of literary, historical, and social contexts, the brief poem invites sustained attention as one component in a series of four related texts produced by Momaday that can be divided into two sets—each set composed of a poem and a piece of prose—published nearly twenty years apart. Each text performs a meditation on the poet's relationship to his Kiowa grandfather, Mammedaty, as well as on his relationship to ceremonial grounds near Carnegie, Oklahoma, that are used by the Kiowa gourd dancers and where, in 1919, Mammedaty was honored in a ritual giveaway. The dates of publication for these texts mark signal events in the U.S. and global commemoration of New World conquest, what in chapter 2 I describe as the "settler celebration." Momaday published the first set of texts in 1976, the year of the U.S. bicentennial observances: a four-part, complex lyric and prose poem, "The Gourd Dancer," which he explicitly dedicates to Mammedaty, and a six-page section of his innovative memoir, *The Names*, that includes a photograph of Mammedaty posed in his gourd dance regalia. Momaday published the second set of texts during and immediately after the Columbus quincentenary: the poem "Carnegie, Oklahoma, 1919" in 1992, followed in 1993 by the essay "Sacred Places," which includes the 1992 poem (without its title) and offers a second prose version of the giveaway ceremony that honored Momaday's grandfather.

Read together, these works create a highly charged intertext that demonstrates Momaday's theories about how memory is passed down the generations within families and communities through storytelling and acts of imagination. Momaday imagines himself into his father's memory of how his grandfather was honored in 1919 by focusing on two details of the event: that his father was a young boy when he witnessed the giveaway ceremony and that another Kiowa boy was charged with presenting the gift, a beautiful horse, to his grandfather. Over the course of the four texts, Momaday constructs his narrative subjectivity so that his "I" occupies various vantage points within and outside the scene of the giveaway, including those of the two Kiowa boys, imagining himself as participant, witness, and chronicler of the event. "Carnegie, Oklahoma, 1919" offers the most condensed version of the giveaway and the most condensed assertion of its ongoing significance. I am interested in Momaday's insistent return to particular personal and familial biographical details in these reimaginings of an auspicious event in his family and community history, as well as in the productive irony of the publication dates for these provocative American Indian texts. They highlight the potential relationships among assertions of Indigenous biography, autobiography, history, and aesthetics and ongoing battles in the United States over the recognition of Native sovereignty.

In terms of form and specific content, several features of "Carnegie, Oklahoma, 1919" immediately garner attention, but these cannot be fully accounted for by conventional contextualization or dominant understandings of aesthetics. For convenience, I have numbered the lines of the poem:

Carnegie, Oklahoma, 1919

This afternoon is older	1
than the giving of gifts	2
and the rhythmic scraping of the red earth.	3

My father's father's name is called,   4
and the gift horse stutters out, whole,   5
the whole horizon in its eyes.   6
In the giveaway is beaded   7
the blood memories of fathers and sons.   8
Oh, there is nothing like this afternoon   9
in all the miles and years around,   10
and I am not here,   11
but, grandfather, father, I am here.   12
    (*In the Presence of the Sun*, 136)

Note, first, that although the title of the poem establishes a specific geographical location and date—a straightforward framework for the action of the poem—the final lines evoke a paradox of space and time.[5] Line 10 sets up this paradox by yoking together "miles and years," while lines 11 and 12 play on the repeated adverb of space and time, *here*. The speaker states in line 11 that he is "not here" (*not* in this specific geographical location and *not* in this specific time) but also, in line 12, that, simultaneously, he is "here" (*in* this place and *in* this time). Second, note that in line 3 the poem locates this paradox at the site of sacred space, specifically at the site of ceremonial dance grounds where a ritual giveaway was celebrated in 1919. The phrasing designating the rhythmically scraped "red earth" echoes the "Oklahoma" of the title in its implicit reference to the original Choctaw derivation for Indian Territory's new name, Okla-houma, "people-red earth" or "red earth people." Third, note that the poem explicitly invokes not only the Indigenous ritual of the giveaway but also, in the central metaphor for the giveaway developed in lines 7 and 8, an Indigenous art form, beading. And fourth, note that the poem deploys at least two and possibly three instances of provocative language that draw attention and that seem intimately linked to the poem's central paradox: the phrase "blood memories" in line 8, which completes and complicates the metaphor of beading; the three-part genealogical sequence "grandfather, father, I" in line 12, which is placed between the paradoxical claims of "not here"/"am here"; and the duplicative adjectival phrase "father's father's" in line 4, which upon completion of the brief poem, can be read retrospectively as an anticipatory echo of the genealogical sequence in line 12. Finally, note, as well, that these instances of provocative language are located in lines 4, 8, and 12, creating a regular pattern of association in the structure of the poem, as well as in its themes and specific diction.

The remainder of this chapter could be devoted to unpacking these early observations in conventional literary-critical terms, and undoubtedly, such work would be productive. In moving to a series of engagements with the poem based in understandings of Indigenous systems of aesthetics, it is not my intention to suggest that dominant critical methodologies are inappropriate or ineffective for this material. Like other scholars, I understand that Indigenous writers appropriate and innovate both Indigenous and settler (in some cases, colonial) artistic and rhetorical traditions to produce texts in all genres. Scholarship on Momaday's own works, especially his Pulitizer Prize–winning first novel *House Made of Dawn* (1968), has made this point abundantly clear. For convenience and to aid my larger argument, the readings I offer are divided into sections and organized around understandings of Kiowa, Navajo, and Māori aesthetic systems, respectively. While each designation indicates the central focus of a particular engagement with the poem, each is related to and builds on the others, and I do not suppress insights that may originate in additional Indigenous traditions or in dominant Western aesthetics and literary-critical modes. My purpose, which I believe is embodied in Momaday's poem and in the work of other contemporary Indigenous writers, artists, and scholars, is to forge productive connections rather than to enforce rigid boundaries. The point is not to denigrate the dominant but to demonstrate the literary and political power of the Indigenous.

A Pictograph for 1919—and for "Now"

Although he is best known as a poet, novelist, and essayist, Momaday is also a visual artist, and since the mid-1970s, he has integrated his own drawings and paintings into his published written works. His father, Al Momaday, was a well-known Kiowa artist, and both father and son can be viewed as working within a tradition of Kiowa and Plains Indian pictorial art that art historians often divide into three basic genres: narrative art, visionary art, and pictorial record keeping (Greene, "Changing," 15). Much attention has been paid in American Indian literary and art history studies to the wide range of Plains Indian art traditions, but especially to the communal and personal pictographic calendars commonly referred to as "winter counts" and to the innovation of the pictographic tradition into pictorial "ledger art" during the so-called reservation period of the late nineteenth and early twentieth centuries.[6] Scholars are especially interested in these art traditions as Indigenous representations of "written" history, biography, and autobiography.[7] Momaday himself describes at some length the calendars and ledger books of the Kiowa and meditates on their contemporary significance in his 1976 memoir.[8]

One way to engage Kiowa and, more broadly, Plains Indian aesthetics for a reading of "Carnegie, Oklahoma, 1919" is to conceive the poem as a contemporary, literary version of the kind of pictographic marker used in the customary Kiowa winter and summer counts. Unlike in some other Plains Indian pictographic record traditions, such as those of the Lakota, the Kiowa historians inscribed two pictographs for each year, dividing time into two annual seasons (Boyd, 2:145; Greene, "Calendars," 300). Conceived as a pictographic marker, the poem can be analyzed as a mnemonic device designed to help organize an event of communal, familial, and personal importance within a temporal framework and to aid in the production of more expansive and necessarily richer oral accounts of this same event. Within the conventions of this aesthetic system, the straightforward title of the poem can be understood to function as a caption for the literary pictograph. I am thinking of the kinds of "captions" Plains Indian artists often added to ledger drawings, written either in English or an Indigenous language or, sometimes, in both, that give basic orienting details, such as the time and location of the event depicted. Alternatively, the entire poem can be conceived as an extended "year name."[9] The condensed, abbreviated, and opaque qualities of the form and language of Momaday's poem can be understood as idiosyncratic to the author-artist, but idiosyncratic within a highly schematic and stylized aesthetic tradition. These features also can be understood as being inextricably linked to other, more detailed and more explanatory texts, but not necessarily in the ways that scholars typically understand instances of literary allusion or intertextuality.

Interpreting the poem in terms of an innovated pictograph or year name invites us to move beyond questions about how the meaning of the poem might be affected by its location as the third component within a sequence of four related and published texts. We can now ask more nuanced questions about how the poem operates as *a particular kind of component* within a *matrix* of related texts that includes but is not limited to the published four. For certain audiences this poem can function, in the way that a drawn pictograph on a Kiowa winter or summer count can function, as the basis for a multimedia event of (re)telling Indigenous history.[10] Lakota scholar Craig Howe describes American Indian history presented from an "indigenous tribal perspective" as having four main aspects, all of which are present in Momaday's poem: it is recited in relation to specific landscapes, waterscapes, and/or skyscapes; it is event centered; it is organized around narrators rather than abstract themes or predetermined sequences; and it often employs drawing so that the telling of history is actually planned as a "multimedia event" (162, 166). Howe focuses especially on what he describes as the four dimensions of an "event-centered" history—spatial, social, spiritual, and experiential—an apt description for Momaday's approach in "Carnegie, Oklahoma, 1919" (162).[11] Thus, for audiences familiar with Momaday's larger body of work, part of the aesthetic pleasure of the poem—part of its "beauty," "power," or "excellence"—is located not in its position within a sequence but rather in its iconicity within a matrix. Momaday's essay "Sacred Places," for instance, can be understood as demonstrating *one version* of such an event of multimedia storytelling. Here, "Carnegie, Oklahoma, 1919," without its distinguishing title/caption, is explicitly embedded within an expanded version of the narrative of the giveaway that honored Momaday's grandfather and within an expanded explanation of the ceremony's evolving significance for Momaday's community, his family, and himself. The brief and highly condensed poem, in other words, operates pictographically.

Similarly, if we place "Carnegie, Oklahoma, 1919" in conversation with the earlier and more descriptive poem "The Gourd Dancer"—part of the literary and extraliterary matrix discussed above—we can better understand how the later poem distills Momaday's broad knowledge of the events of 1919 and his evolving interpretation of their significance into a single ideographic image for the paradox "not here"/"am here."[12] The earlier poem is structured as a narrative, and it organizes its main plot elements into four numbered and named parts.[13] These vary in terms of the number of stanzas per part and the number of lines per stanza, and they alternate in genre between lyric and prose poem: (1) "The Omen" (lyric, two stanzas of four lines each); (2) "The Dream" (prose poem, one stanza of nine lines); (3) "The Dance" (lyric, two stanzas of seven lines each); and (4) "The Giveaway" (prose poem, two stanzas, the first of nine lines, the second of thirteen). Together, the four parts illustrate Mammedaty's experiences leading up to and during the gourd dance of 1919, including his being singled out to be honored by the gift of a black horse. The title of the poem, with its limiting definite article, refers specifically to the historical Mammedaty; this is emphasized by the dedication line immediately following the title, which names Mammedaty explicitly as "The Gourd Dancer" and thus as the subject of the narrative. The dedication line also lists the inclusive dates for Mammedaty's life, 1880–1932, further specifying the subject and, for readers aware that Momaday was born in 1934, marking the events of the narrative as outside the personal memory of the author. The final lines of part 4 reinforce the idea that the poem is meant to commemorate both the life and the name of the poet's deceased grandfather by reimagining how he was honored in his own lifetime: "And all of this [the details of the giveaway] was for Mammedaty, in his honor, / as even now it is in the telling, and will be, as long as / there are those who imagine him in his name" (37).

In its original publication, the poem is preceded by Momaday's evocative, dynamic line drawing of Mammedaty dancing in his regalia, so that the stylized image on the left page of the open book faces the early parts of the poem on the right. Significantly, the drawing is not an image that can stand in for the entirety of the four-part poem; rather, it serves the local purpose of illustrating either the poem's title, "The Gourd Dancer," or, more specifically, the content of part 3, "The Dance." The illustration may be based, in part, on the photograph of Mammedaty that Momaday includes on page 95 of his 1976 memoir, *The Names*. In the sepia-colored photograph, Mammedaty stands in a parlor or photographic studio, posed to display his gourd dance regalia, feet planted firmly on the carpeted floor, arms relaxed at his sides, eyes directed forward into the camera. In contrast, in Momaday's stylized line drawing Mammedaty floats in indeterminate white space in the motions of the gourd dance, his knee bent and his foot raised in midstep, his arms lifting his rattle and eagle feather fan, his blanket and belt swinging about his waist, his gaze directed to the viewer's left to a location beyond the horizon of the page.

Although "Carnegie, Oklahoma, 1919" was also published in a collection that includes examples of Momaday's visual art, the later poem stands on its own, without illustration. Emphasis is shifted away from the historical person Mammedaty and his particular experience of the gourd dance and giveaway performed in 1919 to the contemporary speaker and his experience of *connecting* to his father and grandfather. This shift allows the poet to evoke a paradox of space and time ("not here"/"am here"). The earlier poem inscribes the name of the honored ancestor six times, drawing repeated attention to his specificity, whereas the later poem assiduously avoids inscribing the personal name of this or any ancestor, substituting in place of the personal name the kinship markers "grandfather" and, more precisely, "father's father." The term "giveaway" no longer names the particular ritual that honored Mammedaty in 1919, as it does in "The Gourd Dancer," but a more abstract process of commemorating genealogical bonds. The genealogical sequence in the final line, "grandfather, father, I," now can be understood both as a transgenerational address—the "I" speaking across the generations to the deceased "father" and "grandfather"—and, simultaneously, as an extended nominal phrase for the speaker of the poem that collapses distinctions among three generations of family members—these three classifications within a kinship system—and asserts their equivalence in this particular moment and at this particular location. Read this way, "Carnegie, Oklahoma, 1919" functions as an iconic pictograph not only for the year 1919, as its title/caption announces, but also for "now," the contemporary moment of this connection to the ancestral, what the speaker describes in lines 1 and 9 as "this afternoon": "older / than the giving of gifts" and "like" nothing else "in all the miles and years around." The poem functions, in other words, as a complex pictograph for a significant event that occurred in a named moment in time, 1919, and for a significant event that occurs in a moment *outside* ordinary, named time in which distinctions among the past, the present, and possibly the future are collapsed.[14]

Understanding the "afternoon" of the poem as both inside and outside ordinary time, we can turn our attention to one of the central features of "classic" Kiowa culture evoked in lines 5 and 6, the horse that is made a gift with which to honor Mammedaty. In this reading, the horse stands in, ideographically, for nineteenth-century Kiowa horse culture.[15] When, in line 4, Mammedaty's name is called by an unnamed Kiowa ancestor, this iconic horse "stutters out." The verb is immediately provocative: its tense locates this significant action in an ambiguous present, and its primary definition suggests that the horse's halting performance within the dance arena is also a form of repetitive speech. "Stutters" can evoke the legacy of the Kiowa's subjugation at the hands of the U.S. cavalry and the U.S. government at the end of the nineteenth century, which effectively put an end to classic Kiowa horse culture, a legacy that was felt already in 1919 and was ongoing in 1992. But despite this hobbled and tentative "stutter," the "gift horse"—a fully operational Kiowa culture—arrives in the ritual space of the giveaway "whole / the whole horizon in its eyes."

The repetition of "whole" is suggestive of the primary definition of the verb "stutter"—this action is a form of speech—but it also links thematically to the words "horizon" and "eyes."[16] The process of this "giveaway" offers the poem's speaker an intact worldview, a distinctly Kiowa way of perceiving the whole world. Moreover, this worldview is located not in the "stutter" of the gift horse, in its history of subjugation, but in its "eyes." This word evokes the obvious pun on the "eye" of perception and the "I" of subjectivity, a pun Momaday exploits in other texts.[17] Here, the pun links lines 5 and 6 to lines 11 and 12, where the "I" of the speaker asserts the poem's paradox of space and time. If we are aware that in the Kiowa language the same word is used for both the first-person singular and first-person plural pronouns—for both "I" and "we" (Boyd, 1:28)—we can link the pun on the plural "eyes" also to the genealogical sequence in line 12, "grandfather, father, I." Kiowa culture and Kiowa worldview, these lines assert, are located not in the discrete past of some golden age, such as Kiowa horse culture, or even in discrete ancestors, such as Mammedaty. Rather, the "whole horizon" of Indigenous identity is available to the speaker in a transgenerational conception of self, in all of these "I's" understood as "beaded" together. We can now recast the final lines' paradox of space and time: "and I [understood in the singular] am not here, / but, grandfather, father, I [understood in the plural] am here."[18]

Deep Patterning: The Dynamics of Hózhó

Scholarship on Momaday's literary works and biography has investigated the influence of not only Kiowa and Plains Indian traditions but also Navajo and other Southwestern Indian traditions on his experiments with symbolism, allegory, and allusion, especially in his two novels.[19] Such influences can be explained, in part, by the fact that Momaday spent periods of his childhood living on or near the Navajo reservation and that he has been a lifelong student of Navajo history, language, and culture. In addition, we know that, historically, Kiowa and other Southern Plains Indians, who in their own pictorial art demonstrate a strong preference for graphic patterning and a frequent use of patterned repetition, highly valued Southwestern Indian arts as trade items, especially Navajo weaving in the form of richly patterned blankets (Berlo, "Artists," 30). The pictorial work of nineteenth-century Kiowa and Cheyenne ledger artists often depicts men proudly displaying robes fashioned from distinctive Navajo textiles (Berlo and Phillips, 65; Berlo, "Individuality," 37). In this way, Navajo weaving, which has a long history of borrowing and refashioning materials, techniques, and ideas from other cultural and artistic traditions, also has a long history of participating within other semiotic systems, including other Indigenous semiotic systems, such as that of the Kiowa. At least since the nineteenth century, Navajo weaving has participated in multiple and trans-Indigenous signification.[20]

Less critical attention has been paid to the possible influence of Navajo worldview and aesthetics on Momaday's poetry. Critics of the poetry have noted, however, Momaday's frequent use of syllabics, a poetic technique in which the number of syllables per line is consciously manipulated into legible patterns. An attention to syllabics allows the poet to embed one or more patterns within a poem's line structure, depending on whether he maintains a consistent number of syllables per line, alternates these, or creates a more complex system of relationships. In this section, I investigate Momaday's use of syllabics by analyzing the patterns he establishes in the number of syllables per line through understandings of Navajo worldview and aesthetics, particularly as these are expressed in Navajo weaving. By engaging both syllabics and understandings of Navajo aesthetics, we become aware of several distinct but complementary systems of patterning in the structure of "Carnegie, Oklahoma, 1919." In effect, we can read Momaday's Kiowa poem as though it were conceived as—or fashioned from—a Navajo textile.

Navajo weaving has been the subject of a great deal of critical attention and writing by anthropologists, art historians, museologists, buyers and traders, weavers from various traditions, and Navajo and other Indigenous intellectuals. In several of the more recent studies, different

kinds of scholars and practitioners have worked collaboratively to produce accounts of Navajo textile production, appreciation, and interpretation that is bi- or multicultural and multiperspectivist. While space
does not permit an extended discussion of Navajo systems of aesthetics and their historical development, briefly stated, following the work
of innovative ethnographers and their Navajo collaborators, including
practicing weavers, we can say that Navajo aesthetics are based in understandings of the term *hózhó*, a complex philosophical concept that
"expresses the intellectual notion of order, the emotional state of happiness, the physical state of health, the moral condition of good, and
the aesthetic dimension of harmony" (Witherspoon and Peterson, 15).
Hózhó typically is translated into English as "beauty" (often capitalized as "Beauty"), but the English word does little to convey *hózhó*'s
sense, in the realm of aesthetics, of what the non-Native linguist and
anthropologist Gary Witherspoon describes as "holistic asymmetry" or
"dynamic symmetry." Unlike static symmetry, which creates a mirror
image and absolute balance of its elements, dynamic or what is sometimes called "near" symmetry expresses motion and energy in its use
of opposites, contrasts, and disequilibrium (Witherspoon, *Language*,
172, 198). Dynamic symmetry is undergirded philosophically by a basic
"complementary dualism" that divides all parts of the universe into the
categories "static" (or complete) and "active" (or incomplete and creative).
One model for this binary is the understanding of male and female as
"complementary aspects of a whole, and this whole might appropriately
be described as holistic asymmetry" (Witherspoon and Peterson 24).[21]

This basic Navajo binary is extended in multiple ways. The "static"
category includes the male gender, even numbers, the east (dawn) and
north (night) directions, thought, choreographed undertakings such as
ritual and ceremony, the "inner" forms of things, and both the origins
and culminations of things. In contrast, the "active" category includes
the female gender, odd numbers, the west (twilight) and south (daylight) directions, speech, creative undertakings such as weaving, the
"outer" forms of things, and processes of growth and change (Witherspoon, *Language*, 141–42). Similar to male and female in Navajo understandings of holistic asymmetry, static and active are inseparably
connected, and the tension between them is productive. Witherspoon
describes the Navajo intellectual style as "dynamic synthesis." He describes Navajo aesthetic style in similar terms:

It is not simple or static, but dynamic and active. It is binary and dualistic, but it is not opposed or mirror imagery. Although it often has an axis or axes, it is not split or fragmented. The total impact of Navajo works of art is a unity of diversity, a synthesis of differences, a harmony of divergence, and a confluence of contrast. (*Language*, 200)

The Navajo art of weaving, which is considered "active" and gendered female, is understood as "an act of creative transformation" (Witherspoon, "Cultural Motifs," 372, 373). In some accounts weaving is described as functioning as a language, and the process of weaving is seen as analogous to the process of thought (McLerran, 11, 9). Moreover, many accounts emphasize the importance of the transformative *process* of the act of weaving itself over the importance of the finished textile (Berlo and Phillips, 67; Bonar, 9; Thomas, 33). Witherspoon points out that in contrast to ceremonial sand painting, which employs fixed designs that must be re-created by the artists as closely as possible in order to be used in rituals of restoration and healing—and which is thus considered "static" and gendered male—"in each [textile] composition, the weaver seeks a personal, unique expression of a universal theme" ("Cultural Motifs," 373). Classic Navajo textile designs are distinctive, in part, for the way they hold "static" and "active" elements in productive tension. Static conditions, for instance, are depicted through the use of straight lines and horizontal and vertical stripes, by "static" colors (such as white, black, and gray), and by squares and rectangles. Movement and activity, in contrast, are depicted through the use of diagonal and zigzag lines, by "active" colors (such as yellow/brown, blue/green, and red/pink), by appendages extending from various "static" centers, and by diamond shapes. Motion in these designs is oriented in one of two directions: either linear, continuative, and incomplete or circular, repetitious, and complete (cyclical) (Witherspoon, *Language*, 162). And contrary to the typical expectations of dominant Western aesthetics, in Navajo textiles "most individual design elements mean nothing by themselves"; in other words, individual design elements are not "symbolic" in the conventional sense. Rather, as Witherspoon explains, "they take on their meaning only as a part of a holistic composition. The complete composition is a unique and abstract rendering of *hózhó*" ("Cultural Motifs," 372). For our purposes of engaging Navajo aesthetics to read Momaday's poem, the important point is that Navajo weaving emphasizes "semiotic geometry" over iconicity, patterning over symbolism ("Cultural Motifs," 369). Different types of repetition, including repetition with variation, are therefore essential to Navajo design, and these types of repetition represent energy, activity, and movement that is balanced and under control (Witherspoon and Peterson, 66).[22]

Several kinds of patterning become evident in Momaday's poem if we concentrate not only on the number of syllables per line (syllabics) but also on the placement of end punctuation (the division of the poem into statements) and the presence and forms of verbs (the linguistic representation of activity), especially verbs and verbal forms that indicate language, kinds of speech, and/or physical motion.[23] Figure 2 helps make these patterns more visible. We can begin by noting that all of the lines have an even number of syllables except lines 1, 11, and 12, the beginning and end of the poem, suggesting a basic representation of dynamic symmetry. We can also note that although certain

Line	Syllables	Even or odd	End punctuation	Verbs
1	7	odd	n/a	form of "to be"
2	6	even	n/a	gerund (kind of language)
3	10	even	period	gerund (kind of language)
4	8	even	n/a	passive (actual speech)
5	8	even	n/a	active (kind of motion)
6	8	even	period	none
7	8	even	n/a	passive (kind of speech)
8	10	even	period	none
9	10	even	n/a	form of "to be"
10	8	even	n/a	none
11	5	odd	n/a	form of "to be"
12	9	odd	period	form of "to be"

FIGURE 2. Patterns that emerge in N. Scott Momaday's poem "Carnegie, Oklahoma, 1919" based on the number of syllables per line, the placement of end punctuation, and the presence and forms of verbs.

numbers of syllables per line repeat—8 and 10—there is no regular pattern, certainly no design as an absolute balance or mirror image.

This basic dynamic symmetry at the level of syllables per line becomes more complex when we group the lines into sequences, creating "active" and "static" blocks or spaces, as in Navajo textile designs. The twelve lines of the poem are divisible in multiple ways, and Momaday's sequences of odd- and even-numbered syllables per line lend themselves to multiple patterns. Most obvious is to divide the poem "evenly" into four sets of three lines each. Thus we have the sets 7-6-10 (active), 8-8-8 (static), 8-10-10 (static with variation), and 8-5-9 (active), as seen in Figure 3. This pattern corresponds to one of the typical patterns from the classic period of Navajo weaving identified by Witherspoon: active-static-static-active. Witherspoon explains that this pattern represents thought (static and male) as the inner form of speech (active and female), as well as its complement, speech as the outer form of thought. As opposed to its inverse, static-active-active-static, this

Line	Text	Syllables
1	This afternoon is older	7
2	than the giving of gifts	6
3	and the rhythmic scraping of the red earth.	10
4	My father's father's name is called,	8
5	and the gift horse stutters out, whole,	8
6	the whole horizon in its eyes.	8
7	In the giveaway is beaded	8
8	the blood memories of fathers and sons.	10
9	Oh, there is nothing like this afternoon	10
10	in all the miles and years around,	8
11	and I am not here,	5
12	but, grandfather, father, I am here.	9

FIGURE 3. Basic dynamic symmetry present in N. Scott Momaday's poem "Carnegie, Oklahoma, 1919" becomes more complex when the lines are grouped into sequences, creating active and static blocks or spaces, as in Navajo textile designs. This figure shows the poem divided evenly into four sets of three lines each.

pattern "is often found in Navajo weaving and other art forms where creativity and activity are emphasized" (*Language*, 163).

Other divisions of "Carnegie, Oklahoma, 1919" offer variations on the active-static-static-active pattern and illustrate the complexity of the Navajo sense of dynamic symmetry. For example, we can subtly regroup the lines into the sets 7-6-10 (active), 8-8-8-8 (static), 10-10 (static), and 8-5-9 (active), as seen in Figure 4. More elaborately, we can regroup the lines as the sets 7-6 (active), 10 (static border dividing active and static spaces), 8-8-8-8 (static), 10-10 (static), 8 (static border dividing static and active spaces), and 5-9 (active), as seen in Figure 5. These divisions demonstrate the Navajo idea of the power of asymmetry, oppositions, contrasts, unequal pairing, and disequilibrium to produce variety, tension, and dynamism within an overall design. They also suggest multiple ways of dividing the poem into "blocks" and transitional spaces of specific language and thematic content.

The final, more elaborate division in Figure 5, for instance, suggests a significant connection between line 3 ("and the rhythmic scraping of the red earth.") and line 10 ("in all the miles and years around,"),

Line	Text	Syllables
1	This afternoon is older	7
2	than the giving of gifts	6
3	and the rhythmic scraping of the red earth.	10
4	My father's father's name is called,	8
5	and the gift horse stutters out, whole,	8
6	the whole horizon in its eyes.	8
7	In the giveaway is beaded	8
8	the blood memories of fathers and sons.	10
9	Oh, there is nothing like this afternoon	10
10	in all the miles and years around,	8
11	and I am not here,	5
12	but, grandfather, father, I am here.	9

FIGURE 4. This figure regroups the lines into the sets of three, four, two, and three.

Line	Text	Syllables
1	This afternoon is older	7
2	than the giving of gifts	6
3	and the rhythmic scraping of the red earth.	10
4	My father's father's name is called,	8
5	and the gift horse stutters out, whole,	8
6	the whole horizon in its eyes.	8
7	In the giveaway is beaded	8
8	the blood memories of fathers and sons.	10
9	Oh, there is nothing like this afternoon	10
10	in all the miles and years around,	8
11	and I am not here,	5
12	but, grandfather, father, I am here.	9

FIGURE 5. This figure regroups the lines into the sets of two, one, four, two, one, and two.

each of which is static in terms of the number of syllables per line (10 and 8, respectively) and each of which provides a transition between "blocks" of lines that are static and active. In terms of statement structure, syntax, and specific language use, both line 3 and line 10 appear midstatement, their first words beginning with a lowercase letter. Line 3 opens with a coordinating conjunction ("and") and includes a subsequent preposition that indicates the object of an action ("of"); line 10 inverts and extends this structure by opening with a preposition that indicates spatial relations ("in"), including a subsequent coordinating conjunction ("and"), and ending with a second preposition that indicates spatial relations ("around"). Each line emphasizes a particular kind of connection to the lines that precede it, and internally, each line connects aspects of space and time: "rhythmic scraping" (suggesting time through the gerund's indication of continuous activity) is linked to "red earth" (suggesting space); "miles" (suggesting space) is linked to "years" (suggesting time). These connections potentially intensify our experience of the poem's central paradox of space and time, "not here"/"am here."

Another striking feature of this method of grouping the lines into active and static blocks is that it draws our attention to the fact that the number of syllables in the six lines that compose the active blocks at the beginning and end of the poem never repeat. Each of these six lines has a different number of syllables: 7, 6, and 10 syllables in lines 1, 2, and 3 and 8, 5, and 9 syllables in lines 10, 11, and 12. When we group these numbers of syllables together, we recognize a reordered version of the sequence 10, 9, 8, 7, 6, 5 (or its reverse, 5, 6, 7, 8, 9, 10). The poem's particular ordering of these numbers of syllables per line appears, at first glance, random. However, we can align these active blocks in at least two ways, both of which make visible the possibility of complex relationships. We can either match first, middle, and last lines of the blocks so that line 1 is matched with line 10, line 2 with line 11, and line 3 with line 12, as in Figure 6A, or align the sets as mirror images so that line 1 is matched with line 12, line 2 is again matched with line 11, and line 3 is matched with line 10, as in Figure 6B. If we draw a line connecting the numbers of syllables in these configurations, in either ascending or descending order, in A we produce a circular spiral figure; in B we produce a pair of inward-facing triangles, or a butterfly figure, as seen in Figure 7. The first figure can be associated with the Navajo concept of movement from the center outward (Witherspoon, *Language and Art*, 165), with the Navajo cultural habit of proceeding clockwise/sunwise (Worth and Adair, 176), as well as with the Navajo idea that circular motion is "complete" and therefore "static" and "male." The last aligns the spiral figure with Navajo ceremonial activity (more about this later), as well as with the poem's theme of connection across

A				B			
Line	Syllables	Line	Syllables	Line	Syllables	Line	Syllables
1	7	10	8	1	7	12	9
2	6	11	5	2	6	11	5
3	10	12	9	3	10	10	8

FIGURE 6. Matching the first, middle, and last lines of the poem in *A*, and aligning the first, middle, and last lines of the poem as mirror images in *B*.

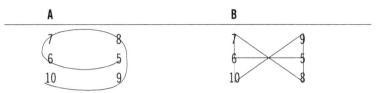

FIGURE 7. When drawing a line to connect the number of syllables per line, a circular spiral figure is produced in *A*, and a pair of inward-facing triangles, or a butterfly figure, is produced in *B*.

three generations of men in a Kiowa family. The second figure can be associated with an emphasis on the triangle as the "generative basis" of Navajo semiotic geometry (Witherspoon, "Cultural Motifs," 369). In this Navajo conception various combinations of bipolar triangles are used to represent "the dynamic, holistic asymmetry found in the Navajo universe, as well as [to provide] the basic design elements from which many of the patterns of Navajo weaving are derived" (Witherspoon and Peterson, 34).

Three of these combinations of bipolar triangles are especially central in Navajo design. The diamond shape, which consists of two triangles pointing outward, is associated with the primary creator deity Changing Woman and suggests "the idea of infinite extension from a center point" (Witherspoon, "Cultural Motifs," 369). The bow pattern, which consists of two triangles pointed in the same direction, is associated with one of the twin sons of Changing Woman, Monster Slayer. And the butterfly pattern, which consists of two triangles pointed inward, is associated with the other twin, Born for the Water. This last figure, when rotated 90 degrees into an "hourglass" figure, is also associated with the Navajo hair bun, first worn by Changing Woman, which is part of girls' puberty rites and is still worn by Navajo men and women today (Witherspoon and Peterson, 33–38, 44). In other accounts, the hourglass-shaped hair bun is associated specifically with women's "disciplined thought" during weaving (McLerran, 23).

These alignments of the opening and closing active blocks of lines in Momaday's poem are also potentially suggestive of Plains Indian artistic practice. We might conceive of the poem's syllabic structure not exclusively in terms of a Navajo textile, then, but also in terms of Plains Indian art production. In particular, we might look to Plains Indian parfleche, which are "containers of folded or sewn rawhide elaborated with painted images on their exposed surfaces" (Torrence,

19).[24] Produced in the eighteenth, nineteenth, and twentieth centuries by women artists from over forty different tribal groups located across the northern, central, and southern plains and into the Southwest—the Kiowa and their allies among them—parfleche were designed for packaging and transporting a variety of everyday and special items, including ceremonial regalia and sacred objects. Like textiles produced by Navajo women, parfleche produced by plains women were highly prized across cultures and thus, through exchange, imitation, and occasionally remaking or repurposing, they participated in multiple and trans-Indigenous systems of signification.

Typically, parfleche are decorated with abstract geometric designs, often brightly painted. The art historian Gaylord Torrence, who has conducted the most extensive comparative study of extant parfleche, describes their "fundamental vocabulary of visual forms" as consisting of "geometric motifs, both straight edged and curved, organized into complex compositions within some type of rectangular frame. These images were based on highly elongated triangles, hourglass shapes, diamonds, rectangles, lines, and circular forms" (30). Perhaps not surprisingly, a number of these figures resonate with the Navajo semiotic geometry discussed above. And similar to the productive tension created in Navajo juxtapositions of active and static spaces, Torrence notes that parfleche paintings "are animated by an active tension arising from the subtle interplay of the highly formal, symmetrical structure of their forms and spatial divisions combined with the dynamic and improvisational quality of their drawing" (51). Parfleche can be divided into four primary forms: folded envelopes, flat cases, cylinders, and boxes. Folded envelopes and flat cases are of particular interest in thinking about how we might conceive the two active blocks of lines in "Carnegie, Oklahoma, 1919"—and perhaps Momaday's poem as a whole—in terms of parfleche design.

Both folded envelopes and flat cases are constructed from a single rectangular piece of rawhide. In the envelope form, two side flaps are folded inward to create a long, vertical rectangle; the top and bottom ends of the rectangle are then also folded toward the center, where they meet, forming the "closure flaps" and "covering the seam formed by the inner flaps" (63). In the flat case form, the piece of rawhide is folded once, and then its sides are sewn shut; the single fold becomes the bottom edge of the case (65). In both forms, but especially in the folded envelope, a significant portion of the pattern of the parfleche's abstract geometric design becomes visible—and complete—only when the single flat piece of rawhide is folded into a three-dimensional package (McLerran, 27; Torrence, 64). Many extant folded envelopes display a three-part vertical division in their design patterns, with the top and bottom flaps completing the center part of the design when they are folded inward to close the container. As Torrence notes, "It was possible for artists to achieve two very different effects utilizing the same basic format" (78): the overall composition lying flat and the overall composition once folded. In addition, artists created designs that were sensitive to the volumetric capacity of the parfleche, since the folded envelope, especially, was "capable of considerable expansion when filled" (61).

In interpreting Momaday's poem, we can think of the "matched" active blocks of lines in *A*, in which a curvilinear "spiral" figure is created when the syllables per line are connected in numerical sequence, as working similarly to the folded envelope form of parfleche, with its double folding of the top and bottom flaps toward the center, which results in a three-part vertical design. And we can think of the "mirror image" alignment of the active blocks of lines in *B*, in which a "butterfly" or "hourglass" figure is created when the syllables per line are connected in numerical sequence, as working similarly to the single-fold flat case form of parfleche. In both a more complex and complete pattern becomes visible only when the separated sections of the poem—the opening and closing active blocks—are brought together and aligned through a kind of metaphoric "folding."

Additional correspondences and productive tensions become apparent when we consider such patterning at the level of syllables per line in relation to other elements in the poem, including marks of punctuation and kinds of verbs, as well as specific linguistic and thematic content. One complementary kind of patterning is evident, for example, at the level of end punctuation. The poem makes four discrete statements, each a full, grammatically complete sentence that begins with a capital letter and ends with a period. The first statement is composed of lines 1, 2, and 3; the second, of lines 4, 5, and 6; the third, of lines 7 and 8; and the fourth, of lines 9, 10, 11, and 12. Thus, we have the pattern three lines, three lines, two lines, four lines, odd-odd-even-even, or active-active-static-static. This pattern is something of a surprise, given the patterning that is produced at the level of syllables per line: active-static-static-active.

The first and last statements in the poem are connected, at the level
of language and theme, by the phrase "this afternoon," the significance
of which we began to explore in the earlier Kiowa section. The phrase
appears first as the beginning of line 1 and, thus, as the beginning of the
three-line (active) first statement; "this afternoon" reappears at the end
of line 9, which begins the four-line (static) fourth statement, creating
another instance of repetition with variation and holistic asymmetry.
The first statement offers readers a condensed but complete rendering
of the poem's primary theme—namely, that orthodox Western conceptions of time and space cannot account for the speaker's experience of this particular "afternoon." Although the moment occurs in the
speaker's present, it is both caught up in the year 1919 announced in
the poem's title/caption and "older" than even this date and thus outside ordinary understandings of time. The fourth statement returns to
the first but offers a fuller, deeper articulation of its central idea. This
explanatory role is announced by the interjection "Oh" that begins line
9. Non-Native anthropologists Sol Worth and John Adair argue that
this structure of returning to the beginning in a different form resembles the structure of Navajo healing rituals, often referred to as chantways: "This going back to the beginning, to where the action started,
is basic to Navajo cognition and is manifested in their mythology and
their ritual and visual arts" (205). Further, they argue that "suspense
of ending is not the point. The process of becoming, of eventing, of
moving toward completion, is what we are made to feel is important;
not *what* will happen, but how it happens" (207). In Momaday's poem
the intervening statements, statements two and three, describe specific actions that illustrate the central idea expressed in the first and
final statements—that is, the details of the giveaway, as understood
historically (statement two) and as understood in the speaker's present (statement three). Together, the four statements move the speaker
(and potentially the reader) rapidly in and out of ordinary time.

The discrete statements, as opposed to the syllables per line, follow
the patterning evident in Navajo chantways, active-active-static-static.
The purpose of such healing ceremonials is to restore the patient to
a state of wholeness and balance.[25] Or put another way, such rituals
work to move the patient from discord to harmony, often from a damaging state of psychological and/or spiritual fragmentation to a more
positive state of psychological and/or spiritual reassemblage. One of
the primary methodologies of such chantways is to place the patient

in the role of the protagonist in an extended narrative of encountering and overcoming some form of discord. The potential ceremonial functions of Momaday's poem become even more apparent if we pay particular attention to the use of terms that either name or suggest circular shapes and concepts: "earth" (line 3), "whole" (lines 5 and 6), "horizon" (line 6), "eyes" (line 6), "beaded" (line 7), "Oh" (line 9), and "around" (line 10). All of these references to circles are suggestive of ritual control, as well as of the way that during Navajo ceremonials ritual grounds become a microcosm for the entire universe. Thus, the invocation of the sky and earth in lines 1 and 3, with the description in line 2 of ceremonial activity occurring literally between them, takes on greater significance as the opening of the poem. Further, the repetition of "whole," which links the "gift horse" to "horizon" and "eyes," centers the poem's ceremonial energy onto the figure of the gift both as a living being and as a symbol: "whole" and with the "whole horizon in its eyes," the horse becomes another microcosm. This is the gift of a worldview. As I began to suggest in the Kiowa section, we can read "Carnegie, Oklahoma, 1919" as a kind of ceremony, with the speaker positioned as the patient in a ritual of restoration. He moves from a fragmented and isolated sense of self—from an "I" understood exclusively in the singular—to a more communal and transgenerational sense of self—to an "I" understood in the plural. In the paradox of the final statement, the speaker articulates an understanding of what we might call the self-in-genealogy or, more broadly, the self-in-narrative. At the conclusion of this ritual, the speaker is able to name his place within an ongoing story of the Kiowa.

We can now shift our focus from the number of syllables per line and the placement of end punctuation to the presence and form of verbs in the poem's four statements—that is, to the linguistic markers of activity. Worth and Adair argue that in Navajo aesthetic systems power accrues from motion (206). In "Carnegie, Oklahoma, 1919," we can locate such motion in the poem's verbal forms. We notice that although every statement and all but three lines in the poem contain some verbal form, the poem includes only a single active verb: "stutters." As noted above, "stutters" occurs in line 5 (statement two) and is marked by the fact that it is not only active and present tense but a verb of motion that specifies, in relation to the gift horse, a particular kind and quality of movement. "Stutters" also can refer to a particular kind and quality of speech, and this sense of the verb potentially adds another dimension to our understanding of the significance of the horse's movement within the context of the ritual giveaway. Although the active verb occurs within a statement of the poem that is also active, it occurs within a specific line that is static (8 syllables); it is preceded and followed by verbs that are passive, both of which are part of statements that obscure agency. The passive verb that precedes the active verb, "is called" in line 4 (also part of statement two), indicates a specific kind of speech. The line does not indicate agency, *who* called, and thus focuses attention on the disembodied *act* of calling. The comma and line ending that immediately follow the passive form only intensify this effect. The use of the unattributed passive verb can be associated with two related Navajo conventions: the general avoidance of speaking a person's name when he or she is present and the more specific avoidance of speaking a person's name when he or she is deceased (Witherspoon, *Language*, 84, 88).

The passive verb that follows the active verb, "is beaded" in line 7 (statement three), indicates a specific kind of artistic practice and a specific kind of patterning. This patterning is most obviously associated with Plains Indian arts but also can be associated with Navajo weaving. In Navajo textiles "beading" can refer to "a narrow band in which tiny blocks of color alternate" (Kent, 17). In lines 7 and 8 (statement three), this sense of the term *beading* reinforces the idea of the integration of the "memories of fathers and sons." If there is agency in this statement, the suggestion is that the giveaway itself, or perhaps its ritual agent, is responsible for this "beading." Here, it may be useful to note, as well, that the passive verb "is beaded" appears to be iterative, indicating repeated or recurrent action: unlike the grandfather's name, which "is called" once, in a specific moment in named time and designated space, this metaphorical "beading" takes place *every time* the "giveaway" is performed. Maurice Boyd, writing in consultation with the Kiowa historian Lynn Pauahty, describes Kiowa "sacred time" in similar terms, as including not only "the past" but also the "present and future." He argues that "relationships presented in Kiowa oral literature reveal a mythical ordering of life that is *perennial*" (2:21; emphasis added). Boyd argues further that "the stories are both a *part of* and *about* the tradition they describe. In the Kiowa oral tradition, individuals are important, but not primary. The tribal stories are already known; it is the traditional function or purpose that bears repetition" (21). Line 8 then completes the third statement. The provocative adjective "blood," here associated with male activities (the ritual of the giveaway and the memories of fathers and sons), echoes the "red" of line 3, associated with the fertility of the female earth, again producing a complementary tension.

In contrast, the opening and closing statements in "Carnegie, Oklahoma, 1919" employ forms of the verb "to be." These linking verbs isolate and draw even more attention to the poem's one active and two passive verbs. The other verbal forms are gerunds: "the giving" and "the scraping." Like the active and passive verbs in the poem, these gerunds also can be associated with speech, in a broad sense, and with kinds of action. "Giving" indicates specific action in the poem with the power to put people and things in motion; "scraping" indicates an action that manipulates the physical environment, either in preparation for the ceremony or during the ceremony itself. The gerund form is suggestive of repetitive, cyclical motion, indicating as well the ritual context of the giveaway and of the poem as a whole.

Overall, such complementary or asymmetrical tension along a male-female axis is suggestive of the potential impact of these types of patterning on reading, interpreting, and enjoying Momaday's poem. Although "Carnegie, Oklahoma, 1919" appears to be focused entirely on male elements—the male speaker, his father and paternal grandfather, ritual activity—attention to the patterning described above reveals that female elements are in fact present in multiple forms throughout the poem. For instance, if we understand the first three lines as active (female), we can note how the poem begins with a juxtaposition of "afternoon" (static and male) and the "red earth" (active and female). The first line, containing the static image, is composed of an odd (active) number of syllables, while the third line, containing the active image, is composed of an even (static) number of syllables. Moreover, although the sky is considered static and male, the specific word "afternoon" indicates a time of daylight when the sun is positioned to the west of its zenith, both of which (daylight and the west) are associated with the active and the female. Similarly, although the earth is considered active and female, with the color red intensifying these designations in its association with menstrual blood, the line's detail of the "rhythmic scraping" suggests either the creation of ceremonial grounds through clearing or the actual ceremonial dancing itself, and in Navajo systems ceremonial activity is considered static and male. Within this "active" set of lines, active and static elements are held in productive tension.

The same is true for the poem as a whole. Its complex patterning on multiple levels transforms its structure into a metaphor for—and a demonstration of—dynamic tension, equally applicable to the semiotic geometry of Navajo and Plains Indian designs. The speaker articulates the paradox of "not here"/"am here" through the specific language of his male descent line, "grandfather, father, I," but the energy of even this, the most thematically male statement in the poem, derives, in part, from the "active," female nature of its number of syllables per line (9, the square of 3) and its three-part genealogical sequence. These odd numbers suggest linear, continuative, and as yet incomplete motion. This transgenerational address and sense of self, this process of understanding the self-in-narrative, does not end with the contemporary speaker of the poem but extends into his familial and communal future.

The Alchemy of Taonga

Kiowa and Navajo systems of aesthetics can be connected to Momaday's biography and poetic process, and their use in the interpretation of his work can be justified by appealing to the tribal affiliation, family history, and personal experience of the author. But what about other systems of Indigenous aesthetics, systems that originate in other parts of North America or in other parts of the globe? Can these, too, elicit productive readings of "Carnegie, Oklahoma, 1919"? In this section I extend my analysis of Momaday's poem by engaging understandings of New Zealand Māori aesthetics, which are part of a larger family of Polynesian aesthetic systems. These derive from worldviews and worldly experiences that are in many ways distinct from those of the Kiowa or the Navajo. And yet in their articulation of key relationships among artist, art practice, art object, viewer, and material, social, and spiritual worlds, Māori aesthetics offer another useful analytic tool and another useful language for better understanding how Momaday's poem can produce meaning and pleasure for multiple audiences, including multiple audiences who identify as Indigenous. In this way, I argue for the possibility of a trans-Indigenous literary criticism—a literary criticism that reads *across* national and geographical borders to engage a broad spectrum of Indigenous conceptions of aesthetic power and pleasure.

As applied particularly to whakairo, the art of carving in wood, stone, and bone (and, in contemporary times, in various other media), customary Māori aesthetics are based in the concepts of ihi, wehi, and wana: power, fear, and authority. In "Nga Timunga Me Nga Paringa O Te Mana Maori: The Ebb and Flow of Mana Maori and the Changing Context of Maori Art," one of the several articles commissioned for the handsome catalog that accompanied the *Te Maori* exhibit, Māori artist and art historian Sidney Moko Mead (Hirini Moko Mead) writes that the Māori artist "strives to imbue his work with ihi (power), wehi (fear), and wana (authority)" (23). These qualities give Māori art its "beauty." An art object or taonga (prized possession) is aesthetically beautiful, Mead explains, "because it has power (ihi), that is, power to move the viewer to react spontaneously and in a physical way to the work of art" (24). Since ihi derives from the gods, Mead argues that within this customary Māori aesthetic system, "an artist is merely a vehicle used by the gods, to express their artistry and their genius" (25). Mead develops this spiritual significance of taonga further by defining these art objects as a bridge between the living and the dead. He emphasizes the ideas of "taonga tuku iho" (taonga "handed down from the ancestors") and "he kupu kei runga" (objects "invested with interesting talk"); the korero (discourse) associated with taonga during their production and use—particularly their ceremonial use—gives them imminent power (21). In a second article included in the *Te Maori* catalog, Māori art historian Piri Sciascia similarly emphasizes the importance of understanding "taonga in their totality—the physical art form, the associated korero [discourse], and, therefore, the resultant dialogue" (164). Sciascia goes on to argue, "When whakairo (carving) is embraced with whaikorero (oratory), the combination has greater mana [power, prestige], it is a fuller expression of the available mauri [life force]" (164).[26] (These ideas are useful for articulating how Momaday's poem functions as a literary pictograph within a larger matrix of texts, as discussed in the earlier Kiowa section.) More recently, Māori scholar and museum curator Paul Tapsell has argued that "taonga are time travelers, bridging the generations, allowing descendants to ritually meet their ancestors, face to face" (13).

It is precisely this power described by Mead, Sciascia, and Tapsell—derived from ancestors and ultimately from the gods—that the viewer responds to emotionally, spiritually, and physically. Pakeha anthropologist Anne Salmond, in her contribution to the *Te Maori* catalog, describes this quality of Māori art objects, this capacity to bridge between the living and the dead, as the "alchemy of taonga" (120). The past is renewed in the taonga by becoming an integral part of the viewer's present reality. Salmond writes that taonga possess the capacity to bring about "a collapse of distance in space-time" and thus "a fusion of men and ancestors" (120). Similarly, Pakeha historian Judith Binney has demonstrated that in Māori oral traditions the telling of history involves "a continuous dialectic between the past and the present" (17). Structured around kin, the traditional telling of Māori history is concerned not with mimetic or historical accuracy but rather "with the holding and the transference of mana [power, prestige] by successive generations" (18). History is seen, in other words, as "an extension of mythology" into contemporary times (20). Similar to an encounter with powerful taonga, in the Māori oral tradition the telling of history "rests on the perceived conjunction between the past and the present, and between the ancestors and the living" (26). In fact, one's right to speak in the present often derives from the mana of specific ancestors, and the contemporary narrator may tell history as though he or she participated in significant past events. Borrowing an evocative phrase from the Danish anthropologist J. Prytz Johansen, the historian Binney refers to this form of storytelling persona as the "kinship I." One aspect of Māori aesthetics, therefore, for both carving and oratory, is the taonga's intersection with whakapapa (genealogy). Art objects and oral narratives enable the viewer or listener to participate in the power of transgenerational address, the power of speaking across generations, and in the understanding of the self-in-genealogy.

We can read "Carnegie, Oklahoma, 1919" as narrating and, potentially, as *performing* a function similar to, if not identical with, the alchemy of taonga, a collapsing of distance in space-time, a bridging of the living and the dead. Situated on ceremonial grounds, Momaday's speaker experiences the past in the present and is enabled to experience ancestors as part of his sense of self. The particular moment of the poem's alchemy—this crucial artistic and spiritual "activity"—occurs in lines 7 and 8 (which, as noted in the Navajo section, are static with variation in terms of their syllables per line [8 and 10] and which form statement three, also static): "In the giveaway is beaded / the blood memories of fathers and sons." Here, in the central metaphor of the poem, we can locate yet another complementary tension, and we can see the significant juxtaposition and compressing of Indigenous ceremony, Indigenous art, and the provocative phrase "blood memories." The genealogical sequence in the poem's final line—"grandfather, father, I"—enunciates this collapse of space-time. The poem's apparent paradox, "not here"/"am here," is undone in the collapse of distinctions among the kinship terms "grandfather," "father," and "I." In the moment of connection, these genealogical terms are rendered equivalent, and the speaker claims a viable contemporary Indigeneity by speaking with and in an ancestral tongue.

The speaker of Momaday's poem, however, never actually speaks within the poem. The only character who does speak is an unnamed Kiowa ancestor. In line 4 the speaker notes, "My father's father's name is called," invoking but not articulating the name of the speaker's grandfather. Mammedaty's name, so prevalent in "The Gourd Dancer," is in fact *unnamed* and *unspoken* in "Carnegie, Oklahoma, 1919." Yet it is the action of "call[ing]" this unnamed name that brings forth the ceremonial "gift horse." And it is this horse—this taonga, this prized possession—that represents for the poem's speaker the heretofore unavailable vitality of Indigenous culture and worldview. In a second apparent paradox, the presence of Indigenous language—the calling of Mammedaty's name—is marked in the poem by its absence, and the speaking of the unspoken Indigenous name effects the process of Momaday's version of the alchemy of taonga, which he subsequently designates with the provocative phrase "blood memories." This "blood memory," this alchemy of taonga, responds to the colonial imposition of the West's alienating fiction of (absolute) individual autonomy by rendering space-time as a palimpsest, a genealogy in the Māori sense of a whakapapa, which means not only to recite in proper order but to place in layers, to lay one generation upon another. In place of an understanding of genealogy as a strictly linear sequence that isolates each generation from its predecessors ("I" understood in the singular), it offers the speaker an understanding of genealogy as a vital, enabling, and, in the end, *demanding* superimposition ("I" understood in the plural).

Elsewhere, I have argued that Momaday's phrase "blood memory," which appears throughout his works published over the past forty years, is a trope that names both a *process* of claiming an Indigenous identity and the *product* of that process.[27] Such understandings confer gifts but also responsibilities. The moment of recognition of this power of the ancestral, this ihi, occurs for the speaker of "Carnegie,

Oklahoma, 1919" in the moment of his articulation of the interjection "Oh" that begins line 9 and statement four, set off by a comma and addressed to himself, to his ancestors, and finally to his audience. If the alchemy of this taonga works, the poem becomes an opportunity not only for the speaker but also for readers to recognize ihi and to respond emotionally, spiritually, and physically.

Politics, Pleasures, and the Contexts of Exchange

It should go without saying that contemporary Indigenous literatures written in English or primarily in English are the products of complicated aesthetic genealogies. Drawn from both Indigenous and non-Indigenous sources, they potentially speak to many audiences. Often, like other contemporary Indigenous arts, these literatures are also the products of complicated and evolving networks of exchange. Writing about the North American context, non-Native art historian and museum curator David Penney explains, "Native artists have always made things for other people, as gifts to forge relationships and for exchange" (54). With the introduction of a Western market economy, the range of "other people" thus engaged expanded. The basic "dialogue between creator and customer," however, continued: "educating the consumer, on the one hand, to the values of the craft; adapting the craft, on the other hand, to the demands of the marketplace" (54). Penney notes that since the mid-1970s, non-Native anthropologists and art historians have rethought their initial dismissal of so-called Indigenous tourist art and reassessed its value, and he himself promotes the use of a more positive alternative term for such creations, coined by Anishinaabe artist and writer Lois Beardslee: "market art" (54). As Penney points out, there are many traditions of Indigenous market art—pottery, baskets, beadwork, carving, painting, sculpture—and the art objects produced typically represent "multigenerational endeavor[s], culturally based, but individually created, traditional yet capable of startling innovation, often rooted in local environments, but globally relevant in [their] insistence upon the value of local knowledge" (56).

We can conceive contemporary Indigenous literatures produced for regional, national, and international markets in similar terms. Scholars have long been interested in how Indigenous literatures educate non-Indigenous readers and how they respond to the demands of the dominant, non-Indigenous literary marketplace. Less attention has been paid, thus far, to how particular Indigenous literatures might educate—and delight or provoke—not only non-Indigenous readers but also readers from other Indigenous communities. Similarly, little attention has been paid to the expansion and diversification of the global literary marketplace over the course of the final quarter of the twentieth century, in part through the development of new print and other media technologies but also through the development of new networks of intellectual and artistic exchange. As the Māori artist and curator Darcy Nicholas remarked in relation to the 2006 *Manawa* exhibit, "We [Māori] are physically connected to our Canadian and American First Nations people by the sea and more recently by modern technology" (8). This expansion and diversification has created more opportunities for Indigenous peoples to publish their works in internationally accessible venues, including not only in print texts, audio recordings, and film and video but also in web-based digital media, and to present their works at international readings, performances, symposia, and academic conferences.

Engaging multiple Indigenous systems of aesthetics expands our appreciation and refines our understanding of how these texts produce meaning and pleasure for multiple audiences, including multiple audiences who identify as Indigenous. In distinct but related ways, Kiowa, Navajo, and Māori conceptions of aesthetic engagement—"beauty," "power," and "excellence"—help explain how Momaday's highly condensed poem both names and overcomes a contemporary anguish over Indigenous separation from ancestors, cultural traditions, and worldviews. Part of the activist power of the poem, within the specific context of its publication during the Columbus quincentenary, is that it voices its political protest, its counterclaim of Indigenous continuity, not exclusively at the level of its language and themes—its "message"—but also at the level of its artistic conception, form, and structure. Its claim that distinctly Indigenous modes of cultural and artistic expression persist into contemporary times actively demonstrates their vitality.

While drafting the early versions of this chapter, I was fortunate to spend the first half of 2005 in Aotearoa New Zealand, supported by a Fulbright Fellowship and hosted at the Turnbull Library, part of the National Library of New Zealand/Te Puna Mātauranga o Aotearoa. As part of my Fulbright duties, I gave a number of invited talks to different academic and community audiences. For four of these, I delivered working versions of my then draft essay. The audiences and contexts for the four talks were diverse, and the experience of interacting with such distinct audiences helped to shape the present version of my analysis and argument.

I gave the first of these talks to the Department of English at Otago University, located in Dunedin on the South Island. I had been invited to Otago by the department head, a Renaissance scholar from the United States who was a recent arrival to Aotearoa. North Americans may be surprised to learn that many on the academic faculty at New Zealand universities are not New Zealanders by birth and did not earn their degrees in New Zealand institutions but come predominantly from Great Britain, Australia, Canada, Europe, and the United States. Only departments of Māori studies and perhaps Pacific studies are likely to have a majority of New Zealand–born and perhaps New Zealand–trained faculty. Neither my American host nor many on her staff had much of a relationship with the university's Department of Māori Studies, and as a result, my talk was scheduled—unintentionally—at a time when the Māori studies staff was unable to attend. My audience was composed almost entirely of non-Māori staff and students and, of its faculty members, was largely non-New Zealand born or raised. Few in the audience had any kind of Māori or Indigenous studies framework for evaluating my experimental approach to Momaday's poem.

It was the first time out with my draft essay, and although I read an abbreviated version, it ran too long. Because we had to vacate the classroom in which I had been scheduled to speak for the next period, the question-and-answer session had to be cut short. Out in the hallway, my host and several students complimented my presentation, but what was most memorable were brief comments from one of the junior members of the English faculty who, like my host, was an American recently arrived in Aotearoa. He was polite, but his critique of my methodology was intense and ultimately dismissive. The main problem, I gathered, was that although my analysis might have momentarily decentered dominant literary traditions and modes of inquiry, it had not disproved them. He had felt no significant shift of paradigm. He found my attempt at engaging Indigenous aesthetics quaint and perhaps a little naïve (my paraphrase, not his actual words); certainly, it was of little genuine importance to literary studies in English.

Undaunted, I delivered a second version of my analysis of Momaday's poem in June 2005 at Massey University, located in the town of
Palmerston North on the North Island, roughly halfway between Wellington and Auckland. I had been invited not by the English department but by a faculty member in the Department of Communications
who happened to be of Ngai Tahu descent (Ngai Tahu are the predominant Māori iwi from the South Island) and who was well connected to
Massey's Māori studies faculty and students. Massey's Department of
Māori Studies specializes in Māori arts production and criticism, so I
was especially pleased that its faculty and students, as well as Māori faculty and staff from other parts of the university, attended my talk in full
force. They composed over half the audience in the large seminar room.
In contrast to my experience at Otago, where I was introduced by the
chair of English in standard Western academic fashion, at Massey I was
given a mihi (formal greeting) in Māori by a member of the Māori studies faculty, followed by a waiata (song) performed by the speaker and
other Māori faculty who stood with him in support. One of the purposes of this type of typical Māori ceremonial greeting is to establish
connections between hosts and visitors and to properly open a space
for the exchange of discourse and ideas. Only then was I introduced in
more typical academic fashion in English by my Māori host.

The talk appeared to go well. I decided beforehand not to read my
paper but to speak from notes, using an overhead projector to display Momaday's poem and examples of Plains Indian pictographs and
Navajo weaving, and this strategy seemed appropriate for my Massey
audience, which represented a diversity of academic training and scholarly interests. During the talk, I felt that Māori in the audience were
especially supportive. When I finished speaking, however, the first
hand to be raised for a question belonged to a Pakeha graduate student
who sat in the front row. Like the American junior faculty member at
Otago, the Pakeha graduate student at Massey wanted to discuss how
my work fit within the Western Tradition—capital W, capital T—of
literary studies. He was not happy when I refused, politely, to answer
the question on his terms and, instead, directed my response to the
historical and ethical, as well as the artistic and scholarly, importance
of clearing space within the dominant academy for (more) Indigenous-
centered approaches to studying Indigenous literatures. (My answer
did score visible and vocal points, however, with the Māori scholars

and students in the room, which I think says less about my specific response than it does about the typical contemporary experiences of Indigenous people in the academy, which are often overwhelmed by dominant interests.) And where at Otago my talk had ended abruptly with the literal ringing of the class bell followed by hurried exchanges in the hallway, at Massey the conversation begun in the seminar room continued over a casual lunch organized by the Māori studies faculty and staff. Sharing a meal, like sharing the mihi and the waiata, was an integral part of the event.

Although I was pleased with my Massey experience, I felt somewhat nervous about presenting the third version of what I had come to think of as my "Indigenous aesthetics" talk in early July 2005 at Victoria University in Wellington. This talk was cosponsored by the single Māori faculty member in the Department of English and by the Department of Māori Studies, and it was scheduled to take place inside the carved wharenui (meeting house) on the campus marae. The setting of a Māori ceremonial space (the marae complex as a whole and the meeting house in particular) placed a certain added pressure on my performance. The talk attracted a small number of faculty and graduate students from the English department and a larger number from Māori studies, as well as the university's vice chancellor for Māori affairs, who happened to be a Māori cultural specialist and art historian, the Pakeha chair of the university's writing program, and several Māori professionals from the National Library and Archives New Zealand. There was some miscommunication about how I would be introduced, given that I was speaking inside the meeting house but would not be formally brought onto the marae, so I was not fully prepared for the formal mihi I received from a member of the Māori studies faculty and the waiata that followed (although I have attended enough Māori events to know that even though I was told beforehand that no formal mihi would be given, it was likely one would be given nonetheless). I fumbled through an appropriate response in Māori and English. I was then given a more standard academic introduction by the Māori studies faculty member in charge of the event.

For this third version of my analysis of Momaday's poem, I discussed the main points of my essay from memory, again using an overhead projector and screen to display the poem and several images. As is customary on most marae, I had removed my shoes before entering the

wharenui, and as I spoke I padded around the warm space of the meeting house in my socks, and I gestured toward the house's taonga (prized
possessions)—its whakairo (carvings of ancestors and their stories) and
tukutuku (woven wall panels of key cultural symbols)—as illustrations
of several of the points I was trying to make about how pictographs,
textiles, and carvings work as mnemonic devices and serve as the bases
for multimedia presentations of narrative. Unlike at the first two talks,
here I took some time to explicitly contextualize the field of Indigenous
literary studies, its dominant methodologies, and some potential limitations of these methodologies for interpreting—and fully enjoying—
Indigenous texts. The talk went well, as did the question-and-answer
period. Inside the wharenui there were no questions about recenter-
ing dominant Western literary and cultural traditions. The Māori vice
chancellor used the question-and-answer period as an occasion to promote his own projects and to comment on his own ongoing feuds with
the dominant academy (as was to be expected), and the Pakeha chair
of the writing program, who happens to be a New Zealander by birth,
a celebrated poet, and no stranger to Māori gatherings, made his own
subtle political statement by having not removed his shoes. After the
talk everyone moved into the adjacent wharekai (dining hall) for good
food and for wide-ranging discussion about Māori understandings of
literary and artistic genres and the paucity of articulated Indigenous
methodologies for use in humanities research and writing. In other
words, although my talk had gone well, in the marae setting I was not
the (only) center of attention (and did not expect to be).

Finally, I gave the fourth version of my talk about Momaday's poem
several days before I left Aotearoa to return to the United States, at
the end of July 2005. I was invited to speak at the Whariki Research
Unit in Auckland, an organization that conducts research on issues af-
fecting Māori health and wellness. Whariki is associated with Massey
University, and one of its leaders had heard about my talk at Massey
in Palmerston North in June. I was surprised to be invited to speak
to them, but I was intrigued. I was told that, among other factors, the
Whariki research team is interested in how Māori health and wellness are affected by issues of identity and representation. My talk was
attended by a Māori physician and the entire Whariki staff, which
included Māori and Pakeha public health researchers and mapping
specialists. In addition, at my invitation, a prominent Pakeha New

Zealand studies scholar from Auckland University also attended, as did a Māori anthropologist who conducts research on land claims. It was probably the most diverse audience for my "Indigenous aesthetics" talk; only one person in the room other than me was equipped with specialized knowledge about literary scholarship.

I again delivered the talk from memory and used an overhead projector. As I had in the meeting house at Victoria University, I contextualized the field of Indigenous literary studies to set up my specific project. The talk went well, and my diverse audience appeared genuinely interested—and perhaps a little relieved that I spoke a language they could understand. Not surprisingly, however, the first hand raised during the question-and-answer period was that of the Pakeha New Zealand studies scholar from Auckland University. He asked a smart, sympathetic, and well-intentioned question. It was more than appropriate for a Western academic setting, but its effect, had I accepted it, would have been to bypass discussion of the Indigenous approaches I had described and, instead, would have refocused attention on the broader and more abstract issue of literary aesthetics in general. Having completed my close analysis, he asked, what did I now have to say about aesthetics with a capital *A*? My response, which also was well intentioned, was to refuse to engage his question and its invitation to universalize my conclusions based on a single experiment of close reading and contextualization. Instead, I asked him to be satisfied, at least for the moment, with the local, to understand what local conclusions might have to say to multiple audiences, before moving up the rungs of the ladder of abstraction and demanding larger claims in the specific realm of literary scholarship within the dominant academy. The remainder of the question-and-answer period was driven by Whariki team members, and the conversation ranged widely as they—and we—attempted to articulate how the issues I had raised in relation to "Carnegie, Oklahoma, 1919" might intersect with the work they do. Afterwards, to my surprise, the Whariki team leader presented me with a koha (gift) before we continued our conversation over a late lunch and coffee.

Is there a portable lesson to be gained from the metanarrative of presenting early versions of my work on Momaday's poem? Thus far, what it has taught me is that the project of engaging multiple Indigenous aesthetics is not exclusively a project of developing new methodologies for close reading and literary interpretation. It is also necessarily a project caught up with better understanding the related issues of audience and context for both literary and critical *reception*. What kinds of primary and secondary audiences do we imagine for the literary works we read and interpret when we approach them with specific methodologies? Which potential audiences for our critical work are privileged by the methodologies we take up and by the critical languages we speak? Which audiences might feel valorized by our practices and which audiences might feel marginalized? Moreover, how are certain kinds of audiences formed, nurtured, and perpetuated through institutions such as undergraduate and graduate programs in literature or in academic and commercial publishing? And how do certain kinds of spaces come to be marked as appropriate or inappropriate contexts for specific modes of inquiry and exchange?

The idea of multiple and multiply informed *Indigenous* audiences has not often occurred to literary scholars in the dominant academy, including those who have devoted their careers to the study of Native American and other Indigenous literatures.[28] And why should it? In all of their—in all of our—training within dominant structures, what could possibly have suggested that such audiences deserve critical attention?

The current system of graduate education in literature and culture studies, especially as these are enacted in most U.S. departments of English, is not designed to enable the kind of engagements with Indigenous aesthetics I am proposing. Quite the contrary.[29] In fact, our greatest challenge in formulating new models for Native American and Indigenous literary criticism may well be to overhaul graduate training so that it will be possible for future scholars to meaningfully engage Indigenous aesthetics and, thus, to more fully engage Indigenous intellectual and artistic sovereignty. We will have to push ourselves to think beyond the typical needs and desires of English literature studies, and we will have to conceive of programs and opportunities that are of interest not only to literary scholars and students within the dominant academy but also to individual Indigenous artists and to Indigenous communities—and we will have to insist that such programs and opportunities be of obvious benefit to both. We have barely begun to imagine what such collaborations might look like within the Indigenous literary and culture studies curriculum. Their potential impact on the future of the field may prove nothing short of revolutionary.

4

Indigenous Languaging

Empathy and Translation across Alphabetic, Aural, and Visual Texts

> I think the comparison will show why American culture is enriched,
> not weakened, by opening the curriculum to these "new" regions of
> our heartland—regions which the Big Guns want us to think are
> deserts, but which I see as *lands of plenty, filled with herbs of healing.*
> To show this, I hope, may help to end the war fomented by those old
> Gunslingers between "Minority Literature" and "Great Books." They
> want, being Gunslingers, to divide and conquer—but (I would ask)
> why shouldn't we unite, and live in freedom and plenty?
>
> ▶ Carter Revard, "Herbs of Healing:
> American Values in American Indian Literature"

In the previous chapter I juxtapose serial readings of a single Indigenous poem, each interpretive installment based in a distinct Indigenous
worldview and system of aesthetics. In this chapter I trace how a chain
of readings can result from staging a series of purposeful juxtapositions of multiple texts composed by multiple, diverse Indigenous writers and artists. Inspiration for this more peripatetic methodology was
seeded, in part, by Carter Revard's essay "Herbs of Healing," in which
the Osage poet and esteemed scholar of medieval literature juxtaposes
contemporary American Indian poems with non-Native U.S. and
British "classics." Revard's project is expansive: Wallace Stevens's abstract "Anecdote of the Jar," a modernist fable in which silent Nature
is conquered by an equally silent Art, introduces the locally grounded
"Speaking" by Simon Ortiz (Acoma Pueblo), whose plainspoken, modernist dialogue connects generations of humans to each other and to
their other-than-human kin; John Milton's majestic sonnet of protest,
"On the Late Massacre in Piedmont," calling for divine vengeance at
the brutal murders of Protestants by Catholics in 1655, segues into the

dramatic monologue "I Expected My Skin and My Blood to Ripen" by Wendy Rose (Hopi/Miwok), lamenting the brutal murders of Lakota by U.S. cavalry in 1890 and protesting the ugly aftermath of Wounded Knee ongoing in the 1970s, when massacre "artifacts" continued to be collected, advertised, and sold; and Robert Frost's love poem "Never Again Would Birds' Song Be the Same" becomes mesmerized in the blinding "Jacklight" by Louise Erdrich (Ojibwe), which draws the delicate sonnet away from its Edenic garden into the wilder woods, where it might choose the unchosen path. More than simply supporting his thesis that "the true values of America are just as vividly and richly present in the 'ethnic' as in the classic poems" (173), Revard's juxtapositions demonstrate a viable method for expanding the reading of all six texts by mobilizing relevant contexts that are unexpected.

Revard began "Herbs of Healing" at least a decade before it was first published in 1998.[1] In the late 1980s, an early live performance included the gift of a remarkable handout: photocopies of the "classic" and American Indian poems, pasted together in collage, were made to fit on a single page, a fitting image for a call for inclusive curricula. Since then, the culture wars have shifted within academe, but versions of their battles remain, and Revard's essay remains, if less ideologically edgy in the new century, still powerful in its methodology. The juxtapositions continue to be arresting and productive. Building from Revard's staging of cross-cultural and transhistorical poetic exchanges, this chapter expands the investigation of the potential impact of drawing on Indigenous aesthetics for contemporary Indigenous literary studies by creating a ranging sequence of textual interactions that are Indigenous-to-Indigenous.

For continuity, I begin the sequence with "Carnegie, Oklahoma, 1919," the focus of chapter 3, but now juxtapose Momaday's poem among a number of similarly evocative texts, all of which can be read through the lens of the productive presence or absence of Indigenous language: "Sad Joke on a Marae" by the Māori poet Apirana Taylor, "Tangata Whenua" by the Māori hip-hop group Upper Hutt Posse, "Blood Quantum" by the Hawaiian poet Naomi Losch, and "When I of Fish Eat" by the Māori poet Rowley Habib (Rore Hapipi), illustrated by the Māori visual artist Ralph Hotere. In the course of staging these juxtapositions, I briefly engage additional texts, including the mixed-media basket *Strawberry and Chocolate* by the Onondaga and Micmac artist Gail Tremblay, the music video produced to augment Upper Hutt Posse's rap composition "Tangata Whenua," a single, linguistically rich sentence from the novel *Potiki* by the Māori author Patricia Grace, and bilingual English–Māori signage produced for the National Library of New Zealand/Te Puna Mātauranga o Aotearoa and for an exhibit at the Museum of New Zealand Te Papa Tongarewa, both located in Wellington. I bring the chapter to closure with brief, additional juxtapositions of the multiple English- and Māori-language versions of *The Whale Rider*, Māori author Witi Ihimaera's inspiring novel originally published in Aotearoa New Zealand in 1987 and adapted into the international feature film *Whale Rider*, released to wide acclaim in 2003. Part of that adaptation was the production of a U.S. edition of Ihimaera's novel (also referred to as an international edition), which self-consciously transforms *The Whale Rider* from a "local" to a "global" Indigenous text.

In the main body of the chapter, I focus primarily on poems and a rap composition, rather than on extended passages of prose, in part because of their potential relationships to Indigenous customary forms of oral composition but also, more pragmatically, because of their relative brevity and formal complexity. I highlight the interpretations that can result from juxtaposing these linguistically, structurally, and thematically dense works in multiple critical and generative conversations. I ask, in other words, What do we learn or see *differently* when we juxtapose a series of diverse but arguably related Indigenous texts?

Rere Kē / Moving Differently

The bilingual phrasing of this section title is meant to convey a sense of highly situated literary interactions created by Indigenous-to-Indigenous juxtapositions. The Māori verb phrase *rere kē* translates into English as "to move" or, more precisely, to "flow" or "fly" (rere) "differently" or "strangely" (kē). The postpositional particle *kē* conveys a sense of the unexpected. Indeed, Māori artist and art scholar Robert Jahnke employs the nominal form of the phrase, *rereketanga* (moving differently-ness), as a rough equivalent to the English term *uniqueness* ("Māori," 42).[2] The "unique" interpretive movements I trace in this

chapter through a sequence of Indigenous-to-Indigenous juxtapositions are linked by a consistent analytic focus on how the presence or
absence of Indigenous language functions in each text, a focus that
emerged over time from working with the juxtapositions themselves.
This focus on Indigenous language raises issues of artistic empathy,
linguistic and literary translation, and what the Latin Americanist
critic Walter Mignolo describes as "bilanguaging"—that is, thinking,
speaking, and writing *among* two or more languages and cultural systems, fully cognizant of the politics of their unequal, often asymmetrical relationships within (post)colonial linguistic and social hierarchies.
Across the main body of the chapter, I demonstrate that this particular
series of juxtapositions, this process of moving "unexpectedly" among
a number of contemporary Indigenous texts, ultimately enables an analysis of how Habib's illustrated poem, "When I of Fish Eat," written
entirely in English and augmented by contemporary, "modernist" line
drawings, can—for certain audiences—produce bilingual and bicultural effects that enrich the poem's potential meaning and amplify its
aesthetic power. The final section then turns to the case of Ihimaera's
translations, deletions, and transculturations to explore the potential
effects of an attempt to globalize the (literary) Indigenous local.

The larger point, however—in line with chapters 3 and 5—is not
the inevitability of any particular juxtaposition or analysis but rather
the productiveness of this kind of interpretive *process* among diverse
Indigenous texts. Revard concludes "Herbs of Healing," "I hope readers will have found the sweet and nourishing, the bitter and healing, in
some measure in this essay. We are talking about a so far undiscovered
country, five hundred years after Columbus mistook it for Japan or
China or India or the Earthly Paradise. We are talking about some
undiscovered writers whose work is good for this America" (192).[3] And
good, we might add, for this shared globe. Following Revard's lead, I
attempt to harness the power of surprising, productive juxtapositions
for a method of literary analysis that is explicitly trans-Indigenous.

Productive Absence

I begin by juxtaposing "Carnegie, Oklahoma, 1919" with "Sad Joke on
a Marae." I first encountered Taylor's poem, part of his 1979 collection

Eyes of the Ruru (Eyes of the Owl), as I struggled to understand how the twelve lines of Momaday's poem, part of his 1992 collection *In the Presence of the Sun*, produce such concentrated power. As discussed in chapter 3, "Carnegie, Oklahoma, 1919" is one of a series of texts— in both poetry and prose forms, and in anticipation of the 1976 U.S. bicentennial observances and the 1992 Columbus quincentenary—in which Momaday meditates on the story of his Kiowa grandfather being honored by the gift of a fine hunting horse during a gourd dance and giveaway performed near Carnegie, Oklahoma, in the year 1919. Reading Momaday's and Taylor's poems together, although they are based in different Indigenous cultures and histories and although they were produced in distinct periods of the twentieth century, helped me to see that the *absence* of Indigenous language in Momaday's poem is highly productive of both situated meaning and aesthetic power. This absence is especially productive for readers familiar with Momaday's larger corpus of published works and thus familiar with a greater range of specific details about the historical events to which this brief poem alludes, as well as with a greater range of interpretations of the ongoing significance of these events that Momaday has submitted to public scrutiny since 1976 with the publication of his narrative poem "The Gourd Dancer" and his memoir *The Names*.

Momaday's and Taylor's poems are related thematically in that each represents and, arguably, performs a moment of emotional, psychological, and spiritual contact between a contemporary speaker and his Indigenous ancestors. Each poem operates, in part, by situating its speaker on culturally relevant ceremonial grounds and evoking a paradox of space and time. In the Taylor poem the speaker, Tu, is explicitly alienated from his Indigenous culture and unable to speak his Indigenous language fluently. Standing on an unnamed marae (Māori ceremonial space) before an unnamed whare whakairo (carved meeting house), he participates in a paradox of space and time when the figure of the tekoteko (carving of an ancestor) offers Tu his own tongue with which to speak. In the Momaday poem, as shown in chapter 3, the speaker is only implicitly alienated from his Indigenous culture and language. Standing on the Kiowa gourd dancing grounds, however, he similarly participates in a paradox of space and time, articulated in the final lines' provocative juxtaposition "not here"/"am here." Consider the poems together:

Carnegie, Oklahoma, 1919

This afternoon is older
than the giving of gifts
and the rhythmic scraping of the red earth.
My father's father's name is called,
and the gift horse stutters out, whole,
the whole horizon in its eyes.
In the giveaway is beaded
the blood memories of fathers and sons.
Oh, there is nothing like this afternoon
in all the miles and years around,
and I am not here,
but, grandfather, father, I am here.

Sad Joke on a Marae

Tihei Mauriora I called
Kupe Paikea Te Kooti
Rewi and Te Rauparaha
I saw them
grim death and wooden ghosts
carved on the meeting house wall.

In the only Maori I knew
I called
Tihei Mauriora.
Above me the tekoteko raged.
He ripped his tongue from his mouth
and threw it at my feet.

Then I spoke.
My name is Tu the freezing worker.
Ngati D.B. is my tribe.
The pub is my Marae.
My fist is my taiaha.
Jail is my home.

Tihei Mauriora I cried.
They understood
the tekoteko and the ghosts
though I said nothing but
Tihei Mauriora
for that's all I knew.

Much can be said about either poem on its own.[4] When the two are juxtaposed, "Sad Joke on a Marae" draws attention to a (now) glaring absence of Indigenous language in "Carnegie, Oklahoma, 1919." Taylor's first stanza deploys the names of five well-known figures, legendary Polynesian explorers and famous Māori prophets, warriors, and rangatira (chiefs). The third stanza announces the speaker's own Māori name, Tu, which can be translated into English as the verbs "to stand," "to fight," or "to be wounded." The name can be read as an allusion to the Māori concept of turangawaewae (standing place, the place from which one derives social standing) and/or as an allusion to the god of war Tumatauenga, whose name is often shortened to Tu. In addition, the poem deploys several words that are likely to be known not only to fluent Māori-language speakers but also to many primarily English-language speakers in Aotearoa New Zealand, including tekoteko (carved figure), Ngati (a term that designates the name of a tribal group), marae (ceremonial space in front of the meeting house), and taiaha (fighting staff, a traditional weapon). Most prominently, the poem repeats the formulaic phrase "Tihei Mauriora," which is likely to be familiar to many readers in Aotearoa New Zealand, whether or not they can translate it into English. In Māori contexts the phrase is often used as a speaker's opening move during whaikorero (oratory) on the marae. It can be translated into English literally as "the sneeze of life," and it refers to the first sound—in English, the first "cry"—produced by a newborn. It thus can be paraphrased and abstracted as evoking "new life."

Through the repetition of this provocative phrase, which appears once in both the first and second stanzas and twice in the concluding fourth stanza, as well as through the use of the formulaic language patterns of formal introductions performed during mihi (greetings) and other Māori rituals of encounter in the third stanza, Taylor's poem emphasizes the role of Māori language and public oratory in this representation of an enabling contact with Indigenous ancestors. Through the primary symbol of the ancestor's tongue, the poem asserts the recuperative power of speaking as an Indigenous person in an Indigenous space and in an Indigenous manner. The assertion is strengthened by the poem's sequence of active verbs for speaking: "I called," "I spoke," "I cried," "I said."

In marked contrast, Momaday's poem deploys no Indigenous language or overtly Indigenous oratorical conventions, and its unusual phrasing and punning in English draws attention to these absences. In lines 4 through 6, the speaker declares, "My father's father's name is called, / and the gift horse stutters out, whole, / the whole horizon in its eyes." The duplicative adjectival phrase "father's father's" focuses attention on the significant ancestral "name," but this name remains unnamed and unspoken. The passive verb that follows, "is called," adds to this effect, since unlike Taylor's sequence of active verbs, the passive verb obscures agency and concentrates attention on the disembodied *act* of calling rather than on its agent. Absence is further emphasized in the lines that complete the statement. Although the auspicious act of calling produces "the gift horse," this gift is immediately associated with the repeated word "whole," which puns "hole," another word readily associated with absence. (This pun is echoed at the beginning of line 9 with the pun Oh / O, creating another "hole" in the poem.) The statement ends with the word "eyes," linking line 6 with lines 11 and 12, where the repeated "I" of the speaker declares his paradox of "not here"/"am here." Moreover, combined with the statement's one active verb, "stutters"—which, as discussed in chapter 3, suggests both movement and speech that is halting and difficult—the pun between the plural "eyes" of perception and the repeated "I" of subjectivity draws further attention to those "I's" absent from the poem: the father, the father's father, and the unnamed Kiowa ancestor who calls his name.

Once these absences are made visible, how might we refine our understanding of the ways in which the absence of Indigenous language in "Carnegie, Oklahoma, 1919" is actually productive of meaning and aesthetic power?

Let us turn to a second juxtaposition by adding the rap track "Tangata Whenua" by the Māori hip-hop group Upper Hutt Posse, who are led by MC Dean Hapeta (also known as D-Word and Te Kupu [The Word]), which I encountered several years after first reading "Carnegie,

Oklahoma, 1919" and "Sad Joke on a Marae."⁵ "Tangata Whenua" appears on Upper Hutt Posse's 1995 CD *Movement in Demand*, and this track can be read as a representation of the political and cultural development of the generation of urban Māori youth that followed the generation represented in Taylor's poem from the 1970s. (Given the purposes of this chapter, I read "Tangata Whenua" primarily in the context of contemporary Indigenous literary composition and reception rather than in the context of global rap and hip-hop cultures.) Building on Tu's experience in "Sad Joke on a Marae," the young, unnamed speaker/MC of Upper Hutt Posse's rap has reconnected with Māori language. Instead of repeating a single formulaic phrase as a pathetic plea to the ancestors and as a call for a much-needed "new life," this speaker/MC is able to produce whaikorero, formal oratory, and he is able to do so within an enabling structure of community rather than in a context of debilitating isolation. Significantly, he is able to do so completely and deftly in the Māori language.

The phrase *tangata whenua* can be translated into English literally as "land people" or "people of the land," and it carries both the more specific connotation, on the marae, of "hosts" (as opposed to "guests" or "visitors"), as well as the more expansive connotation, on the national or global scene, of "Indigenous people" (as opposed to "outsiders" or "settlers"). On the CD the rap is performed entirely in the Māori language with no English translation. The lyrics are presented exclusively in Māori in the CD liner notes, as well. Moreover, the track evokes a particularly "tribal" sound in its juxtapositions of complementary female and male voices, conventional rap and the Indigenous haka form of vigorous chant, and bass guitar supported by the stirring sound of the purerehua (bull-roarer, a disk of wood or stone strung on a cord and twirled through the air to produce a distinctive whirring), conventional drums, Polynesian log drums, and Afro-Cuban congas. The track opens with a female voice performing a brief but piercing karanga (call), which is appropriate protocol for beginning any ceremony on the marae. The rap itself begins, as is often the case with whaikorero, with the recitation of whakapapa (genealogy). The male rapper asserts that he is the child of Papatūānuku, the earth mother, and Ranginui, the sky father. In the background a male voice calls out the central formulaic phrase from Taylor's poem, "Tihei Mauriora," another indication that the rap is meant to evoke a speech on the marae. The rapper goes on to assert that the "root" (te take) of his genealogy is Io Matua Kore, Io the Father of the Void, the first principle in some versions of Māori cosmology.

Following this brief whakapapa, the rap's hook (chorus) makes bold assertions about what it means to be tangata whenua, people of the land:

Tangata Whenua Te Pake Whakapapa
Tangata Whenua Te Take Me Te Mana
Tangata Whenua Te Hana O Te Haa
Tangata Whenua Te Ahi Kaa

These lines can be translated into English as "Tangata whenua is the persistent genealogy / Tangata whenua is the root and the power / Tangata whenua is the flame of the essence of life / Tangata whenua is the home fire."[6] Together, they make strong claims for Māori land rights based in Māori philosophy and customs of land tenure. Other verses describe Māori aspirations for "knowledge" (mātauranga) and "unity" (kotahitanga) and contrast these with the "evil" deeds of the "enemy." The rap's closing lines return to the idea of an expansive genealogy connecting contemporary Māori to the earth and cosmos and assert, more specifically, "E rere ana te toto o oku Tupuna i roto i toku Manawa" (The blood of my ancestors runs in my heart), and, "E rere ana te wairua o oku Tupuna i roto i toku tinana" (The spirit of my ancestors runs in my body).

Juxtaposed with "Carnegie, Oklahoma, 1919" and "Sad Joke on a Marae," "Tangata Whenua" reveals a similar collapsing of distance in space and time, a similar connection of the contemporary with the ancestral, in at least two ways. For audiences fluent in Māori language and familiar with Māori cultural concepts, such as *ahi kā roa* (the long-burning home fires, a customary claim to land rights), that connection is evoked in the rap's specific content, which explicitly links the rapper to Māori ancestors and the gods. But the rap potentially evokes this kind of connection for those listeners who do not possess this level of skill in the Māori language or this level of knowledge of Māori culture. Similar to Taylor's use of the formulaic phrase "Tihei Mauriora," which gains force and builds meaning through its strategic repetition,[7] the rap's extensive use of "tribal" acoustic elements—including called, chanted, and sung Māori language, but also Māori musical instruments and distinctive Māori vocal performance customs such as the karanga and the haka—evokes contemporary Māori connection to the ancestral. Even in the absence of a high level of Māori linguistic skill or semantic understanding, these sound elements can be productive—at least for certain audiences—of particular kinds of meaning and aesthetic power. Within a contemporary, global music form, these sound elements can defiantly signify Māori Indigeneity.

Visual and Aural Empathy

How might we conceptualize the potential of a performed rap composition to evoke a contemporary Indigenous connection to the ancestral at the level of its acoustic elements, as opposed to exclusively at the level of its linguistic content? One approach is to situate the creation, performance, recording, and editing of Upper Hutt Posse's rap within a broader context of contemporary Māori arts practices. Māori artist and art scholar Robert Jahnke has developed a conceptual model for contemporary Māori visual art that imagines a continuum running between the pole "customary" (art created by Māori that maintains "a visual correspondence with historical models") and its opposite pole, "non-customary" (art created by Māori in which "visual correspondence and empathy with historical models [is] absent") ("Māori," 49–50). Much of contemporary Māori art is produced in the vast middle space between these poles, Jahnke argues, and it is neither "hybrid" nor caught "between" but "trans-customary": art that establishes not a strict correspondence with customary forms but rather a "visual empathy with customary practice" through the use of "pattern, form, medium, and technique" (48). Note that Jahnke draws his key distinction between "strict correspondence" with "customary forms" and "visual empathy" with "customary practice."

Jahnke's model makes immediate sense when viewing a wide range of contemporary Māori or other Indigenous works of art. In the North American context, for example, we can look to the baskets constructed by the Onondaga and Micmac poet, scholar, and weaver Gail Tremblay. One striking example of Tremblay's work, *Strawberry and Chocolate* (2000), is on permanent display at the National Museum of the American Indian in Washington, DC.[8] A "customary" Northeastern Indian basket typically is woven from thin splints of wood. In contrast,

Tremblay has crafted her contemporary basket from a combination of strips of standard 16 mm motion picture film and strips of full-coat magnetic film. The material for the basket is "non-customary" within Jahnke's model, but how this material is used—the physical practice of the basket's making—nonetheless demonstrates "empathy" with the "customary practice" of making northeastern baskets. Specific manipulation of the strips of film produce the basket's distinctive shape and textures: its square mouth and reinforced lip, the contrast between its smooth inner walls and curled, three-dimensional exterior. Even the luminous red and brown colors of the film strips demonstrate empathy with a "customary" strawberry basket produced from dyed splints of brown ash, while at the same time evoking the playfulness and sensuality of the contemporary basket's title. The juxtaposition of materials and practices in Tremblay's piece make suggestive statements about relationships between a contemporary art form, such as film production, and a customary art form, such as basket making. Similar to a strawberry basket, a film can be a tool for gathering and storing items of value that nourish and delight the community, and it can be both strong and beautiful, utilitarian and aesthetically accomplished. Tremblay's *Strawberry and Chocolate* is easily situated along Jahnke's continuum as an example of "trans-customary" American Indian visual and plastic art.

Upper Hutt Posse's Māori-language rap occupies a similar position along a continuum between "customary" and "non-customary" Māori music. "Tangata Whenua" fits Jahnke's criteria for the "trans-customary" in its use of recognizably customary sound elements, patterns, and techniques, only in an aural rather than in a visual or plastic medium. Following Jahnke, we can describe their techniques as creating "aural empathy" with customary practice.

If we take into account the 1998 video produced to augment the effects of "Tangata Whenua," we can investigate the multiple possibilities for aural and visual empathy within a single, multimedia text. Space does not permit full analysis of the visual component of the music video, and that level of analysis is not necessary to make my point. Instead, I focus on a visual motif that recurs over the course of the video's three minutes and ten seconds. This visual component narrates a dramatic story in which the practices of industry threaten the land, water, and traditional food resources of Aotearoa New Zealand with toxic pollution and, thus, threaten the health of the people of the land, the tangata whenua. Throughout the visual narrative, the frame repeatedly returns to images of a whare whakairo (carved meeting house) on a rural marae. Exterior shots of the whare focus on the elaborate, ochre-colored carvings of ancestors decorating the front of the house. Interior shots focus similarly on the walls, which feature alternating carved pou (wood slabs) and woven tukutuku panels. Similar to the house's exterior, the interior pou are carved into highly stylized likenesses of the Indigenous community's ancestors and record its whakapapa (genealogy).

For the greater part of the visual narrative, in these interior shots the pou are consistently centered within the frame, so that the alternating tukutuku panels can be partially seen on either side of the wood carving; the tukutuku create a woven and geometrically patterned border for the centered, curvilinear carvings. Toward the end of the video, however, following the visual narrative's climax, in which the poisonous effects of industry are reversed through Māori spiritual practices, there is a brief, twenty-second sequence in which the composition of this repeated interior shot is also reversed. In this sequence the interior shot of the whare's wall repeats eight times. In each shot a woven tukutuku panel—rather than a carved pou—is centered within the frame so that now the partially seen pou create a carved ochre border on either side of the woven tukutuku. In addition to this reversed composition, each of these eight interior shots includes a Māori child positioned at the center of the frame; that is, each child is positioned as *centered* in front of a patterned tukutuku panel. Each child's relatively small upper body is thus framed on either side by the visible woven panel behind him or her, which is then flanked on either side by carved pou. Read from left to right, each frame is organized as the sequence pou, tukutuku, child, tukutuku, pou. Through the visual empathy of this positioning, each child becomes, in effect, a living pou within the alternating sequence of carved pou and woven tukutuku. That eight different children appear in the eight interior shots is both noticeable to the viewer and striking. Although each shot is on screen only briefly, the different children are visually distinctive, not only in terms of their gender, relative physical sizes, apparent ages, and clothing but also in terms of their skin and hair color and Polynesian facial features. All of the children, whether they have darker or lighter skin or hair, are positioned identically as pou within the interior of the house. They are all identically positioned as carvings of Māori ancestors. Each becomes a part of the whaka-papa encoded in the walls of the whare whakairo. All of these chil-dren, the visual empathy asserts, are equally tangata whenua, equally people of the land. Linked to the Māori past through whakapapa, all of these children represent *future* ancestors of the Māori people—future tupuna—as understood in Māori terms.

We can extend this analysis by including the visual imagery of the shots placed *between* those of the Māori children in the twenty-second sequence. These alternating frames depict a dramatic sunrise over a low, perfectly level horizon of a calm ocean. In each, the sun emerges slightly higher from behind the dark horizon and the sky becomes in-creasingly orange, until the final shot in the sequence, following the eighth shot of a Māori child positioned before a tukutuku panel, in which the sun emerges as a perfect orange disk, filling the sky and the frame with golden light. This movement from darkness to light can be linked to versions of the Māori creation story, which moves through multiple stages of darkness until the dramatic revelation of the world in which we now live, designated te ao mārama, "the world of light."

The audio component of the video supports the above analysis and helps connect the two sequences of alternating images. The concluding lines of the rap's final verse introduce and then play over the interior shots of the eight Māori children and the exterior shots of the dra-matic sunrise: "E rere ana te toto ō ōku tūpuna / I roto i te ngaringari nei, I te ngaringari nei / I te tinana nei, i te waiata nei." On their web-site, Upper Hutt Posse translates these lyrics into English: "Flowing is the spirit of my ancestors / In this unity song, this unity song / This body, this waiata [song]." The alternating visual sequences of the chil-dren and the sunrise begin precisely with the repetition of the phrase "I te ngaringari nei." Thus, the sequence of visual images of the Māori children positioned as pou and the sun rising over the ocean are edited to coincide with the rapping of the three parallel phrases "this unity song," "this body," "this song." These lyrics represent a slight revision from the lyrics of the original version of "Tangata Whenua" recorded in 1995. The addition of the Māori term *ngaringari* (unity song), along with its explicit juxtaposition with the terms *tinana* (body) and *waia-ta* (song), introduces a meaningful and productive Māori pun. As Upper Hutt Posse's posted translation indicates, as a noun, *ngaringari* translates into English as "a song to make people pull together"—that is, a "song" (waiata) that helps the community become a single "body" (tinana). As a verb, however, *ngaringari* translates into English as "to increase in numbers." Combined with the images of the Māori children positioned as pou inside the whare whakairo, itself the "body" of an ancestor, and with the bright sun emerging out of the dark ocean horizon as though both it and the world were being born anew, the repetition of *ngaringari* links the "unity" of the Māori community to its generational "increase." Positioned as the conclusion to the visual narrative's story of the community's response to destructive elements from the colonial world, generational increase is linked, as well, to the ability of both the human community and the greater cosmos to build anew a world marked specifically as Indigenous. *Tihei mauriora*, indeed.

Bilingual Punning, Bilanguaging, and Double Translation

The link between operations of visual and aural empathy through various types of patterning leads to a third juxtaposition and a fourth primary text for analysis. Published in the 2003 anthology *Whetu Moana: Contemporary Polynesian Poems in English*, "Blood Quantum" by Naomi Losch provokes on a number of political and aesthetic levels. Of particular interest here are the poem's strategic deployment of Hawaiian language and use of complex visual and aural patterning, which, for lack of a more precise term, I will call *bilingual punning*. Losch's poem is written primarily in English. Similar to "Sad Joke on a Marae," it includes several names of illustrious ancestors and of significant sites in the landscape (lines 2–4). "Blood Quantum" draws additional attention to Indigenous language, however, in its deployment of a single line written entirely in Hawaiian. Positioned at line 10 in the nineteen-line poem, the line divides the English-language text into equal halves. In effect, it forms an Indigenous fulcrum, with nine lines of English balanced above the Hawaiian and nine lines of English balanced below. In line 1, Losch's speaker opens the first half, "We thought we were Hawaiian"; in line 11, which immediately follows the line of Hawaiian language and begins the second half, the speaker states, "And yet, by definition we are not Hawaiian." Together, these lines describe a paradox of contemporary Indigenous identity created by official blood quantum standards that echoes Momaday's paradox of space and time, "not here"/"am here":

Blood Quantum

We thought we were Hawaiian	1
Our ancestors were Liloa, Kuali'i and Alapa'i.	2
We fought at Mokuohai, Kepaniwai, and Nu'uanu,	3
And we supported Lili'ulani in her time of need.	4
We opposed statehood.	5
We didn't want to be the 49th *or* the 50th,	6
And once we were, 5(f) would take care of us.	7
But what is a native Hawaiian?	8
Aren't we of this place?	9
"O ko mākou one hānau kēia."	10
And yet, by definition, we are not Hawaiian.	11
We can't live on Homestead land,	12
Nor can we receive OHA money.	13
We didn't choose to quantify ourselves,	14

¼ to the left	½ to the right	15
⅜ to the left	⅝ to the right	16
⁷⁄₁₆ to the left	⁹⁄₁₆ to the right	17
¹⁵⁄₃₂ to the left	¹⁷⁄₃₂ to the right	18

They not only colonized us, they divided us.[9]	19
(*Whetu Moana*, 120)	

The line of Hawaiian, moreover, is framed by quotation marks, drawing further attention to its difference: "'O ko mākou one hānau kēia.'" The glossary included at the back of *Whetu Moana* translates this line into English as "This is our birthplace/homeland (a Hawaiian phrase)" (267). The translation makes clear that the line of Hawaiian is a response to the questions posed in the two lines immediately preceding it: "But what is a native Hawaiian? / Aren't we of this place?" Losch's poem articulates—and, in its columns of separated fractions, visually manifests—how U.S. federal and Hawaiian state governments have worked to divide the Hawaiian community through imposed policies, such as blood quantum requirements, that limit who can claim Hawaiian status and therefore access both to tangible resources, such as land, and to symbolic and social resources, such as recognition and legitimacy. The single line of Hawaiian works as an expression of collective Indigenous self-identification despite the pronouncements of official policies. It literally centers the ancestral, in the form of Hawaiian language, in a text that describes ongoing colonial practices of domination, division, and erasure.

Potentially more is asserted in the line than the fact that the Hawaiian Islands constitute an Indigenous "birthplace" or "homeland." Literally, *one hānau* translates into English as "birthing sands."[10] As in the Māori language, in Hawaiian as a noun *one* refers most specifically to sand; *hānau*, like the Māori word *whānau*, refers to both giving birth and being born. The visual and aural patterns of these words create additional levels of meaning and aesthetic power. The Hawaiian word *one* is located at almost the horizontal center of line 10, the vertical center of the nineteen-line poem, with nine lines balanced above and nine balanced below. The line's semantic content in Hawaiian thus locates *sand/land* at the center of this meditation on an embattled contemporary Hawaiian identity. In a poem that announces a quantitative and mathematical methodology as its subject—blood quantum and its colonial system for translating Indigenous identities into tables of descending fractions—Losch's horizontal and vertical centering of Hawaiian language and *sand/land* can be read as an assertion of an alternative system for articulating Indigeneity. Where dominant, official policy measures fractionated "blood," Losch responds with geographic coordinates, intersections of meridians and parallels. Determining location by means of these lines of longitude and latitude requires a fundamental plane from which to measure all possible positions within the system—that is, an equator. Losch's line of Hawaiian language functions as this great, defining circle. It asserts an alternative system for reckoning Indigeneity measured not by "blood" but by enacted relationships to land.

In the otherwise English-language poem, the line of Hawaiian and its precise centering of *sand/land* draws attention, as well, to its potential to create bilingual punning. On the page, in its visual (alphabetic) representation, the Hawaiian word *one* (oh-nay) looks exactly like the English word *one* (wun). In other words, the Hawaiian and English terms are homographic (spelled the same) but heterophonic (sound different) and heteronymic (carry different meanings). At the geographic center of the poem, therefore, a bilingual pun joins the idea of land to the idea of unity (oneness), further supporting the poem's activist message that all Hawaiians, regardless of their status under imposed rules of blood quantum, are united in their regenerative relationships to the homeland—*one hānau*, the place of giving birth and being born.

Within conventional English-language literary studies, we are accustomed to think that sound patterning and semantic relationships within poetic structures (including punning) work to "defamiliarize" the ordinary, to emphasize the possible connotations of a given word or set of words over their explicit denotation. As a form of wordplay, both monolingual and bilingual punning are typically deployed to create humorous or satiric effects. Losch's Indigenous bilingual pun works toward different ends. To a greater degree than those of either monolingual or more typical bilingual puns, its effects are highly dependent not only on the specific and specialized linguistic skills of particular listeners or readers but also on their level of cultural and historical knowledge. For readers who are actively bilingual and bicultural, Losch's pun offers the possibility of a synchral experience of (at least) two distinct language and cultural systems. Her bilingual pun is thus a form of repetition with variation. It is also a form of reiteration, saying the same thing and not saying exactly the same thing (at least) twice. Rather than defamiliarizing "ordinary" language, Losch's Hawaiian–English bilingual pun works to create additional layers of meaning for particular audiences by engaging multiple denotations (both *one* as "sand/land" and *one* as "a single entity"), as well as multiple connotations (both "birthplace/ homeland" and "unity/lack of division"). Instead of creating an obvious hierarchy of meaning, this bilingual punning stresses simultaneity. And this simultaneity is precisely the source of the Indigenous bilingual pun's potential for political and aesthetic power.

Losch's bilingual (and bicultural) punning responds to the ongoing subordination of Hawaiian individuals, communities, and culture within the (post)colonial context of the state of Hawai'i and to the ongoing subordination of Hawaiian language within the U.S. and global contexts of (post)colonial translation. Walter Mignolo, in *Local Histories/ Global Designs: Coloniality, Subaltern Knowledges, and Border Thinking* (2000), describes similar interactions among colonial power relations, the history of translation, and contemporary discursive strategies produced from "subaltern" perspectives within Latin American and U.S. Latino contexts in terms of "languaging," which he defines as "thinking and writing between languages" (226). More specifically, Mignolo analyzes "bilanguaging," which he defines as "not precisely bilingualism where both languages are maintained in their purity" but rather a practice where both languages are maintained "at the same time in their asymmetry." Such practices, Mignolo argues, are "not a grammatical but a political concern," since "the focus of bilanguaging itself is redressing the asymmetry of languages and denouncing the coloniality of power and knowledge" (231). These concepts describe the conditions for the production and reception of Losch's specific Indigenous pun. And they articulate the conditions for Indigenous literary production and reception more generally within contexts of settler colonialism, where Indigenous languages and cultures are engulfed and often overwhelmed by the sheer force of colonial languages and cultures and by a history of active suppression by imperial and settler governments.

Instances of what we might now call Indigenous *bilanguaging* can be either less or more overt than that evidenced in Losch's "Blood Quantum." Consider, for instance, a single sentence from the celebrated 1986 novel *Potiki* (The Final Born) by the Māori writer Patricia Grace. Although written primarily in English, Māori words and phrases appear throughout this text without direct translation or a glossary, and the novel's final moment is rendered in an extended Māori passage with no translation. Thus, the novel's overall linguistic composition reveals the status of te reo Māori within a New Zealand language hierarchy, as well as the role Māori language plays in ongoing Indigenous resistance to colonial and neocolonial power.[11] The sentence in question is written exclusively in English; for bilanguaging readers, however, it can produce effects similar to those of Losch's more obvious bilingual pun:

Every day the sounds came closer until one day we could see the *yellow* cuttings that the *yellow* machines had made, and the *yellow* clothes and the *yellow* hard hats that the men wore who worked the *yellow* machines. (106; emphasis added)

Set in the early 1980s, *Potiki* narrates ongoing colonial relations between Māori and Pakeha through the story of a Māori family's battles to save its homeland from developers who want to build a luxury resort there. The sentence appears at the point in the narrative when the developers attempt to physically force the Māori family off its land: with large earth-moving machines, they destroy the hills above the coastal village, causing dangerous flooding.

Grace's sentence draws attention because it repeats the adjective *yellow* five times among the sentence's thirty-nine words. The repetition connects the destruction of the land ("yellow cuttings") to the earth-moving equipment ("yellow machines") and to the working men—some of whom are Māori—forced to become agents of destruction through employment with the Pakeha company ("yellow clothes," "yellow hard hats"). In addition, the repetition connects these elements to the European-derived cultural connotations and literary allusions of *yellow*, including negative associations of cowardice (yellow-bellied), disease (jaundice), insanity (the 1891 short story "The Yellow Wallpaper" by Charlotte Perkins Gilman), irresponsible representation (yellow journalism), and greed (one of Christianity's seven deadly sins). For actively bilingual and bicultural readers, the repetition of *yellow* and the aural and visual patterns it creates across the sentence can suggest that Grace's strategy involves more than exclusively English-language and European-derived literary emphasis, connection, and allusion. Within the greater context of the novel, where the interplay of dominant English and subordinate Māori indicates more than a century of ongoing linguistic and cultural interactions, the repetition can suggest, as well, an active Indigenous negotiation—a Māori intervention *within* the lexical and semantic structures of (post)colonial New Zealand English.

One of the Māori translations for *yellow* is "renga." As an adjective, *renga* can mean "yellow" or "light-colored." When discussing water, it can also mean "discolored" or "turbid," potential references to scenes earlier in Grace's novel when the developers pollute the ocean near the Māori family's home with runoff from their digging and when they dam the local stream in order to flood the family's gardens and cemetery with muddy water. In other contexts *renga* can mean "scattered about," a potential reference to the developers' attempts to dislocate the family through tactics that include offers of service jobs and money, as well as verbal threats and physical violence. *Renga* can also be used as a verb, and then it means to "overflow" or "fill up," more potential references to the flooding caused by the developers. Like many Māori words, *renga* can be doubled, producing the form *rengarenga*. As an adjective, in addition to "scattered about," *rengarenga* can mean "crushed," "pounded," "destroyed," and "beaten," as well as "strident" and "raucous." All of these meanings resonate in the scene described by the sentence and in the larger plot of the novel. In a subsequent scene a group of rangatahi, Māori young adults, destroy the yellow machines and effectively put an end to the developers' digging, drawing positive connotations of "strident" and "raucous" to their activism (166).

Unlike Losch's strategic positioning of the Hawaiian–English homograph "one/one," Grace's repetition of the English adjective "yellow" does not easily fit the typical definition of punning: a word or phrase that exploits confusion either between similar-sounding different words or between two senses of the same word. And yet, similar to Losch's bilingual pun, the aural and visual patterning of Grace's English-language sentence can provoke connections and allusions across English and Māori languages and Pakeha and Māori cultures. The interplay among the connotations the sentence and the scene accrue through the repetition of the English adjective *yellow* and the connotations added by an awareness of the multiple meanings of the Māori words *renga* and *rengarenga* create a potential third text. While the monolingual reader of English can understand the basic meaning of the sentence, the actively bilingual and bicultural reader—the bilanguaging reader of English and Māori—is privy to more complex associations and interpretations. In addition to pointing up the novel's larger engagement with the asymmetrical power relations of colonial translation, the sentence points to an understanding of translation not simply as knowledge *transference* but also as knowledge *production.*

Indigenous bilanguaging—thinking and writing between languages, engaging the politics of their asymmetry within (post)colonial relations—can be more overt than either Losch's single heteronym or Grace's repetition of a single adjective. Cross-linguistic association and wordplay can actively display two (or more) languages side by side, so that readers have little choice but to register at least the *potential* for multiple meanings within gaps in translation and within the fertile interactions among words and phrases originating in different languages and cultures, especially when the languages and cultures in play are part of a (post)colonial hierarchy, as in Aotearoa New Zealand and other settler nations. When languages are presented together, of course, the potential effects of bilanguaging, like those of bilingual punning, are no less dependent on the language skills and cultural and historical knowledge of particular readers.

In Aotearoa New Zealand one encounters texts presented in side-by-side English and Māori versions with some regularity, especially within civic, governmental, and educational institutions. Both English and Māori are official languages of the contemporary settler nation-state, and publicly financed entities all bear two names. The dual name for the National Library of New Zealand/Te Puna Mātauranga o Aotearoa, located in the capital city of Wellington, is a good example. The Māori version, typically positioned either directly below or directly to the right of the English version on official signs, documents, web pages, and so forth, is an approximate but not "equivalent" translation of the English. The English noun *library*, derived from the Latin for "book," can be translated into Māori more directly as *te whare pukapuka*, "the book house." The Māori phrase *Te Puna Mātauranga*, in contrast, can be translated into English as "The Knowledge Source" or "The Source of Knowledge." The primary meaning of the noun *puna* is a "spring" (of water); in certain contexts it also can carry the connotation of *tupuna*, "ancestor." The noun *mātauranga*, "knowledge," derives from the verb *mātau*, which means "to know," "to be acquainted with," "to understand," and so forth. From this reading, we might conclude that the Māori version is a metaphorical gloss for the more mundane English: rather than simply a place for storing the nation's books (a national "book house"), the Māori metaphor reveals that the building and its textual contents can be conceived as a productive source—a natural "spring" and a generative "ancestor"—for the nation's collective body of knowledge.[12] In this sense, the Māori-language version serves a complementary function to the English, one often assigned to (subordinated) Indigenous languages within colonial relations: placed in a position secondary to the imposed colonial language and allowed to provide linguistic "flare" and cultural "novelty" but no defining substance. Other, more activist readings of the bilanguaging practices evidenced in the dual name are possible, however, if readers reject the linguistic hierarchy imposed by settler colonialism and do not assume that translation works in only one direction.

A striking example of activist bilanguaging is evident in the signage produced for an exhibit that opened in April 2006 at the National Museum of New Zealand Te Papa Tongarewa, also located in Wellington. Titled *Blood Earth Fire/Whāngai Whenua Ahi kā: The Transformation of Aotearoa New Zealand*, the exhibit is described in promotional literature as "an extraordinary journey of discovery through the changing landscape of New Zealand" that "tells the dramatic story of how people have interacted with, and had an impact on, New Zealand's land and resources over the last 800 years." On the signage displayed inside the museum, in promotional posters, and in images on the museum's website, the juxtaposition of English and Māori versions of the exhibit's primary title create multiple visual patterns, including the alignments and spacing of individual words, the relative sizes of their typeface, and the use of contrasting colors. The English version typically is rendered in a larger and bolder typeface than the Māori. Against a black background, the larger English is colored white in contrast to the smaller Māori, colored red. These juxtapositions of size and color can suggest ongoing colonial hierarchies, as well as contemporary demographic realities in which Māori make up approximately 15 percent of the total population of Aotearoa New Zealand. The proximity of the words also can imply that the smaller Māori version is a direct or equivalent translation of the larger English rather than an additional, complementary, or alternative text. None of the English and Māori terms used in the title are either homophones or homographs; they neither sound nor look the same. For audiences limited to reading only the English, the exhibit in effect carries only a single meaningful title, although the presence of Māori language may suggest the possibility of additional or excess meaning.

This is not the case for an actively bilanguaging—bilingual, bicultural, and politically aware—audience. This audience may interpret the sign's white and red lettering, set against a black background, as signaling visual empathy with the intertwining black, white, and red colors typical of kowhaiwhai scroll painting, often applied to the interior rafters of wharenui (meeting houses), that indicate genealogy as well as connection to the natural world. The combination of black, white, and red is often deployed in contemporary Māori artwork and in contemporary icons for Māori political organizing and activism. For this audience the exhibit carries at least two titles—and possibly three. There is the English title on its own, *Blood Earth Fire*; there is the Māori title on its own, *Whāngai Whenua Ahi kā*; and there is a potential third text created when bilingual and bicultural readers move back and forth among the three English-language and three Māori-language terms and their many possible connotations, allusions, and other associations, creating multiple sets and multiple patterns of juxtapositions, translations, interpretations, and situated meanings.[13]

The two versions of the title are not equivalent in any direct sense. The English terms fit the official description of the exhibit, in which the story of Aotearoa New Zealand is about a "changing landscape." Part of the immediate appeal of these terms is their invocation of well-known, European-derived conceptions of the natural world as composed of primal elements: earth, air, fire, and water. The addition of "Blood" is startling, but it suggests the human drama driving the organization of an exhibit about the transformation of land. The sequence of English terms also invokes language that is specifically biblical—in particular, passages from the Old and New Testaments that describe the manifest power of the Judeo-Christian God to wreak destruction on His creation. Readers may recall, for example, Ezekiel 21:32: "You will be fuel for the *fire*, your *blood* will be in the midst of the *land*. You will not be remembered, for I, the Lord, have spoken"; Joel 2:30: "I will display wonders in the sky and on the *earth, blood, fire* and columns of smoke"; or Acts 2:19: "And I will grant wonders in the sky above and signs on the *earth* below, *blood*, and *fire*, and vapors of smoke" (emphasis added). Flanked by "Blood" and "Fire," the centered "Earth" of the English-language title appears distinctly imperiled. The juxtaposed Māori terms also fit the exhibit's official description. At the same time, for readers fluent in Māori language and familiar with Māori culture, these terms invoke specific conceptions of social relationships and political organization. *Whāngai* literally means "to feed" or "to nourish" and is used to describe a type of kinship relation expressed in English by the related but distinct concepts of fostering or adopting a child. *Whenua* means "land," the physical ground upon which we stand, but also carries the equally primary meaning of "placenta" or "afterbirth," the nurturing soil of the womb. Finally, *ahi kā* means "burning fire," a phrase that suggests human occupation keeps land "warm." As discussed in relation to "Tangata Whenua," *ahi kā* therefore connotes the concept of land rights asserted through continuous occupation.

Understood in their own linguistic and cultural contexts, the exhibit's English and Māori titles, along with their immediate connotations, create a stark contrast. In conventional terms, we might say productive gaps exist between the translations; for bilingual and bicultural readers, these gaps create a highly charged intertext. In a 2003 follow-up to *Local Histories/Global Designs*, Walter Mignolo, collaborating with Freya Schiwy, investigates a specific example of bilanguaging, "a particular kind of translation/transculturation […] in which a dense history of oppression and subalternization of language and knowledge is being unlocked." Mignolo and Schiwy name this operation a "double translation" (10). This is a form of translation "in multiple directions" in which dominant, colonial thinking is "transformed" and "interpreted" according to the worldview of the subaltern (12). In Mignolo and Schiwy's examples (speeches and published writing by leaders of the Zapatista activist movement in Mexico), double translation does not result from "first contact" but rather emerges "out of a border space where contact has already been taking place" (15). This context of ongoing contact is similar for the dual-language signage at the National Museum of New Zealand.

The concepts of bilanguaging and the double translation articulate the activist possibilities of the English–Māori intertext created by bilingual and bicultural readers of the museum signage. Consider the matrix in Figure 8 of associated concepts emanating from the dual-language exhibit title, rendered as lists extending above and below the three English and three Māori terms. These lists create distinct but related layers of bilingual and bicultural connotations, allusions, and associations. Reading across and among the English and Māori terms, the patterns of interplay demonstrate complex practices of bilanguaging and double translation that involve not simply linguistic substitutions but also cultural, social, and political reckoning. These practices are necessarily caught up in issues of identity and power. Within the specific context of a Māori response to the Pakeha museum, the patterns of interplay demonstrate a potential empathy with the customary practices of Māori whakapapa (genealogy). *Whakapapa* means not only "to recite in proper order" but also "to lay one thing upon another." This empathy with whakapapa creates an additional discourse rhetorically more rich and politically more complex than that of either the sequences of English terms or Māori terms on their own. That is, it creates a double translation situated specifically within the (post) colonial history of Aotearoa New Zealand. Note, for instance, that potential interactions between "Whenua" and "Earth" are placed at the generative center of this matrix of terms. Beginning with the tension of this central juxtaposition, additional relationships can be traced either vertically or horizontally or through multiple combinations of vertical and horizontal "moves." There are many provocative possibilities,

	Indigenous hosts land people	ongoing land rights
Maui	tangata whenua	long-burning fire
adopt	afterbirth	ahi kā roa
foster	placenta	land rights by occupation
nourish	ground	continuous occupation
feed	land	burning fire
Whāngai	**Whenua**	**Ahi Kā**
Blood	**Earth**	**Fire**
toto	Papatūānuku	ahi
Maui	mother	Maui
whanaunga	whenua	
blood relations	Aotearoa	
whakapapa	Te Ika a Maui	
genealogy		

FIGURE 8. Associated concepts emanating from the dual-language exhibit title of *Blood Earth Fire / Whāngai Whenua Ahi kā: The Transformation of Aotearoa New Zealand* rendered as lists extending above and below the three English and three Māori terms.

and particular bilingual and bicultural—bilanguaging—readers will produce their own trajectories across and among the terms and their possible connotations, allusions, and associations.

One trajectory might begin vertically. "Whenua" does not immediately evoke the idea of "Earth," especially with a capital *E*, which is typically translated into Māori as Papatūānuku (Earth mother). Rather, as noted, "Whenua" more immediately evokes the idea of land, the ground upon which we stand, as well as its other primary meaning, "placenta" or "afterbirth." "Earth" links to "Whenua" through these connections: *Papatūānuku* and *mother*. "Whenua" also suggests the phrase *tangata whenua*, which translates into English as "land people" or "people of the land" and which, as discussed earlier, carries both the specific connotation of "local hosts," as opposed to "traveling visitors," and the more expansive connotation of "Indigenous." "Earth," as land and whenua, also suggests one of the Indigenous names for New Zealand, Aotearoa (Land of the Long White Cloud), which can also suggest a more specific Indigenous name for the North Island, Te Ika a Maui (The Fish of Maui). Te Papa, the museum housing the exhibit, is located in Wellington at Te Upoko o te Ika a Maui (The Head of the Fish of Maui).

The trajectory of relationships might then move horizontally. Maui is the Polynesian culture hero. In addition to being credited with fishing up the North Island, Te Ika a Maui, he is credited with harnessing the power of fire (ahi). Ahi suggests the phrase *ahi kā* (burning fire), a term connoting "continuous occupation of land" and, therefore, "land rights by occupation," typically designated in Māori by the phrase *ahi kā roa* (the long-burning fire), a term for land rights that are ongoing so long as some part of the community remains on the land to keep it "warm." In the stories about his life and exploits, Maui is the first whāngai, the first child to be fed and nourished by other than his own parents. *Whāngai*, literally "to feed" or "to nourish," is used to describe a relationship expressed in English by the related but distinct concepts of fostering or adopting. *Whāngai* thus seems an odd choice to juxtapose with the English term *blood*, since European-derived cultures often draw a sharp distinction between children related to parents by blood and children who enter families through temporary fostering or permanent legal adoption. The word for literal blood in Māori is *toto* and can be associated with the story of how Maui fished Te Ika a Maui out of the sea: he used a magical fishhook made from the bone of an ancestor, smeared with blood from his own nose as bait. *Blood* can suggest the Māori concept of whanaunga (blood relations), which suggests the concept of whakapapa (genealogy). Whāngai relationships (fostering, adoption) place children within the matrix of whakapapa and secure relations.

Other possible trajectories abound. My point is that we can understand this overt juxtaposition of bilingual terms as Indigenous bilanguaging and double translation, related to Losch's bilingual punning and to works of "trans-customary" art. Through its empathy with the customary practices of tracing relationships through the matrix of whakapapa, the bilingual title is able to provoke multiple messages, at least for certain audiences, including activist messages about land rights. "The changing landscape of New Zealand" is not simply *natural* but significantly *political*. As patrons of the National Museum of New Zealand enter the exhibit, they are confronted with the assertion of an *enduring* Aotearoa still "warmed" by ahi kā, Māori home fires—that is, a continuously occupied and nourishing Indigenous homeland.

It is tempting to return to the National Library's official dual-language name, as well. For the bilanguaging reader, what kinds of activist messages are possible within its own matrix of juxtapositions? What pressure, for instance, might the Māori noun *puna* apply to the English adjective *national*?

Although "Carnegie, Oklahoma, 1919" contains no obvious bilingual puns, bilanguaging, or double translations, part of the power of the absence of Indigenous language in this text can be described by the concepts of synchral experience and simultaneity. In Momaday's brief poem the emphasis placed on the sequences of genealogical terms "father's father's" and "grandfather, father, I" is suggestive of their equivalence. All of these subject positions—all of these "I's"—are "beaded" together in the speaker's experience of apparent paradox ("not here"/"am here"). As noted in chapter 3, in the Kiowa language the same word is used for the first-person singular and first-person plural pronouns, for both "I" and "we" (Boyd, 1:28). The majority of readers will be unaware of this linguistic fact and semantic potential. Yet the patterning of the poem's English, its puns on words such as "eyes" and the visual and aural empathy created between "father's father's" and "grand*father*, *father*, I," produces a similar effect, especially read within the context of Indigenous responses to the 1992 Columbus quincentenary. Along with the speaker, at least some readers can experience the "I" of subjectivity understood not only in the (settler) singular but also in the (Indigenous) plural.

Cultural Seizure

The idea of a single work creating different kinds of meaning for different audiences through a combination of visual and aural cues brings me to a fifth text and final juxtaposition. Rowley Habib's poem "When I of Fish Eat" was first published in the September 1962 issue of the Department of Maori Affairs journal, *Te Ao Hou*, then edited by the

Pakeha scholar of Māori language and literature Margaret Orbell. Part of Orbell's contribution to the long-running journal was to improve the overall quality of its production and the aesthetic quality of its layout. In addition, with the assistance of her husband, the acclaimed Pakeha artist Gordon Walters, Orbell increased the number and quality of illustrations included in each issue.[14] Habib's poem is accompanied by two illustrations created by the (now) renowned Māori artist Ralph Hotere. Although I encountered Habib's poem and Hotere's drawings when I was first working with Momaday's and Taylor's poems, I did not see them as especially related until I encountered Upper Hutt Posse's Māori-language rap and Losch's Hawaiian–English bilingual pun.

Similar to "Carnegie, Oklahoma, 1919" and "Sad Joke on a Marae," "When I of Fish Eat" stages a scene of emotional, psychological, and, especially, spiritual connection between the speaker and his Indigenous ancestors (see Figure 9). In Habib's poem the connection between the contemporary and the ancestral is effected not through contact with ceremonial grounds but through the speaker's act of eating fish "with knife and fork." Through a series of explicit linguistic associations in English, the poem links the "sensual" act of eating fish to the "sacred" experience of "revelation." The speaker experiences a vision of the Māori past, as well as a deep understanding of how that past exists in the present. Like Momaday's poem, Habib's is written entirely in English, but it, too, offers the potential of a synchral experience of English and Indigenous languages and cultural connotations. Hotere's modernist line drawings, positioned above left and below right of the printed text, actively contribute to the poem's ability to provoke, for certain readers, bilingual punning and Indigenous bilanguaging. More than illustration, Hotere's pictorial frame offers a visual, perhaps pictographic interpretation of the poem's dominant theme. For the actively bilingual and bicultural reader/viewer, these configurations of lines and shadows point toward Māori linguistic puns on the poem's key English-language words and concepts.

The poem's distinctive syntax and careful use of punctuation and line endings, along with several internal rhymes, alliterations, and repetitions, create formal rhythms and verbal patterning suggestive, foremost, of ritual recitation. Notice, for instance, the balanced and nearly palindromic sequence created across the poem by the purposeful placement and repetition of the rhyming adverbs of time "when" and "then" and

When I of Fish Eat

When I of fish eat; when, with knife and fork,
I break the tender segments of flesh within my plate
I feel the pulling back. Strong I feel it;
Pulling me back to my forefathers,
To shores not yet trodden by white men.
It is, then, not a mere eating of the flesh,
A delighting in the sensual taste.
It is, for me, more than this: it is a revelation.
The sea surges before me, washing upon long shores;
Heaving against jagged rocks; as it did of old.
And this sea holds more than just its beauty,
Its aboundingness. It is something sacred;
It is like a parent to me. For think I then
That the sea was my forefathers' very existence.
Fishermen were they. From the sea came their very life.
This then is what it is when, with knife and fork
I lift a morsel of fish to my mouth.

ROWLEY HABIB

FIGURE 9. "When I of Fish Eat" by Rowley Habib, with illustrations by Ralph Hotere. Image of page from *Te Ao Hou* 40 (September 1962): 4. Republished with the permission of the National Library of New Zealand Te Puna Mātauranga o Aotearoa and the Maori Purposes Fund Board.

their near rhyme, the comparative conjunction "than"—"when," "when," "then"; "than," "than"; "then," "then," "when." Notice, too, the strategic placement of the poem's five semicolons and single colon. That the body of the poem is printed in italics only adds to the effect of speech that has been set apart. The poem's specific content creates a chain of associations that resonate with the particular ritual of the Christian sacrament: "fish" is associated with "flesh," which in turn is associated with "revelation" and "sacred," and finally with "a parent." The consumption of this flesh made sacred facilitates a communion with the spiritual father. At the same time, the poem resists reduction to a Christian formula. The explicit chain of linguistic associations that begins with "fish" also includes "fore-fathers," "shores," and "the sea." While the act of eating the flesh of fish is explicitly named a "revelation," it is the "sea" that is explicitly described as "something sacred," "like a parent to me," and "my forefathers' very exis-tence." Although these "forefathers" are described as "fishermen," linking them to Christ as a fisher of men, this act of communion connects the speaker with the sea god Tangaroa as much as with the Christian father.

Looking closely at the content of the poem, we realize that it does not, in fact, describe the speaker's actual consumption of fish, but rather the moments *between* his act of breaking into segments the flesh "within my plate" "with knife and fork" and his act of "lift[ing] a morsel of fish to my mouth," also with "knife and fork." The poem describes and, in a sense, enacts the significant pause between the acts of breaking and consuming flesh. And it is within this pause that the speaker experienc-es his "revelation" of a spiritual connection to the ancestral. Positioning draws attention to the concrete details at the ends of the two opening and two closing lines that describe these acts of breaking and lifting: the "knife and fork," which are the instruments of both the breaking and the lifting of flesh; "my plate," which is the site of both the breaking of the flesh and its contemplation during the speaker's revelation; and "my mouth," the human aperture for ingestion, which is distinctly unlike the inanimate objects that precede it in the poem. Within the colonial history of Aotearoa New Zealand, knife, fork, and plate can be read as symbols of the European "civilization" brought by settler-invaders. In this reading, local nature, represented by the fish, is subjected to a colonial "civilizing" process that can connote not only the conventions of European-derived table manners but also the conventions of Euro-pean-derived aesthetic display (the plate suggesting the white space of the gallery wall or museum case) and scientific study (the segmenting of flesh suggesting a form of dissection). Over the course of the poem, European processes of eating/displaying/dissecting are reconfigured as Māori customary practice, as ritual for remembering history.

The repetition of the phrase "with knife and fork," which appears at the ends of the first and penultimate lines, emphasizes the European convention of holding the knife in the right hand and the fork in the left hand; the repeated phrase can be read "with right and left." Here, we have the potential for a type of bilingual punning and for bilanguaging, thinking and writing between English and Māori languages and engaging the politics of their asymmetry within Aotearoa New Zealand. In Māori, right and left, matau and maui, carry multiple ritual connotations, including the idea, on the marae, of taha matau (the right side, usually designated for manuhiri, visitors) and taha maui (the left side, usually designated for tangata whenua, hosts). The emphasis on right and left, in other words, suggests a marae setting. We can now read the "plate" as suggesting a marae atea, the open space in front of the meeting house that is used during ceremonies where visitors (positioned on the right side) and hosts (positioned on the left side) formally encounter one another and exchange words and song before entering. When the connotative potential of the poem's associations are combined with the connotative potential of these bilingual puns on "knife and fork," a scene whose *form* is multiply recognizable as Pakeha can be reconfigured as the site of a distinctly Māori *practice*.

This potential reconfiguration of the European plate as a marae atea resonates with Jahnke's analysis of contemporary Māori art installations. Jahnke argues that European-derived spaces for the public display of art, such as galleries or museums, are often reconfigured by Māori artists and curators to conform to Māori cultural practices and cultural conventions, such as those enacted on the marae or within the meeting house ("Voices," 199). Similar reconfigurations of public spaces for display also occur in the staging of Māori theater, dance, and other performances. Jahnke names this reconfiguration of significant cultural spaces "the ritual seizure of site" (199). In a different context, I analyze the Indigenous appropriation and redeployment of the conventions of dominant discourses, such as the discourse of treaties, as an "activist occupation of significant sites of colonial discourse" (*Blood Narrative*, 21). Habib's poem can be read as operating in this activist vein, performing what Jahnke calls an "act of cultural seizure" (197) in its movements to realign the mundane act of eating the flesh of fish, first, with the spiritual context of Christian communion and, then, with the customary paradigms of Māori rituals of encounter. In a sense, Habib's associations make the speaker's act of eating the flesh of fish doubly significant. These connotations of different kinds of ritual encounter also link Habib's poem to similar encounters in Momaday's and Taylor's poems.

Hotere's illustrations, in their potential to provoke further bilingual punning and bilanguaging, advance these kinds of realignments. The first drawing, a skeletal fish positioned above the title of the poem, emphasizes the horizontal line of the fish spine, which supports a string of intersecting, perpendicular bones, as well as the skeleton's large, empty head and vacant eye. The second drawing, positioned below the text of the poem, represents a teeming mass of living fish. Each fish is formed by two intersecting arcs, in the style of the fish symbol for Christianity.[15] The mass of fish is divided by a vertical line that suggests the act of fishing. This drawing emphasizes life and abundance, as well as vertical and horizontal movement. Both drawings emphasize intersections and the crossing of boundaries, again linking "When I of Fish Eat" to "Carnegie, Oklahoma, 1919" and "Sad Joke on a Marae." Taken together, the drawings suggest the Christian idea of resurrection and illustrate a central paradox of Habib's poem: consumption leads not to depletion but to increase. More specifically, this consumption leads to an increase of knowledge and a spiritual connection to the past. It is a version of the idea that life follows from death in a natural cycle. But Hotere's visual frame does more than simply illustrate this aspect of Habib's poem. For actively bilingual and bicultural readers/viewers, the drawings direct attention to specific words and concepts. These juxtapositions of graphic images and alphabetic writing signal specific bilingual puns and specific acts of bilanguaging that add additional meaning and aesthetic power to the experience of the poem.

The first drawing focuses attention on specific words in the first half of Habib's poem, especially "fish," "segments," "flesh," and associated concepts. The most common Māori word for "fish," as both noun and verb, is *ika*. As a noun, *ika* can also be used figuratively to refer to any prized possession. (Historically, this includes warriors slain in battle or other kinds of victims.) In addition, *ika* is suggestive of Te Ika a Maui (The Fish of Maui), which is commonly used to refer to the North Island of Aotearoa and also can be used to refer to the group of stars known in English as the Milky Way. The poem's "fish" is thus a prized possession linking the speaker not only to the sea but also to the land and cosmos.[16] The drawing emphasizes not simply the fish, however, but more precisely the skeletal fish, that which is revealed when the speaker "break[s] the tender segments of fish within my plate": it emphasizes the bones. In English this emphasis supports the paradoxical theme of life following death. In Māori the word for "bones" or "skeletal remains" is *iwi*, which also carries a primary meaning of "people" or "tribe" and, by extension, "nation." A familiar Māori pun, *e nga iwi o nga iwi* ("the bones of the people" or "the people of the bones"), exploits the potential of these multiple meanings. Māori writer Keri Hulme draws on the connotative power of this pun in the title of her 1984 novel, *The Bone People*; the pun emphasizes the connections between the living community and the ancestors whose remains are buried in their homeland.

In "When I of Fish Eat," the pun on *iwi* is highly productive of additional meaning. As the speaker segments the flesh of fish, he reveals the iwi, in the sense of the bones of the ancestors, and he is "pull[ed] back," similar to the speakers in both Momaday's and Taylor's poems, to the iwi, in the sense of the ancestors, and to the land itself, the whenua—and, in the case of the North Island, the ika, the fish—that holds their remains. (As noted above, *whenua* carries the additional primary meaning of "afterbirth" or "placenta," linking the land not only to ancestors and to Te Ika a Maui but also to the womb and, thus, regeneration.) We may infer that as a result of this revelation, the speaker is subsequently "pull[ed] back" to the iwi in the sense of the living community. Hotere's drawing emphasizes this aspect of *iwi* in the way its components correspond to the parts of a meeting house, which is both the literal embodiment of the principal ancestor and the contemporary community's meeting place. The central spine of the drawn fish can be read as the ridgepole (tahuhu) of a house, the backbone of the ancestor and his or her main line of descent; the intersecting bones can be read as the rafters (heke) of a house, the ancestor's ribs and descent lines; the large head can be read as the front porch (mahau) of a house, with the mouth representing the doorway (kuwaha) and the eye the window (matapihi), the ancestor's brains, mouth, and eye. Through this visual empathy, Hotere's skeletal fish unites the primary meanings of *iwi*.

"People, tribe, or nation" is not a precise equivalent for one of these primary meanings of *iwi*, however, since the English words carry specific connotations of European-derived political and economic structures that do not convey the genealogical imperatives that underpin Māori customary concepts of social organization. As Jahnke explains:

> The holistic union between the body as a critical notion of regeneration and nature as personification of being is often absent from contemporary translations of "iwi.""Iwi" is more than "people" or "tribe." It is the essential component of the spine, the fulcrum that articulates the nerve centre of Maori culture. It is the "bone" that protects the marrow of culture. It encompasses hapū [subtribe; to be pregnant] and whānau [extended family; to give birth or to be born] as sustenance for the regeneration of iwi. It exists as a cultural backbone whose strength and durability carry the essential ingredients of culture. The concept of nurture within the womb has been trivialized in the translation of "hapū" as sub-tribe. "Whānau," in its colonized translation as "extended family," is rendered as an economically viable unit. Unfortunately, the erasure of the inseparability of genealogy and birth in the latter translation epitomizes the imposition of Pakeha terms of reference. As such these colonial categories of capture attempt to render the metaphysical as illogical or human potential as capitalist units of production or servitude. ("Voices," 196)

Jahnke's explanation points up both the inadequacy of these common English translations for key Māori concepts and their potential for colonial distortion and appropriation. For the purposes of the present discussion, Jahnke's explanation also points up the centrality of the theme of regeneration in Habib's text and Hotere's drawings, which work together to link the idea of the regeneration of the human body and human community to both natural and spiritual worlds. Indeed, as the above juxtapositions demonstrate, complex understandings of regeneration are central not only to the texts produced by Habib and Hotere but also to those produced by Momaday, Taylor, Upper Hutt Posse, and Losch.

Hotere's second drawing is linked thematically to the first—both evoke ideas related to "fish"—but the mass of living fish also can direct attention to the specific word "aboundingness" in the second half of Habib's poem. This word already draws attention as a neologism in

English. If the reader has knowledge of te reo Māori, this joining of the adjective *abounding* with the noun suffix *-ness* can be read as following a similar pattern for creating new nouns in Māori by adding the noun suffix *-tanga*. In addition, linking "fish" and "aboundingness" in Māori is suggestive of an alternative word to *ika*. Among Hotere's Te Aupouri iwi (tribal group), *ika* is often avoided as a word for "fish" because Te Aupouri venerate a famous ancestor named Te Ika Nui (The Great Fish). In place of *ika*, Te Aupouri may substitute *ngohi*, which carries the connotation of "hundreds" or, more generally, "abundance," alluding to the experience of generous fishing grounds off the coast of the Te Aupouri homeland in the far north of the North Island (the Tail of the Fish of Maui).[17] In H. M. Ngata's *English–Maori Dictionary*, the first Māori translation given for *abound* is "hāwere" (plentiful, prolific; a variety of kumara [sweet potato]). Ngata gives the following example of its use: "I te ūnga mai o Kupe ki konei, hāwere ana te ika i te moana" (When Kupe landed here, fish abounded in the sea). In the association of *hāwere* with a variety of kumara, a staple food, fishing is linked to horticulture, the abundance of the sea to that of the land, emphasizing the sustenance of the community.

The vertical line dividing the mass of fish in Hotere's second drawing suggests a fishing line (hī ika, to catch fish with a line and hook), although neither the fisherman nor the hook is represented on the page. These absences, in other words, are productive. Like Momaday's absent Indigenous language in "Carnegie, Oklahoma, 1919," the absences at the ends of Hotere's vertical line can produce meaning and aesthetic power, but such production depends on the specific knowledge of particular audiences, including the knowledge of other texts. Two "other" texts are immediately available to help interpret these absences: Habib's poem, which explicitly invokes images of fishermen and fishing, and Hotere's first drawing, which implicitly emphasizes the horizontal fish spine. The spine of the skeletal fish suggests not only a ridgepole in a meeting house but also a horizon line. Note that either end of this line extends beyond the perpendicular lines of the intersecting fish bones. Similarly, the vertical line in the second drawing suggests a border that extends beyond the immediate, visible scene. This border is actively crossed by the mass of fish. Their movement is oriented from the right (taha matau, the side of visitors on the marae) toward the left (taha maui, the side of hosts). At

this point in the analysis, we may suddenly notice that in the first drawing the skeletal fish is oriented so that it faces toward the right.[18]

Righting a Target Language

The spatial arrangements and specific orientations of Hotere's line
drawings thematize interpretive movements in multiple directions
and argue for their productiveness for multiple audiences. Both the
individual drawings and the graphic relationships between them signal
the potential for bilingual punning and Indigenous bilanguaging in
Habib's English-language poem. For bilingual and bicultural readers/
viewers, these multiple interactions among graphic and linguistic elements add complexity to understandings of the written text's "meaning" and depth to experiences of its aesthetic power. Hotere's drawings
provide something of a Māori-language gloss for Habib's English-
language text. Although that characterization does not feel fully adequate, it is interesting to note that, in 2006, when Habib reprinted this
early poem as part of the first volume of his collected works—on its
own, without Hotere's evocative drawings—he revised its title from
the original, monolingual "When I of Fish Eat" to the overtly bilingual
"Ika (Fish)" (73).

At first glance, Habib's revision simply rehearses a typical scene of
(post)colonial translation. Positioned on the left side of this conventional juxtaposition, the unmarked *ika* indicates the priority of the
Māori term's role as exotic object, as a "source" language in need of explanation; positioned on the right side, the English term *fish*, marked by
punctuation, indicates its complementary role as the "target" language
that not only explains the exotic term preceding it but also contains the
potentially multiple meanings of that term through the juxtaposition's
suggestion of equivalence and substitution. In the conventional practice, monolingual readers of English are invited to equate *ika* with *fish*.
Similar to Hotere's drawings, though, the spatial arrangements and use
of punctuation in the bilingual title also enact practices of Indigenous
bilanguaging. For bilingual and bicultural readers, the juxtaposition
of Māori and English terms can be seen as binding them together in a
productive tension. The curved brackets of parentheses not only suggest translation as a process of substitution but reveal the direction of

that substitution and engage its particular politics within the (post) colonial context of Aotearoa New Zealand. The placement of the unmarked—or, more precisely, the *unenclosed* and *unrestricted*—Māori term on the left side of the bilingual title not only indicates its role as a "source" language for (post)colonial translation but also suggests its enduring occupation of taha maui, the side of tangata whenua (hosts) on the marae. Similarly, the placement of the marked—*enclosed* and *restricted*—English term on the right side not only indicates its role as the "target" language of (post)colonial translation but also suggests its assigned position of taha matau, the side of manuhiri (visitors) on the marae. We might note, too, that parentheses are conventionally used to indicate not only the process of translation but also the source of quotation, paraphrase, or summary, as in an academic citation. In this way, Habib's bilingual revision acknowledges its monolingual source, again enacting practices of bilanguaging.

More subtly, Habib's revised title suggests key aspects of Hotere's second drawing, the teeming mass of fish that cross the seemingly infinite border of the drawing's central vertical line *i matau ki maui*, from right to left. The intersecting arcs that form the fish symbol for Christianity, repeated over and over in Hotere's drawing, have been separated, rotated, and further abstracted into the mirrored brackets of the parentheses placed around the English term *fish*. The recognition sign for belief in the Christ who died on the *cross* is remade into a recognition sign for the asymmetrical process of (post)colonial translation, in which "to carry *across*" often meant—and often continues to mean—"to carry *a cross*." In these ways the revised title points to the power of Hotere's original graphic gloss, how it can highlight the poem's participation in an ongoing Māori negotiation with the colonial power of English-language, European-derived Pakeha culture and, perhaps especially, imported Christianity. The poem's explicit Christian symbolism is reconfigured—but not erased—through visual and aural empathy with Māori customary practices. That symbolism becomes multivalent and more complex. Along with the poem's speaker, bilanguaging readers are invited, perhaps provoked, to contemplate various "shores"—horizons, borders—"not yet trodden by white men." For these readers "(Fish)" contextualizes and complicates but cannot contain "Ika."

The series of juxtapositions among texts by Momaday, Taylor, Upper Hutt Posse, Losch, Habib, and Hotere highlights the ability of English-language poems to resonate with meaning and aesthetic power that can be marked as specifically Indigenous. Although radically diverse in many respects, these contemporary compositions offer up mutually recognizable symbols of Indigenous persistence and renewal—Momaday's gift horse, Taylor's ancestral tongue, Upper Hutt Posse's tribal acoustics, Losch's birthing sands, Habib's and Hotere's fish—as well as mutually empowering poetic strategies for articulating their activist claims. These juxtapositions also suggest that reading *across* texts offers a number of avenues for Indigenized methodologies of literary analysis and interpretation. Paradigms for juxtaposition, which I describe throughout this book as trans-Indigenous, do not obligate scholars to force diverse Indigenous texts from distinct Indigenous worldviews and from distinct Indigenous histories into categories of sameness. On the contrary, radical literary comparison through Indigenous juxtapositions can provoke more complex analyses of specific texts. "Moving differently" will not produce definitive readings, but it will place a more consistent and productive emphasis on the intellectual and artistic sovereignty of Indigenous writing (primarily) in English.

Writing (and Wronging) a Tale of a Whale

To bring the diverse engagements and "different" movements of this chapter to closure, I conclude with a final set of Indigenous juxtapositions that trace the process through which a "local" Indigenous text was revisioned as self-consciously "global." In this process, linked as it is to the pursuit of international audiences and global capital, we can discern a (not so) surprising movement away from privileging the practices of Indigenous bilanguaging and multimedia expression toward the primacy of English translation, substitution, and representational simplification. This set of juxtapositions involves the several editions of *The Whale Rider*, Witi Ihimaera's humorous, politically savvy, and highly engaging novel for young adults. Although first published in Aotearoa New Zealand in 1987, Ihimaera's story of a young girl destined to become a leader in her rural community is best known in the United States (and elsewhere) in its adaptation to the internationally financed feature film *Whale Rider*, directed by the Pakeha filmmaker Niki Caro and released in 2003.[19] This circuitous route to a U.S. audience is ironic, since Ihimaera drafted the original version of the novel in New York City while on diplomatic assignment for New Zealand. As he writes in his 2003 author's note, "In this American edition, *The Whale Rider* makes a return visit to the country in which it was written" (n.p.). I leave it to others to trace the considerable changes Caro and her production team made in adapting and updating Ihimaera's representation of East Coast Māori culture, history, politics, gender relations, and spirituality into a film for global and, perhaps especially, U.S. consumption. Instead, I focus on the changes Ihimaera himself made for the U.S./international edition of his novel, released as a marketing tie-in for the film's U.S. distribution.

The changes to the print text are more difficult to chart than are the more dramatic changes made for the film. For example, Caro all but eliminates the several scenes in the novel written from the perspective of a pod of migrating whales, which in the original text accentuate the mythic dimensions of the story and voice protest against nuclear testing in the Pacific and its devastating impact on the environment. These scenes would have been difficult to re-create on screen without breaking the film's predominantly realistic conventions. In place of Ihimaera's original five brief chapters of contemporary description, memories, and dialogue from the whales' perspectives, Caro substitutes documentary footage of whales at sea, overdubbed with haunting, ethereal music. In contrast, the U.S. edition of the novel retains Ihimaera's original chapters but revises their diction. Although subtle, these changes to the language of the U.S. edition are nonetheless significant in their effects. While international audiences of Caro's film can assess the merits of her work as an audio-visual "version" or "translation" of the novel *The Whale Rider*, the U.S. audience has little choice but to read the U.S. edition as an accurate representation—a verbatim copy—of Ihimaera's original. Since no version of the novel was widely available outside Aotearoa New Zealand until 2003, few U.S. or other international readers will have access to the New Zealand edition, and few are likely to make comparisons. For most it will be as though the New Zealand edition never existed. It is only when the several editions are placed side by side that the full extent and impact of Ihimaera's translations, substitutions, and deletions become evident.

Similar to Patricia Grace in her 1986 novel *Potiki*, in the original 1987 edition of *The Whale Rider* Ihimaera employs Māori-language words and phrases without italics (a common practice in Aotearoa New Zealand), mostly without direct translation in the text and without a glossary. This first version of *The Whale Rider* also includes six grayscale illustrations by the Māori artist John Hovell. In each of the novel's six sections, the section title appears on its own page, followed by its corresponding grayscale illustration printed across two open pages, followed by the numbered chapters of the section. Hovell's evocative illustrations are "trans-customary," following Jahnke's definition, in that they demonstrate visual empathy with the curvilinear patterns of Māori carving in wood, stone, and bone, evoking koru (spiral) and matau (fishhook) designs, especially in their stylized depictions of adult whales and calves. Several demonstrate empathy, as well, with broader Polynesian visual art practices, such as the distinctive geometric patterning of tapa (bark cloth) and the distinctive floral patterning of other textiles and with European visual art practices, such as the distinctive patterning of stained-glass windows in Christian churches.

In 1995, in the wake of successful Māori-language activism in the 1980s, a Māori-language edition of *The Whale Rider* was published in Aotearoa New Zealand under the title *Te Kaieke Tohorā*, translated by the Māori language and culture specialist Timoti Karetu. This version is faithful to Ihimaera's original, and it reprints Hovell's six grayscale illustrations. However, Karetu's monolingual Māori translation is unable to maintain at least one defining aspect of Ihimaera's original. In the first edition Ihimaera repeatedly juxtaposes Māori and English words and phrases. These juxtapositions of language systems are productive throughout, but they are especially central to chapter 19 in the epilogue, the final section written from the perspective of the whales, since the whales' dialogue is rendered exclusively in Māori without translation. The potential aesthetic and, importantly, cultural and political effects of these juxtapositions are necessarily lost in Karetu's monolingual translation to Māori.

In 2003, the novel was published for the first time in the United States, again in the original English, as a marketing tie-in for the award-winning international film *Whale Rider*. In this third version, published under the original title, Ihimaera translates a significant portion of the Māori language included in the New Zealand edition into English; he deletes certain Māori passages altogether; he places the novel's remaining Māori in italics, following U.S. rather than New Zealand publishing conventions, marking Māori language as "foreign"; and finally, he creates a glossary of English translations for the remaining eighty-six "foreign" Māori words and phrases.[20] Not surprisingly, the U.S. edition replaces New Zealand (British) spellings with American spellings. And perhaps understandably, as part of its marketing function, the U.S. edition features photographic stills from the film *Whale Rider* on its covers. Less expectedly, this third edition deletes Hovell's grayscale illustrations and does not replace them with either new illustrations or film stills. Instead, the first page of each section and the first page of each chapter feature a less evocative graphic of a faded koru (spiral figure).

It would require an additional chapter to fully juxtapose these three editions of Ihimaera's novel and explicate the different effects created by each version's specific deployments or deletions of English and Māori languages and Hovell's illustrations.[21] To close this chapter, I juxtapose three brief passages to demonstrate how the different versions privilege—and thus acknowledge—different categories of readers. Similar to Habib's "When I of Fish Eat" and Grace's *Potiki*, the first edition privileges bilanguaging readers of Māori and English. These actively bilingual and bicultural readers have access to more of the novel's potential meaning than do monolingual or monocultural readers of English. In an obvious contrast, the second edition, the Māori-language translation, privileges bilingual readers of Māori and English. In 1995, as well as today, few if any potential readers in Aotearoa New Zealand (or elsewhere) will be monolingual readers of Māori. The most likely audience for the second edition is current or former students of Māori language, who will likely have access to the original edition for comparison. Finally, the third edition privileges U.S. (and international) readers with limited or no knowledge of Māori language or culture. This audience is unlikely to have access to the original edition and may be unaware of its existence.

Many of the differences across the three editions reflect relatively minor changes, especially when considered separately. Their individual effects are often subtle. Consider, for instance, the opening sentences from the novel's prologue. In the 1987 New Zealand edition, the prologue is titled "The Coming of Kahutia Te Rangi"; in the 1995 Māori-language translation, it is titled, similarly, "Te Haerenga mai o Kahutia-te-rangi"; in the 2003 U.S. edition, it is revised as "The Whale

Rider."[22] Kahutia Te Rangi is the name of a legendary ancestor, also known as Paikea, who journeyed from central Polynesia to the east coast of Aotearoa riding on the back of a whale. His mythic story and its cultural symbolism underpin the novel's contemporary conflicts and resolution. In the juxtapositions below, I have added italics to draw attention to elements that change across the three versions:

> In the old days, in the years that have gone before us, the land and sea felt a great emptiness, a yearning. The mountains were like *the poutama, the* stairway to heaven, and the lush green rainforest was a rippling *kakahu* of many *colours.* The sky was iridescent *paua,* swirling with the *kowhaiwhai* patterns of wind and clouds; sometimes it reflected the prisms of rainbow or southern aurora. The sea was ever-changing *pounamu,* shimmering and seamless to the sky. (1987, 4)

> I ngā rā o nehe, i ngā tau o mua noa atu i a tātou, e kuatau ana te whenua me te moana, i te hematanga o te rangi me te whenua. Ko ngā maunga i rite tonu ki *te poutama, te* ara piki ki te rangi, ā, ko te ngahere e matomato ana, e mata ana anō nei he *kākahu* tae huhua e hāki ana. Anō nei he kākara *pāua* te rangi, i reira e koromiomio ana te hau me te kapua, pēnei i te *kōwhaiwhai,* he wā anō whakaatatia ai ngā mata tīhoi o te kōpere, o te hīnga ake rānei o te rā i te tonga. Ko te moana anō nei he *pounamu* e rite tonu ana te huri o te āhua, e ārohirohi ana, e maurua kore ana, ā, tae noa ki te rangi. (1995, 10)

> In the old days, in the years that have gone before us, the land and sea felt a great emptiness, a yearning. The mountains were like *a stairway to heaven,* and the lush green rainforest was a rippling *cloak* of many *colors.* The sky was *iridescent,* swirling with the *patterns* of wind and clouds; sometimes it reflected the prisms of rainbow or southern aurora. The sea was *ever-changing,* shimmering and seamless to the sky. (2003, 3)

In the original New Zealand edition, Ihimaera's imagery evokes the customary practices of Māori arts, several of which are typically associated with the wharenui (meeting house), as well as artistic materials indigenous to Aotearoa and the waters off its coasts. The poutama, "stairway to heaven," is a pattern often used in woven tutkutuku panels placed between carvings on the interior walls of meeting houses. Similarly, the exposed rafters of meetings houses are often painted with highly stylized kowhaiwhai patterns, which reference elements of the natural world and indicate whakapapa (genealogy). The shell of the pāua, a species of abalone, is often used to decorate the eyes of ancestors carved on the meeting house's exterior and interior walls; pāua also is used to decorate other types of carving. A kakahu can be described as a "cloak" or "cape," but in the context of "a rippling kakahu of many colours," it suggests, more specifically, a customary and highly prized Māori garment decorated with the bright feathers of birds. Pounamu refers to nephrite jade or "greenstone," which is indigenous to the South Island of Aotearoa (in Māori, Te Wai Pounamu, "The Greenstone Waters"); this stone occurs naturally in many color variations, from dark to milky green, and is highly prized as a medium for carving. Traditional stories link pounamu's creation to the sea.

Taken together, these elements from the opening sentences of the 1987 edition situate Ihimaera's story within a world distinctly Māori. The passage is preceded by the prologue's title, which invokes the name of the Māori ancestor who became "the whale rider," as well as by Hovell's first grayscale illustration, which depicts this ancestor riding the famous whale across the sea. In Hovell's stylized image, the face of the ancestor features prominent moko, distinctive Māori tattooing. The whale he rides demonstrates visual empathy with the customary practices of Māori carving; unlike the face of the ancestor, which is highly representational, the head of the whale has been abstracted into a series of interlocking koru (spirals). The waves of the sea are similarly abstracted, creating the suggestion of vitality and movement. Not surprisingly, all of the above elements are carried over in the 1995 Māori-language translation, with the exception of Ihimaera's original juxtaposition of Māori and English. (Karetu even maintains Ihimaera's explanation of the poutama as "the stairway to heaven": "te ara piki ki te rangi.") In stark contrast, all of the specifically Māori elements from the first edition are either deleted from the 2003 U.S. edition or translated into a less specific English-language term or phrase. No Māori terms remain in the passage, and thus, no juxtapositions remain of Māori and English. This edition deletes Hovell's illustration and its trans-customary visual effects. The overall impact is to make the passage less distinctly Māori and less rich in terms of its imagery and symbolism. Arguably, though, these changes do not significantly alter the narrative or its impact.

Now consider the three versions of a brief passage taken from the final paragraphs of the prologue, which provide information essential to the novel's main plotline and eventual resolution. Again, I have added italics to indicate elements that change:

He [the whale rider] saw far off the land long sought and now found, and he began to fling *small spears of mauri* seaward and landward on his magnificent journey toward the land.

Some of the *mauri* in mid flight turned into pigeons. (1987, 6)

Ka kite atu i te whenua i tawhiti, kua roa e kimihia ana, ā, i nāianei kua kitea ka tīmata tana hōreke *tao iti, tao mauri* ki uta, ki tai i a ia e rere whakahirahira rā ki uta.

Ko ētahi o ngā *mauri* i te wā e rere tonu ana i huri hei kererū. (1995, 12)

He [the whale rider] saw far off the land long sought and now found, and he began to fling *small spears* seaward and landward on his magnificent journey toward the land.

Some of the *spears* in midflight turned into pigeons. (2003, 6)

Although these changes are similar to those in the first passage, the effect of deleting the Māori term *mauri* from the 2003 U.S. edition is far more significant than the earlier deletions of *poutama, kakahu, paua, kowhaiwhai,* and *pounamu.* Mauri is typically translated into English as "life force" or "life principle." (Recall the discussion of the formulaic phrase *Tihei mauri ora,* "the sneeze of life.") Mauri also can mean a material symbol of a specific life force. In Ihimaera's original version, one of the whale rider's "small spears of mauri" represents the specific life force of pigeons; he carries this force to Aotearoa to animate its forests. As the passage continues, another mauri flung by the whale rider toward the sea represents the specific life force of eels, which then animates the surrounding waters. In the original edition, "spears" describes the *shape* of the mauri, these material symbols of animating life force brought from central Polynesia to Aotearoa. This adjectival use of "spears" carries over in the 1995 Māori translation. In the U.S. edition, however, "spears" becomes the significant noun, which for U.S. (or international) readers with limited or no knowledge of Māori language or culture, cannot signify "animating life force." In the revised passage the whale rider flings "small spears" toward the land and sea; readers are left to wonder why these inanimate objects, typically associated with violence, magically transform into pigeons and eels. As the novel develops, the deletion of the spiritual and philosophical concept of mauri affects the audience's ability to make sense of the narrative's central conflict and ultimate resolution, which hinges on understanding that the contemporary whale rider, a young girl, is connected to one of these "spears of mauri" brought to Aotearoa by her ancestor, the original whale rider. The specific animating life force of this mauri has been held in reserve until needed by the community.[23]

Finally, consider the three versions of a passage that occurs in the epilogue, the full understanding of which also depends on the spiritual and philosophical concept of mauri. The epilogue includes chapter 19, one of five written from the perspective of the whales at sea; like the others, chapter 19 is printed in italics in all three editions, which I have omitted for ease of analysis. As in the previous examples, I have added italics to highlight elements that change across the versions:

> The *kai karanga* saw the *toa taiaha* preparing to give her a sharp nip in the behind. *She* moved quickly toward the *koroua* and let a fin accidentally on purpose caress the place of his deepest pleasure. "*Engari,*" she told the *koroua*, "*i titiro ahau i te tekoteko, aua.*" She gave her head two shakes to *emphasise* that when she had looked at the *tekoteko* it didn't look like Paikea at all. Instead, the *tekoteko* looked like a human girl. "*He mokopuna na Paikea, pea?*" she asked modestly. "*He mauri no Paikea?*" Her song inflected the questions with graceful ornamentation. (1987, 114)

> Kua kite atu te *kaikaranga* i te *toa taiaha* e whakatika ana ki te wero mai i a ia ki te tou. Tere tonu tana neke atu ki te *koroua*

ka tuku i tētahi o ana pakipaki kia pā noa tau ki te wāhi *o te kor;oua* e tino rongo ai ia i te reka, anō nei i tūpono noa engari he mea āta whakapā atu e te *kaikaranga*. Ka kī atu ia ki te *koroua*, *"Engari i titiro atu ahau ki te tekoteko, aua."* E rua ngā rūrūtanga i tōna māhunga hei whakaū noa i tāna kōrero i a ia i titiro atu ai ki te *tekoteko* kāore i rite ki a Paikea te āhua. I rite kē te *tekoteko* ki te kōtiro, tangata nei. Ka pātai ia me te paku whakamā anō, *"He mokopuna pea nā Paikea? He mauri nō Paikea?"* Ko tana waiata i pātai i ana pātai me ngā whakapaipai i te taha. (1995, 135)

The *old mother whale* saw the *warrior whales* preparing to give her a sharp nip in the behind. She moved quickly toward the *ancient bull whale* and let a fin accidentally on purpose caress the place of his deepest pleasure. *"But,"* she told *him*, *"I can see the rider and it's not who you think it is."* She gave her head two shakes to *emphasize* that when she had looked at the *rider*, it didn't look like Paikea at all. Instead, the *rider* looked like a human girl. *"Perhaps it's a descendant of your lord?"* she asked modestly. *"Think back, husband."* Her song inflected the questions with graceful ornamentation. (2003, 140–41)

Similar to the first example, the 1987 New Zealand edition resonates with specifically Māori imagery and deploys Māori language that is either revised or deleted in the 2003 U.S. edition. The "tekoteko" of the original, for instance, is not equivalent to the "rider" of the revision; rather, as discussed in relation to "Sad Joke on a Marae," *tekoteko* refers to a *carving* of an ancestor, such as that placed on the gable of a meeting house. Thus, the imagery of the original aligns the young girl riding the whale with her significant ancestor, Paikea, whose carved likeness sits atop the community's house. This alignment is emphasized, as well, in Hovell's final grayscale illustration, which precedes the epilogue in the original and Māori translation editions. The girl riding the whale is positioned as a mirror image of her ancestor riding the whale in the first illustration. The head of the whale she rides is similarly abstracted into interlocking koru (spirals). Where her ancestor is depicted amid abstracted representations of waves moving in the sea, indicating perhaps his isolation during migration, the girl is depicted amid stylized representations of other whales, which demonstrate visual empathy with matau (fishhook designs) and other customary Māori icons and which indicate the girl's integration within a vibrant community.

The language of the original version, moreover, evokes a specifically Māori familial and social world, creating parallels between the individual whales and members of the human community. The Māori "kai karanga," for example, does not translate into English literally as the "old mother whale," as the U.S. edition suggests, but rather designates the senior female elder responsible for performing the karanga (call) that brings visitors onto the marae, aligning her with Nanny Flowers, the young girl's great-grandmother, and emphasizing less her age or role as a mother figure and more her gendered social power within the community. Similarly, "toa taiaha" does not translate literally as "warrior whales" but designates a warrior (toa) skilled in the martial art of the taiaha (fighting staff), a traditional weapon, aligning him with the young men of the community who work to maintain Māori traditions. And "koroua" does not translate literally as the "ancient bull whale" but designates a male elder, aligning him with Koro Apirana, the young girl's great-grandfather, and emphasizing his genealogical relationships to the larger community and his social, political, and spiritual responsibilities as its leader.

In addition to these changes, the U.S. edition again deletes the significant concept of mauri. In the first and second versions, the wise kai karanga asks the koroua, who mourns the loss of the original whale rider, not one but two distinct questions: first, if the person riding the koroua's back might be a *descendant* (mokopuna) belonging to Paikea and, second, if this person might be a *mauri* belonging to Paikea. The grammatical construction of the Māori-language dialogue both in the original and in the Māori translation distinguishes between two categories of "belonging to." When the kai karanga refers to the possibility that the rider is a mokopuna, she uses "na," indicating Paikea's *dominant possession* of his possible descendant—that is, indicating that ancestors are dominant in relation to their descendants. When she refers to the possibility that the rider is a mauri, she uses the contrasting "no," indicating Paikea's *subordinate possession* of this possible animating life force—that is, indicating that all humans, including illustrious ancestors, are subordinate in relation to spiritual forces. Thus, in the concise grammar of the original dialogue, the kai karanga suggests that the contemporary girl riding the koroua occupies a complex position vis-à-vis both the whale pod and the human community—as well as vis-à-vis both the past and the present—a mediating position that is socially and spiritually potent. This meaning is lost in the Māori deletions and English substitutions of the U.S. edition.[24]

These brief examples indicate the kinds of changes Ihimaera made in revising *The Whale Rider* for U.S. and international audiences. Most of these readers likely came to the novel through its association with the international film *Whale Rider* rather than through its association with Ihimaera, Māori language, or Māori culture. Part of the activist potential of Ihimaera's original version lies in its visible—and, read aloud, audible—process of bilanguaging, its Indigenous intervention within New Zealand English, its production of meaning from within the linguistic and cultural space between Māori and English languages, and its active engagement with the politics of their asymmetry in contemporary Aotearoa New Zealand. The 1987 edition privileges—and thus acknowledges—a bilanguaging audience. The 1995 Māori-language translation declares its own activist potential: its very existence argues for the ongoing vitality of te reo Māori, its ability to adapt to alphabetic writing and to the conventions of longer works of prose fiction. It asserts an audience of readers of te reo. In practice, the majority (if not all) of these readers will be bilingual readers of Māori and English rather than monolingual readers of Māori. They will have access to the original as a resource, making the two versions an excellent pedagogical tool in the ongoing activist promotion of Māori-language literacy. One can imagine a future, fully bilingual edition that maintains the original's practices of bilanguaging by juxtaposing the two versions on facing pages. The U.S. edition, however, in both its minor and more significant changes, revises or deletes much of the original version's potential for Indigenous bilanguaging. In the process, these changes undermine much of the novel's potential to contribute to Indigenous activism abroad, especially its potential for specifically literary assertions of artistic sovereignty.

The trajectory of Ihimaera's revision process represents one possible, perhaps unanticipated result of attempting to revision the Indigenous "local" as the self-consciously Indigenous "global." Although successful in its wide distribution for bringing attention (and, no doubt, tourism) to New Zealand, the U.S. edition of *The Whale Rider* is less successful as a distinctly Māori text. The contrast with Momaday's trajectory in producing "Carnegie, Oklahoma, 1919" from "The Gourd Dancer" and *The Names* is instructive. Whereas Momaday moves toward condensation, Indigenous aesthetics, and situated exposition in the several versions that he authored, from the mid-1970s into the 1990s, of the story of the giveaway that honored his grandfather, Ihimaera moves toward expansiveness, globalized aesthetics, and situated opacity (those unexplained "spears") in retrofitting his 1987 novel for the world market in 2003. Where Momaday asks audiences to work harder at Indigenous interpretation and, in essence, to understand *more* in order to fully appreciate and enjoy his work on its own terms, Ihimaera invites audiences to assume they already understand everything they might need or want to know.

Siting Earthworks, Navigating Waka

Patterns of Indigenous Settlement in Allison Hedge Coke's
Blood Run and Robert Sullivan's *Star Waka*

The stars are very important to me mythically. To think of losing the
stars represents to me a very deep wound.

▶ N. Scott Momaday

In a 1986 interview with Louis Owens (Choctaw/Cherokee), N. Scott
Momaday warns that increasing light pollution in the U.S. desert
Southwest represents far more than a technical problem for astronomers or an aesthetic nuisance for artists and romantics who turn their
eyes skyward alongside professional watchers of the stars. For all citizens, Momaday argues, light pollution represents a moral dilemma.
For those who identify as Indigenous, whether living in the southwestern deserts of what is now the United States or in diverse land- and
waterscapes around the globe, such pollution represents a potential
crisis of kinship. If light pollution continues to escalate, will future
generations be able to see the stars and other celestial bodies moving
above them? In so many cultural traditions, the bright stars and re-
flecting planets—along with the life-giving sun and the earth's primary
traveling companion, the moon—are coded into story, image, and ritual that tether their regular orbits and provocative arrangements in
the night sky to the ongoing histories of human communities. Without their visible presence, will future generations, like their ancestors
before them, be able to imagine kinship with the larger cosmos and,
ultimately, with each other?

Technologies for recording cosmic kinship abound in Indigenous
traditions, as do technologies for utilizing the observed movements
of celestial bodies for a wide range of "applied" and "theoretical" arts
and sciences, from the calendrical, orientational, cartographic, and

navigational to the aesthetic and spiritual, the social and political. In twentieth-century Indigenous literatures written (primarily) in English, such technologies feature both as metonymic markers for ancient forms of knowledge and as devices for developing themes and advancing plot. One thinks, for instance, of the "star map of the overhead sky in late September" that recurs in Leslie Marmon Silko's acclaimed 1977 novel *Ceremony*. Silko's story of personal and communal healing reveals itself to revolve around this map of the "Big Star constellation" (214). Drawn in a ceremonial sand painting by the medicine man Betonie and painted on the surface of an "old war shield [...] made from a hide," the star map guides the protagonist, Tayo, toward his dramatic encounter with—and resistance to—the "destroyers": "But he saw the constellation in the north sky, and the fourth star was directly above him; the pattern of the ceremony was in the stars [...]. His protection was there in the sky, in the position of the sun, in the pattern of the stars" (247). As the novel draws toward conclusion, Tayo is able to articulate the multiple functions of the star map in its ancient and modern forms. It helps him and others to align the present with significant events of the past and with possibilities for the future:

> He had arrived at the convergence of patterns; he could see them clearly now. The stars had always been with them, existing beyond memory, and they were all held together there. Under those same stars the people had come down from White House in the north. They had seen mountains shift and rivers change course and even disappear back into the earth; but always there were those stars. Accordingly, the story goes on with these stars of the old war shield; they go on, lasting until the fifth world ends, then maybe beyond. (254)

What sustains the power and relevance of the technology of the star map, Tayo understands, is its connection to multiple levels of natural and human patterning. The patterns converge at regular intervals; for those initiated into Indigenous technologies, these points of convergence can be predicted and, thus, engaged for healing and survival, continuance and resurgence.

More recently, as the dominant West anticipated and then marked the turning of a new century and the dawn of a new millennium—

acknowledging, at last, the global dilemmas and deep wounds of many kinds of pollution—at least two Indigenous writers rendered technologies similar to Silko's star map as central dramatic features of their work and as central sustaining logics for defining Indigenous identities, survivals, and resurgence in the contemporary world. In 1999, the Māori poet Robert Sullivan published *Star Waka*, a book-length sequence of related poems that explores the multiple meanings of *waka*, a term that indicates any kind of actual or figurative "vessel" but signifies, preeminently, large, ocean-voyaging "canoes." Guided at night by their knowledge of the patterns and perceived movements of stars, Polynesians migrated on waka to the South Pacific islands of Aotearoa and there transformed themselves into Māori.[1] In 2006, the American Indian poet Allison Hedge Coke (Cherokee/Huron/Creek) published *Blood Run*, also a book-length sequence of related poems organized around an Indigenous technology. Hedge Coke's sequence evokes the art, engineering, culture, and history associated with the Native American earthworks—often described as "mounds"—of the little-known Blood Run site located on both sides of the Big Sioux River on what is now the South Dakota–Iowa border. Similar to other earthworks sites located across the North American continent, the so-called mounds at Blood Run were built to mirror significant patterns and celestial movements in the sky.

In both their explicit contents and their more implicit poetic forms, Sullivan's and Hedge Coke's contemporary texts emphasize waka and earthworks as Indigenous technologies and, more precisely, as Indigenous technologies for settlement. *Star Waka* emphasizes themes of ancient, ongoing, and possible future histories of Polynesian exploration and migration; *Blood Run* emphasizes themes of ancient, ongoing, and possible future histories of Native American construction and trade. In this way, both texts disrupt the typical coding of these activities in dominant discourses as demarcating superior, fully human European or U.S. "settlers" from inferior, less than fully human "Natives." Moreover, the focus in each poetic text on Indigenous tenacity, survival, and endurance in the face of settler colonialisms complicates the concept of the *historical* settlement of "new" lands with implications of activism, legal battles, and public acts of moral suasion in the contemporary cause of *political* settlement. In their focus on Indigenous technologies that link human communities to earth and sky, these poetic texts assert the ability of the authors' Indigenous ancestors to embrace change and to create complex civilizations, and they assert the abilities of the descendants of those remarkable ancestors to continue to move, build, and grow, to continue, that is, to not only re-create themselves as individuals and communities but also to re-create their symbolic and physical worlds.

The emblematic technologies of ocean-voyaging waka navigated beneath stars and monumental earthworks sculpted to mirror sky suggest both a literary focus based on common Indigenous themes and a contextual framework based on shared Indigenous politics. By juxtaposing Sullivan's and Hedge Coke's book-length sequences of poems, in this chapter I demonstrate that each poet's literary achievement and each poet's activist message is located not exclusively in the explicit content, overt themes, or wordplay of his or her individual poems. Rather, those achievements and messages are located, as well—and perhaps more profoundly—in each book's complex formal structures and multiple structural patterns.[2]

Sullivan's sequence is composed of a core of one hundred poems and 2,001 lines, numbers that anticipate the new century and the new millennium. These poems are divided into three sections, indicated by three distinct systems of numbering that also can suggest temporal movement: Roman, Arabic, and Sullivan's own Indigenous "waka" numbering. In terms of style and form, the individual poems range from contemporary personal reflections to epic-inspired narratives based in oral traditions to iconic visual poems to dramatic personas who tell their own versions of the stories of sky, earth, and sea. Sullivan indicates in an introductory note that each poem must contain "a star, a waka or the ocean" (n.p.). Framing the sequence of one hundred numbered poems are two additional poems that are unnumbered: an opening "prayer" to "guide" the book on its journey across open water and a "sail" printed on the book's back cover with which to "launch" the sequence once again. The lack of numbering for this prayer and sail situates the poetic frame outside the multiple systems for counting time acknowledged in the poetic core.

Hedge Coke's book-length sequence is structured even more elaborately as a series of frames within frames. The table of contents lists a total of seventy-one distinct components. A core of sixty-four dramatic persona poems that animate the Blood Run site are framed by two longer, epic-inspired narrative poems that overview and predict history; these, in turn, are framed by five nonpoetic pieces that provide definitions of key terms and relevant site details for Blood Run and that position Hedge Coke as author, teacher, and activist. The poetic sequence is preceded by a formal introduction written by the Anishinaabe scholar and poet Margaret Noori, an author's foreword, and an author's note, while sets of extensive acknowledgements and dedications follow its conclusion. In addition, the sequence of two narrative and sixty-four persona poems is arranged into five formal sections of varying length. In the initial four, numbering and titling suggest both temporal and thematic movement, from a utopian distant past in sections 1, "Dawning," and 2, "Origin," to a disrupted near past and volatile present in section 3, "Intrusions," to an anticipation of further danger in section 4, "Portend." The unnumbered fifth section, "Epilogue," then points toward the still unknown future(s) of Blood Run.

My argument in this chapter is that Sullivan and Hedge Coke make their strongest literary assertions and most forceful activist claims in *Star Waka* and *Blood Run* at this primary yet subtle level of sequencing. In the macrostructures of these book-length poetic works, Sullivan and Hedge Coke actively demonstrate the efficacy of ancient, historical, and ongoing Indigenous technologies, for it is at this level that they literally embody aspects of these technologies in their contemporary poetic practice. (This is another instance of Jahnke's notion of artistic "empathy" discussed in chapter 4.) Each book's poetic structures, built upon the distinct technologies of Polynesian waka and Native American earthworks, respectively, are highly suggestive of the artist, cultures, and histories behind their production. But while the two sequences share this aspect, each is based in distinct principles of organization and in distinct modes of patterning.

In the following sections I map the macrostructure of each poetic sequence and trace a number of the parallels, complements, inversions, and other regular patterns of relationships created in the interactions between these macrostructures and the structures of specific subsections, poems, stanzas, and lines in each sequence. Though not exhaustive, these analyses demonstrate how multiple relationships among levels of poetic structures generate particular forms of aesthetic pleasure and particular modes of activist discourse within each book's thematic anchoring in a specific Indigenous technology. Similar to the multiple representations of Silko's star map, the multiple modes of structural patterning evident in Sullivan's *Star Waka* and Hedge Coke's *Blood Run* align to orient readers to interpret waka and earthworks technologies from particular perspectives that are culturally and politically situated. Oriented to see regular, persistent systems of natural, cosmic, and human patterning, readers are positioned to imagine the persistence and resurgence of Indigenous worlds rather than to submit to the dominant culture's ongoing assertions of their inevitable erasure.

Earth Sculpted to Mirror Sky

For thousands of years, Indigenous peoples living across the North American continent layered rock and packed soil into durable, multiply functional, highly graphic constructions of large-scale earthworks. These raised forms marked territorial boundaries and significant roadways; they created focal points within urban settlements and within centers for economic trade, technological and artistic exchange, and intellectual and spiritual practice. Platform, conical, pyramid, ridgetop, geometric, and effigy "mounds" thus represent achievements of science and aesthetics on a monumental scale. They integrate the precise observation of natural phenomena with geometry and other abstract forms of knowledge, as well as with practical skills in mathematics, architectural design, engineering, and construction. Many earthworks were sculpted to mirror perceived patterns in the sky, both in the bodies of individual works and in the arrangements of multiple works into complex sites and cities; moreover, particular works were often aligned with specific celestial events, such as an equinox or solstice sunrise or sunset point on the horizon.

The best-known examples of extant Indigenous earthworks are the well-preserved and, in some cases, reconstructed ceremonial, burial, and boundary-marking works in Cahokia, Illinois, located along the Mississippi River outside of what is now St. Louis, Missouri. The earthworks at Cahokia date from about a thousand years before the present, and they include the majestic Monks Mound, a platform rising in multiple terraces to a height of nearly one hundred feet. Within this solar-focused complex, Monks Mound is sited to correspond to the sunrise points of the vernal and autumnal equinoxes and the summer and winter solstices. Other well-known examples include the large-scale geometric earthworks (outlines of circles, squares, and octagons) and the large-scale effigy earthworks (including Eagle Mound, Alligator Mound, and Serpent Mound) situated along the waterways of what is now central and southern Ohio. The oldest of these works date from more than two thousand years ago, and depending on their specific locations, they are sited to correspond to key solar, lunar, or other celestial events.

Contemporary researchers have determined, for instance, that the Octagon Earthworks located at what is now Newark, Ohio, is both a mathematically perfect octagon the size of a football field and a type of lunar calendar that marks the 18.6-year cycle of the moon's northernmost and southernmost rise and set points along the horizon. Remarkably, the accurate observation of these sky phenomena is possible in North America only within a restricted range of latitude. The Octagon Earthworks is thus uniquely sited to facilitate a particular set of astronomical observations.[3] Researchers also have determined that the complex of geometric earthworks at Newark, which includes relatively few burial mounds, is connected to a related complex, the High Banks Works, located sixty miles to the southwest, near the town of Chillicothe, which includes a relatively large number of burial mounds and charnel houses. The two sites, each of which features the mounded outline of a large octagon connected to the mounded outline of a large circle, appear to have been connected by a straight and bounded roadway approximately two hundred feet wide. At certain times of the year, this roadway became aligned beneath the visible stars of the Milky Way, creating a "star path" between the lunar observation site at Newark and the mixed solar and lunar internment site at Chillicothe.[4] In response to these and other types of archaeologically based evidence, including the presence of natural materials and trade items originating great distances from central and southern Ohio (copper, obsidian, mica, silver, meteoric iron, marine shells, bear and shark teeth), researchers speculate that beginning roughly two thousand years ago, the region was a center for Indigenous North American social, spiritual, and, importantly, intellectual and artistic activity and exchange. Archeologists have located over six hundred earthworks within the contemporary borders of Ohio, and there are literally thousands of individual earthworks and earthworks complexes sited across the North American continent, some dating to more than five thousand years ago.

Earthworks have been sketched, mapped, and surveyed, some-times excavated, and too often looted by non-Indigenous settlers and their descendants since at least the eighteenth century. However, it is a twentieth-century technology—aerial photography—that has en-abled contemporary viewers to see individual earthworks, bounded roadways, and earthwork complexes from a great height, the only per-spective from which these works can be viewed as complete wholes. (Some archaeologists and art historians suggest that the geometric shapes and aesthetic forms of earthworks can be appreciated *only* from this overhead perspective and, thus, argue that earthworks may not have been intended primarily for human viewing at all.[5]) Aerial photography has made it possible to consider how these large-scale constructions of packed earth function as and within sign systems in what are increasingly revealed to be regularized patterns.

Drawing on knowledge gained from conventional surveying, map-ping, and excavation, as well as from aerial photography, the legibility of earthworks and their systematic patterning has been further en-hanced by the development of computer-generated models for par-ticular sites.[6] In addition, in 2008 researchers in Ohio began to sur-vey earthworks through the aircraft-based use of the optical remote-sensing technology known as Light Detection and Ranging (LiDAR), which deploys laser pulses to measure ground elevation. Combined with Global Positioning Satellite (GPS) data, LiDAR creates highly detailed, three-dimensional, color-coded imaging of topographic data. These vivid pictures make it possible to see evidence of earthworks no longer visible to the naked eye, as well as to conceptualize more pre-cisely the specific siting, geometric patterning, and celestial alignments of individual earthworks, roadways, and earthwork complexes. The archaeologist William Romain and his colleagues have demonstrated how LiDAR imaging strengthens hypotheses about Ohio earthworks that are based on ground-level observations and measurements, such as the finding that these works are consistently located near water and that they typically align with solar and/or lunar events. LiDAR has validated additional speculations, as well, confirming that Ohio earthworks are consistently oriented to the lay of the land, often run-ning parallel to natural ridges or embankments, and that geometric earthworks (outlines of circles, squares, and octagons) are typically "nested"—that is, calibrated to fit within each other, even when located at some distance apart. Perhaps most intriguingly, LiDAR has confirmed speculation that the sizes of the major Ohio earthworks all appear to be based on a consistent unit of measurement, that unit's multiples, and that unit's key geometric complements.[7] Romain suggests that any one of these aspects constitutes a striking achievement in the construction of earthworks. That Indigenous mound-building cultures spanning roughly fifteen hundred years of earthwork activity in Ohio were able to incorporate all of these aspects into the construction of specific sites at the same time is truly astounding.

In short, the more legible the earthworks become through aerial-based technologies—that is, the better contemporary viewers are able to see these works both as individual constructions and as multigenerational components within larger sign systems and patterns—the better we are able to understand earthworks as technologies and the better we are able to conceptualize earthworks as a form of Indigenous writing that inscribes knowledge not simply *on* the land but literally *through the medium of* the land itself.[8]

Although Hedge Coke did not have access to LiDAR imaging technology when she wrote *Blood Run*, her multiply coded, three-dimensionally imagined, and highly patterned sequence of poems—dense with data—similarly reveals new ways of seeing and new ways of conceptualizing an important earthworks site. In contrast to the three-dimensional images produced by LiDAR, however, Hedge Coke's sequence of poems provides a fourth dimension: perspectives that are explicitly and distinctly Indigenous.[9] *Blood Run* is the first American Indian literary text to give voice to the traditions of Indigenous mound-building cultures and, most strikingly, to the earthworks themselves.[10] And although she does not attempt to speak *for* the Oneota peoples of the past who built and then flourished at Blood Run, or for their descendants scattered across the region, who she believes can and should speak for themselves, Hedge Coke creates a series of sixty-four persona poems through which a range of elements associated with the Blood Run site and its long history are enabled to "speak."[11] These voices include the site's Ceremonial, Burial, and effigy Snake mounds, which speak both individually and collectively across the sequence, as well as the central River along which the site was constructed and the distant Horizon that marks its physical and conceptual borders. They also include "wild" and "domesticated" flora and fauna associated with the site, Dog, Starwood, Corn, Redwing Blackbird, Sunflower, Deer, Beaver, Buffalo, and Fox; the celestial bodies Morning Star, Sun, Moon, Blue Star, and North Star that move above and mirror back the site; an abstracted Memory that pervades the physical space across time; a Tree that marks time's passage since the "interruption" of natural life at Blood Run; and evidence of Indigenous writing systems on Cupped Boulder and Pipestone Tablets. In addition, there is an ambiguous spiritual guide who moves among these different aspects of space and time called Clan Sister and an ambiguous medicine called Esoterica, Skeletons and Ghosts of the interred dead, and, perhaps least expectedly, multiple non-Indigenous human and mechanical intruders to the site: Jesuit, Squatters, Tractor, Looters, Early Anthro, and Early Interpreter.[12]

In their discussion of the possibilities for LiDAR technology in the interpretation of earthworks, Romain and his colleague Jarrod Burks remark, "In the 19th century, when many of these sites were first mapped, thousands of years of erosion had already obscured the earthwork outlines. Thus, many of these earthwork sites have hidden discoveries waiting to be revealed by modern investigators and LiDAR imagery represents one avenue for reexamining these monumental sites."[13] The archaeologists caution, however, that

It is important to recognize that the process of creating a LiDAR image is part science and part art. Similar to a map, or drawing, what the viewer is presented with reflects what the image-maker wishes to show and is based on a series of subjective decisions. By changing perspective, lighting intensity and angle, height exaggeration, and color, very different results are achieved. Certain features can be exaggerated, others minimized.[14]

Hedge Coke harnesses this ambiguity between "science" and "art" in the animation of multiple personas and multiple perspectives in order to make visible at Blood Run what has not been seen with the human eye for over three centuries. What she creates is neither static nor simply a poetic "map" or "drawing." Rather, in her core sequence Hedge Coke creates a series of dramatic monologues spoken by thirty-seven distinct personas, some of which recur across the book's sixty-four persona

poems and some of which speak only once. Simultaneously, she creates a series of staged dialogues spoken between some twenty-nine
personas that become paired across the central and defining spine of
the open book. More than a sequence of related poems, at the core of
Hedge Coke's *Blood Run* is a script meant for embodied performance,
an activist play. In contrast to work produced by archaeologists, the
purpose of *Blood Run* is not to reveal "discoveries" about an exotic or
past culture. Rather, Hedge Coke's highly patterned, multidimensional
script endeavors to move audiences (and performers) in the present
so that they might act in the future, to persuade readers (and speakers and listeners) that the Blood Run site continues to carry intrinsic
value and thus deserves to be treated as sacred and preserved for future
generations.

Despite potential tensions between "science" and "art," the reading
practices developed for interpreting aerial photography and LiDAR-
produced three-dimensional imaging of earthworks are suggestive of
reading practices appropriate for interpreting the structural patterning
of Hedge Coke's *Blood Run*. Viewed from the surface—that is, moving among the intricate language and specific content of Hedge Coke's
five nonpoetic and sixty-six poetic pieces—the formal structures of
the sequence appear rather flat or two-dimensional; they do not stand
out as especially developed or regularized. Viewed from an "overhead"
perspective and at a relatively great height, however, the book's macrostructure becomes more clearly visible and increasingly legible. The
patterning of Hedge Coke's sequence of diverse but multiply related
poetic and nonpoetic forms is revealed to be highly complex—even,
one might argue, as three- or possibly four-dimensional.[15] From an
aerial position we can better see the mathematics and geometry at the
foundation of Hedge Coke's carefully constructed "earth"-works and
better determine the specific units of measurement on which the poet
has based individual constructions and complexes and their multiple
alignments and, indeed, multiple nestings.

Viewed from above, the world built in Hedge Coke's *Blood Run* is
revealed to be based on a principle of layering diverse forms and materials, the construction technique for actual Indigenous earthworks.
This textual world of sections, poems, stanzas, lines, words, and syllables is also revealed to be based on the repetition, recombination, and
reconfiguration of a limited set of natural numbers—four; three; their

sum, seven; and multiples of all three—as well as on the repetition, recombination, and reconfiguration of the sequence of primes, those natural numbers that can be divided only by themselves and the number one, which is itself unique in the sense that one is neither a prime nor a composite number.[16] An aerial analysis of the title page of *Blood Run* begins to reveal the significance of these repetitions, recombinations, and reconfigurations for building Hedge Coke's conception of Indigenous settlement. The title and author information Hedge Coke presents is organized into four horizontal lines or layers, and each is made distinct not only through variable spacing but also through differences in typeface, font, size, and capitalization (see Figure 10). Reading from the top down, the sequence begins with the primary title, "Blood Run," in a large, bold typeface, followed by a space and then by a secondary title, "Free Verse Play," in a smaller, italicized typeface. The second layer is followed by a second, larger space and then by a tertiary title and preposition, "Earthworks By," in small caps. The third layer is followed by a more narrow space and then by the author's full name, "Allison Adelle Hedge Coke," in bold small caps. An excavation of the four layers moves from the bold surface of the physical site— that is, the boldly marked surface of Blood Run itself—to the italicized "slopes" of the book's two primary genre classifications—"free verse" poetry and embodied dramatic "play"—to the central, "capital" concept of the construction of "earthworks" "by" a particular people, and finally to the four-part, boldly "capitalized" base of the author's full name.[17]

The most significant unit of measurement in the title page, as in the book as a whole, is the number four. In many Indigenous North American cultures, the number four is associated with the cardinal directions and recognized in the regular patterns of the seasons and other natural phenomena. Moreover, in these cultures four is often associated with ritual activity, with completed action, and with balance or harmony; four is thus often associated with the sacred. In the specific context of contemporary literary production, these and other associations have meant that four has been used as a primary organizing structure in a number of twentieth- and twenty-first-century American Indian poems, plays, and novels, including Momaday's *House Made of Dawn*, Silko's *Ceremony*, and Thomas King's *Green Grass, Running Water*, among others. Mathematically, while four is not prime, it is the square of two, the first and only even prime. Four thus

Blood Run

Free Verse Play

EARTHWORKS BY

ALLISON ADELLE HEDGE COKE

SALT

CAMBRIDGE

FIGURE 10. The title page of *Blood Run* by Hedge Coke is organized into four horizontal lines or layers, and each is made distinct not only through variable spacing but also through differences in typeface, font, size, and capitalization.

evokes balance, harmony, and completion by making the first and only even prime two-dimensional.

Hedge Coke's second basic unit of measurement for *Blood Run*, three, is the second (and first odd) prime. As noted in chapter 3 in the discussion of the semiotic geometry of Navajo weaving, in at least some Indigenous North American cultures three, in contrast to four and other even numbers, is associated with creative activity and with action that is incomplete and ongoing. The sum of four and three is seven, Hedge Coke's third basic unit of measurement for *Blood Run*. Seven is the fourth prime, and like the natural number four, it is associated with the sacred in many Indigenous North American cultures. Cherokee social organization, for instance, with which Hedge Coke identifies, is arranged into seven principal clans. Moreover, within Cherokee medicinal texts, these numbers calibrate the geographical world with the cosmological world: while the number four indicates a two-dimensional, horizontal schematic of the world divided into the four cardinal directions, the number seven describes a three-dimensional, spherical schematic that adds to the four cardinal directions the three complementary spatial positions zenith (above), nadir (below), and center.[18] As we shall see, in addition to the auspicious numbers four, three, seven, and their multiples, the sequence of the first twenty-four primes, which range from two to eighty-nine, and the condition of "primality" are also significant for measuring Hedge Coke's earthworks and for building her conception of Indigenous settlement in *Blood Run*.

Consider the following measurements in Figure 11 of the words and syllables in each layer of the *Blood Run* title page and how each can be mapped onto information presented in the book's table of contents. The recurrence of Hedge Coke's basic units of measurement becomes increasingly visible when we examine the title page in relation to the table of contents' schematic overview of the macrostructure for *Blood Run*. As noted, the table lists a total of seventy-one distinct components to the book; seventy-one is the twentieth prime.[19] Similar to the title page, the table of contents reveals a technique of layering diverse forms and materials. Of the seventy-one components, five are nonpoetic; three of these precede the book's sixty-six poems (Noori's introduction, Hedge Coke's foreword and note), and two follow (the acknowledgements and dedications).[20] Two, three, and five are the first,

Layer	Words	Syllables	Mathematical results	Correspondences
1	2	2	2×2 or $2^2 = 4$	basic unit of measurement
2	3	3	$3 \times 3 \times 3$ or $3^3 = 27$	poems in section 3
3	2	3	$2 \times 2 \times 2$ or $2^3 = 8$	poems in section 4
4	4	7	$4 \times 7 = 28$	poems in section 2

FIGURE 11. Measurements of the words and syllables in each layer of the *Blood Run* title page.

second, and third primes. The book's central core, however, is the sequence of sixty-four persona poems, which are divided across sections 2 (twenty-eight persona poems), 3 (twenty-seven persona poems), and 4 (eight persona poems) and the epilogue (one persona poem). Sixty-four is the square of eight, a number associated with the third layer of the title page and the number of poems included in section 4, "Portend." Sixty-four also can be factored as four raised to the third power, $4 \times 4 \times 4$, or four cubed—what we might think of as the sacred basic unit of measurement, four, made three-dimensional.

By now the significance of the book's larger sequence of sixty-six poems organized into four numbered and titled sections will have become increasingly legible.[21] In addition, we can note again that one, the number of poems in section 1, "Dawning," is neither a prime nor a composite number; one stands alone as itself and can be multiplied by itself infinitely—squared, cubed, quadrupled, and so forth—and produce the consistent result of one. Section 1 is composed of the first narrative poem, "Before Next Dawning," which offers an expansive overview of the history of Indigenous peoples in the Americas in a total of 176 lines.[22] At first glance this number appears arbitrary. However, 176 indexes the number of earthworks still extant when the Blood Run site was mapped at the end of the nineteenth century, a fact to which Hedge Coke draws attention in her author's note (xiv). It can be factored as 4×44, emphasizing the book's sacred basic unit of measurement, four, and in effect evoking its cube and, thus, its three-dimensionality; this factoring of 176, in other words, evokes the number sixty-four ($4 \times 4 \times 4$), the number of persona poems that make up *Blood Run*. Hedge Coke's alignment of the numbers one and 176 thus asserts both the singularity and the multidimensional sacredness of Indigenous settlement at the Blood Run site.

The measurement of other sections is equally suggestive of thematic connections to Indigenous settlement. Section 2, "Origin," is composed of twenty-eight persona poems, the result of four, the book's basic unit of measurement and primary but not prime sacred number, multiplied by seven, the fourth prime and another number aligned with the sacred. Section 3, "Intrusions," is composed of twenty-seven persona poems, the cube of three ($3 \times 3 \times 3$), the second prime and a number associated with ongoing and incomplete action. And section 4, "Portend," is composed of eight persona poems, the result of four multiplied by two, the first prime, and also the cube of two ($2 \times 2 \times 2$). Cubing suggests not only geometric three-dimensionality but also movement in multiple directions and general vitality. Indeed, the cubing of the first (and only even) prime—multiplying two by itself three times—is suggestive in section 4 of the possibility of a restorative, fully functional future at Blood Run that is both three-dimensional and balanced. Finally, the unnumbered epilogue is composed of two poems, the sixty-fourth and final persona poem and the second narrative poem, "When the Animals Leave This Place." The latter is composed of eighty-nine lines, the twenty-fourth prime.[23] Ending with a section of only two poems repeats and emphasizes the first prime, two, the square root of the basic unit of measurement, four, potentially adding a fourth dimension—time—to section 4's prophecy for the future.

This line of aerial analysis of the book's macrostructure can be extended, as well, to Hedge Coke's core sequence of sixty-four persona poems, which is composed of thirty-seven distinct personas. Thirty-seven is the twelfth prime, and twelve is the product of the two basic units of measurement for *Blood Run* (4×3). Of these thirty-seven distinct personas, twelve can themselves be considered prime if we enumerate the order of their first appearance in the sequence. (Thus, the second, third, fifth, seventh, eleventh, thirteenth, seventeenth, nineteenth, twenty-third, twenty-ninth, thirty-first, and thirty-seventh personas can be considered prime.)[24] Ten of the sequence's thirty-seven distinct personas speak more than once, while twenty-seven speak only once.[25] Of the twelve personas considered prime, four speak more than once: the second, third, fifth, and seventh personas, corresponding to the first, second, third, and fourth primes. The number of times specific personas speak in the sequence varies considerably: two personas speak seven times each; three personas speak four times each; one persona speaks three times; and four personas speak two times each. These ten "repeating" personas speak in a total of thirty-seven poems, which, as already noted, is the number of distinct personas and the twelfth prime, the result of four multiplied by three.

The repetition of basic units of measurement and the sequence of the first twenty-four primes across multiple levels of organization, including not only the title page, table of contents, and distinct personas but also the number of lines and stanzas for each of the book's sixty-six poems, creates more than a regular system of poetic patterning for *Blood Run*. Such repetition conveys on the printed page a sense of the architectural, geometric, and astronomical patterning evidenced at actual earthworks sites. The packed earth at Cahokia, the Octagon Earthwork, or Blood Run is sculpted not only to mirror sky but also to orient human bodies that approach, enter, or move among their structures; they guide the physical movements of those human bodies into particular ritual, social, and civic patterns. Similarly, Hedge Coke's packed repetitions of key natural numbers and primes orient human minds that enter her poetic structures toward particular intellectual and aesthetic patterns. Hedge Coke's elaborate patterning works, as well, to bolster the message of her book's specific content by guiding readers to move toward rather than away from the difficult moral issues raised by the history of Blood Run and the difficult political issues raised by its specifically Indigenous settlement.

Siting—and Defending—a City of Mounds

Hedge Coke's book-length sequence of poems was published as part of the Earthworks series of Native poetry produced by Salt Publishing, based in the United Kingdom with printing and distribution networks in the United States and Australia.[26] *Blood Run* appears designed for a broad primary audience of U.S., British, and other English-speaking readers who are likely to be unfamiliar with the technology of Indigenous earthworks and with the histories and ongoing legacies of North American mound-building cultures. Hedge Coke guides readers into her poetic city of mounds through elaborate procedures of mediation, and she offers readers extensive metacommentary on her literary project and its activist goals. Before the "free verse play" begins among the dramatic monologues and staged conversations of her persona poems,

Hedge Coke first provides readers with multiple layers and multiple genres of introductions that define key terminology, relate relevant history and specific site details for Blood Run, and establish her own ethos. Her opening narrative poem, "Before Next Dawning," then provides readers with a panoramic overview of Indigenous history in the Americas and a précis of the book's larger argument for preserving and protecting earthworks and other sacred sites. The narrative poem ends in a brief ceremony that promotes the earth's restoration. The multiple introductions and the panoramic narrative poem literally set the stage for the drama that will be performed by Hedge Coke's cast of Blood Run personas.

Another model for conceiving these layers of introductions is provided by the archaeologist William Romain. In *Mysteries of the Hopewell: Astronomers, Geometers, and Magicians of the Eastern Woodlands* (2000), Romain notes "an ancient belief among many peoples that spirits can only travel in straight lines and not in zigzags. To obtain entrance or exit, however, into or out of [an Ohio earthwork] enclosure that has a gateway or guardian mound, a zigzag path is required" (182). We might conceive of Hedge Coke's layers of introductions as functioning like a "gateway or guardian mound" that requires readers to take a "zigzag path" into her sequence of "earth"-works.

The first of these gateways is the three-page formal introduction by Noori, which provides historical and site details for Blood Run, identifies major themes in the book, and positions Hedge Coke not only as poet and teacher but also as Indigenous activist.[27] The second gateway, the two-page foreword by Hedge Coke, builds on Noori's introduction by guiding readers toward a series of key concepts that, together, create a site plan or schematic map both for Blood Run and for the book's core sequence of persona poems. These concepts include the ancient activities of North American "trade relationships" and the "archetypal practice" of Indigenous humanitarian "relations," as well as physical "throughways" and "language systems," including specifically "trade languages." Toward the end of the foreword, Hedge Coke writes, "Blood Run is *such a place*, one of significant trade, once a great city" (xiii). In this formulation the place that was and is Blood Run is defined not in terms of static geographical coordinates, fixed points on an imagined grid, but rather in terms of "relations," "ways," and "systems" that are multiple and dynamic. Finally, Hedge Coke defines Blood Run as "this

memory […] of these civilizations at their peak." Her sequence of
personas will enact this memory of the dynamic relations, ways, and
systems of the historic Blood Run site and argue for their potential, in
the future, to be fully dynamic once again.

In the third gateway, the two-page author's note that follows the
foreword, Hedge Coke offers more precise statistics for Blood Run
and more precise descriptions of the "building culture" of the Oneota
peoples who lived there.[28] Many of the numerical details she cites are
identical to those provided by Noori; others are rounded up or down.
Hedge Coke notes, for instance, that although first occupancy of the
site "dates back over 8,500 years ago," Blood Run was most heavily
populated at "the beginning of the 18th century"—not in the so-called
prehistoric deep past but rather within the period of written history.[29]
Like Cahokia in Illinois, Blood Run was an urban space, a large city,
and a regional trade center. Hedge Coke relates that the available
evidence indicates that "as many as 400 mounds existed in upward
to 2300 acres" at the site. An 1883 survey documented "276 mounds"
spread "over 1200 acres," while subsequent mapping indicated "only 176"
earthworks as still visible. Hedge Coke states that at the time of her
writing, after more than a century of looting, physical removal, and
agricultural cropping, "less than 80" earthworks remained visible at
Blood Run. The numbers Hedge Coke relates in this metacommentary are foundational—though not fully adequate—for explaining the
complex systems of numerical patterning that develop among individual poems and across the larger sequence of *Blood Run*. Although
Hedge Coke does not name the number four explicitly as her basic
unit of measurement, every number she lists in her note that describes
a relevant statistic for Blood Run is, in fact, a multiple of four.[30] As
demonstrated, however, four is but one of several basic units of measurement for the *Blood Run* sequence.

Hedge Coke's opening narrative poem, "Before Next Dawning,"
continues the process of guiding readers through gateways into the city
of mounds by providing an expansive overview of the history of Indigenous peoples in the Americas. In these 176 lines, which reinscribe
the number of mounds surveyed in an earlier era and emphasize the
basic unit of measurement, four, Hedge Coke establishes a broad and
highly politicized context for Blood Run's history of creative building,
vibrant life, multiple intrusions by European and American settlers,

and finally decimation, decline, and near erasure. Indigenous *settlement* and its link to earthworks as technologies for "Marking worldly occurrence" and "[becoming] part of this landscape" develop as a primary theme across the poem (5). "In building earthworks, effigy, / community civic sculpture, structure," the speaker states, the mound-building community creates a "safe barrier bound by / earth," a barrier suitable for "taking in the bones of The People upon their untimely / passing" (9). Through the building of multiple earthworks, and through the interment of the dead within specific works, the human community becomes both "part of this landscape" and "Immortal" (5). Finally, following an account of the destruction brought to "this great civilization" at Blood Run by "new disease" and "new ways" from "The Lands Across the Waters" (8), "Before Next Dawning" ends in prayer, with the final twenty lines arranged into six stanzas that emphasize repetition and a four-part ritual structure.[31] Readers are invited to pray for the restoration of the endangered land, the violated earthworks, the desecrated human remains at Blood Run, and, ultimately, for the restoration of the entire planet: "May she breathe. / May she breathe again" (10).

Taken together, Hedge Coke's layers of introductions, historical overview, and prayer—these multiple gateways into the city of mounds—position readers not at ground level to walk among the earthworks themselves but rather high enough overhead to see the monumental and multidimensional whole. The zigzag perspective these gateways create is aerial, panoramic, schematic, a dynamic map of the physical site and its long history within which to situate the dramatic monologues and staged dialogues of the persona poems that follow.[32]

The persona poems draw attention to what outsiders, invaders, and looters have viewed as mere inanimate objects and revivify these as living and articulate entities situated within multiple contexts, relationships, and narratives. Their voices bear witness to the site's former glory, historical and ongoing violation, and possible reclamation, repatriation, and renewal. The collective and singular personas of the earthworks at Blood Run (The Mounds, Ceremonial Mound, Burial Mound, and Snake Mound) describe themselves as technologies for relating the human community to the earth and cosmos—that is, as technologies for connecting the "middle world" of their raised surfaces to both a "lower world" and an "upper world."[33] The earthworks form part of a vital middle space that is simultaneously natural and artistic, spiritual and civic. The mounds assert that the activities that take place on, in, and among their bodies of packed and sculpted earth place humans within a matrix of relationships—with each other, with the natural forces of the universe, with the spirit world—that produce significant meaning. These assertions narrate an evolving story about place identity and sacred geography. Understood as extensions of the mathematics and geometry at the structural foundation of Hedge Coke's poetic sequence, these assertions develop, as well, a highly nuanced definition of what it means for humans to legitimately settle—not simply to occupy a particular place or to exploit its resources but to become integral to the regularities and harmonies of its dynamic systems.[34]

Seven poems spread across sections 2, "Origin," 3, "Intrusions," and 4, "Portend," voice the collective persona of The Mounds. Five of these are arranged on the page as distinctly visual poems whose shapes mimic the slopes of terraced earthworks. One poem situated in section 2 voices the persona of Ceremonial Mound; three poems spread across sections 2 and 3 voice the persona of Burial Mound. In addition, a single poem positioned in section 2 voices the persona of the effigy Snake Mound, who reappears in section 3 in the altered form of the persona Stone Snake Effigy.[35] The Mounds persona describes its collective self as the physical embodiment of prayer, "the love of man honoring mystery" (55), its "purposes" as "funerary, fundamental, immaculate" (82). More precisely, the collective Mounds assert that they were constructed in alignment with "constellation rise, cyclic phenomena, lunar cycle, / solar event" (17), "positioned relevant to all that was" and "will be" (17), made to "model / each rise, fall; Sun, Moon" (30) and to "mirror" not only specific "constellations" (30) but the entire "universe" (52). Ultimately, they "were meant to make matters meaningful" (82). It is the singular Ceremonial Mound, however, positioned early in section 2, "Origin"—aligned, that is, with the era before non-Indigenous intrusions into Blood Run—that outlines a detailed model for how the earthworks relate the human community to the earth and cosmos (18). Similarly, the third appearance of the Burial Mound persona, positioned as the fourteenth poem—and the precise midpoint—of section 3, "Intrusions," outlines a detailed model for how the earthworks relate the living to both their interred dead and to unborn generations yet to come (58). Each stresses the relational function of the earthworks, how these structures of embodied knowledge position the living human community, either as a whole or through designated representatives, at the center of ongoing processes. And each poem deploys unexpected wordplay and a type of bilanguaging in English (a concept discussed in detail in chapter 4 and redefined below) to suggest the nuances of this Indigenous technology of settlement.

Ceremonial Mound describes itself as a sacred altar "raised from flatland" upon which "The People" can come together as a body to "praise / what holds the unending universe intact." In twenty lines divided into nine stanzas, the mound emphasizes the role its elevation "above mortal reach" and "higher than common ground" plays in "positioning" humans in closer proximity to the cosmos and, by analogy, in closer proximity to the spirit world while keeping The People literally grounded: "eyes to Sky; feet on Earth." The raised surface of Ceremonial Mound is thus a transitional space between "Earth" and "Sky," a middle world where one can not only "diagram the phases / of Sun, [and] Moon" but also engage in reciprocal relations with cosmic forces. Indeed, in the fourth stanza, the conclusion of the first half of the poem, in a moment of subtle wordplay the mound invites humans to "Climb upon my table, my bone plate. / From here, you can touch the clouds. / From here clouds embrace."

Although "table" indicates the flat surface of the terraced mound, it also suggests a place of sustenance, a supply and source of food, as well as a place of assembly. More abstractly, it points to elements arranged in horizontal rows and vertical columns. Within the context of Hedge Coke's poetic sequence, "Climb upon my table" connotes this sense of entering into a set of complex relations. Like the common word "table," the unusual phrase "bone plate" can suggest sustenance. It also can suggest a Native breastplate constructed from animal bones, an esteemed piece of regalia, a type of armor to protect a warrior from injury. But "bone plate" refers, as well, to a contemporary medical procedure for holding together a fractured bone when a solid cast cannot be used; these plates help healing bones to regain strength and allow tissue to regenerate. Ceremonial Mound's invitation to "Climb upon my table, my bone plate" thus suggests a process of healing bodies, renewing strength, regenerating the reciprocal, living tissue of cosmic and spiritual connections. Although these lines are composed entirely in English, their wordplay is suggestive of the potential for Indigenous bilanguaging discussed in chapter 4: not simply the grammatical act of translating from one distinct language to another but the political act of operating between two or more languages and cultural systems, actively engaging the politics of their asymmetry within (post)colonial relations. Walter Mignolo discusses similar examples of "bilanguaging in the same language" in other contexts (264). In *Blood Run* the singular voice of Hedge Coke's Ceremonial Mound intervenes in the politics of contemporary U.S. settler English by juxtaposing multiple discourses—topographic, cultural, medical—in order to provoke unexpected connections.

The third Burial Mound poem, composed of seventeen lines (the seventh prime) divided into six stanzas, enlists similar wordplay to create similar effects in its alliterative opening line: "My seed coat meant for sheltering, chambers choate." Across these eight words of erudite, somewhat obscure, ambiguous English, the mound enacts a process of Indigenous bilanguaging as it shifts its discourse among botany, architecture, human biology, and law. A "seed coat" is a protective covering for a plant's technology for regeneration. "Sheltering" and "chambers" suggest functions and forms of architecture, with "chambers" carrying the specific connotation of private rooms and, more precisely, private rooms used by judges in a court of law. "Chambers" also connotes cavities within a body or organ, such as the human heart. The mound's use of the unusual word "choate," which works across the line as an echo of "coat" that picks up the morphing "sh" and "ch" sounds from "sheltering" and "chambers," draws particular attention. "Choate" is a back formation from the more familiar "inchoate"—with its typical meanings of rudimentary, incomplete, disordered, or otherwise imperfectly formed—and "choate" is used almost exclusively within legal discourses to signify the exact opposite of "inchoate": the idea of a legal order, such as a lien against property, being completed and perfected in and of itself and, thus, superior to all other legal orders that might attempt to challenge its authority. Through this process of bilanguaging, in asserting the "perfection" of its body, the voice of Burial Mound asserts both a biological necessity and a legal authority for its civic role at Blood Run. The line and the poem as a "perfect" whole work to disrupt colonial practices of containing Indigenous technologies within settler metaphors of the rudimentary, the incomplete, the disordered, and the otherwise imperfect.[36]

Moreover, in contrast to Ceremonial Mound, which emphasizes its raised surface as a ritual platform, the third Burial Mound describes its surface as a "tremendous testa," an old term for "seed coat," a protective covering. Following this logic, Burial Mound describes its primary function as providing a "womb" that "shield[s]" the human remains buried within it.[37] These roles are described in more precise detail in the poem's ongoing wordplay and bilanguaging, especially through the juxtaposition (in line four at the end of the first stanza and line eight at the end of the second stanza) of the near homographs "anthesis" and "antithesis." At the conclusion of the opening four-line stanza, the mound states that its role is to "nurture" the "blooming spirits" of The People until they are prepared for "anthesis." A botanical term, "anthesis" describes the period during which a flower is fully open, in its most receptive state—in "bloom"—when the anthens release their pollen and pollination occurs. To explain this particular process of pollination, in the second four-line stanza Burial Mound invokes the philosophical concept and rhetorical device of antithesis:

> Their heritage seed below at Macy, in Omaha—
> They speak to me, from both sides,
> turnip hole; still breathing.
> Each needing antithesis to fare well through me.

Burial Mound asserts its function as the point of contact between the world of the living and the world of the spirits, the human community and their dead, a function that the mound links to the story of Sky Woman (also known as Feather Woman) in its reference to a central "turnip hole" through which contact can be made. A culture hero, Sky Woman left the human community to marry a star but later returned to earth through a turnip hole she dug in the sky world, bringing home both new blood in the form of her children and various new technologies.[38] The mound names the community "at Macy, in Omaha"—the location of the contemporary Omaha Reservation—as the "heritage seed" of the interred dead. These descendants are the enduring, genetic link to Blood Run and to the Indigenous ancestors who built its earthworks. The mound states that each world needs the other in order to achieve the benefits of the mound's particular technology: "Each needing antithesis to fare well through me." The use of "antithesis" complements the earlier use of its near pun "anthesis," abstracting literal into spiritual pollination and growth. The spirits of the dead require the living for their "flowering," but the living require the spirits of the dead, too, if they are to "fare well"—with that phrase's connotations of travel, sustenance, and success—and prosper in their own futures and in those of the coming generations. Through these poetic strategies, the voices of Ceremonial Mound and the third Burial Mound convert the dead objects of settler nostalgia—mapped, surveyed, excavated, and looted "mounds"—into sites of Indigenous technological power, civic celebration, and physical resurgence.

The contrast between Indigenous and non-Indigenous technologies of settlement is rendered particularly acute within the specific drama and patterning of the thematically volatile section in which the third Burial Mound speaks, section 3, "Intrusions." This section enacts a sequence of twenty-seven persona poems in which six historical, non-Indigenous entities "intrude" among eight distinct Indigenous elements of the Blood Run site. The six intruders appear in seven poems (the fourth prime), and their names indicate spiritual, physical, and intellectual intrusions into Blood Run: Jesuit, Squatters, Tractor, Looters, Early Anthro, Looters, Early Interpreter. Only the Looters speak twice, and their repetition creates a pattern of alternating individual and collective intrusions. The eight Indigenous personas that speak in the section—The Tree at Eminija Mounds, Burial Mound, Ghosts, Skeletons, Clan Sister, The Mounds, Horizon, River, Stone Snake Effigy, and Memory—appear in the twenty remaining poems of the section; five of these personas (the third prime) speak more than once, and three (the second prime) speak only once. Within the sequence of twenty-seven poems in section 3, the "intruders" speak in poems five, seven, nine, thirteen, fifteen, seventeen, and nineteen. Five of these numbers are prime: five, seven, thirteen, seventeen, and nineteen (corresponding to the third, fourth, sixth, seventh, and eighth primes). The other two, however, are also prime within the book's larger sequence of sixty-four persona poems: poem nine in section 3 corresponds to poem thirty-seven in the overall sequence, the twelfth prime, and poem fifteen in section 3 corresponds to poem forty-three in the overall sequence, the fourteenth prime. Similar alignments become apparent if we look at the position of all of the intruder personas within the book's larger sequence.

The prime status of these non-Indigenous, destructive intruders seems to challenge what we might call the thematic geometry of Hedge

Coke's carefully coded macrostructure. The condition of primality suggests *originality* and *primacy*, positive qualities Hedge Coke consistently aligns with the Blood Run site personas and with the concept of Indigenous settlement. Primality also suggests the positive quality of *indivisibility* or, put another away, the positive state of an activist *unity*. At the same time, primality can suggest the negative qualities of *primitiveness* and *baseness*, a lack of sensitivity and sophistication. Rather than an unbreakable *unity*, this understanding can suggest a potentially debilitating *singularity* and *self-focus*, a lack of complexity and an unwillingness—or inability—to become associated with others—that is, to become "composed" like a composite number, formed into a balanced whole. These last qualities align with the six intruders and their seven poems.

The actual intrusions of section 3 occur in an interior sequence of fifteen poems (3 × 5, the second and third primes) whose individual voices and staged interactions articulate competing understandings of settlement. Four poems precede the initial intrusion, while eight poems follow the final. Poem four in the section, which immediately precedes the first intrusion, is also poem thirty-two (4 × 8) in the book's overall sequence of sixty-four and thus marks its midpoint. Poem twenty (4 × 5) in the section, which immediately follows the final intrusion, is also poem forty-eight (4 × 12) in the sequence of sixty-four and thus marks the beginning of its final quarter. The precise midpoint of the interior section of fifteen poems is poem twelve (4 × 3), "Skeletons," one of the Indigenous elements that speaks three times within section 3. "Skeletons" is composed of twelve lines divided into three stanzas of four lines each. It is positioned in dialogue with poem thirteen, the first "Looters," which is similarly composed of twelve lines but divided into four stanzas of varying lengths: two, five, three, two. Across the central river of the open book's spine, "Skeletons" warns "Looters," "Do not *unsettle* us. / [...] Until there is dust we must remain / *settled* here where we were lain" (56; emphasis added). The significant conceptual movement from *unsettle* to *settled* is positioned not in lines that correspond to multiples of four, the book's sacred basic unit of measurement, but rather in lines five and ten. When "Looters" responds to "Skeletons," however, its most damning phrases are placed precisely at line four: "Nothing is sacred in this world. Nothing" (57). Seven poems (the fourth prime and another number aligned with the sacred) precede poem twelve, "Skeletons," in this interior section, and seven poems follow. In the former, three intruders are sequenced with four Indigenous personas; in the latter, four intruders are sequenced with three Indigenous personas. Thus, although the interior section is focused thematically on challenge, disruption, and *imbalance,* its numeric structures are not simply inverted but surprisingly *balanced.*

The precise midpoint of section 3, however, is not poem twelve, "Skeletons," but rather poem fourteen, the third "Burial Mound," previously discussed in some detail, which shifts emphasis back to sculpted earth and recenters its particular kind of balance. (At this point we may notice that the number of Indigenous personas that speak, eight, and the number of intruder personas that speak, six, add up to a total of fourteen distinct personas in the section.) Burial Mound is the seventh persona (the fourth prime) introduced in the book's overall sequence, and it is also one of the Indigenous elements at Blood Run that speaks multiple times: once in section 2 and twice in section 3. In section 3, poem fourteen is both preceded and followed by thirteen poems (the sixth prime). It is composed of seventeen lines (the seventh prime), divided into six stanzas of varying but related lengths. Despite this variation, the poem's stanzaic structure is "balanced" and describes its own precise midpoint—a fulcrum or hinge—at line nine, a number that squares and thus emphasizes the active number three within the volatile section 3. The stanzaic structure is organized as four, four, *one,* four, two, two. Eight lines divided into two stanzas of four are positioned above the midpoint at line nine; eight lines divided into three stanzas of four, two, and two are positioned below, guiding readers to the pivotal center:

My seed coat meant for sheltering, chambers choate.	1
Though now my beauty furrowed, furled so	2
I can scarcely shield the remains of my People,	3
nurture their blooming spirits for anthesis.	4
Their heritage seed below at Macy, in Omaha—	5
They speak to me, from both sides,	6
turnip hole; still breathing.	7
Each needing antithesis to fare well through me.	8
So lamentable, what was!	9

I was a fine, broad hull, tremendous testa.   10
From far distance, rivaling hills   11
lain like kernelled landscapes, ideal body.   12
Before the novices came chiseling ruins.   13

I endure wrath of the till   14
bludgeoning of benighted.   15

Take pity on me! I appeal.   16
Without my womb, they but dust.   17
        (58)

In line nine, the midpoint of section 3's midpoint, the intruded upon Burial Mound exclaims, "So lamentable, what was!" The mound's exclamation condenses the section's theme of Indigenous response to a history of multiple violations into four words and seven syllables, repeating and realigning, once again, the book's sacred "primary" but not prime basic unit of measurement, four, and the similarly sacred fourth prime, seven. As noted, the product of four and seven is twenty-eight, the number of preintrusions persona poems presented in section 2, "Origin."[39] Moreover, a comma divides this pivotal line in two, signaling both space and breath at the center of the poem's center, creating a caesura crucial not only to the line's potential meaning (the two parts suggestive of a *thesis* and its *antithesis*) but also to its visual, aural, and even somatic effects—that is, how it looks on the page and sounds when spoken aloud, but also how it is experienced by the speaking body. While subtle on the fixed page, in performance the caesura can be rendered especially provocative: its extended beat of silence creates dramatic tension, heightens the force of both the alliteration in the repeated *w* sounds of the line's penultimate and final syllables and of the exclamation point at its end. The caesura suggests that the purpose of the poem is not to record irretrievable loss—"So lamentable"—but rather, in its emphasis on life-giving *breath*, to assert Indigenous endurance beyond the interruptions of recent history—"what was!" Indeed, such alignments gesture toward the possibility of future *regeneration* (not to be confused with a nostalgic *return* to the past) even at the very center of destructive "Intrusions."[40] This central exclamation also can be aligned with the fourth layer of the *Blood Run* title page, the author's full name, which is similarly composed of four words and seven syllables. The assertive sentiment expressed at the midpoint of the midpoint of the volatile section 3 can thus be aligned with that of the contemporary Indigenous poet. The center of destructive action, in other words, directs attention not only to the constructive beginning of the mound but also to the constructive beginning of Hedge Coke's text, emphasizing the purposefulness of both the historic earthworks at Blood Run and the contemporary sequence of activist poems that bears their name.

This focus on the potential for new construction and new beginnings reverberates, as well, in the second narrative poem of *Blood Run*, "When the Animals Leave This Place." This final poem in the sequence offers a prophetic vision in which the River at the center of the Blood Run site reasserts "its greatest force": animals seek higher ground, and clouds gather in auspicious forms; the waters of the resultant storm flood the River, which reclaims and, in its reclaiming, remakes and renews the land.[41] Hedge Coke's description of "gathering clouds" forming "sculptured swans, mallard ducks, and giants" can be read as an oblique reference to the North American myth of the Earth Diver, in which various animals and birds attempt to retrieve earth from beneath the depths of a flood in order to begin the process of world creation and renewal. Romain hypothesizes that Ohio earthworks built on river floodplains were designed, in fact, to demonstrate the pervasive Earth Diver story:

> Imagine, then, the stunning effect during a flood [...] as [the mounds] slowly emerged from the surface of a retreating expanse of floodwater. As the [people] looked on, they would have been witness to an ever-expanding bit of earth, slowly gaining in size as the lowering floodwaters revealed more and more of a circular earthwork or burial mound. What better visual metaphor could there be for the creation of the earth, just as told in the Earth Diver myth? (194)

Hedge Coke's final poem and the larger sequence end at line eighty-nine (the twenty-fourth prime) with the stark phrase "It has begun." Read as either prophetic warning or celebration of the next turn in this cycle, the three words and four syllables of the final line repeat

Hedge Coke's basic units of measurement for *Blood Run* as they herald a reclaiming of the land and a new beginning for Indigenous peoples through seeming destruction.

Hedge Coke's closing emphasis on the renewal of the local— "When the Animals Leave *This Place*"—extends to the final, nonpoetic components of *Blood Run*, the two pages of formal acknowledgements and four pages of formal dedications, and ties this emphasis explicitly to her activism on behalf of the Blood Run site. She states in the acknowledgements, "This volume was written in effort to move the state and its citizens to protect, preserve and honor an Indigenous mound site." More precisely, she reveals that the opening narrative poem, "Before Next Dawning," "is a version of the author's oral testimony that urged the State of South Dakota Game Fish & Parks Department to vote unanimously to secure the site after twenty-three years of deliberation" and that "a portion of the proceeds from this volume will go to the preservation of this site" (94).⁴² These remarks, along with the long list of activist poets named in the dedications, effectively reframe "When the Animals Leave This Place," linking its vision of renewal of the natural world to the unresolved human conflicts in the Americas detailed in the opening poem—"[. . .] lands were overrun in Strangers, settling in, erasing, / erasing. [. . .] Yes, this is a story of Blood Run, of sudden / regional mound culture departure. [. . .] let us not / erase what has happened here before" (8)—and in the persona poems of section 3, "Intrusions"—"So lamentable, what was!" (58).

Launching a Changing Vessel

Similar to Hedge Coke's *Blood Run*, Sullivan's *Star Waka* orients its readers to view individual poems and the larger poetic sequence from a particular perspective that is culturally and politically situated. *Star Waka* was published by Auckland University Press and appears to have been designed for a primary audience of New Zealand readers familiar with the basic history of Polynesian voyaging and with basic aspects of Māori culture, including words and phrases in te reo Māori (the Māori language). In contrast to Hedge Coke, Sullivan "launches" readers upon his poetic vessel with relatively little mediation and metacommentary. Before the sequence of one hundred numbered poems begins—while the poetic vessel rests on shore, as it were—Sullivan offers directions for navigating *Star Waka*'s complex journey through an author's note that explains the book's kaupapa (overall plan) in four brief statements. He then offers a ceremony for safe voyaging through an unnumbered opening poem, "He karakia timatanga" ("A beginning prayer" or "A prayer for beginning"), of thirty-two lines. Thus launched, readers are left mostly on their own to notice and to interpret signs provided by the various guidance systems embedded in specific poems—star paths and the shapes of clouds, wave movements and floating debris, the flight patterns of birds—to navigate the poetic waka.[43]

Following the expected title page, copyright page, and table of contents, Sullivan provides his brief navigational note, in which he makes four explicit statements about the book's kaupapa, the overt scheme of the sequence's methodology, themes, and organization. To aid analysis, I have numbered these brief paragraphs:

> I wrote *Star Waka* with some threads to it: that each poem must have a star, a waka or the ocean. This sequence is like a waka, members of the crew change, the rhythm and the view changes—it is subject to the laws of nature.   1
>
> There are three sections, indicated by the change in title numbering from Roman to Arabic to "waka" numbering. Occasionally a poem's numbering breaks into another part of the sequence.   2
>
> There is a core of one hundred poems, and 2001 lines.   3
>
> For references to Maori mythology see Margaret Orbell's *Encyclopedia of Maori Mythology*. Other references are built into the text.   4

At first glance, similar to Hedge Coke's, Sullivan's metacommentary appears to provide a comprehensive map for navigating *Star Waka*. Read against the actual sequence, however, this map turns out to be surprisingly ambiguous and less than complete. In the first statement, for example, Sullivan draws attention to the three terms that organize his sequence—*star, waka*, and *ocean*—but offers no explicit rationale for these choices (or for this combination of English- and Māori-language terms) and, notably, no definition for the Māori term *waka*. An explicit definition does not appear until poem "xvii: Some definitions and a note on orthography": "in English the waka / is a canoe /

but the ancestral waka / were as large / as the European barks / of the eighteenth century explorers" (21). In the second statement, Sullivan draws attention to his three-part numbering system—Roman, Arabic, and "waka"—but again offers no rationale for these choices and no explanation for why the three numbering systems contain different numbers of poems: thirty-four Roman, nineteen Arabic, and forty-seven waka. Do the three systems align with "a star, a waka or the ocean," the three organizational terms designated for the sequence? Do changes in numbering indicate changes in speaker or changes in temporal, geographical, or cultural positioning? Something else? Sullivan draws attention in this statement, as well, to the fact that there are occasional "breaks" in the three-part numbering sequence, suggesting that a "break" of one numbering system into another will in some way affect meaning. But such breaks in the numbering occur only twice, and in both cases waka numbering from the third section disrupts the Roman numbering of the first. Again, no rationale is given.[44]

In the third statement, Sullivan draws attention to the fact that his sequence, published in 1999, anticipates the turn of the twenty-first century with its "core" of one hundred poems, as well as passing into the second millennium with its 2,001 lines.[45] These numbers draw attention, as well, to the general significance of numbering and patterning in *Star Waka*, suggesting a possible link to *Blood Run*. As we shall see, similar to the numbers Hedge Coke relates in her own explicit metacommentary in her author's foreword and author's note, Sullivan's explicit rationale of one hundred and 2,001 is less than fully adequate for explaining the complex numerical patterning that develops among his individual poems and across his book's sequence—which, in addition to the "core" of one hundred, includes the unnumbered opening poem located within the pages of the book and a second unnumbered poem printed on the book's back cover. Although the "total" of 2,001 lines stated in the metacommentary includes the opening poem's thirty-two, it does not include the cover poem's fourteen.

Finally, in the fourth statement, Sullivan draws attention to the need for a secondary text to decode allusions to Māori culture made in the sequence. He lists Margaret Orbell's *Encyclopedia of Maori Mythology*, a title that does not actually exist.[46] As noted in chapter 4, Orbell is a preeminent Pakeha scholar of classical Māori texts; she is the author of two encyclopedias, *The Illustrated Encyclopedia of Maori*

Myth and Legend (1995) and *A Concise Encyclopedia of Māori Myth and Legend* (1998). These books will be readily available to the primary audience but much less accessible to potential readers outside Aotearoa New Zealand. Sullivan also indicates that additional texts will feature in his poems. Alongside classic works of literature (sonnets by Shakespeare), works of art from the nineteenth and twentieth centuries (paintings by C. F. Goldie and Peter Robinson), popular culture texts from the twentieth century (the 1969–1971 U.S. children's television series *H. R. Pufnstuf*, the 1997 film *Boogie Nights*), and Internet resources (the NativeNet Listserv), a number of works of scholarship are either quoted, paraphrased, alluded to, or discussed in various poems. These secondary sources include the classic work of anthropology *The Maori Canoe* by Elsdon Best, originally published in 1925, and the ocean survival guide *The Raft Book: Lore of the Sea and Sky* by Harold Gatty, published in 1943, as well as more recent scholarship on waka, such as *Nga Waka Maori: Maori Canoes* by Anne Nelson, published in 1991, and *Nga Waka o Nehera: The First Voyaging Canoes* by Jeff Evans, published in 1997.[47] One secondary source, however, is especially generative of the complex patterning developed across Sullivan's sequence: *We, the Navigators: The Ancient Art of Landfinding in the Pacific* by David Lewis, originally published in 1972 and reissued in a second edition in 1994. Sullivan refers explicitly to this book in two poems positioned in the third section, "Waka 60: Dead Reckoning" and "Waka 67: from *We the Navigators*." But the details of Lewis's seminal investigation and first-hand account of extant Oceanic navigation techniques are implicit in many other poems. Although Sullivan does not name Lewis or his scientific study in his metacommentary, *We, the Navigators* is, in fact, an important guide for navigating the systems that structure the elaborate patterning of *Star Waka*.

Following the brief, four-part note, before the first of the numbered poems, Sullivan begins his poetic text with the unnumbered poem "He karakia timatanga" ("A beginning prayer" or "A prayer for beginning"), composed of thirty-two lines divided into sixteen two-line stanzas. The poem establishes a pattern of bilanguaging movements between Māori and English languages and between Māori and Pakeha (European) cultures that recur across the book. It also enlists powerful imagery that links the landscape of the (mythical) Polynesian homeland, Hawaiiki, to the landscape of the human body.[48] In addition, two features stand out as especially relevant to how the opening poem formally launches Sullivan's core of one hundred numbered poems and, similar to Hedge Coke's layered introductions, establishes a specific perspectival orientation for readers.

First, the poem links the genre announced in its title, karakia (chant or prayer), to the genre of tuki waka (a chant or song used to count time for paddlers). The poem's opening phrase of English, "A prayer to," repeats a total of four times in the first half of the thirty-two-line poem; a variation, "A prayer [...] / for," follows in lines seventeen to eighteen, stanza nine, the first stanza of the second half of the poem. The italicized chant in Māori, "*hoea hoea ra*" (*hoea* = "to paddle," "to row," "to convey by waka"), then repeats four times in the second half of the poem. The poem ends with a second repetition of the phrase "a prayer for" in the final line.[49] Second, each repetition of the italicized paddling chant in Māori is preceded by a word or phrase in English. The series of associations created across these two-line stanzas moves readers through four elements that emerge as significant to Sullivan's larger poetic sequence: "the chanted rhythms," which emphasizes human agency; "storms," which emphasizes uncontrollable natural forces; "a thousand years," which emphasizes the passage of time (and, more specifically, Māori tenure in Aotearoa); and "fleet mothers of tales," which emphasizes the relationship between technology—a group of waka—and the production of story, discourse, mediated experience. The four lines that follow the four stanzas of these elements and the repeated tuki waka end the poem with a bilanguaging emphasis on the potential "combination" of natural forces with human agency and technology that is necessary for successful voyaging:

I greet you in prayer oh star oh waka ...
and pray for your combination here.

He karakia mo korua, e te waka, e te whetu o te ao nei.
Star and waka, a prayer for you both.[50]
(2)

Taken together, the explicit metacommentary of the note and the more subtle metacommentary of the opening poem launch Sullivan's core of one hundred numbered poems by positioning readers at sea level, either inside the waka with the crew or outside the waka at parallel points on the ocean or horizon. Like the crew and its observers, readers of *Star Waka* are oriented to look toward the sky and its guiding stars.

Steering the Waka, Conceptualizing Sea and Sky

Discussions of *Star Waka* have focused on Sullivan's exploration of the term *waka* itself, which indicates any kind of literal or figurative "vessel" but signifies most preeminently the ocean-voyaging "canoes" that brought Māori adventurers and settlers from central Polynesia to the large islands of Aotearoa.[51] Over the course of his core sequence of one hundred poems, Sullivan reveals the expansiveness of the term's potential meanings—those historical, those contemporary, and those imagined into possible futures—through multiple strategies: reworkings of relevant oral and literary traditions; citation and critique of authoritative representations of waka, their technologies, and their histories; and personal reflections on contemporary life in New Zealand, the broader Pacific, and a world increasingly interconnected by technology. Toward the end, in preparation for the final poems, Sullivan embeds a minisequence of twelve distinct personas.[52] Although their combined effect is equally dramatic as that produced by the thirty-seven distinct personas of *Blood Run*, the twelve persona poems in *Star Waka* do not offer the most productive juxtaposition with Hedge Coke's extensive structural patterning. Rather, it is Sullivan's similar evocation of a worldview and spatial conceptual system that can be divided into upper, middle, and lower worlds that suggest the most provocative intersections with Hedge Coke's schematic structuring of *Blood Run*.

In the Oceanic context, these three worlds correspond to the positions of Sullivan's key terms "star," "waka," and "ocean." The poem "Waka 16: Kua wheturangitia koe" (You have appeared above the horizon), for instance, which is the first of the two "waka" poems that "break" into the section of Roman numbering, indicates Oceanic systems of star navigation in its title and, in its closing lines, directs attention to the two earthly locations where stars—which in Polynesian understandings represent not only guiding *lights* but also guiding *ancestors*—can still be seen clearly in contemporary times, despite the presence of "machines / [that] lighten blackness" and cause "many stars / [to be] lost in the lightning." These locations for sighting stars, removed from the threat of light pollution, are designated on land as "from [the] tops of pa"—that is, from fortified Māori villages, which often include earthworks built atop hills or mountains—and at sea as "from [the] middle of ocean," "from these places stars / meant to be seen can be" (20).[53] Similar to Hedge Coke's description, voiced by Ceremonial Mound, of the civic and spiritual purposes of raised platforms of earth, Sullivan indicates that carved waka located in the "middle of ocean" are positioned in a "middle" place that makes possible significant contact between worlds above and below.

Much of the power of Sullivan's book-length sequence, similar to that of Hedge Coke's *Blood Run*, derives not exclusively from its explicit content but also from its manipulations of poetic form and its high level of structural patterning. Sullivan's attention to lineation is signaled in the explicit metacommentary of his opening note. But he pays careful attention, as well, to line grouping, indentation, intra- and interlinear white space, punctuation, capitalization, and size and style of typeface within individual poems and across the sequence. These aspects of poetic form, however, do not map easily onto the specific numerical alignments that are significant in Hedge Coke's own sequence; in line with Sullivan's commentary, these aspects of form map, instead, onto the technologies and traditions of Oceanic voyaging, especially the systems for Oceanic navigation described in detail in Lewis's *We, the Navigators*.

Lewis's study is driven, in large part, by the two questions that have dominated debates over how to conceptualize and how to value Oceanic voyaging. First, were exploration and settlement "intentional" (as Indigenous traditions assert) or merely "accidental" (as many Western researchers and settler-invaders have assumed)? And second, were voyaging routes "repeatable" (again, as Indigenous traditions assert) or merely the result of "luck" or "guesswork" (again, as many Western researchers and settler-invaders have assumed)?[54] Lewis's experiences in the 1960s convinced him—and persuaded many of his readers—of the validity of Indigenous claims. In *Star Waka*, Sullivan follows Lewis's lead by evoking the critical concepts of *intention* and *repetition* that Lewis examined in his several experiments at sea with contemporary Oceanic navigators, as well as by evoking the critical observation of the *regularity* of oceanic and celestial movements by which Oceanic peoples navigated the open sea.[55] Beyond the explicit content of individual poems, Sullivan evokes such regularity more implicitly through regularized variation in the number and length of lines within poems and of stanzaic patterning within, between, and among poems across the sequence.

In several poems Sullivan's lineation and especially his stanzaic patterning are suggestive of the concept of whakapapa (genealogy) as a Māori and Polynesian epistemology, a technology for organizing knowledge into genealogical "lines." *Whakapapa*, as discussed in chapter 4, can be translated into English as both "to recite in proper order" and "to place in layers, one upon another." These definitions, as well as *whakapapa's* less explicit connotation of positioning humans and other entities within webs of narrative interconnections, are evoked in poem "xx: a whakapapa construction." Sullivan enlarges the amount of white space between the eighteen lines of the poem so that they separate into eighteen distinct stanzas or genealogical "layers," iconically rendering the organizational methodology of whakapapa on the page. This visual arrangement enhances the semantic impact of the poem and reinforces its primary theme that whakapapa continues to operate as a viable technology for ordering all knowledge.

Most striking in this regard, Sullivan's core of one hundred poems, divided into three sections through the use of three systems of numbering, includes three poems that are distinctly visual—that is, three poems composed as much (or more) for the eye as for the ear. In poem "Waka 29: waka taua" ("war canoe," the second of the two waka poems that break into the early section of Roman numbering), and in the untitled "51" and "53," the visual arrangement of the brief linguistic text of each poem can be apprehended in its own terms, as a meaningful image, prior to as well as in conjunction with each text's potential semantic meaning or meanings. Similar to several of Hedge Coke's persona poems written in the collective voice of The Mounds, the arrangement of each of Sullivan's three visual poems is recognizably figurative and arguably mimetic. More precisely, the linguistic text of each of the three visual poems is arranged into a distinct combination of two primary geometric figures: straight lines and curved arcs. In this way, Sullivan's three visual poems draw attention to themselves not only individually, since they stand out from the ninety-seven core poems arranged in standard verse patterns of single or double columns, but also collectively, similar to Hedge Coke's The Mounds poems, since their figures appear related to each other both structurally and thematically.

The three visual poems in *Star Waka* thus form a provocative sub-set, another minisequence, within Sullivan's larger sequence of one hundred poems. On their own the visual figures of the three poems represent key aspects of the book's exploration of waka technology within the context of Polynesian voyaging, especially concepts related to intentional and repeatable Oceanic navigation. Taken together, the three figures demonstrate the flexibility and situated versatility of this Indigenous technology, and they argue for its effectiveness in keeping Indigenous voyagers intact and on course at open sea even when buffeted by unexpected storms.

Where Hedge Coke's multiply interrelated configurations of basic numerical units and primes evoke the schematic nature of a mapped, cosmically aligned, and "nested" Indigenous city, Sullivan's three-part visual intertext distills several of his book's activist assertions and predominant themes into iconic geometric figures that evoke primary tools for Indigenous open-water navigation. Through spacing and parallel syntax, for example, the eleven words that comprise the brief text of "Waka 29: waka taua" (war canoe) are composed into five discernible lines, which are arranged in the upper half of the page as a sine wave form (a pair of side-by-side, inverted, continuous arcs) situated above a diagonal straight line.[56] These figures "float" above the white space of the lower half of the page (see Figure 12).

The iconic geometric form of the sine wave is printed in a font larger than that used in the ninety-seven nonvisual poems in the book's core. The form is composed of the poem's first four lines, with the first and second lines, "A taniwha / brushes the sides," arranged as the "upper," convex arc of the sine wave, and the third and fourth lines, "uenuku / touches the eyes," arranged as the corresponding "lower," concave arc. The fifth line, "waka pitches," is printed in a font that is noticeably larger than that used in the first four, and it is arranged as a diagonal straight line running at a forty-five degree angle below the second, concave arc. The diagonal line is positioned so that it points to and perhaps suggests an intersection with the word "uenuku" in the third line.

The poem's arrangement as a sine wave (two arcs) and a diagonal straight line creates a highly abstracted visual figure of a swell or rolling ocean wave "pitching" a single-hulled waka. Sullivan thus places the viewer/reader at sea level, as though aboard a second vessel, watching the waka's "pitched" encounter with waves. The sine wave also can

Waka 29 waka taua

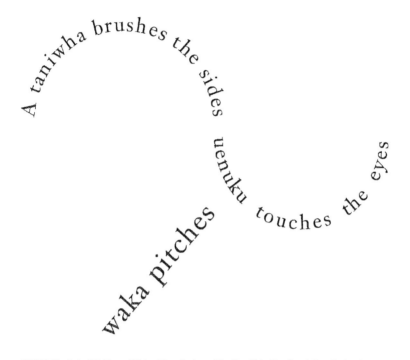

FIGURE 12. Robert Sullivan, "Waka 29: waka taua," in *Star Waka* (Auckland, New Zealand: Auckland University Press, 1999), 33.

suggest other forms of regular movement, such as sound, potentially playing on an alternate meaning of "pitches," and light, potentially playing on the Polynesian figure of Uenuku, a man whom the gods transformed into a rainbow—that is, a man transformed into *light* passing through droplets of rain, mist, spray, dew, or other forms of water—and whose name has come to mean rainbow, itself an iconic *arc*.[57] Within the context of Oceanic voyaging, the sine wave form can suggest, as well, the sinuous body of a taniwha, a water-dwelling creature that is understood both as a "spirit" able to assume multiple physical manifestations and as a fantastic sea or freshwater "monster." In either conception a taniwha is often described as a protective guardian, which underlines Sullivan's suggestion that the waka is under control and protected rather than in peril. Orbell emphasizes this aspect of taniwha in *A Concise Encyclopedia of Māori Myth and Legend*:

> Taniwha: Spirits in the water. These beings live in the ocean and the inland waters, and some can move through the earth. Most are associated with humans, because every people have a taniwha of their own. Many famous taniwha arrived from Hawaiki, generally as guardians of ancestral waka, then settled down in Aotearoa with the descendents of the crew of the vessel they had escorted. (149)

In "Waka 29" the expected relative positioning of taniwha and uenuku is inverted in the visual poem's mimetic figure of a waka "pitching" at sea. The taniwha, a spirit-creature associated with water (and thus with the abstracted position *below*), forms a segment of the convex arc of the sine wave (positioning it *above*), while uenuku, a transformed person-spirit and an optical phenomenon associated with the sky (and thus with the abstracted position *above*), forms a segment of the concave arc of the sine wave (positioning it *below*). According to some Māori traditions, the spirit of the transformed Uenuku was brought to Aotearoa on board the Tainui waka within a sacred stone.[58] Sullivan's inversion of expected above and below positions draws additional attention to the *action* depicted by the textual figure: the upward "pitch" of the waka appears to have been caused by the rising taniwha "brush[ing] the [waka's] sides," which in turn has resulted in uenuku descending to "touch[ ] the eyes" of the waka crew and/or sea-level observers. Rather than a scene of oceanic calamity as might be imagined by Western researchers or settler-invaders—a small vessel attacked by fierce creatures or wracked by the waves of a menacing storm—the verbs in these lines indicate the gentle "brush" of a guardian companion and the light "touch" of a guardian spirit. That the waka figured in the poem points directly toward uenuku, the man become a rainbow become a traveling spirit, may indicate an emphasis on the theme of voyaging as both continuity (carrying the Polynesian past into the Māori future) and transformation (literally changing worlds and becoming a distinct people). Less expectedly, perhaps, the potential intersection of waka and uenuku may invoke the biblical story of the Great Flood, a connection that exposes potential in the poem for multiple levels of visual and aural punning and for bilanguaging between Māori and English linguistic elements and Māori and Pakeha cultures. As related in the book of Genesis, God creates the rainbow (an *arc*) as the sign (read *sine*) of His promise to Noah and his family aboard the *ark* (a primal *waka*) that never again will He send a deluge (read above-and-below-inverting, waka-pitching sine *wave*) to destroy creation. The "touch" of uenuku, in other words, signals vitality and survival.

Sullivan's poem "51" similarly evokes ideas of "above" and "below" worlds. Here, the two arcs and diagonal straight line of "Waka 29" are reconfigured into the iconic geometric figure of a circle bisected into upper and lower halves by a horizontal straight line (see Figure 13). Similar to "Waka 29," "51" is printed in a font that is larger than that of the core's ninety-seven nonvisual poems. Also similar to "Waka 29," eleven words comprise its brief text; these are composed into three lines, which are arranged into the figure of a split, open circle. Although the figure is literally two-dimensional, its open arrangement is suggestive of three-dimensionality. Centered on the vertical axis of the page and positioned slightly above center of the horizontal axis, the figure of the open, bisected circle appears to "float" within (white) space like a celestial orb. The first line, "Uenuku Bird Flight," is arranged as the upper, convex arc of the implied circle/orb. The second line, "Waka Light Dark Shift," is arranged as a horizontal straight line that runs through the center of the implied circle/orb, measuring its full diameter. And the third line, "Leaf Ocean Ocean Mist," is arranged as the lower, concave arc. The arcs that should form the left and right sides of the implied circle/orb are blank white space, their shapes suggested by the mirrored curves of the upper and lower arcs and by the beginning and end points of the bisecting center line.

A number of interpretations are possible for the geometric figure created in "51." Viewed from a cosmic perspective, as noted, the figure of a bisected, open circle is suggestive of a celestial orb, a planet or globe.[59] In this interpretation the bisecting center line functions as an equator, whereas the upper and lower arcs suggest a planet's northern and southern poles. Viewed as an abstract model for our own, watery planet—perhaps especially as an abstract model for our world conceived from the perspective of Oceania—the bisecting line becomes a horizon dividing the dome of the sky from the bowl of the sea. The line "Waka Light Dark Shift" supports the idea of a horizon line

Uenuku Bird Flight

Waka Light Dark Shift

Leaf Ocean Ocean Mist

FIGURE 13. Robert Sullivan, "51," in *Star Waka* (Auckland, New Zealand: Auckland University Press, 1999), 56.

and evokes, as well, versions of the Māori story of creation in which Ranginui, the sky father, and Papatūānuku, the earth mother, are separated from their marital embrace by their son Tāne, god of forests and birds and father of humankind, who pushes the cosmic parents apart, allowing light to stream into the world, which becomes te ao mārama, "the world of light."[60] And viewed from above, from an aerial perspective, the bisected circle can suggest the figure of a compass, itself an abstract model for our world. This compass need not be conceived as the magnetic variety but as a star compass, wind compass, solar compass, or compass based on currents, all of which are part of Oceanic systems for open-water navigation investigated and confirmed by Lewis in *We, the Navigators* and all of which Sullivan evokes within other poems in the *Star Waka* sequence.[61]

In addition to reconfiguring the two arcs and single straight line of "Waka 29," "51" repeats two words from the earlier poem: "Uenuku" and "Waka." As in the first configuration, in the second these Māori words are positioned in close proximity to each other, suggesting their significant relationship. In "51," Uenuku, the man transformed into a rainbow, is restored to the expected *above* position within the convex arc; moreover, he is aligned in this sky world with the phrase "Bird Flight." If we return to the biblical story of the Great Flood, we can note that the use of "arcs" in both poems suggests an aural pun on "ark," the waka Noah constructs and then captains in order to save his family—and the world's animals—from the deluge.[62] The rainbow becomes God's perennial promise of no future flood of devastating proportions. The specific sign for Noah and his crew that the waters have receded and dry land again exists—the sign that, indeed, there has been a "shift" in worldly circumstances—is not the rainbow, however, but rather the dove that returns to the ark bearing an olive branch in "leaf." In poem "51" we can correlate these details from the biblical story with the phrase "Bird Flight," positioned alongside the iconic rainbow in the convex "upper" arc, and "Leaf," positioned directly across the circle from "Bird Flight" in the concave "lower" arc. In this reading, Sullivan's figure of the bisected circle represents the immediately postdiluvian moment, man as vital survivor still aboard the sacred vessel, his "shifted" world washed new and made full of potential for new life.[63]

Sullivan's arrangements of "Uenuku," "Bird Flight," and "Leaf" along the arcs of the visual poem's implied circle/orb do not require interpretation within the context of biblical allusion. The positioning of "Bird Flight" across the circle from "Leaf" is equally suggestive of Māori mythology (as Orbell emphasizes, Tāne is god of both forests—and thus leaves—and birds) and of Oceanic systems of voyaging, especially techniques for open-water navigation during daylight.[64] At sea both birds in flight and leaves carried by currents can be read as signs indicating the presence and position of nearby land. In *We, the Navigators*, Lewis points out that navigating on the open ocean during daylight hours—when stars and other celestial bodies with predictable paths across the sky are no longer visible—requires the processing of multiple kinds of available data (84, 99). Leaves and other drift objects can signal the presence of land (211), and the flight paths of various bird species at morning and evening—at the "Light Dark Shift" of dawn and dusk—can indicate the specific position of a nearby land mass (163).[65] In poem "51" Uenuku is positioned directly across the implied circle/orb from the word "Mist." Within the context of voyaging, both meteorological phenomena indicate varying levels of visibility at sea. But the specific pairing also can invoke the full story of Uenuku's transformation: because of his overwhelming love for Hine-pūkohurangi, the Celestial Mist Maiden, the Polynesian gods took pity on Uenuku in his old age (when he had become physically bent like an arc) and allowed him to join the Mist in the sky world as the rainbow.[66] Thus, all four elements balanced on intersecting axes that cross the visual poem's geometric figure of an implied circle or orb—Uenuku, Bird Flight, Leaf, and Mist—can be read within a specifically Oceanic as well as a specifically biblical context. Like "Waka 29," "51" demonstrates Sullivan's playful and productive bilanguaging across Māori and English languages and Indigenous Polynesian and Western settler cultures.

Oceanic voyaging is the apparent context for the second reconfiguration of arcs and straight lines that Sullivan creates in his third visual poem, "53" (see Figure 14). The fourteen words of this poem's linguistic text are composed into ten discernible lines, which are arranged into a complex figure of three small circular "islands" and four horizontal entities that "float" in the sea either between or near them. Similar to the geometric figures created in "Waka 29" and "51," the six lines that comprise the three "islands" in "53" are printed in a font that is larger than that of the ninety-seven nonvisual poems in the book's core. The four horizontal lines that create the figure's four floating entities, however, are printed in the smaller font used in the majority of the text. Also similar to "Waka 29" and "51," the visual figure created in "53" is positioned in the upper half of the page, above an expanse of white space. The overall effect of the figure is to suggest an overhead view of an abstracted Oceania, an aerial map depicting a range of entities—an object, a creature, and two human personae—situated at various locations within a "sea of islands."[67]

Each of the three island figures is composed of a tightly closed, two-line circle; each of these lines consists of a single word, "island," which is bowed into a small arc. Unlike the arcs that form the sine wave in "Waka 29" or the bisected circle in "51," these one-word arcs are set on the diagonal, with the effect of deemphasizing their separateness and emphasizing, instead, the complete circle of the "repeating" island-island.

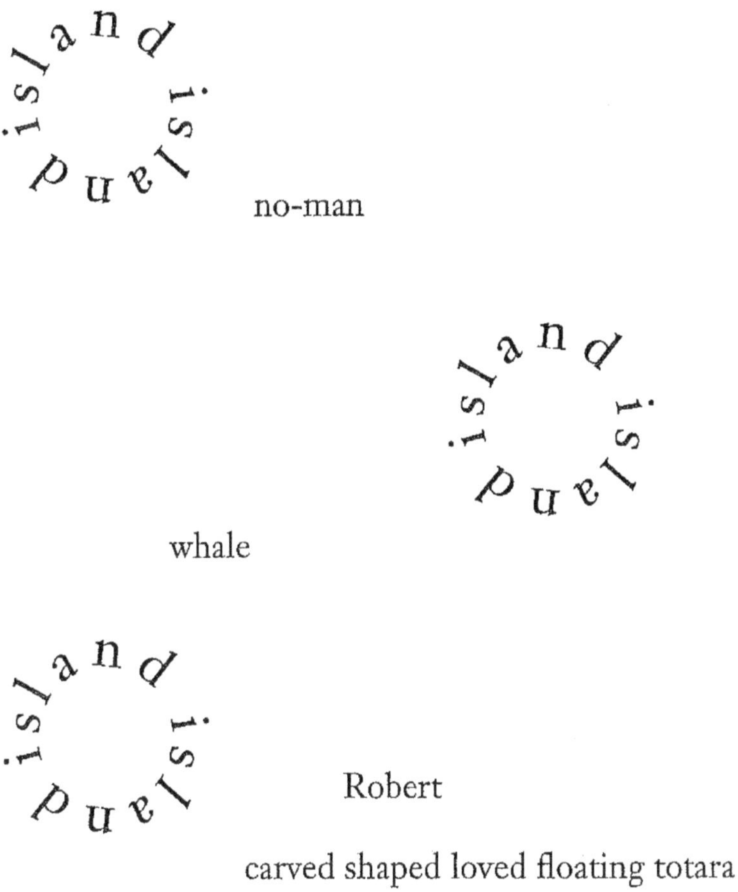

island / island / island / island

no-man

island / island / island / island

whale

island / island / island / island

Robert

carved shaped loved floating totara

FIGURE 14. Robert Sullivan, "53," in *Star Waka* (Auckland, New Zealand: Auckland University Press, 1999), 58.

If we read the figure of the aerial map from top to bottom, the text of the poem begins with the first two-line "island / island," set to the left of center, followed by the first one-word horizontal straight line, the persona "no-man," which sits close by to the right of the first island, at roughly center page. The second two-line "island / island" then sits to the right of and below "no-man." Next, the second one-word horizontal straight line, the creature "whale," is positioned below and to the left of the second island. The third two-line "island / island" sits close by, below and to the left of "whale," positioned almost directly beneath the first island. The third one-word horizontal straight line, the persona "Robert," sits to the right of the third island. And finally, the longer, five-word fourth horizontal straight line, the described object "carved shaped loved floating totara," sits directly below the third line, so that the word "shaped" aligns directly below "Robert."

This figurative "map" of an object, a creature, and two personae floating in a sea of three islands evokes numerous specific puns, allusions, and internal and extratextual references. Perhaps most obvious is the first island's and first persona's pun on Donne's often-quoted line "no man is an island, entire of itself" from his 1623 "Meditation 17."[68] This line may also allude to adventurer Odysseus's encounter with the Cyclops; the clever Greek, who speaks in *Star Waka* as one of the twelve personae near the end of the sequence, fooled the one-eyed giant by claiming his name was "no man." The proximity of the creature "whale" to the third island can suggest Whale Island, also known as Moutohora (sometimes rendered Motuhora), located in Aotearoa New Zealand's Bay of Plenty, off the coast and visible from the town of Whakatane, whose name records an important event from the era of Polynesian voyaging to Aotearoa.[69] For bilingual readers this association can evoke not only one of the Māori words for whale, *tohorā* (specifically, the southern right whale) but also the Māori words for "island," *motu*, which means "isolated," "cut off," "separated," and *moutere* (or *motutere*), which suggests, as well, the condition of drifting, floating, or swimming (*tere* = "to drift," "to float," "to swim," "to flow"). Although Whale Island/Moutohora has a long history of Māori occupancy and use, within recent history it has been protected, through a partnership between its customary Māori caretakers and the New Zealand government, as a refuge for indigenous wildlife. Perhaps this "floating" "whale / island / island" (two arcs) represents a bicultural reconfiguration of the biblical "arks" and Indigenous "arcs" evoked in "Waka 29" and "51." Bilingual and bicultural readers may think of the story of the famous Māori ancestor Paikea, whose waka was destroyed and who then traveled to Aotearoa on the back of a whale, and they may note, too, that whales (such as Paikea's) can be understood as manifestations of taniwha. According to Orbell, "On the ocean, taniwha often appear in the form of a whale or large shark" (150). Thus, "53's" reconfiguration of the arcs and straight line of "Waka 29" can be read as repeating and reconfiguring this element, as well.

The most intriguing specific feature of the figure of the aerial map in "53" is the persona "Robert," whose name implies the author Sullivan. His positioning directly above the word "shaped" in the final line, which describes the object of a "carved shaped loved floating totara," strongly suggests that the persona and the object are meant to be viewed—and read—as a single unit. The totara is a tree native to Aotearoa often used in carving and in the making of waka; moreover, *totara* can be used figuratively to indicate a waka. "Robert" is thus positioned as aboard this vessel. In his opening note, Sullivan states that "this sequence [of poems] is like a waka," and indeed, many individual poems support this idea explicitly or implicitly. The position of "Robert" directly above "shaped" suggests his specific role in the production of this totara, this waka, this sequence of poems: not "creating" the sequence out of nothing, like some originary cosmic force, but rather "shaping" material found within communal, familial, and personal histories. We may note here, as well, that the sequence of four adjectives that precede totara in the final line include three completed actions—"carved," "shaped," "loved"—and one action that is continuous—"floating." We have arrived, once again, at the theme of vital survival.

If we read the aerial map of "53" only in terms of these specific pairings—which potentially move us through ancient Greek and British voyaging, Polynesian migration, and Māori poetic production—we will have missed the overall effect of the visual poem's complex figure. That there are three small "islands" in the figure (rather than two or four or some other number) can be read as corresponding to the three main islands of Aotearoa: Te Ika A Maui (the North Island), Te Wai Pounamu (the South Island), and Rangiura (Stewart Island). The three islands are not arranged on the page into the relative positions of the islands of Aotearoa, however, but rather into the shape of a triangle. This triangle might suggest, in highly abstract terms, the so-called Polynesian triangle, the points of which indicate the northernmost, easternmost, and southernmost extents of Polynesian migration and settlement: the islands of Hawai'i, Rapa Nui (Easter Island), and Aotearoa. The positioning of the various floating entities, however, especially of "Robert" and the "totara," suggest that such a reading is at best partial. Rather than a specific map, the figure may point attention, instead, to the Oceanic navigation system described in *We, the Navigators* as "dead reckoning." Dead reckoning refers to a system of provisional positioning—a system of conceptual models for visualizing one's position on the open sea—by which a navigator takes account of currents, winds, storms, and other factors that may have thrown his waka off its intended course (see Lewis, chapter 4).[70] In this reading, the visual poem "53" and, perhaps, the visual poem "51," as well, functions to conceptualize and visualize the poetic sequence *thus far* in order to take critical measurement of its location and, if necessary, to reorient *Star Waka* at roughly the midpoint of its core of one hundred poems and 2,001 lines.

The precise midpoint of *Star Waka* can be measured in more than one way, depending on whether one counts poems or lines. In terms of the declared core of one hundred poems, the midpoint occurs in the white space *between* poems "50" and "51," whereas if we take into account the 101 poems listed in the table of contents (the enumerated core plus the unnumbered opening poem, "He karakia timatanga"), the midpoint occurs at poem "50": fifty poems precede it, and fifty follow. A further complication, however, is the additional unnumbered poem printed on the back cover of *Star Waka*, "A Cover Sail," which brings the total to 102. If this final poem is included, the midpoint now occurs in the white space between poems "51" and "52." Sullivan announces in his opening note that precisely 2,001 lines appear between his book's covers. (Recall that this number includes the lines that compose the one hundred core poems plus the lines of the unnumbered opening poem.) Based on Sullivan's 2,001 lines, the midpoint of *Star Waka* occurs at line eighteen in poem "52": 1,000 lines precede this line, and 1,000 lines follow.

Poem "52" is situated between the visual poems "51" and "53" with their iconic figures of a waka positioned within a planetary orb or compass and a waka positioned among other floating entities within a sea of islands. In the more conventionally lyric poem "52," the speaker explicitly positions himself in relation to Karetu, his mother's home village near the Bay of Islands in the north of Aotearoa's North Island.[71] In a subtle pun on the Oceanic navigational technique of dead reckoning, the speaker asserts that his maternal homeland was "planted" in him by his mother's "stories" of deceased elders and ancestors. It is this oral tradition, appropriated into the speaker's sense of self through years of listening, absorbing, remembering, and retelling—this reckoning of the dead—that insures his repeated reorientation toward the whanau (extended family) and his repeated return to the homeland.[72] The structure of the poem

supports and enhances this message in the way that it subtly emphasizes the concepts of centering and balance. The thirty lines of the poem,
which correspond to Sullivan's age at the time of writing, are divided
into seven stanzas of unequal lengths.[73] These can be arranged into at
least two related symmetries. The first symmetry emphasizes two halves
to the poem and divides the stanzas into two sets, each with a total of
fifteen lines: a first set of five stanzas divided into line groupings of four,
three, three, two, and three and a second set of two stanzas divided into
line groupings of twelve and three. The second symmetry emphasizes a
more complex four-part organization. In the first half of the poem, a set
of four stanzas totaling twelve lines, divided into groupings of four, three,
three, and two, is followed by a single stanza of three lines, for a total of
fifteen; this pattern is repeated with variation in the second half of the
poem, where a single stanza of twelve lines is followed by a single stanza
of three lines, again for a total of fifteen.

This second symmetry, especially, emphasizes the poem's thematic
content and movement. The first set of twelve lines, organized as four
stanzas, introduces the theme of visiting the familial and tribal home of
Karetu; the three-line stanza that immediately follows then introduces
the theme of the significant relationship between belonging to a place
and having heard and appropriated its stories as one's own: "but my
mother is from Karetu / and that is how I know the place / through all
the stories she's told me." The second set of twelve lines, organized as a
single stanza, joins these themes in its first ten lines by briefly catalog-
ing the stories told by the speaker's mother, each of which is marked by
the prepositions "like" or "about," and then reemphasizes the conjunction of the themes in its final two lines: "that's why I go back because
of my mother / who planted Karetu in me." The final three-line stanza
links the poem to the book's larger themes related to waka and tribal
ancestors but also links directly to the three-line stanza at the end of
the first half of the poem: "not just because of my ancestors / buried
in the cemetery and the cave nearby / whose waka navigated to the
soil there." These lines could directly follow the earlier three, without
the intervening catalog of stories, and still make sense. The speaker
resists a biological essentialism and asserts the importance of cultural
memory and oral traditions in defining personal identity.

Line eighteen of poem "52," the precise midpoint of *Star Waka's*
2,001 lines, is part of the catalog of specific stories told by the mother

and now recalled in the speaker's own voice: "about Nanny Pu who lived to be over a hundred."[74] The line begins with the preposition "about," linking it to the mother's stories. It ends with the phrase "over a hundred," the grandmother's age, which also can refer to the number of poems in the *Star Waka* sequence. Between "about" and "over a hundred," the line's reference to Nanny Pu can suggest the well-known whakataukī (saying, proverb) *ka pu te ruha, ka hao te rangatahi* (the old net *lies in a heap*, the new net goes fishing). The whakataukī indicates how the younger generation takes up the responsibilities of its elders and carries the community forward through its own actions. In "52," readers witness the thirty-year-old speaker taking up his mother's role as the teller of the family stories that link them all to the ancestral homeland at Karetu. It is yet another iteration of the themes of continuance and vital survival. Although the book is organized around elements of historic Polynesian voyaging and migration, "star," "waka," and "ocean," the precise midpoint of the sequence returns the speaker—and readers—to the *settled* land of Aotearoa and to the stories that shore up contemporary identities defined as Māori.

Patterning Indigenous Worlds

Flanking the precise midpoint of *Star Waka*, Sullivan's poems "51" and "53" manifest Oceanic navigational techniques for visualizing the position of the waka at sea so that necessary corrections can be made to keep the vessel on course. An additional technique for handling these "waka pitches" is demonstrated in the poem "Waka 74: Sea anchor," positioned roughly three-quarters of the way through the sequence.[75] Sullivan writes:

> In storms the waka would lower
> a sea anchor halfway to help control
>
> the vessel. In a way this poem
> is a sea anchor. We are waiting
>
> for a storm to pass, one preventing
> control of the narrative.[76]
> (83)

Having regained control in poems "Waka 75" and "Waka 76," Sullivan's speaker moves first toward the minisequence of persona poems (wakas 84 to 90 and 92 to 96) and then on to the final four poems in the core of one hundred. "Waka 97" returns to the potent combination of a prayer for the waka crew paired with the italicized tuki waka—"*hoea hoea ra*," again repeated four times—created in "He karakia timatanga," the unnumbered opening poem. "Waka 98" allows the speaker's own waka, this sequence of poems, to respond to the vexed question, "when will you stop tasting the wind?" In an italicized voice the waka replies, *"when the wind relinquishes its salt taste / then like my ancient cousins I will turn to stone / and stay here forever"* (108). "Waka 99" explicitly links the "resurrection" of ancient waka turned to stone and otherwise rendered dormant with the "resurrection" of the Māori nation, a theme that has been developed across the sequence.[77] "Waka 100," the final poem in Sullivan's core and one of its longest at sixty-eight lines divided into eleven stanzas, then closes the sequence by positioning the book's meditation on waka of the past, present, and possible future within distinctive European and Māori conceptions of time.

The first half of Sullivan's "Waka 100" functions similarly to Hedge Coke's opening narrative poem, "Before Next Dawning," in its panoramic overview of Indigenous–settler contact—here, in Aotearoa New Zealand. In the opening seven lines, Sullivan reorients orthodox contact history from the seventeenth- and eighteenth-century European technology of the *bark* to the transhistoric Oceanic technology of the *waka*, emphasizing Indigenous rather than settler agency and creating an account that is distinctly Māori:

Stroke past line 1642
into European time.
Stroke past 1769
and the introduction of the West.

Stroke on the approach to 1835
and formal Northern Maori sovereignty.

Stroke into the New World and stop.[78]
(110)

The second half of "Waka 100," however, functions more similarly to Hedge Coke's closing narrative poem, "When the Animals Leave This Place," in its prophetic look toward the possibility of future worlds:

And you, Urizen, Jupiter, Io Matua Kore,
holder of the compasses—
wind compass, solar compass,
compass encompassing known
currents, breather of the first breath
in every living creature,
guide the waka between islands,
between years and eyes of the Pacific
out of mythologies to consciousness.[79]

But in contrast to Hedge Coke's vision of the River's highly localized cycle of world renewal and the reclamation of specific geographic sites, Sullivan's "Waka 100," whose number indicates the new century, imagines a Māori world extending beyond known conceptions of both time and space. When Sullivan writes in the seventh stanza that "we ask our ancestors to wake, / [...] our ancestors of a culture / that has held its breath / through the age of Dominion," it is in preparation not for the reclamation of specific territory but rather for his speaker's exhortations for temporal and spatial expansion. In the first six lines of the eleventh and closing stanza of "Waka 100," Sullivan's speaker exhorts "you stars, the ancestors" to "burn brilliantly" on waka from the present and the past. But in the seventh and final line (line sixty-eight of the poem "Waka 100" and line 2,001 of the larger sequence), the speaker exhorts these same stars and ancestors to "burn on waka past the end of the light" (112). The final phrase indicates time and space beyond te ao mārama, "the world of light," the known configuration of our contemporary world situated between Ranginui, the sky father, and Papatūānuku, the earth mother. This vision of Indigenous culture and technology continues far beyond the local. This vision of Oceanic voyaging extends beyond the Earth's sea of islands into the cosmos and into futures unknown.[80]

Vital Indigenous survival, and the possibilities of other voyages, indeed.

Coda: Always Be-*coming* Indigenous

Hedge Coke's and Sullivan's book-length sequences of poems disrupt the typical coding, within dominant discourses, of construction and trade, exploration and migration, and intentional system and complex and repeatable pattern as "superior" activities that distinguish (civilized) "settlers" from (savage) "Natives." Similar to the star map in *Ceremony*, the earthworks in *Blood Run* and the waka in *Star Waka* represent Indigenous technologies that aid in resistance to various "destroyers" and that guide users toward Indigenous resurgence.

The particular emphasis Hedge Coke and Sullivan place on Indigenous technologies for settlement is also not without precedent. Twenty-five years before Silko published her novel *Ceremony* and a half century before Hedge Coke and Sullivan published their turn-of-the-twenty-first-century sequences of poems, a prominent U.S. American Indian intellectual and a prominent New Zealand Māori intellectual each published a nonfiction book of history and anthropology similarly focused on revealing the complex patterns of Indigenous exploration, migration, trade, and settlement. *They Came Here First: The Epic of the American Indian* by D'Arcy McNickle and *The Coming of the Maori* by Te Rangi Hiroa (Sir Peter Buck) were both published in 1949, in the wake of the demographic upheavals of World War II and on the eve of the many social changes that would continue to accelerate for Indigenous peoples in the United States and in Aotearoa across the decade of the 1950s.[81] Moreover, McNickle and Buck produced their substantial works not exclusively for specialist scholars but rather for broader audiences of educated readers, including educated Indigenous readers.[82] Like the early twenty-first-century "creative" and "imaginative" works produced by Hedge Coke and Sullivan, these mid-twentieth-century "scientific" and "factual" works were meant to be widely accessible.

As expected within their fields of expertise, McNickle and Buck each surveys scientific evidence and analyzes historical data. Each demonstrates as well, however, an explicit literariness: storytelling conventions and imaginative techniques that build interest and drama; a subjective, insider's perspective; a narrative voice that is often surprisingly personal.[83] Perhaps most striking is the coincidence that each Indigenous intellectual anchors the magisterial title of his work with a different form of the verb *to come*. There is a potentially sharp distinction to be drawn between the declarative sense of completion created by McNickle's simple past tense, *They* Came *Here First*, and the dynamic sense of process created by Buck's gerund, *The* Coming *of the Maori*. Each author's invocation of epic, however, which is explicit in McNickle but equally present in the grand syntax offered by Buck, suggests a shared commitment to not simply recount the historical settlement of Indigenous peoples but to record in detail how they became a distinct people and, thus, to herald the heroic founding of distinctive Indigenous *nations*.[84] This is a commitment Hedge Coke and Sullivan will advance, too, a half century later.

My point is not to argue that McNickle's and Buck's works of nonfiction prose provide direct antecedents for the poetry produced by Hedge Coke and Sullivan, as tempting as that argument is for establishing a continuity of Indigenous intellectual traditions and artistic practices across the second half of the twentieth century and into the twenty-first. There are too many differences in the personal visions, experiences, and commitments of the four writers, too many differences in their historical, social, and political contexts, too many differences in the scope and emphases of their respective careers. Rather, my point is that despite these significant differences, McNickle's and Buck's works of history and anthropology share with Hedge Coke's and Sullivan's dramatic sequences of poems an implicit interest in defining Indigenous identities as the result of ancient and ongoing *processes* of making, trading, moving—in a word, of *be-coming* or coming into being. The "literary" aspects of the earlier set of works, especially—what their contemporary reviewers called the "speculative" and "imaginative" sections of McNickle's and Buck's factual studies—work similarly to Hedge Coke's and Sullivan's efforts to decolonize dominant, orthodox scholarship on Indigenous technologies and settlement by actively revivifying the Indigenous past and by linking that vital past to an ongoing Indigenous present and to possible Indigenous futures. This emphasis, this strong belief in the persistence and resurgence of Indigenous peoples and cultures within the context of contemporary politics, represents a significant continuity of Indigenous intellectual traditions across the twentieth and twenty-first centuries.

One can only speculate that had they lived to see the "new worlds" of the twenty-first century and the second millennium, McNickle and

Buck would have heralded Hedge Coke's and Sullivan's efforts to defy orthodox scholarship and to disrupt dominant metaphors that continue, in our own era, to ignore Indigenous knowledges and to subsume and erase Indigenous histories within settler constructions. Like their younger counterparts, McNickle and Buck responded to the settler's situated nostalgia of "So lamentable" with the defiant exclamation, "what was!"

Notes

Introduction

1. In *Blood Narrative* I offer an extended explanation for my use of parentheses in the term *(post)colonial*, which is meant to emphasize the irony of an often asserted postcolonial situation for Indigenous peoples in settler nations (where the *post-* implies beyond) that is never quite one. I also offer an extended definition of the term *Indigenous* and an extended justification for comparing U.S. American Indian and New Zealand Māori literary and activist texts.

2. My remarks are not meant as a comprehensive account of the historical development or the current state of the established field of comparative literature or the emerging field of world literature studies.

3. My reading of "Comparatively Speaking" assumes the speaker addresses white Australian tourists; the poem produces similar effects if the reader assumes the speaker addresses Pakeha New Zealanders.

4. This settler-driven form of colonial comparison also can be understood through Edward Said's concept of *orientalism* or through Gerald Vizenor's concepts of *manifest manners* and *terminal creeds*.

5. In the United States, see, for instance, Kenneth Lincoln, *Native American Renaissance* (1983); Louis Owens, *Other Destinies: Understanding the American Indian Novel* (1992); James Ruppert, *Mediation in Contemporary Native American Fiction* (1995); James Cox, *Muting White Noise: Native American and European American Novel Traditions* (2006); and Sean Teuton, *Red Land, Red Power: Grounding Knowledge in the American Indian Novel* (2008). My own comparative study, *Blood Narrative*, discusses several celebrated mid-twentieth-century American Indian novels but attempts to expand the body and types of texts under discussion, as does Robert Dale Parker's *The Invention of Native American Literature* (2003). This list is by no means exhaustive.

6. Reclamations of nineteenth-century texts include the 1997 republication of *Wynema, A Child of the Forest* by S. Alice Callahan (Creek), originally published in 1891; the 2007 republication of *The Life and Traditions of the Red Man*, by Joseph Nicolar (Penobscot), originally published in 1893; the 2010 publication of *Changing Is Not Vanishing: A Collection of American Indian Poetry to 1930*, edited by Robert Dale Parker; and the 2011 republication of *Queen of the Woods* by Simon Pokagon (Potawatomie), originally published in 1899. Reclamations of early twentieth-century texts include the 1987 republication of *The Moccasin Maker* by E. Pauline Johnson (Mohawk), originally published in 1913, and the 2007 first publication of *The Singing Bird* by John Milton Oskison (Cherokee). Reclamations of mid-twentieth-century texts include the 2003 republication of *Winter Count* by Dallas Chief Eagle (Lakota),

originally published in 1967. Robert Warrior (Osage) argues the need for more attention to nonfiction texts in *The People and the Word: Reading Native Nonfiction* (2005).

7. I am drawing on Diana Taylor's distinction in *The Archive and the Repertoire: Performing Cultural Memory in the Americas* (2003) between the "archive" of supposedly enduring materials—texts, documents, buildings, and bones—and the supposedly ephemeral repertoire of embodied practices and knowledges, such as spoken language, dance, sports, and ritual (19).

8. Many Native and non-Native scholars have called for increased attention to issues of aesthetics within Indigenous literary studies. The Indigenous Australian scholar Marcia Langton, for instance, writes, "I contend that the central problem is not one of racial discrimination, although I do not deny that it might be a factor in specific or general encounters. Rather, the central problem is the need to develop a body of knowledge and critical perspective to do with aesthetics and politics, whether written by Aboriginal or non-Aboriginal people, on representations of Aboriginal people and concerns in art, film, television or other media" (115).

9. Book-length studies published in the United States that also endeavor to engage various Indigenous aesthetic systems and/or technologies include Greg Sarris, *Keeping Slug Woman Alive: A Holistic Approach to American Indian Texts* (1993); Lisa Brooks, *The Common Pot: The Recovery of Native Space in the Northeast* (2008); and Penelope Kelsey, *Tribal Theory in Native American Literature: Dakota and Haudenosaunee Writing and Indigenous Worldviews* (2008). Other scholars pursuing this line of work include Malea Powell and Angela Haas in the field of Indigenous rhetorics.

10. Such calls are often traced to their articulation in Robert Warrior's *Tribal Secrets: Recovering American Indian Intellectual Traditions* (1995) and Jolene Rickard's (Tuscarora) "Sovereignty: A Line in the Sand" (1995). They can be traced further to goals articulated by early activist organizations, including on the global stage the World Council of Indigenous Peoples (WCIP), beginning in the 1970s.

11. Although not an enrolled citizen of the Chickasaw nation, I trace Chickasaw ancestry through my maternal line.

12. For an account of the formation of NAISA, see Robert Warrior, "Organizing Native American and Indigenous Studies."

13. I was fortunate, for example, to spend six months in 2005 at the Turnbull Library in Wellington, Aotearoa New Zealand.

14. In 2006 and 2007, Māori scholar Alice Te Punga Somerville and I collaborated on several related projects in comparative Indigenous literary studies. We cofacilitated an interactive workshop on pedagogy; we copresented a plenary address for a symposium, which led to a special issue of the *Journal of New Zealand Literature*, which we coedited with Alex Calder and Witi Ihimaera and for which we cowrote an introduction staged as a back-and-forth exchange; and we copresented, along with Steven Salaita, in an interactive conference session.

15. See N. Scott Momaday, *The Gourd Dancer* (1976), *In the Presence of the Sun* (1992), and *In the Bear's House* (1999); Wendy Rose, *Lost Copper* (1980) and *The Halfbreed Chronicles* (1985); Peter Blue Cloud, *Elderberry Flute Song* (1982); Gail Tremblay, *Indian Singing in 20th Century America* (1990); Nora Naranjo-Morse, *Mud Woman: Poems from the Clay* (1992); Eric Gansworth, *Nickel Eclipse: Iroquois Moon* (2000) and *A Half-Life of*

Cardio-Pulmonary Function: Poems and Paintings (2008); Joy Harjo, *Letter from the End of the Twentieth Century* (1995), *Native Joy for Real* (2004), *Winding through the Milky Way* (2008), and *Red Dreams: A Trail beyond Tears* (2010); Sherman Alexie, *The Business of Fancydancing* (2002); and Diane Glancy, *Flutie* (1998) and its film adaptation, *The Dome of Heaven* (2010).

16. While a visiting professor at the University of Oregon in 2007–2008, I organized Indigenous Literatures and Other Arts: A Symposium and Workshop, held at the Many Nations Longhouse on campus. I experimented with collaboration enacted along several axes at once and tested my hypothesis about the productiveness of the trans-Indigenous staging of unexpected conversations across genres, forms, and media; across academic fields and arts practices; across Indigenous nations; and across historical periods and geographical locations. Rather than a keynote or panel format, the symposium was organized around staged conversations between an artist and/or arts scholar and a writer and/or literary scholar and hands-on workshops led by one or more workshop leaders.

17. Kauri is a species of tree native to Aotearoa; swamp kauri is kauri wood that has been recovered from a swamp. Pāua is a species of abalone.

18. For more information on Northwest Coast style, see Bill Holm, *Northwest Coast Indian Art: An Analysis of Form* (1965). Graham's use of interlocking spirals to form the whale's head is reminiscent of paintings made by the Māori artist John Hovell to illustrate Witi Ihimaera's 1987 novel *The Whale Rider*, which I discuss in chapter 4.

19. I am thinking of newspaper journalism but also of academic essays, broadcast and published speeches, government reports, and book-length works of scholarship in several fields, as well as biography, legal and political analysis, and social commentary.

20. See, for instance, Momaday's foreword to *Earth Is My Mother, Sky Is My Father.*

21. Mignolo, *Local Histories/Global Designs.*

22. Jahnke, "Māori Art towards the Millennium."

23. Survivance, Gerald Vizenor's concept of "active native presence" and "survival as resistance," was first demonstrated in a series of provocations about American Indian representation, published in 1994 as *Manifest Manners: Postindian Warriors of Survivance* (reissued in 1999 as *Manifest Manners: Postindian Narratives on Survivance*). Vizenor continues this demonstration in *Fugitive Poses: Native American Indian Scenes of Absence and Presence*, published in 1998. He provides a more straightforward definition in his 2008 essay "Aesthetics of Survivance: Literary Theory and Practice."

1. "Being" Indigenous "Now"

1. The *Midcontinent American Studies Journal*, now *American Studies*, was associated with the University of Kansas and the Midcontinent American Studies Association (MASA), now the Mid-American American Studies Association. The 2005 special double issue of *American Studies* was published jointly with the journal *Indigenous Studies Today*. An earlier version of this chapter was titled "Unspeaking the Settler: 'The Indian Today' in International Perspective."

2. For a detailed account of the AICC and its *Declaration of Indian Purpose*, see Allen, *Blood Narrative*, 103–6.

3. For an additional account of the development of the 1965 special issue and its relevant historical and political contexts, see Valandra, "National Coexistence Is Our Bull Durham."

4. Vine Deloria Jr. begins *Custer Died for Your Sins: An Indian Manifesto* (1969), "To be an Indian in modern American society is in a very real sense to be unreal and ahistorical" (2). He argues, further, that "the deep impression made upon American minds by the Indian struggle against the white man in the last century has made the contemporary Indian somewhat invisible compared with his ancestors. [. . .] Indians are probably invisible because of the tremendous amount of misinformation about them" (12). Writing about the representation of American Indians in popular discourses in the 1950s and 1960s, the non-Native historian Robert F. Berkhofer Jr. notes in *The White Man's Indian: Images of the American Indian from Columbus to the Present* (1978) that "no matter how new the media were, the old White stereotypes of the Indian generally prevailed in their presentations" (103).

5. Of course, in either version, emphasis can be shifted so that "Today" becomes the significant noun, modified by "The Indian" or "The American Indian," which become its adjectives. In this reading—more against the grain than with it—the special issue announces its subject as the contemporary moment as experienced, understood, or imagined by Indigenous North Americans. While intriguing for its suggestion of subverting dominant discourses, this possibility is not realized in the special issue. For an extended definition of "imperialist nostalgia," see Resaldo, *Culture and Truth*.

6. The time marker "today" is common in "contemporary" assessments of all categories of difference. From the 1960s and early 1970s, such texts include Herbert Aptheker's *The Negro Today* (1962) and expanded *Soul of the Republic: The Negro Today* (1964); Robert Penn Warren's essay "The Negro Now" published in *Look* magazine (1965), an excerpt from his book *Who Speaks for the Negro?*; J. I. Simmons and Barry Winograd's *It's Happening: A Portrait of the Youth Scene Today* (1966); *Seventeen* magazine's *The Teen Age Girl Today* (1968); and Edward Simmen's edited collection *Pain and Promise: The Chicano Today* (1972).

7. The Indian Affairs Branch became part of Canada's Department of Citizenship and Immigration in 1950.

8. Information about Dunstan is taken from William J. Megill, "Editor's Note-Book."

9. The 1964 edition of *The Indian in Transition* was reprinted in 1969.

10. Here and throughout, I refer to the indigenous Polynesian inhabitants of what are known as the Hawaiian Islands and their descendants as Hawaiians rather than as Native Hawaiians.

11. A third printing appeared in 1976, the year of the U.S. bicentennial, and a fourth, in 1995; the most recent editions were published by Ku Pa'a Publishing.

12. An earlier overview survey was published in Australia in March 1962 by the Council for Aboriginal Rights, located in Victoria. Titled *The Struggle for Dignity*, the brief book carries this explanatory subtitle on its front cover: *A Critical Analysis of the Australian Aborigine Today, the Laws Which Govern Him, and Their Effects*. Edited by William M. Murray, it includes chapters written by Shirley Andrews, Mary M. Bennett (in whose memory the book is dedicated), Alastair H. Campbell, Len Fox, and Barry E. Christophers. In the front matter the editor claims, "In presenting this book

the Council for Aboriginal Rights has completed a unique project. For the first time a picture of Aboriginal life on a nation-wide scale is given" (n.p.). The five contributors are described only as "experts in their field." Bennett, who died in 1961, is described in more detail as a "crusader" for Aboriginal rights and an author of a short book, *The Australian Aboriginal as a Human Being* (1930), and several articles on Aboriginal history and culture. Additional overview surveys with similar titles were produced in the 1970s, including Susan Reid's 1972 *The Aborigine Today*, published by the Victoria Education Department for use in middle schools, and Chris Mullard's 1974 booklet *Aborigines in Australia Today*, commissioned and published by the newly organized National Aboriginal Forum. The latter text is of particular interest. As described in the preface, Mullard, "a black British sociologist and author, was invited to Australia by the National Aboriginal Forum to report on the conditions under which many Aborigines are living" (6). Mullard had recently published the 1973 study *Black Britain* (released in the United States in 1975 as *On Being Black in Britain*), one of the first books published by a black writer born and raised in the United Kingdom. Outside Australia, R. D. Cartwright's *Aborigines Today* was published in 1977 by the New Zealand commercial press Smith/Methuen for use in elementary and junior high schools; Survival International, based in London, published its booklet *The Aborigines Today: Land Rights, Uranium Mining, Social Disruption, Anthropology* in 1978. Several texts with titles similar to that of the 1965 special issue were published both in Australia and abroad in response to Australia's bicentennial in 1988, including a double issue of the journal *Kunapipi*, "Aboriginal Culture Today"; Julian Burger's *Aborigines Today: Land and Justice*, published by the Anti-Slavery Society in London; and Penny Taylor's *After 200 Years: Photographic Essays of Aboriginal and Islander Australia Today*, published by Cambridge University Press.

13. Reay does not capitalize Aborigine in her introduction or in any of her contributors' essays. The phrase "aboriginal life today" is taken from the blurb on the dust jacket.

14. By 1968, Schwimmer had left New Zealand to become a professor of anthropology at the University of Toronto. For a history and analysis of *Te Ao Hou*, see Allen, *Blood Narrative*, 43–72.

15. See Allen, *Blood Narrative*, 103–6.

16. Curiously, the map insert is not listed in the table of contents or front matter. Titled "The North American Indians: 1950 Distribution of Descendants of the Aboriginal Population of Alaska, Canada and the United States," the map was prepared between 1956 and 1959 under the direction of Sol Tax at the University of Chicago and originally published in December 1960 in preparation for the 1961 American Indian Chicago Conference, which Tax and Lurie helped organize. In the Penguin paperback edition, the map is listed in the table of contents and integrated into the final pages of the book.

17. Holt mentions in passing the history of systematic violence against American Indians. Similarly, several writers in *Aborigines Now* make passing reference to American Indians or New Zealand Māori. I have identified only one comparative survey from the period with a title similar to "The Indian Today," published by the Inter-American Indian Institute based in Mexico. In December 1962, the institute published

an English translation of its "Indianist Yearbook," an annual supplement to its quarterly journal *America Indigena*. Titled "Indians in the Hemisphere Today: Guide to
the Indian Population," it offers brief profiles of the contemporary demographics and
economic development of Indian communities in eighteen nation-states across the
Americas, arranged alphabetically from Argentina to Venezuela. Included are entries
for the predominantly English-speaking United States (a member of the institute) and
Canada (a nonmember). Edited by the institute's director, Miguel León-Portilla, and
supported financially by the Wenner-Gren Foundation for Anthropological Research,
the guide's eighteen monographs were written by several Latin American and one U.S.
anthropologist; their primary audience appears to be governments and nongovern-
mental organizations involved in community and socioeconomic development across
the hemisphere. The institute was established in 1940 at the First Inter-American
Indian Congress. Prior to 1962, the annual supplement to *America Indigena* was titled
"Boletín Indigenista." The English translation for "Indians in the Hemisphere Today"
was prepared by Virginia B. García.

18. In their introduction to "Indigeneity at the Crossroads of American Studies,"
D. Anthony Tyeeme Clark and Norman Yetman overview the careers of Thomas and
Witt (20n17).

19. The other is "Tight Shoe Night" by the non-Native researcher Carol K. Rachlin.

20. We might compare Holt's description of this "vicarious sense of courage" with
the American Indian intellectual and writer Ella Deloria's description of "vicarious
honor" in her historical novel *Waterlily* (85). We might link Holt's specific statement
about "the fantastical navigational feats of our ancestors" to the work of Māori poet
Robert Sullivan in his sequence of poems *Star Waka*, which I discuss in chapter 5.
Here and elsewhere, I use square brackets to indicate when ellipses are mine rather
than the author's.

21. Holt's emphasis aligns with what I describe in *Blood Narrative* as the "blood/
land/memory complex."

22. Information on the publication history and promotion of *The Maori Today* is
from files held at Archives New Zealand in Wellington (file GP1 W2714 5/32/1, Maori
Affairs: "The Maori Today").

23. New Zealand sent troops to Malaya in 1956 as part of a Commonwealth effort
to fight communist insurgents. The so-called emergency lasted until 1960.

24. Information on the publishing background for *The Maori People in the Nine-
teen-Sixties* is from files held at Archives New Zealand in Wellington (file ABJZ 869
W4644 18 9/3/28 1, Maori Purposes Fund Board—Publications, "Aspirations and
Stresses of a Minority").

25. The committee hoped to actually receive at least eighteen completed essays
from the invited contributors by the publisher's deadline.

26. Beaglehole agreed to write a new essay for the collection but died before its
completion.

27. This passage begins: "One of the authors has suggested to me that 'the term
"Aborigines" has clearly taken on a "nationality" aspect . . . their being singled out as
a special group seems to require the capital that one would normally give to other
nationalities'" (168).

28. In the obituary for Marie Reay (1922–2004) published in the *Australian Journal of Anthropology*, Paula Brown Glick and Jeremy Beckett remark that Reay was not "comfortable with the increasing radicalism of the 1970s and 1980s, and never had much sympathy for Aboriginal land rights." Beckett is one of the young anthropologists featured in *Aborigines Now*.

29. Information on the production of the film *The Maori Today* is from files held in Archives New Zealand in Wellington (files AAPG W3435 16 3/2/87, "The Maori Today," and AAMK 869/1160A 52/1/8 1, "The Maori Today—16 mm film").

30. September 25, 1968, file AAPG W3435 16 3/2/87, "The Maori Today," Archives New Zealand, Wellington.

31. Numerous scholars have analyzed this early ethnographic photography. For a contemporary Indigenous analysis and response, see Ortiz, *Beyond the Reach of Time and Change*.

32. The American Indian writer Thomas King, who is also an accomplished photographer, writes, "That's really what photographs are. Not records of moments, but rather imaginative acts" (43).

33. A one-thousand-year Hawaiian time line runs down one side of each cover, beginning with the year 960 and ending with 1960. A one-inch margin above "960" and a quarter-inch margin below "1960" indicate that Hawaiian history extends before and after these markers of a Hawaiian millennium. Five other designated years punctuate the space between these markers, dividing the millennium into rough periods; these are illustrated in a vertical mural on each cover. At the top of the mural, corresponding to the period around 960, are images of double-hulled Polynesian canoes with triangular sails; next, for the period from 1350 to 1630, are images of well-organized and highly developed Hawaiian villages; below these, corresponding to the period around 1770, are representations of the first appearances of European sailing ships, as well as representations of classic Hawaiian artifacts; further down, near "1820," are images of the Hawaiian kingdom, Euro-American architecture, and plantations; finally, for the period between 1920 and 1960, the mural illustrates the contemporary coexistence of rural communities and the large modern city of Honolulu, with images of a commercial airliner and a cruise ship to indicate the importance of modern travel and tourism.

34. It is a surprise, then, that the more recent editions of *On Being Hawaiian* appear with a different cover. Instead of the time line and mural, the later printings use one of the historical sketches included in the original edition, a representation titled "Masked Kahuna" that is described in the 1964 edition as "Secret alii sect in gourd helmets, sketched by Webber at the time of Captain Cook's last visit to Hawaii." The sketch depicts a group of Hawaiian leaders paddling a double-hulled canoe, suggesting that *On Being Hawaiian* is about Hawaiian identity in the historical past. Moreover, the later editions include only forty-four illustrations rather than the fifty-three of the first printing; the final images are now "Pa'u Riders, after annexation" (63) and "Unidentified singers of the early 20th century" (64), which also link the text with the past rather than with the present or possible future.

35. The photograph is captioned "David Mathewson, 3 years, of Hamilton, Ontario, has a chat with an Indian, Perry Williams, also 3 years, at the Six Nations Indian Fair

at Ohswekan" (186). Most of the photographs that illustrate Dunstan's essay, including this one, were provided by the Department of Citizenship and Immigration.

36. The 1970 Penguin paperback edition of *The American Indian Today* includes a different image on its cover. In this black-and-white photograph, an apparently Plains Indian woman wearing a "traditional" beaded and fringed buckskin dress, moccasins, and headband stands inside the doorway of a decorated tipi, cooking on a modern range and looking down at an Indian child wearing a "modern" girl's party or perhaps church dress and white shoes. No caption accompanies the unattributed photograph. Gilda Kuhlman is credited with cover design.

37. Similar to other familiar terms for peoples indigenous to North America, the term Sioux is actually foreign, an abbreviated form of an Odawa term that was borrowed into Canadian French during the seventeenth century and later anglicized. Today, peoples typically designated Sioux tend to refer to themselves as Lakota, Nakota, or Dakota, indicating their particular dialect, or by specific nation names. Throughout the book, I try to follow the usage of particular authors.

38. Levine mentions Haskell in his introduction to the special issue only in passing: "A colleague of mine and his wife hired a teen-age girl from Haskell Indian Institute to do housecleaning." The brief anecdotes he tells about this Pima girl and her interactions with the "modern" world of Lawrence, Kansas, are meant to suggest her difference as Indian ("Even months after coming to Haskell, this intelligent youngster was still bewildered by the elementary artifacts of the larger civilization"), but the stories are awkward in their telling. They say more about Levine's assumptions about what counts as Native difference and why difference might or might not matter than they do about the diverse lives of American Indian young people in the 1960s (13).

39. A billy can or billy is a metal pot or kettle used for camp cooking.

40. The Pintubi are referred to in a subsequent essay, "Papunya: Westernization in an Aboriginal Community" by Jeremy Long, an investigation officer for the Welfare Branch of the Northern Territory Administration. Long's statements make more sense as captions for the photographs—such as, "Newcomers to the settlement who have seldom if ever worn clothes exhibit shame at nudity within weeks of their arrival" (78).

41. Lois Briggs was the first Indigenous Australian fashion model, appearing on both runways and television. Although her skin is visibly lighter than that of the unnamed subjects on the same page, she is marked as "Aboriginal" rather than "Part-aboriginal."

42. According to the *Australian Dictionary of Biography*, Robert Tudawali, also known as Bobby Wilson, was born c. 1929 on Melville Island off the coast of the Northern Territory to Tiwi parents and died tragically of severe burns and tuberculosis in 1967. He served in the Australian military during World War II and was an outstanding athlete before being cast as the male lead, Marbuck, in the 1955 film *Jedda*, directed by Charles Chauvel. He played subsequent roles in the 1958 film *Dust in the Sun* and in the Australian television series *Whiplash*. An advocate for Aboriginal justice, in 1966 Tudawali was elected vice president of the Northern Territory Council for Aboriginal Rights. See Forrest, "Tudawali, Robert (1929?-1967)."

43. Tudawali is also mentioned in "The Popular Image: Aborigines and the Newspapers" by Ted Docker, a journalist and historian. Echoing Beckett, Docker writes:

"What of Robert Tudawali, of the flashing teeth and the frank engaging personality? [. . .] If you look for Robert Tudawali or one of a dozen other bright alert young full-bloods who have been favoured at one time or another by the special approval of Darwin's native administration, you will find most likely he is in jail. Search in Kempsey for one of its famous aboriginal boxing heroes. He cannot be found. His wife has not seen him for six weeks. He is probably drunk somewhere" (18).

44. *Aborigines Now* includes "Negritude for the White Man" by Randolph Stow, a lecturer in English at the University of Western Australia and a published poet and novelist. In his analysis of white representations of Indigenous Australians, Stow laments, "What is needed, of course, is an aboriginal writer, a literary Namatjira [the Indigenous painter], an Australian Camara Laye [the West African novelist]" (6). Stow appears unaware of Kath Walker, an Aboriginal poet who published a first book in 1964. In her introduction, however, Reay includes Walker in a preemptive rebuttal to Stow that is also another instance of barely veiled paternalism: "Kath Walker, an aboriginal poet, has shown considerable promise in a volume of verse that is mainly propagandist for her people, but I see a real danger that she and others may find recognition before their grasp of the craftsmanship of writing gives them the literary stature to justify it. I would not like to see their work acclaimed just because it is written by aborigines and not because of any intrinsic merit it may have: the prospect calls to mind a circus in which fleas and elephants are applauded because they perform actions that are commonplace in humans" (xvi).

45. "Canadian Indians Today" includes a photograph of Micmac artist Michael Francis at work at his desk, with six of his "wildlife paintings" clearly visible on the wall behind him (193). In *Aborigines Now*, "Totemic Designs and Group Continuity in Walbiri Cosmology" by the anthropologist Nancy Munn includes three "figures" of contemporary Walbiri drawings, although there are no photographs of the artists.

46. Thompson's *Getting to Know American Indians Today* is part of Coward-McCann's Getting to Know series of juvenile books, which "cover today's world." In 1965, the series included seven titles devoted to explaining various United Nations agencies and many more titles set in various parts of Africa (eleven), the Arctic (one), Asia (twelve), the Caribbean and Central America (eight), Europe "East and West" (twelve), the Middle East (six), the Pacific (six), and South America (seven), as well as in North America (five). The publishers described the books in these terms: "This round-the-world series not only covers everyday life in many countries and regions and includes their geography and history—it also highlights *what's new today*" (n.p.).

47. Unfortunately, I have been unable to secure Larsen's short book. I assume it takes an explicitly Mormon perspective, based on descriptions of Larsen's other publications: *You and the Destiny of the Indian* (1966), *Free to Act* (1989), and *People of Destiny* (2001).

48. Robinson's revisions, however, amount to only an additional four pages.

49. Kirk often produced several books related to a particular geography. *David, Young Chief of the Quileutes: An American Indian Today* (1967), is part of a series that includes *The Olympic Seashore* (Port Angeles, Wash.: Olympic Natural History Association, 1962), *Exploring the Olympic Peninsula* (Seattle: University of Washington Press, 1964), and *The Olympic Rain Forest* (Seattle: University of Washington Press,

1966). In this period Kirk also produced another book with Harcourt, Brace and World focused on a "foreign" child, *Sigemi: A Japanese Village Girl* (1965).

50. Lurie uses similar language in the opening sentence of her contribution to the 1965 special issue, "An American Indian Renascence?" [sic]: "American Indian people constitute one of the smallest yet most durable minority groups in the United States" (25).

51. Information about Roessel is taken from the Navajo Nation's press release upon his death; see Navajo Nation, "Navajo Nation Bids Farewell." Much of this information is also included in the 1969 revised and expanded edition of Robinson's *Navajo Indians Today* (see 46–49).

52. These efforts were successful. In the Fall 1967 issue of the *MASJ*, Levine writes, "Our last special issue, the one devoted to the American Indian, is a case in point: it's all sold out. Please stop adopting it as a text for the time being. Adoptions continue to pour in, and we have no way to fill the orders. It will be reprinted, in expanded and much-revised form, this spring, and will then be permanently available" (2).

53. Levine's language about "fences" alludes to Robert Frost's 1914 poem "Mending Wall."

54. In his introduction Levine states, "The Editor conceives of this journal as a kind of *Scientific American* for American Studies, a place where specialists can 'report in' on the direction in which new research is going in their areas and on the implications of that work for people in other fields" (4). Near the end of the "MASA Bulletin," he argues further that "in practical terms responsibility for transmitting such information lies on the shoulders of our growing group of interdisciplinarians, people who as a professional commitment keep in close touch with a number of disciplines" (188). He then states, "It is one of the functions of the present *Journal*, and this issue in particular, to serve as a medium through which such contact [among different disciplines] can be established and maintained" (188). He ends the bulletin by stating, "Thus another one of the purposes of the present collection is to provide information, observations and recommendations which will be of use not merely to people working directly with the complex problems faced by the American Indian community, but to others, in fields as diverse as diplomacy and education as well" (189).

55. Although it was not published in the United States, we might include the scholarly collection *The North American Indian Today* (Toronto, Canada: University of Toronto Press, 1943), proceedings of a seminar conference jointly sponsored by the University of Toronto and Yale University from September 4 to 16, 1939, and coedited by C. T. Loram, chair of the Department of Race Relations at Yale, and T. F. McIlwraith, professor of anthropology at Toronto. Contributors include the U.S. anthropologist Ruth Underhill and the commissioner of Indian affairs John Collier. Attendees include the American Indian intellectuals Ruth Muskrat Bronson, then an associate guidance officer in the Office of Indian Affairs, and D'Arcy McNickle, then also an employee of OIA.

56. We might also include the national newspaper *Indian Country Today*, which began publication in 1981.

57. In the new century versions of the word Indigenous are increasingly used in similar ways. See, for example, the 2007 collection of scholarly essays titled *Indigenous Experience Today*, edited by Marisol de la Cadena and Orin Starn, which concludes with an afterword by Mary Louise Pratt titled "Indigeneity Today."

58. We might also ask what it means that only one title in this list includes an explicit reference to Alaska Natives.

59. Curtis is listed in the 1936 edition of *Indians of Today* as "Kaw—one-eighth" (38).

60. The 1936 edition includes an entry for the now infamous Gray Owl, who claimed various Indigenous identities during his lifetime—he is listed here as "Apache—three-eighths"—but is now known to have been non-Native.

61. Unlike McNickle and Peterson, Dozier is not identified as American Indian in the volume itself. However, Dozier is among the notable living Indians profiled in the 1960 and 1971 editions of *Indians of Today* (17–18; 208–9). He is also listed among prominent American Indians at the end of Hildegard Thompson's 1965 *Getting to Know American Indians Today* (58).

62. For a more detailed history of these events, see Allen, *Blood Narrative*.

2. Unsettling the Spirit of '76

1. A history of Australia Day is available at www.australiaday.com.au.

2. Local Aborigines were not invited to participate in the reenactment of Phillip's landing in 1938. Instead, a small group from western New South Wales were brought in to perform a brief corroboree (ritual). The reenactment did not include settler contact with any Indigenous peoples. For an overview, see www.australiaday.com.au.

3. For original documents, see Attwood and Markus, *The Struggle for Aboriginal Rights*, 82–91. Also see Heiss and Minter, *Anthology of Australian Aboriginal Literature*, 30–37.

4. "Active Indigenous presence" is one of the definitions Gerald Vizenor (Anishinaabe) has given for his politically charged term *survivance*.

5. Foley notes, in particular, that the *New York Times* ran a page 2 article about the protest (Seth Mydans, "Aborigines Cast a Shadow over Australia's Party," *New York Times*, January 26, 1988). *Australia Daze* (1988) is a seventy-five-minute "observational documentary" shot on January 26, 1988. Twenty-nine directors and their camera crews were posted to different parts of the country to record the bicentennial celebrations. Five of the directors were charged specifically with recording the Indigenous protest march. See http://australianscreen.com.au/titles/australia-daze.

6. Similar sentiments were voiced by other Aboriginal leaders, including Philip Morrissey, who developed and managed the Bicentennial National Aboriginal and Torres Strait Islander Program. Writing in the special double issue of the journal *Kunapipi*, Morrissey stated that "the march itself was considerably broader in its cultural implications than a straightforward boycott. One Aboriginal leader's speech, following the march, would not have been out of place coming from an advocate of the 'Living Together' theme of the Bicentenary and the striking news photographs of the march and its individual participants point to a victory of the spirit over historical circumstance" (11).

7. See Lonetree (Ho-Chunk), "Museums as Sites of Decolonization," for a discussion of the need for "truth telling as a decolonizing strategy" within the museum context. Lonetree's work draws from the important collection *For Indigenous Eyes Only: A Decolonization Handbook*, edited by Waziyatawin Angela Wilson and Michael Yellowbird.

8. I quote from the version of "The Burnum Burnum Declaration" reprinted in the *Anthology of Australian Aboriginal Literature*, 124–25. For brief accounts of Burnum's life and activism, see Milliken, "Obituary: Burnum Burnum," and the foreword to *Burnum Burnum's Aboriginal Australia* (7–9). A detailed account is available in Norst, *Burnum Burnum*.

9. Philip Morrissey argues that "Burnum's irony in part exemplifies his refusal to be imprisoned by history or to accept a moral or a political dimension of the Bicentenary as being the only one." Morrissey also notes, "Speaking of his own Bicentennial grant to prepare a traveler's guide to Aboriginal Australia [...] Burnum has sometimes said that he is celebrating 250 Bicentenaries [that is, 50,000 years of Aboriginal tenure in the land]" (11). In the travel guide itself, Burnum includes a photo of the Aboriginal protest of the bicentennial First Fleet reenactment in the section titled "Aboriginal Sydney today" (51). For an analysis of the 1969 Alcatraz proclamation, see Allen, *Blood Narrative*, 162–68.

10. For an account of the Aboriginal demand for a treaty, see, for example, Kevin Gilbert, "Aboriginal Sovereignty: Justice, the Law and Land: A Draft Written in Consultation with Aboriginal Members of the Sovereign Aboriginal Coalition at Alice Springs on 19–21 June 1987" (cited in Attwood and Markus, 310–13); and the "Barunga Statement" of June 12, 1988 (cited in Attwood and Markus, 316). The call for a treaty went unfulfilled, as documented by the Aboriginal rock group Yothu Yindi in their 1992 hit single "Treaty." For an account of the Bicentennial National Aboriginal and Torres Strait Islander Program, see Morrissey, "Restoring a Future to a Past."

11. See Heiss and Minter, *Anthology of Australian Aboriginal Literature*, 6, 40.

12. The case of *The Education of Little Tree* has been reported in numerous accounts. Dan T. Carter (no relation) broke the story of Carter's identity in "The Transformation of a Klansman," *New York Times*, October 4, 1991. Among other Indigenous scholars, Gerald Vizenor has written extensively about Carter; see, for instance, his remarks in *Fugitive Poses*, 114–17. Vizenor includes the detail that "*The Education of Little Tree* has sold close to a million copies, more copies sold than *The Way to Rainy Mountain* [1969] by N. Scott Momaday, which once was the best seller at the University of New Mexico Press" (116). See also Huhndorf, "The Making of an Indian: 'Forrest' Carter's Literary Inventions," in *Going Native*.

13. July 4 has been used by American Indian writers and activists (as well as by other so-called minority writers and activists) as a key symbol of (hypocritical) U.S. ideals of freedom and justice, beginning as early as William Apess's 1836 *Eulogy on King Philip* (see Apess, 286). For a discussion, see Lopenzina, "What to the American Indian Is the Fourth of July?"

14. Warner was a veteran of World War II and the Korean War, a lawyer, and secretary of the navy under President Nixon from 1972 to 1974. He served as a five-term Republican U.S. Senator from Virginia between 1979 and 2009.

15. Information on Thomasine Hill is taken from *The Desert Yearbook, Class of 1974* (Tucson: University of Arizona, 1974), 24, www.e-yearbook.com.

16. Office of Native American Programs, *Annual Report*, n.p.

17. McNickle makes similar references to recent activism and the power of a collective Indigenous voice in the revised edition of *They Came Here First*. In *Behind the Trail*

of Broken Treaties, Deloria lays out the historical and social contexts for this activism. Drawing from the recent history of Israel, he asks readers to contemplate alternative futures for Indigenous Americans: "Who is to say that Indians cannot regain their independence some time in the future?" (83).

18. Harris gives few production details for the Reader's Digest film, which she would have been able to screen only in a theater. A footnote indicates Harris viewed a "matinee showing . . . in Tallahassee, Florida (1974)" (8n6). Released in 1973, *Tom Sawyer* was directed by Don Taylor for Reader's Digest/Apjac International and distributed by United Artists. In 1976, it aired on the CBS television network, a fact Harris could not have known but appears to have anticipated in 1974.

19. The speech appears to have been given to a Rotary Club or similar organization.

20. Revard subsequently published "Discovery of the New World" in *Ponca War Dancers* (1980), and it has been reprinted, in slightly revised versions, in several places, including Revard's *How the Songs Come Down: New and Selected Poems* (2005).

21. For a reading of Revard's poem in relation to Vizenor's novel, see, for example, Wilson, "Nesting in the Ruins," 183. For an account of Indigenous responses to the Columbus quincentenary in the museum context, see, for example, Cooper (Cherokee), "No Celebration for Columbus," in *Spirited Encounters*, 109–19. For Indigenous responses to 1992, see, for example, Gonzalez, *Without Discovery*, and Gentry and Grinde, *The Unheard Voices*.

22. The Luiseño artist Fritz Scholder, for instance, painted his provocative "Last Indian with [U.S.] Flag" in 1975, included in the bicentennial exhibition *The American Indian and the American Flag*, Flint Institute of Arts, Flint, Michigan. The exhibition also showed in New York, Wisconsin, Houston, and Phoenix during 1976 and 1977. A number of other exhibitions of American Indian arts, "traditional" and contemporary, were organized in the United States and abroad to commemorate the bicentennial, including *One with the Earth*, Institute of American Indian Arts; *I Wear the Morning Star: An Exhibition of American Indian Ghost Dance Objects*, Minneapolis Institute of Arts, cosponsored by the Minneapolis Regional Native American Center; *The Artistic Spirit of the North American Indian*, Roberson Center for the Arts and Sciences, Binghamton, New York; *Interwoven Heritage: A Bicentennial Exhibition of Southwestern Indian Basketry and Textile Arts*, Memorial Union Art Gallery, University of California at Davis; and *Sacred Circles: Two Thousand Years of North American Indian Art*, Arts Council of Great Britain and Nelson Gallery of Art in Kansas City.

23. Davids also participated in the First Convocation of American Indian Scholars in 1970.

24. A similar range of sentiments appeared in *Akwesasne Notes*. In the issue dated Late Summer 1975, for instance, the paper published a series of readers' letters under the banner "Native Perspectives on Bicentennial" and included a center fold-out titled "The Native American Revolution Bicentennial 1776–1976: 200 Years of Resistance."

25. The Newberry Library event was held February 21–22, 1975. In addition to Deloria, the conference featured Reginald Horseman, "The Image of the Indian in the Age of the American Revolution"; Bernard W. Sheehan, "The Ideology of the Revolution and the American Indian"; Mary E. Fleming Mathur, "Savages Are Heroes, Too, Whiteman!"; Francis Jennings, "The Imperial Revolution: The American Revolution

as a Tripartite Struggle for Sovereignty"; James Axtell, "The Unbroken Twig: The Revolution in America Indian Education"; and James H. O'Donnell, "The World Turned Upside Down: The American Revolution as a Catastrophe for Native Americans." Robert Berkhofer Jr. and Barbara Graymont provided commentary. I am grateful to Scott Stevens and the staff at the D'Arcy McNickle Center at the Newberry Library for their assistance in confirming the conference dates and presentation titles.

26. Douglas Latimer edited the Harper and Row series. Preceding *Indians' Summer* were *Seven Arrows* by Hyemoyohsts Storm (1972), *Ascending Red Cedar Moon* by Duane Niatum (1974), and *Winter in the Blood* by James Welch (1974). Immediately following *Indians' Summer* was *Carriers of the Dream Wheel: Contemporary Native American Poetry*, edited by Duane Niatum (1975).

27. According to its website, the Shawnee Nation, United Remnant Band, which is not a federally recognized tribe, reorganized in 1971 and, through a Joint Resolution passed in 1979–1980, received recognition as a "historical tribe" from the State of Ohio. In 1995, after raising its own money, the United Remnant Band was able to purchase a small land base in Ohio, a historical homeland of the Shawnee. See www.zaneshawneecaverns.net.

28. In addition to his novel published with Harper and Row, Nasnaga (sometimes rendered Nas'Naga) self-published two volumes of poetry, *Faces beneath the Grass* (completed in 1975, published in 1979) and *The Darker Side of Glory* (n.d.), as well as a book titled *Warriors* (1979). Like his novel, these works feature examples of Nasnaga's art. Nasnaga also published at least one short story in a national journal, "Two Paths to Eternity." Correspondence between Nasnaga and his publisher written between 1972 and 1976, held in the American Heritage Center archives at the University of Wyoming, indicates Nasnaga worked closely with Douglas Latimer on completing the manuscript between 1972 and mid-1974, while he was living in Texas, and then returned to Ohio in late 1974, after the manuscript had gone through copyediting and Nasnaga had completed his illustrations. The novel was published in January 1975, with an official release date of February 28. The initial printing of 3,000 sold out in March 1975 (2,600 in actual sales, 400 given away), and an immediate reprint was ordered of an additional 2,000 to 3,000 copies.

29. Vernon Bellecourt, interview by Richard Ballard, *Penthouse*, July 1973, 58–64, 122, 131–32. Nasnaga slightly alters the original. Bellecourt made similar statements in other venues, including the speech "American Indian Movement" published in the anthology *Contemporary Native American Address* (1976): "We recognize that in 1976 when this country is going to celebrate its 200th birthday, they will be celebrating in our backyard. And, by then, they had better have involved the host, or we are going to be very much concerned whether they are going to have a *Happy Birthday* or not" (74–75). The editors do not provide the date or site of the speech. Bellecourt's *Penthouse* interview also appears to have influenced Michael Dorris's language of "... we'll blow out / Your candles, one by one."

30. Nasnaga appears to follow a trend in this period, among some Native activists and intellectuals, to use Anishinabe as a pan-Indian term across North America or across North and South America. See, for example, Jack D. Forbes's pan-Indian and pan-hemispheric use of Anishinabe and the related term Anishinabe-waki (Indian

country) in "It's Time to Throw Off the White Man's Names" and *Aztecas del Norte.* Nasnaga also follows Forbes in spelling Anishinabe with only one *a,* rather than the more typical spelling of Anishinaabe.

31. For original readers this structure may have suggested the "Bicentennial Minute" vignettes regularly aired on the CBS television network between 1974 and the end of 1976. CBS aired 732 different versions of these vignettes.

32. The Battle of the Hundred Slain on December 21, 1866, also known as the Fetterman Massacre, was the worst U.S. Army defeat—and the greatest Indian military victory—on the plains before the Battle of the Little Big Horn on June 25, 1876. The Battle of the Hundred Slain can be viewed as part of the larger Red Cloud's War, also known as the Bozeman War or the Powder River War, fought between the Lakota and their allies and U.S. forces in the Wyoming and Montana Territories from 1866 to 1868, ending with victory for the Lakota and the signing of the 1868 Treaty of Fort Laramie.

33. *Booklist,* unsigned review of *Indians' Summer.* Nasnaga's *Indians' Summer* is included in the University of Iowa's Books for Young Adults program's annual "poll" of "contemporary books selected by juniors and seniors in local schools" for 1975. The program staff reports, "These books have been chosen by popular appeal," and the books "represent the viewpoint of the adolescent who has found them relevant" (95). *Indians' Summer* is grouped with other popular books under the subheading "Intense Encounters," which includes works of "science fiction, the supernatural story, and the whodunit mystery," such as Peter Benchley's *Jaws* (1974), William Goldman's *Marathon Man* (1974), Laird Koenig's *The Little Girl Who Lives down the Lane* (1974), and Stanley Konvitz's *The Sentinel* (1974). The program staff describes *Indians' Summer* as an "angry, often humorous novel" and quotes one of their young adult readers as saying, "My fear is that the incidents in this book could really happen" (96). Carlsen, Manna, and Yoder, review of *Indians' Summer.*

34. *Virginia Quarterly Review,* review of *Indians' Summer.*

35. Freling, review of *Indians' Summer.* Mt. Pleasant, Michigan, is located near the Saginaw Chippewa (Anishinaabe) Reservation.

36. Evers, review of *Indians' Summer.*

37. Press, review of *Indians' Summer.*

38. CH, review of *Indians' Summer.* The language of this final sentence echoes the opening line of the plot summary given on the inside of the novel's dust jacket: "Indians' Summer is a warning, and quite possibly a prophecy." This summary ends by noting that "Americans should remember that in the summer of 1976, when one group of Americans is celebrating the 200th anniversary of the United States, a different group—the Native American people—will be celebrating the 100th anniversary of the Seventh Cavalry's annihilation at the Battle of the Little Bighorn."

39. Other novels considered in this chapter are George Pierre's *Autumn's Bounty* (1972), James Welch's *Winter in the Blood* (1974), and Leslie Marmon Silko's *Ceremony* (1977).

40. I offer extended definitions for "treaty discourse" in "Postcolonial Theory and the Discourse of Treaties" and in *Blood Narrative.*

41. Akwesasne Notes also published an account of the events at Wounded Knee, *Voices from Wounded Knee, 1973: In the Words of the Participants* (1974).

42. Many accounts have been written about the efforts of Tecumseh and Tenskwa-tawa. See, for example, Colin G. Galloway's *The Shawnees and the War for America* (2007).

43. Nasnaga appears to follow Forbes in his use of the term Cabolclo, as well. In his 1972 article published in *Akwesasne Notes*, "It's Time to Throw Off the White Man's Names," Forbes similarly defines Caboclo (his spelling) as "a Tupi-Guarani word meaning 'copper colored,'" adding, "This word is used in Brazil in the same way that Indian is used in the United States (to include all people of Indian race, Indian appearance, or Indian culture)." Later in the article, he states, "Since the word *Caboclo* is already available and already refers to 'Pan-Indian' people, I would suggest that we adopt it for use in North Anishinabe-waki. If we do so, then a *Caboclo* would be an Anishinabe living away from a specific native, traditional homeland" (31).

44. Martin Cruz Smith is best known for *Gorky Park* (1981) and for his five subsequent novels featuring Arkady Renko, a Russian investigator: *Polar Star* (1989), *Red Square* (1992), *Havana Boy* (1999), *Wolves Eat Dogs* (2004), and *Stalin's Ghost* (2007). At least two of Smith's post-1970 works feature American Indian characters and/or themes, *Nightwing* (1977) and *Stallion Gate* (1986). He was born in 1942, a year after Nasnaga. Smith's mother, a Pueblo Indian, was a jazz singer and, in her later years, an advocate for American Indian rights. Smith adopted the middle name Cruz, the maiden name of his maternal grandmother, in 1977, when he published *Nightwing*. For an overview of his career, see Wroe, "Crime Pays."

45. Red Shirt was a Lakota leader who fought at the Battle of the Little Big Horn.

46. My attempts to contact Smith about his awareness of activism at the time have been unsuccessful.

47. Tension between the past of Indigenous–settler history and possible Indigenous futures is prevalent in literary discourses published throughout the bicentennial year. In "The Red / White Blues: Bicentennial Poem," published in her collection *Lost Copper* (1980), Wendy Rose (Hopi/Miwok) individualizes the collective emotional, psychological, and spiritual legacies of invasion and colonization on Indigenous peoples. The speaker states, "I know / of passing for the unreal, / I know / of bloodlessness." She wishes for "a chrysalis / [. . .] without human doubts" but feels unable to "burrow" into the reviving earth and its cleansing waters without "my father's badger claw, / my mother's buckeye burden basket" (25).

48. Toni Morrison is featured under the heading "The Black Experience."

49. The *Times* artist appears to respond to Deloria's point that "it seems to be the general Indian consensus that the Washington Monument should be renamed the Indian Memorial because it represents the shaft the Indians got when the white man came to the continent" (80).

50. In 1976, Momaday also gave a radio interview to CBS News, "Tradition, Arts and Future of the American Indian."

51. The American Indian scholar Clara Sue Kidwell (Choctaw) expressed similar views in a speech she delivered in 1976, "American Indian Attitudes toward Nature: A Bicentennial Perspective." She opens, "The history of Native American nations in North America extends far beyond that of the American nation whose 200th anniversary occurs this year. For millennia, the native people of this continent lived in a

state of harmony and balance with the natural environment around them" (277). After comparing European to Native worldviews and discussing the current ecological crisis, she concludes: "Let the traditional values and attitudes of American Indian people toward nature here serve as models for American society" (292).

52. Stephen Harper, prime minister of Canada, delivered a similar apology to Indigenous peoples in June 2008 in the House of Commons: "The government of Canada sincerely apologizes and asks the forgiveness of the Aboriginal peoples of this country for failing them so profoundly." See "Canada Apologizes for 'Failing' Native People," *Indianz.com*, June 12, 2008, http://64.38.12.138/News/2008/009265.asp; and Sarah van Gelder, "Canada Apologizes to Its Native People. Will We?," *Yes! Magazine*, June 16, 2008, http://www.alternet.org/module/printversion/88325. For broader analysis of the Canadian apology, including comparisons with Australia, see Henderson and Wakeham, "Aboriginal Redress."

53. "Brownback Applauds Committee Passage of Native American Apology Resolution," Senator Sam Brownback's official website, May 11, 2007, accessed October 7, 2010, www.brownback.senate.gov (site discontinued).

54. See www.crazyindn.com.

55. The Saami are Indigenous to northern Scandinavia and southern Russia. The title of the Crazy Ind'n world map may allude to *Fear of a Red Planet: Relocation and Removal* (2000), a 7-by-160-foot mural painted by Steven Joe Yazzie (Navajo/Laguna) for the Ullman Learning Center of the Heard Museum in Phoenix, Arizona.

3. Pictographic, Woven, Carved

1. Quoted in Sciascia, "Ka Pu Te Ruha, Ka Hao Te Rangatahi," 160.

2. The most cited analysis of Indigenous aesthetics in American Indian film remains the work of Leuthold. On the need to develop critical understandings of Hawaiian aesthetics, see Dudoit and Ho'omanawanui.

3. This type of museum practice has become more common since the 1970s. In 1995, for instance, critical dialogues were organized among Navajo weavers, art historians, and anthropologists while developing the exhibit *Woven by the Grandmothers*. See Bonar, *Woven by the Grandmothers*.

4. See Allen, "Blood (and) Memory," *Blood Narrative*, and "N. Scott Momaday."

5. Momaday's title may do additional work in its allusion to Andrew Carnegie, the celebrated philanthropist, who was born in Scotland in 1835 and died, coincidentally, in the United States in 1919. Carnegie funded many libraries, schools, and universities that bear his name, and we might link his association with philanthropy and education to themes central to Momaday's poem (e.g., "the giving of gifts"). The town of Carnegie, Oklahoma, was originally called Lathram; when it was incorporated in 1903, city leaders changed the name in the hope that Carnegie would build a library there. He did not.

6. Christina E. Burke explains, "The term *winter count* comes from the Lakota name for these pictographic calendars: *waniyetu wówapi*. The first word is glossed as 'winter' and refers either to the season or to the span of a year from first snow to first snow, as reckoned by the Lakota. […] The second word (*wówapi*) can refer to

anything that is marked and can be read or counted, from the root verb *owá*, meaning 'to draw, paint, color, or mark'" (1–2).

7. See, for example, Blish, *A Pictographic History of the Oglala Sioux*; Wong, *Sending My Heart Back across the Years*; Donnelley, *Transforming Images*; Greene, *Silver Horn*; and Greene and Thornton, *The Year the Stars Fell*. Also see my discussion of how pictographic traditions are innovated in contemporary written literature in *Blood Narrative*. Contemporary artists continue to innovate the conventions of ledger art.

8. See *Names*, 47–52.

9. Burke notes, for the Lakota, "By the end of the 19th century, some winter counts were solely texts; pictographs were replaced by written year names as the mnemonic device of choice" (4).

10. In *Telling Stories the Kiowa Way*, the Kiowa linguist Gus Palmer Jr. praises Momaday as a writer but remarks that he is not a "storyteller [. . .] in the Kiowa sense [. . .] as the term applies to the oral Kiowa world," because Momaday "writes exclusively in English" and "does not speak the Kiowa language" (58).

11. Howe designates these four dimensions as the spatial, in which people and lands are seen as intimately connected; the social, which emphasizes relationships between a distinct community and its "remembered landscape" (165); the spiritual, which guides the relationships between tribal peoples and their lands; and finally, the experiential, which emphasizes the community's ongoing relationship with higher spiritual powers (161–66).

12. Boyd notes the Kiowa continued to hold their summer dances from 1890 to the 1930s despite the federal ban and "today the Kiowa Gourd Dance has replaced the annual Sun Dance" (1:114).

13. The number four is important to many American Indian aesthetic and ritual traditions, including Kiowa and other Plains Indians, as well as the Navajo. Four typically is associated with balance, harmony, and completion.

14. My understanding of a "now" that collapses distinctions among past, present, and future is influenced by the novels *Potiki* (1986) and *Baby No-Eyes* (1999) by Patricia Grace (Māori).

15. See Berlo, "Artists, Ethnographers, and Historians," on the importance and prominence of horses in Plains Indian graphic arts.

16. Gila River Pima philosopher David Martinez argues, "The horizon, too, is like the wind—a phenomenon we can perceive but never really apprehend. For as we move about any given place, the horizon is that which constantly moves away from us as we approach it, yet which never leaves our perceptual field" (260).

17. See Allen, *Blood Narrative*, for an analysis of Momaday's use of the pun on "eye/I" in his well-known essay "The Man Made of Words."

18. Martinez argues that *here* "is emphasized as a term defining place because it is *being here* from which our knowledge and understanding of place truly derives. It is from *here* that we ultimately organize our perception of the world, at least as we experience it" (258).

19. See, for instance, the work of Lawrence Evers, Matthias Schubnell, Susan Scarberry-Garcia, and Kenneth Roemer.

20. Art historian Jennifer McLerran makes a similar point in relation to how Navajo weaving has participated within non-Native semiotic systems in the context of

the non-Native purchase, trade, and collection of Navajo textiles, and she borrows art historian Ruth Phillips's concept of *dual signification* to describe how these textiles produce meaning within two distinct aesthetic systems (10). McLerran does not consider the possibility of trans-Indigenous purchase, trade, and collection, however, or the possibility of multiple rather than dual signification.

21. Harry Walters (Navajo), director of the Hatathli Museum at Navajo Community College in Tsaile, Arizona, states similarly, "The male and the female not only signify sex, but principles. There are male principles and female principles, and the male and female should have equal power. When they work together in balance, they establish harmony and peace. The word we use is *hozho*. Hozho means, 'I will walk in the Beauty Way'" (30).

22. In this analysis I follow the innovative work of Witherspoon, a non-Native linguist and anthropologist married into a Navajo family, and other ethnographers who have worked collaboratively with Navajo to understand weaving not simply as a commodity but as what the non-Native anthropologist, curator, and weaver Kathy M'Closkey calls "cosmological performance" (242). In *Swept under the Rug: A Hidden History of Navajo Weaving* (2002), M'Closkey overviews the conflicting accounts of Navajo aesthetics produced by the majority of non-Native ethnographers, museologists, and traders, on the one hand, and Witherspoon and the majority of interviewed Navajo weavers, on the other (see, especially, chapter 7, "Toward an Understanding of Navajo Aesthetics"). M'Closkey is particularly critical of accounts of Navajo weaving and aesthetics produced by non-Native museologists, which, she demonstrates, reflect "the imposition of the dominant society's ideas" onto Indigenous concepts and practices (9).

23. Trudy Griffin-Pierce notes, "What [the folklorist Barre] Toelken calls 'the metaphor of movement' permeates Navajo mythology, religion, language, and thought," and she states, in her own words, "The structure of Navajo language clearly emphasizes movement" (24). See also M'Closkey, *Swept under the Rug,* 236.

24. The word *parfleche* is a French Canadian term derived from the French *parer* (to parry or turn aside) and *fleche* (arrow)—that is, "to deflect arrows." This etymology may suggest a connection between the syllabic structure of "Carnegie, Oklahoma, 1919" and Momaday's telling of the Kiowa story of the arrow maker, part of *The Way to Rainy Mountain* (1969).

25. Momaday includes an extended passage from the Navajo Night Chant, in English translation, in *House Made of Dawn* (146–47). See Scarberry-Garcia's analysis of Momaday's use of Navajo ceremony in this novel.

26. Sciascia's description of how Māori carving produces more power when "embraced" by discourse resonates with Wesley Thomas's (Navajo) description of how Navajo weaving is "personified" through the weaver's elaborate process, which includes the raising of sheep and the production of wool and dyes in preparation for weaving, as well as the weaver's singing, praying, and talking during the weaving itself.

27. See Allen, "Blood (and) Memory" and *Blood Narrative.*

28. See, for example, Krupat, "*Atanarjuat, the Fast Runner* and Its Audiences," in *All That Remains.* In his analysis of the reception of the Inuit film *Atanarjuat,* Krupat designates "three distinct audiences": (1) "a local and quite specific indigenous community"— that is, the Inuit in Canada; (2) a non-Inuit "southern—French and English Canada and

the United States, but also more generally metropolitan—audience" that is willing to be challenged "to see with a Native eye"; and (3) an audience of non-Inuit "southerners who are either unwilling or unable to alter their habits of perception" (132–33). Although Krupat is willing to acknowledge the possibility of a "fourth audience" of other Indigenous peoples, at my urging, he does so only in a footnote (196n9). The possibility of non-Inuit Indigenous perspectives does not inform his reading, analysis, or argument.

29. For an example of how little attention is paid to Indigenous arts in the current "multicultural" approach to expanding ideas about literary aesthetics, see Elliott, Caton, and Rhyne, *Aesthetics in a Multicultural Age.*

4. Indigenous Languaging

1. Some readers may recognize in the phrasing of Revard's title an allusion to *Black Elk Speaks,* the popular as-told-to autobiography of an Oglala holy man written by the non-Native poet John G. Neihardt and first published in 1932. In Neihardt's reworking of Black Elk's voice, it is this "herb of healing" and its as yet unrealized potential for rebuilding a broken Indigenous nation that is emphasized by the Lakota elder when he describes the life-altering vision revealed to him as a child. Despite the allusion to Neihardt's Black Elk, and despite stated overtures to healing, Revard's essay is at times openly combative. In this way it reminds readers that in the more expansive account of Black Elk's powerful vision, detailed in the stenographic notes made during Neihardt's interviews with him in the early 1930s but not published until 1987 under the title *The Sixth Grandfather,* edited by the non-Native anthropologist Raymond J. DeMallie, the vibrant herb for healing is balanced by an equally potent herb for war. Although Revard's "Herbs of Healing" is an awe-filled celebration of the poetic and human *possible,* unlike Neihardt's text, it is no work of imperialist nostalgia.

2. In a personal communication, Jahnke indicated that he is following Māori art historian Hirini Moko Mead in his use of *rereketanga.* In his *English–Māori Dictionary,* Ngata translates the English adjective *novel* as "rerekē."

3. Revard's reference to "this America" appears to be a purposeful echo of the opening poem in Simon Ortiz's *from Sand Creek* (1981): "This America / has been a burden / of steel and mad / death, / but, look now, / there are flowers / and new grass / and a spring wind / rising / from Sand Creek" (9).

4. I offer a reading of "Sad Joke on a Marae" in *Blood Narrative.*

5. Upper Hutt Posse's name refers to their hometown of Upper Hutt, located in the Hutt valley north of Wellington.

6. Upper Hutt Posse released a new version of "Tangata Whenua" as part of their 2002 CD *Te Reo Māori Remixes* (Māori-language remixes). The rap has an updated musical and vocal arrangement, and some of the lyrics have been changed to convey an even more explicitly activist message. The hook (chorus) remains unchanged. On their website Upper Hutt Posse offer this translation of the hook: "People of the land, the durable ancestral connections / People of the land, the root and the authority / People of the land, the glow of the breath / People of the land, the ever burning fire" (www.tekupu.com).

7. Robert Sullivan makes a similar point about how the phrase "Tihei Mauriora"

accrues meaning through its repetition in Taylor's poem in his essay "A Poetics of Culture" (16–17).

8. For a photograph of *Strawberry and Chocolate*, see National Museum of the American Indian, *Essays on Native Modernism*, 51.

9. In a footnote Losch explains several of her specific references in the poem: "In 1920, the United States Congress created the Hawaiian Homes Commission Act. Persons of 50 percent Hawaiian blood or more were eligible to lease homestead lots for 99 years at $1 a year. Since then, other programs which have been established to help the Hawaiian people have had the 50 percent blood quantum imposed. 5(f) is a clause in the Admissions Act (for Statehood) which provides for Hawaiians as defined in the 1920 Act. The Office of Hawaiian Affairs (OHA), a multi-million dollar State of Hawai'i agency, also has a provision for native Hawaiians as defined in 1920."

10. Haunani-Kay Trask translates *one hānau* as both "birthsands" and "homeland"; see also *From a Native Daughter*, 126, 140.

11. See Allen, *Blood Narrative*, 146–56.

12. Created by an act of Parliament in 1965 and originally administered by the Department of Education, the National Library of New Zealand received its Māori designation when it became an autonomous government department in 1988. On the library's website, the Māori phrase is translated as "The Wellspring of Knowledge."

13. In *Blood Narrative* I analyze a similar interaction across and between languages in a dual-language Māori–English literary text. There, I refer to this potential third text as "te korero i waenganui/the text between"; see 64–65.

14. For a detailed discussion of the history of *Te Ao Hou*, see Allen, *Blood Narrative*.

15. Often referred to as the "Jesus fish," the simple fish symbol of two intersecting arcs is thought to have been used as a recognition sign by Christians since the first three centuries of the common era.

16. *Ika* also carries the meanings of "cluster," "band," "troop," and "heap." The phrase *Ika whenua* can be used to refer to a main line of hills, and the phrases *Te ika o te rangi* and *Ika whenua o te rangi* can be used to refer to the Milky Way.

17. I am grateful to Hugh Karena (Te Aupouri) for helping me understand these aspects of the use of the word *ngohi*.

18. Note the Māori pun on *matau*, which means both "right side" and "fishhook."

19. Before publishing *The Whale Rider*, Ihimaera explored several of its key themes and invoked much of its key imagery in a short story titled "The Whale," part of his early collection *Pounamu, Pounamu* (1972). See Allen, *Blood Narrative*, 133–35.

20. Ihimaera's revisions for the U.S. edition are notable for a number of reasons. Part of their context is Ihimaera's decision to rewrite and essentially update many of his early works, including his first collection of short stories *Pounamu, Pounamu* (1972), his first novel *Tangi* (1973), his second novel *Whanau* (1974), his second short story collection *The New Net Goes Fishing* (1977), and his third novel *The Matriarch* (1986). In a May 2009 interview with Peter Mares for the Australian Broadcasting Corporation, Ihimaera states that "from *The Whale Rider* on I'm really happy [with my work]" and that he has not—and has no intention of—rewriting *The Whale Rider*. Moreover, in the interview Ihimaera asserts, "I never translate my Maori words into English. It doesn't matter whether or not it's an edition that's appearing in England or

the USA or whatever. And so my work is not really all that amenable overseas"; see www.abc.net.au/rn/bookshow/stories/2009/2558016.htm.

21. In 2007, to mark the twentieth anniversary of its original publication in 1987, Ihimaera produced yet another edition of *The Whale Rider*. Published by Reed Books in New Zealand, the 2007 anniversary edition retains most of the language of the U.S. edition and makes further changes, including the addition of color photographs from the film, an expanded glossary, a list of film and literary awards, and an expansive set of author's notes that runs twenty-three pages. In the author's notes Ihimaera describes his work on the 2003 U.S. edition in these terms: "For that edition I *reversioned* the novel" (180, emphasis added).

22. This is the only section title that is revised in the U.S. edition. The original title is restored in the 2007 anniversary edition.

23. Although *mauri* has been added to the expanded glossary of the 2007 anniversary edition and defined as "life principle," neither the Maori word nor its English translation appears in the passage quoted from the prologue. Ihimaera retains the language of the 2003 U.S. edition.

24. The language of the U.S. edition is maintained in this passage in the 2007 anniversary edition (157).

5. Siting Earthworks, Navigating Waka

1. Sullivan continues these themes in his 2005 collection *Voice Carried My Family*.

2. In making this claim, I am reminded of Thomas King's claim in *The Truth About Stories* that "the magic of Native literature—as with other literatures—is not the themes of the stories—identity, isolation, loss, ceremony, community, maturation, home—it is the way meaning is refracted by cosmology, the way understanding is shaped by cultural paradigms" (112). Indigenous technologies are one of those cultural paradigms.

3. See Lepper, *Newark Earthworks*.

4. For an early account of the research for establishing the so-called Great Hopewell Road, see Lepper, "Tracking Ohio's Great Hopewell Road." Many of Lepper's theories, based on archival data, ground survey, and aerial photography, have been substantiated and expanded by more recent work involving LiDAR technologies, which I discuss in the following paragraphs.

5. Joyce M. Szabo, "Native American Art History," 74.

6. Computer-based interactive exhibits of earthworks sites have been developed by the Center for the Electronic Reconstruction of Historical and Archaeological Sites (CERHAS) at the University of Cincinnati. See their website at www.cerhas.uc.edu and follow links for the EarthWorks project. Also see the website for the Ancient Ohio Trail, a collaborative site geared toward earthworks tourism created by the Ohio Historical Society, the U.S. National Park Service, the Newark Earthworks Center at The Ohio State University–Newark, and CERHAS at www.ancientohiotrail.org.

7. In 2008, Romain and his colleague Jarrod Burks published several online essays on the preliminary findings of their LiDAR research in Ohio, from which my information is taken. Romain presented many of these findings in a lecture at Ohio State University, "LiDAR Imaging of Ohio Hopewell Earthworks: New Images of Ancient

Sites," October 23, 2008. The base unit of measurement for Ohio earthworks appears to be 263.5 feet; its double, 527 feet; and its quadruple, 1,054 feet. Another key unit of measurement appears to be 1,178 feet, which is the length of the hypotenuse of a right triangle when the two legs of the triangle are 527 and 1,054 feet, respectively.

8. Scholars working in several fields—archaeology and anthropology, art history, history, literary and cultural studies, literacy studies, and rhetoric—identify a range of writing systems in use across the Americas prior to the introduction of alphabetic literacy, including not only the Mayan codices but also petroglyphs and pictographic rock art; pictographs painted on tanned animal hides (Plains Indian winter counts and brag skins) or inscribed in birch bark (Anishinaabe and Passamaquoddy birch-bark scrolls); and strings or belts of wampum. These and other writing systems and mnemonic devices were used to complement oral performance traditions. A number of these systems continued to be used into and through the so-called contact era, often in modified forms that responded to changes in social conditions and available resources (such as the development of a more narrative style of Plains Indian led-ger art on paper or the incorporation of alphabetic writing in French or English into birchbark scrolls); many continue into the present. I am suggesting that we add the construction of earthworks to our broadening understanding of Indigenous writing systems and their multiple media.

9. Existing scholarship and interpretive materials on earthworks include almost no information about Indigenous understandings of these sites.

10. Although it is the first text to animate an earthworks site and give voice to the mounds, Hedge Coke's sequence of poems is not the first *representation* of earthworks in contemporary American Indian literature. LeAnne Howe (Choctaw), for instance, incorporates the Nanih Waiya, a large platform mound located in what is now Missis-sippi that is sacred to the Choctaw and other southeastern peoples, into the plot of her 2001 novel *Shell Shaker*. The Choctaw filmmaker Ian Skorodin incorporates the Nanih Waiya into the elaborate website built to support his 2007 and 2009 stop-motion *Crazy Ind'n* animated films, discussed in chapter 2.

11. Hedge Coke made statements to this effect during her presentation on *Blood Run* at Indigenous Literatures and Other Arts: A Symposium and Workshop, held at the Many Nations Longhouse, University of Oregon, May 2–3, 2008. See also Hedge Coke's account of how she came to write *Blood Run* in her introduction to the anthol-ogy *Sing: Poetry from the Indigenous Americas*.

12. Here is a complete list of the thirty-seven distinct personas, in the order of their first appearance: River, Clan Sister, Memory, Horizon, The Mounds, Ceremonial Mound, Burial Mound, Morning Star, Sun, Dog, Starwood, Corn, Redwing Black-bird, Sunflower, Moon, Blue Star, North Star, Snake Mound, Esoterica, Deer, Bea-ver, Buffalo, Fox, Cupped Boulder, Pipestone Tablets, The Tree at Eminija Mounds, Ghosts, Skeletons, Jesuit, Squatters, Tractor, Looters, Early Anthro, Early Interpreter, Stone Snake Effigy, Prairie Horizons, and Skeleton.

13. Romain and Burks, "LiDAR Analyses."

14. Romain and Burks, "LiDAR Analyses," note 1.

15. Previously, I have employed the concept of a fourth dimension metaphorically to highlight the activist politics of Hedge Coke's inclusion of explicitly Indigenous

perspectives in *Blood Run*. Within Western mathematics and philosophy, however, the concept of a fourth dimension generally refers to time. Here, I evoke the possibility of a four-dimensional quality to Hedge Coke's poetic structures to suggest their potential to link the present to the past and to project into the future.

16. Hedge Coke's subtle manipulations of four, three, seven, and the sequence of the first twenty-four primes illustrates what Tewa scholar Gregory Cajete describes in *Native Science* as the "proper role of mathematics" within Indigenous scientific systems. As in contemporary physics, a field often engaged with phenomena "that cannot be explained in words," Cajete argues that within Indigenous fields of science, mathematics helps render "transparent" certain "basic relationships, patterns, and cycles in the world" through their quantification and symbolic "coding" (65, 234).

17. The word *capital* carries a number of potentially significant meanings and connotations for this analysis. As a noun, *capital* can refer either to a city that is the seat of government for a larger political entity or to a city or region that is the center of a particular activity, such as trade or artistic production. The noun *capital* also can refer to any form of material wealth used or available for the production of additional wealth. In a similar vein, it can refer to any asset. As an adjective, *capital* can indicate the qualities of being first or foremost, being first rate or exceptional, but also the qualities of being extremely serious or of involving death or calling for the death penalty. The verb *capitalize* can mean to utilize or take advantage of some thing or some situation, to provide financial support for an enterprise, or to estimate the present value of an asset. The common preposition *by* also carries a number of potentially significant meanings and connotations. For instance, it can indicate not only agency (through the action of or with the help or use of) but also the physical positions of next to or close to and up to and beyond or past, as well as the temporal position of in the period of or during.

18. Margaret Bender, "Writing, Place and Indigeneity in Cherokee," Global Script of Indigenous Identities, international symposium, Michigan State University, October 30, 2008.

19. Twenty is the result of four (the book's sacred and primary—but not actually prime—basic unit of measurement) multiplied by five, the third prime. The number five is also significant because it is the hypotenuse of a right triangle whose legs are four and three.

20. The two brief and unmarked dedications included in the front matter of *Blood Run*, one of which precedes the table of contents and one of which follows the author's note, are not listed in the table of contents and, thus, are not part of this official measurement.

21. The total number of poems in *Blood Run*, sixty-six, mirrors the number of books in the Christian Bible. In standard Protestant and Catholic versions, the Bible is composed of an Old Testament with thirty-nine books and a New Testament with twenty-seven books.

22. The elaborate intraline spacing in the poem suggests the purposefulness of the poem's division into 176 lines.

23. The number twenty-four is the *factorial* of the number four. A factorial is the product of all the positive integers from one up to a given number, typically designated

within mathematics by a given number followed by an explanation point. Thus, the factorial of four (4!) is 1 × 2 × 3 × 4 = 24.

24. The midpoint of the thirty-seven distinct personas, number nineteen—eighteen personas precede it and eighteen follow—is "Esoterica," which speaks only once in the sequence. Nineteen is the eighth prime (4 × 2). "Esoterica" is further distinguished by the fact that it is the only poem that is divided into numbered sections; not surprisingly, there are seven (the fourth prime). The poem is composed of fifty-three lines; fifty-three is the sixteenth prime (4 × 4).

25. Ten is the result of two, the first prime, multiplied by five, the third prime. And twenty-seven, as noted, is the cube of three, the second prime; it is also the number of books in the New Testament.

26. The Earthworks series is edited by the U.S.-based poet and scholar Janet McAdams.

27. "The poems of Blood Run are cupmarks," Noori writes, for example, "small indentations on the surface of our souls, invocations that cannot be ignored. Allison says it all when she writes, 'no human should dismantle prayer.' [...] By writing this book, she begins the mending of a rent in the fabric of sacred spaces on earth" (xi).

28. Hedge Coke lists the Ho-Chunk, Ioway, Kansa Otoe, Osage, Omaha, Quapaw, Ponca, Missouri, Arikira, Dakota, and Cheyenne nations as having "history in the Blood Run site" (98).

29. In contrast, Noori states that the site "extends back in time to as early as 8,505 years ago," when the site may have been occupied by as many as "10,000 individuals," but that "the heaviest years of use may have been between 1675 and 1705 A.D." Noori's figures appear to come from the Iowa State Historical Society's web page for Blood Run.

30. 8,500 years = 4 × 2,125; 400 mounds = 4 × 100; 2,300 acres = 4 × 575; 276 mounds = 4 × 69; 1,200 acres = 4 × 30; 176 mounds = 4 × 44; 80 mounds = 4 × 20.

31. The first and sixth stanzas, each composed of two lines, introduce and conclude the ritual sequence. The four stanzas situated between them, each composed of four lines, "perform" the ritual prayer (10).

32. Our exit from the dramatic world of *Blood Run* is similarly mediated. Hedge Coke's final persona poem is followed by the second narrative poem, "When the Animals Leave This Place," which is followed by a series of acknowledgements and another set of dedications. In contrast, no material follows the final poem of Sullivan's one-hundred-poem sequence, unless we count the additional poem included on the book's back cover, "A Cover Sail," which most readers are likely to read before beginning the book rather than after its completion.

33. Romain and other scholars describe the mound-building cultures of Ohio and elsewhere as having this kind of three-worlds worldview. See Romain, *Mysteries of the Hopewell*.

34. Hedge Coke's ideas about place identity can be linked to Momaday's ideas about how individuals and communities "invest" themselves in particular landscapes and at the same time "incorporate" those landscapes into their "fundamental experience" and thus into their sense of self. See Allen, "N. Scott Momaday."

35. In her acknowledgements, Hedge Coke writes, "Once, a snake mound effigy of

a mile and a quarter length, much like the worldwide lauded Snake Mound in Ohio State, existed in this very place—Blood Run. The railroad used it for fill dirt" (93). I analyze the poems "Snake Mound" and "Stone Snake Effigy" and their relation to the extant Serpent Mound in Ohio in "Serpentine Figures, Sinuous Relations."

36. Here, I am following Mignolo and Schiwy (5).

37. In its first appearance, the Burial Mound describes its body as a "venter," the swell of a muscle but also a belly or uterus, or any swollen structure, suggesting the state of pregnancy (19). In its second appearance, the Burial Mound states, "I do my best to shelter, keep them" (46).

38. James Welch (Blackfeet/Gros Ventre) tells a Blackfeet version of the Feather Woman story in his 1986 historical novel *Fools Crow*.

39. The twenty-eighth persona in the book is Skeletons, which speaks four times: three times in the "Intrusions" section and once in the fourth, future-oriented section, "Portend."

40. This central exclamation can be aligned with Hedge Coke's opening narrative poem in section 1, "Dawning," which ends with a meditation on the power of breath and breathing (9–10).

41. The title of this narrative poem is anticipated in the seventh and final appearance of "The Mounds": "When the animals leave this place, / now without protective honorary sculpture. / When River returns with her greatest force." This "The Mounds" poem also anticipates the theme of renewal through flooding: "when the Reclaiming comes to pass, / all will know our great wombed hollows, / the stores of Story safely put by" (82). Lines from several persona poems anticipate the final narrative poem as well, including the fourth "Clan Sister" (62), the third "Horizon" (67), the third "Skeletons" (69), and the sixth "Clan Sister" (80).

42. The long number of years of the state's deliberation about preserving Blood Run, twenty-three, can be worked into the earlier analysis of the structural patterning of *Blood Run*. Twenty-three is the ninth prime, and twenty-three is a factor in two of the key numbers listed among the site statistics in Hedge Coke's author's note: 2,300 acres at the site (23×100) and 276 mounds surveyed in 1883 (23×12). Twenty-three also points to specific poems in the sequence of personas. The first twenty-third persona poem, located in section 2, "Origin," marks the single appearance of "Beaver" and is composed of twelve lines ($12 \times 23 = 276$). The second twenty-third persona poem, in section 3, "Intrusions," marks the third appearance of "Horizon" and is composed of twenty-three lines.

43. Sullivan offers additional (minor) metacommentary about the sequence in several specific poems. See, for example, "xvii: Some definitions and a note on orthography" (21), "Waka 62: A narrator's note" (70–71), and "Waka 74: Sea anchor" (83).

44. The Roman section includes poems 1–36, with two "waka" interruptions at 16 and 29; the Arabic section includes poems 37–55, with no interruptions; and the "waka" numbering section includes poems 56–100, also with no interruptions. Thus, thirty-four of the core one hundred poems are Roman, nineteen are Arabic, and forty-seven are "waka."

45. The 2,001 lines may also allude to the iconic science fiction film *2001: A Space*

Odyssey, directed by Stanley Kubrick and released in 1968 (incidentally, the year following Sullivan's birth in 1967). Explicit reference to *2001: A Space Odyssey* is made in "Waka 58: Waitangi Day." The film's title, of course, alludes to Homer's *Odyssey*, which makes explicit appearances in "Waka 62: A narrator's note" and "Waka 88."

46. It is unclear whether this is a genuine mistake (which seems unlikely) or part of Sullivan's artistic depiction of navigational uncertainty (which seems more likely).

47. *The Maori Canoe* by Elsdon Best appears in "Waka 59: Elsdon Best"; *The Raft Book: Lore of the Sea and Sky* by Harold Gatty appears in "Waka 67: from *We the Navigators*"; *Nga Waka Maori: Maori Canoes* by Anne Nelson appears in "xxvi," "Waka 69: Kupe," and "Waka 72: Hawaikinui's 1985 journey"; *Nga Waka o Nehera: The First Voyaging Canoes* by Jeff Evans appears in "Waka 69: Kupe" and "Waka 70."

48. Sullivan uses the term Hawaiiki throughout to name the Polynesian "homeland." This is a variant of the more common spelling, Hawaiki.

49. There is a subtle play in these lines on the puns to/two and for/four: "A prayer to" is repeated four times, while "A prayer for" is repeated two times.

50. The final line of English is a translation of the preceding line of Māori. A more literal translation would be, "A prayer for you two, waka, star of this world." Other poems in the sequence reveal that "stars" also can refer to ancestors, who are believed to become stars after death. See, for example, the lines "yet stars are / ancestors / they are stars / our ancestors / and we will be stars" in "Waka 16: Kua wheturangitia koe" (20) and the line "And you stars, the ancestors" in "Waka 100" (112).

51. See, for example, the review by Perez and the essay by Marsden.

52. Sullivan's twelve personas, in order of their appearance in poems 84–90 and 92–96, are "the waka of memory"; "the star Kopua" (Venus) and its "cousins" the Southern Cross; the Polynesian explorer Kupe; "the anonymous [British] settler"; Homer's archetypal voyager Odysseus; the Polynesian culture hero Maui; the Kurahaupo Waka; the Polynesian homeland Hawaiiki; the ocean; the Māori god of forests, Tane Mahuta; the Māori god of the sea, Tangaroa; and finally, the "star waka" itself.

53. *Pā* can refer to any type of stockade or fortification, but especially a fortified village. In addition to palisades (takitaki), pā often involved some kind of earthworks (maioro), such as terracing or moats.

54. For an overview of such debates, see, for example, Finney, "Myth, Experiment, and the Reinvention of Polynesian Voyaging," and Turnbull, "Pacific Navigation."

55. In "Waka 57: El Nino Waka," the speaker contrasts the past, when navigators could count on "the reliability of the sea," with the contemporary situation "Today," when "the sea / is unreliable" because of environmental degradation (64).

56. Twenty-nine is the tenth prime; eleven is the fifth prime; and five is the third prime.

57. See Orbell's version, "Hine-pūkohurangi: Woman of the Mist" (*Concise Encyclopedia*, 39–40). Many other versions have been recorded. In a separate entry, Orbell also notes that in some traditions Uenuku is the name of "a great rangatira [chief] in Hawaiki" who forced many people to migrate (198–99).

58. See, for instance, Te Awamutu Museum online at www.tamuseum.org.nz.

59. Sullivan develops the idea of the planet as both the earth mother and a waka

moving through space in "Waka 57: El Nino Waka": "The planet, as you are aware, / is not only our mother, but the mother of all / living creatures here, from the latest computer virus / to the greatest of the primates. She carries us / through the universe" (64).

60. In Orbell's version, "The world is made up of Rangi the sky and Papa the earth, but it was their son Tāne who pushed them apart and gave the world its proper form" (*Concise Encyclopedia*, 145).

61. Sullivan begins "Waka 57: El Nino Waka": "Among the compasses of navigators—/ star compass, wind compass, solar compass—/ a compass based on currents, such was / the reliability of the sea" (64). And in "Waka 100," the final poem in the book's core, Sullivan writes in the penultimate stanza: "And you, Urizen, Jupiter, Io Matua Kore, / holder of the compasses—/ wind compass, solar compass, / compass encompassing known / currents, [. . .]" (111).

62. Sullivan evokes the pun on *arc* and *ark* and the connection of the waka to the biblical Noah in "Waka 83," which begins: "I ask you, waka, ark, high altar / above the sea, your next destination?" (93).

63. In Christian contexts the story of Noah can be read as prefiguring the sacrament of baptism.

64. Orbell notes that "birds singing loudly at dawn are 'Tāne's mouth' [Te waka o Tane]" (*Concise Encyclopedia*, 146).

65. In "Waka 60: Dead Reckoning," Sullivan writes: "The heights and shapes of waves, flotsam / and jetsam, indicate the direction of currents. // Lewis says that a line of jetsam clearly delineates / the meeting point of two currents—" (68). In poem "ix," Sullivan includes the line "following birds across an Ocean" (13), and in "Waka 67: from *We the Navigators*," he follows Lewis to describe in more detail how "Boobies, noddies, terns—these and other birds / indicate the presence of land, most particularly / in the early morning and the evening when // they return home. They fly straight / to their perches" (76).

66. Uenuku is positioned directly above the word "Leaf" on the left side of the lower arc, which can be read as invoking the contemporary practice of placing leaves at the base of the Uenuku stone as a sign of aroha (affection). See www.tamuseum .org.nz.

67. The phrase is from the seminal 1993 essay "Our Sea of Islands" by Oceanic scholar Epeli Hau'ofa.

68. See John Donne's "Meditation 17" in *Devotions upon Emergent Occasions* (1624).

69. Orbell relates this story in her entry "Wairaka: The woman who acted like a man" (*Concise Encyclopedia*, 202).

70. The map created in "53" may refer to the system of "etak" Lewis describes (133–45).

71. Sullivan refers to his mother's home village as Te Kaaretu in poem "xv: Sullivan Whanau" (Sullivan Family). As a noun, *kāretu* refers to a species of sweet-smelling grass.

72. DeLoughrey exploits this pun on the navigational technique of dead reckoning in chapter 3 of *Routes and Roots*.

73. See poem "xxx," which begins, "in three weeks I turn 30" (34).

74. *Nanny* is commonly used in New Zealand for either "grandmother" or "grandfather."

75. We can link the imagery of the sea anchor here also to Sullivan's depiction of his maternal homeland, Karetu, in poem "52" and especially in poem "xv: Sullivan Whanau," where he writes, "We move around / like the four winds, but when we gather / at Te Kaaretu, we are anchored / and hold fast to one another" (19).

76. Sullivan reveals the nature of the storm in the poem that follows, "Waka 75: A Storm": "a storm so violent / waka and coracles [Irish boats] slam into each other / tohunga [Māori "experts"] and filiddh [Irish poets] swap notes / sing each other's airs / and before you know it the bloodlines / race in and out at crazy angles" (84). As in other poems, the speaker acknowledges mixed descent—"my Irish and Scottish inheritance" (90)—but ultimately reconfirms his Māori identity. "Waka 75: A Storm" ends with the lines "again the wave slaps his face / try harder / slaps him again / portray me as I am." The poem that follows, "Waka 76," then asserts a Polynesian understanding of the human–ocean connection based in whakapapa (genealogy). Humans are related to the sea god Tangaroa because they are his brother "Tane's kids" (85).

77. See "xxii: Te ao marama II" (The world of light II) and "Waka 62: A narrator's note."

78. These dates correspond to the first European sighting and naming of New Zealand in 1642 by the Dutch captain Abel Tasman; the first voyage to and mapping of New Zealand in 1769 by the English Captain James Cook; and the declaration of formal sovereignty in 1835 by northern Māori rangatira (chiefs).

79. Urizen is the embodiment of conventional reason and law within the philosophy of the Romantic poet William Blake; Jupiter is the Roman equivalent of the Greek god Zeus; and Io Matua Kore (Io, Father of the Void) is the first principle in some versions of Māori cosmology.

80. Sullivan imagines future waka as "rocket ship[s]" in "iv: 2140 AD" and as "spacecraft" in "46" and "Waka 62: A narrator's note"; he also imagines future waka as "submarines" in "49 (environment I)."

81. For extended biographical accounts of each author, see Parker, *Singing an Indian Song*, and Condliffe, *Te Rangi Hiroa*. McNickle (1904–1977) significantly expanded *They Came Here First* and published a revised edition in 1975. Buck (1877–1951) added an epilogue to *The Coming of the Maori* and published a second edition in 1950.

82. McNickle published *They Came Here First* as the first volume in the popular Peoples of America series edited by Louis Adamic for the U.S. commercial press the J. B. Lippincott Company. The book runs 300 pages in the original hardback edition, plus a series of eight photographic illustrations, source notes, acknowledgements, and an index. Buck arranged publication of *The Coming of the Maori* through the Maori Purposes Fund Board of the New Zealand Department of Internal Affairs, and it was distributed in New Zealand by the commercial press Whitcombe and Tombs. It runs 538 pages in its original hardback edition, plus a foreword written by the minister of Māori affairs, a bibliography, an index, and a series of twenty-four photographic illustrations. Buck was already well known for his earlier book-length study of Polynesian voyaging, *Vikings of the Sunrise*, first published in 1938. In his prologue to *Vikings*, Buck

writes, "This work is an attempt to make known to the general public some of the romance associated with the settlement of Polynesia by a stone-age people who deserve to rank among the world's great navigators" (v).

83. In his foreword to *The Coming of the Maori*, the minister of Māori affairs, the Rt. Hon. P. Fraser, writes, "Sir Peter has infused into his writing much of his own compelling and charming personality and his quick, incisive humour. Many readers will wonder which they more appreciate—the ever interesting, indeed fascinating subject-matter of the volume, or the captivating and delightful style in which it is written" (n.p.). Early reviewers, all of whom were non-Native professional anthropologists and historians, were more hesitant about the explicitly literary aspects of either Buck's or McNickle's work and described them as "speculative," "imaginative," and even "picturesque." These readers reserved their highest praise for those sections of the books that are based in each author's acknowledged areas of professional expertise: Buck on Māori and Polynesian material cultures, which he had documented in extensive and precise detail over a long career that included directing the Bishop Museum in Honolulu and lecturing in anthropology at Yale University; McNickle on twentieth-century federal Indian policy and especially on the legacies of the 1934 Indian Reorganization Act, legacies he had worked to secure as an official in the Bureau of Indian Affairs under John Collier. See, for example, reviews of *The Coming of the Maori* by Ralph Linton in *American Anthropologist* (1950) and by Raymond Firth in *Man* (1951) and reviews of *They Came Here First* by Joseph Green in *American Historical Review* (1950), by William Fenton in *American Anthropologist* (1950), by Robert Raymer in *Pacific Historical Review* (1950), by Ruth Underhill in *Western Folklore* (1951), and by E. E. Dale in *Americas* (1951).

84. For a more detailed discussion of McNickle's *They Came Here First*, see Allen, *Blood Narrative*, 94–102.

Bibliography

Akiwenzie-Damm, Kateri. "Preface: We Remain, Forever." *Skins: Contemporary Indigenous Writing*, edited and compiled by Kateri Akiwenzie-Damm and Josie Douglas, vi–ix. Alice Springs, Australia: Jukurrpa Books, 2000.

Akwesasne Notes. *Trail of Broken Treaties: B.I.A. I'm Not Your Indian Anymore*. Rooseveltown, N.Y.: Akwesasne Notes, 1973.

Allen, Chadwick. "Blood (and) Memory." *American Literature* 71, no. 1 (March 1999): 93–116.

———. *Blood Narrative: Indigenous Identity in American Indian and Maori Literary and Activist Texts*. Durham, N.C.: Duke University Press, 2002.

———. "N. Scott Momaday: Becoming the Bear." *Cambridge Companion to Native American Literature*, edited by Kenneth Roemer and Joy Porter, 207–19. Cambridge: Cambridge University Press, 2005.

———. "Unspeaking the Settler: 'The Indian Today' in International Perspective." *American Studies* 46, nos. 3–4 (Fall/Winter 2005): 39–57.

———. "Engaging the Politics and Pleasures of Indigenous Aesthetics." *Western American Literature* 41, no. 2 (Summer 2006): 146–75.

———. "Rere Kē/Moving Differently: Indigenizing Methodologies for Comparative Indigenous Literary Studies." *Studies in American Indian Literatures* 19, no. 4 (Winter 2007): 1–26. Also in special issue, *Journal of New Zealand Literature* 24, no. 2 (2007): 44–72.

———. "Serpentine Figures, Sinuous Relations: Thematic Geometry in Allison Hedge Coke's *Blood Run*." *American Literature* 82, no. 4 (December 2010): 807–34.

———. "A Transnational Native American Studies? Why Not Studies that are Trans-Indigenous?" *Journal of Transnational American Studies* 4, no. 1 (2012).

American Revolution Bicentennial Administration. *The Bicentennial of the United States of America: A Final Report to the People*. 5 vols. Washington, D.C.: Government Printing, 1977.

Apess, Willam. *On Our Own Ground: The Complete Writings of William Apess, A Pequot*. Edited by Barry O'Connell. Amherst: University of Massachusetts Press, 1992.

Aptheker, Herbert. *The Negro Today*. New York: Marzani and Munsell, 1962.

———. *Soul of the Republic: The Negro Today*. New York: Marzani and Munsell, 1964.

Attwood, Bain, and Andrew Markus, eds. *The Struggle for Aboriginal Rights: A Documentary History*. Sydney, Australia: Allen & Unwin, 1999.

Beckett, Jeremy R., ed. *Past and Present: The Construction of Aboriginality*. 1988. Reprint, Canberra, Australia: Aboriginal Studies Press, 1994.

Berkhofer, Robert F., Jr. *The White Man's Indian: Images of the American Indian from Columbus to the Present*. New York: Random House, 1978.

Berlo, Janet Catherine. "Artists, Ethnographers, and Historians: Plains Indian Graphic

Arts in the Nineteenth Century—and Beyond." In *Transforming Images: The Art of Silver Horn and His Successors*, by Robert G. Donnelley, 27–45. Chicago: University of Chicago Press, 2000.

———. "'It's Up To You—': Individuality, Community and Cosmopolitanism in Navajo Weaving." In *Weaving Is Life: Navajo Weavings from the Edwin L. & Ruth E. Kennedy Southwest Native American Collection*, edited by Jennifer McLerran, 34–47. Athens, Ohio: Kennedy Museum of Art, Ohio University / Seattle: University of Washington Press, 2006.

Berlo, Janet C., and Ruth B. Phillips. *Native North American Art*. Oxford History of Art. New York: Oxford University Press, 1998.

Best, Elsdon. *The Maori Canoe: An Account of Various Types of Vessels Used by the Maori of New Zealand in Former Times, with Some Description of Those of the Isles of the Pacific, and a Brief Account of the Peopling of New Zealand*. Wellington, New Zealand: Board of Maori Ethnological Research, for the Dominion Museum, 1925. Reprint, Wellington: Government Printer, 1976. Reprint, Wellington: Te Papa Press, 2005.

Binney, Judith. "Maori Oral Traditions, Pakeha Written Texts: Two Forms of Telling History." *New Zealand Journal of History* 21, no. 1 (1987): 16–28.

Blish, Helen H. *A Pictographic History of the Oglala Sioux*. Ledger art by Amos Bad Heart Bull. Lincoln: University of Nebraska Press, 1967.

Blue Cloud, Peter. *Elderberry Flute Song: Contemporary Coyote Tales*. Buffalo, N.Y.: White Pine Press, 1982.

Bonar, Eulalie H., ed. *Woven by the Grandmothers: Nineteenth-Century Navajo Textiles from the National Museum of the American Indian*. Washington, D.C.: Smithsonian Institution Press, 1996.

Booklist. Unsigned review of *Indians' Summer*, by Nasnaga. June 15, 1975.

Boyd, Maurice. *Kiowa Voices*. With Lynn Pauahty. 2 vols. Fort Worth: Texas Christian University Press, 1981–83.

Brooks, Lisa. *The Common Pot: The Recovery of Native Space in the Northeast*. Minneapolis: University of Minnesota Press, 2008.

Buck, Sir Peter (Te Rangi Hiroa). *Vikings of the Sunrise*. Philadelphia: J. B. Lippincott Company, 1938.

———. *The Coming of the Maori*. Wellington, New Zealand: Maori Purposes Fund Board, Whitcombe and Tombs, 1949.

Burke, Christina E. "*Waniyetu Wówapi*: An Introduction to the Lakota Winter Count Tradition." In *The Year the Stars Fell: Lakota Winter Counts at the Smithsonian*, edited by Candace S. Greene and Russell Thornton, 1–11. Lincoln: University of Nebraska Press, 2007.

Burnum Burnum. "The Burnum Burnum Declaration." *Anthology of Australian Aboriginal Literature*, edited by Anita Heiss and Peter Minter, 124–25. Montreal: McGill-Queen's University Press, 2008.

———. *Burnum Burnum's Aboriginal Australia: A Traveller's Guide*. Edited by David Stewart. North Ryde, Australia: Angus and Robertson, 1988.

Cajete, Gregory. *Native Science: Natural Laws of Interdependence*. With a foreword by Leroy Little Bear. Santa Fe, N.Mex.: Clear Light, 2000.

Callahan, S. Alice. *Wynema, A Child of the Forest.* 1891. Reprint, Lincoln: University of Nebraska Press, 1997.

Calloway, Colin G. *The Shawnees and the War for America.* New York: Penguin Books, 2007.

Carlsen, G. Robert, Tony Manna, and Jan Yoder. Review of *Indians' Summer*, by Nasnaga. *English Journal* 65, no. 1 (January 1976): 96.

Carter, Jacq. "Comparatively Speaking, There Is No Struggle." In *Whetu Moana: Contemporary Polynesian Poems in English*, edited by Albert Wendt, Reina Whaitiri, and Robert Sullivan, 40–41. Auckland, New Zealand: Auckland University Press, 2003.

CH. Review of *Indians' Summer*, by Nasnaga. *New Republic* March 29, 1975, 33.

Chaudhuri, Joy, ed. *Indians and 1976: Native Americans Look at the American Revolution Bicentennial Observance.* Tucson: University of Arizona Amerind Club, 1973.

Chief Eagle, Dallas. *Winter Count.* 1967. Reprint, Lincoln: University of Nebraska Press, 2003.

Clark, D. Anthony Tyeeme, and Norman R. Yetman. "'To Feel the Drumming Earth Come Upward': Indigenizing the American Studies Discipline, Field, Movement." *American Studies* 46, nos. 3–4 (Fall/Winter 2005): 7–21.

Condliffe, J. B. *Te Rangi Hiroa: The Life of Sir Peter Buck.* Christchurch, New Zealand: Whitcombe & Tombs, 1971.

Cooper, Karen Coody. *Spirited Encounters: American Indians Protest Museum Policies and Practices.* Lanham, Md.: AltaMira Press, 2008.

Cox, James H. *Muting White Noise: Native American and European Novel Traditions.* Norman: University of Oklahoma Press, 2006.

Dale, E. E. Review of *They Came Here First: The Epic of the American Indian*, by D'Arcy McNickle. *The Americas* 7, no. 3 (January 1951): 382–84.

Deloria, Ella Cara. *Waterlily.* Lincoln: University of Nebraska Press, 1988.

Deloria, Vine, Jr. *Custer Died for Your Sins: An Indian Manifesto.* New York: Collier-Macmillan, 1969.

———. *God Is Red.* New York: Grosset and Dunlap, 1973.

———. *Behind the Trail of Broken Treaties: An Indian Declaration of Independence.* New York: Delta, 1974.

———. "The Next Three Years: A Time for Change." *The Indian Historian* 7, no. 2 (Spring 1974): 25–27.

———. "1976: The Desperate Need for Understanding." *Cross Talk* 3, no. 4 (December 1974-February 1975): part 8.

———. "Why Indians Aren't Celebrating the Bicentennial." In *Spirit and Reason: The Vine Deloria, Jr. Reader*, edited by Barbara Deloria, Kristen Foehner, and Sam Scinta, 199–205. Golden, Colo.: Fulcrum, 1999.

———. "A Last Word from the First Americans." *New York Times Magazine*, July 4, 1976, 80.

———. "We Pledge Allegiance: A Conversation with Vine Deloria, Jr." *Journal of Current Social Issues* 13, no. 1 (Winter 1976): 12–17.

———. "The American Revolution and the American Indian: Problems in the Recovery of a Usable Past." In *Spirit and Reason: The Vine Deloria, Jr. Reader*, edited by Barbara Deloria, Kristen Foehner, and Sam Scinta, 206–22. Golden, Colo.: Fulcrum, 1999.

DeLoughrey, Elizabeth M. *Routes and Roots: Navigating Caribbean and Pacific Island Literatures.* Honolulu: University of Hawaiʻi Press, 2007.

Department of Citizenship and Immigration, Indian Affairs Branch. *The Indian in Transition: The Indian Today.* Ottawa, ON: Queen's Printer, 1962.

Department of Maori Affairs. *The Maori Today.* 3rd ed. Wellington, New Zealand: Government Printer, 1964.

Donnelley, Robert G. *Transforming Images: The Art of Silver Horn and His Successors.* With contributions from Janet Catherine Berlo and Candace S. Greene. Chicago: University of Chicago Press, 2000.

Dorian, Edith, and W. N. Wilson. *Hokahey! American Indians Then and Now.* New York: McGraw-Hill, 1957.

Dudoit, D. Māhealani. "Carving a Hawaiian Aesthetic." *ʻŌiwi: A Native Hawaiian Journal* 1 (1998): 20–26.

Duffek, Karen, and Charlotte Townsend-Gault, eds. *Bill Reid and Beyond: Expanding on Modern Native Art.* Vancouver, Canada: Douglas & McIntyre / Seattle: University of Washington Press, 2004.

Dunstan, William. "Canadian Indians Today." *Canadian Geographical Journal* 67, no. 6 (December 1963): 182–93.

Dutton, Bertha Pauline. *Navajo Weaving Today.* Rev. ed. Santa Fe: Museum of New Mexico Press, 1975.

———. *New Mexico's Indians of Today.* Santa Fe: Tourist Division of the New Mexico Department of Development, 1964.

Eastman, Charles A. (Ohiyesa). *The Indian To-day: The Past and Future of the First American.* Garden City, N.Y.: Doubleday, Page, and Company, 1915. Reprint, New York: AMS Press, 1975.

Elliott, Emory, Louis Freitas Caton, and Jeffrey Rhyne, eds. *Aesthetics in a Multicultural Age.* New York: Oxford University Press, 2002.

Evans, Jeff. *Nga Waka o Nehera: The First Voyaging Canoes.* Auckland, New Zealand: Reed Publishing, 1997.

Evers, Lawrence J. Review of *Indians' Summer,* by Nasnaga. *American Indian Quarterly* 1, no. 4 (Winter 1974–1975): 294–95.

———. "Words and Place: A Reading of *House Made of Dawn.*" In *Critical Perspectives on Native American Fiction,* edited by Richard F. Fleck, 114–33. Washington, D.C.: Three Continents Press, 1993.

Fenton, William N. Review of *They Came Here First: The Epic of the American Indian,* by D'Arcy McNickle. *American Anthropologist* 52, no. 4 (October/December 1950): 546–47.

Finney, Ben. "Myth, Experiment, and the Reinvention of Polynesian Voyaging." *American Anthropologist* 93, no. 2 (June 1991): 383–404.

Firth, Raymond. Review of *The Coming of the Maori,* by Sir Peter Buck. *Man* 51 (August 1951): 112–13.

Foley, Gary. "The Australian Labor Party and the *Native Title Act.*" In *Sovereign Sub-*

jects: Indigenous Sovereignty Matters, edited by Aileen Moreton-Robinson, 118–39. Crows Nest, New South Wales: Allen & Unwin, 2007.

Forbes, Jack. *Aztecas del Norte: The Chicanos of Aztlan.* Greenwich, Conn.: Fawcett, 1973.

———. "It's Time to Throw Off the White Man's Names." *Akwesasne Notes* 4, no. 2 (March 1972): 31.

Forrest, Peter. "Tudawali, Robert (1929?—1967)." In *Australian Dictionary of Biography,* 16:419–20. Melbourne: Melbourne University Press, 2002.

Freling, Anne. Review of *Indians' Summer,* by Nasnaga. *Library Journal* 100, no. 9 (May 1975): 882.

Gansworth, Eric. *Nickel Eclipse: Iroquois Moon.* East Lansing: Michigan State University Press, 2000.

———. *A Half-Life of Cardio-Pulmonary Function: Poems and Paintings.* Syracuse, N.Y.: Syracuse University Press, 2008.

Gatty, Harold. *The Raft Book: Lore of the Sea and Sky.* New York: G. Grady Press, 1943.

Gentry, Carole M., and Donald A. Grinde Jr., eds. *The Unheard Voices: American Indian Responses to the Columbian Quincentenary 1492–1992.* National Conference Proceedings Series 3. Los Angeles: American Indian Studies Center, University of California, 1994.

Gilbert, Kevin, ed. *Inside Black Australia: An Anthology of Aboriginal Poetry.* New York: Penguin, 1988.

Glancy, Diane. *Flutie.* Wakefield, R.I.: Moyer Bell, 1998.

Glick, Paula Brown, and Jeremy Beckett. "Marie Reay, 1922–2004." *Australian Journal of Anthropology* 16, no. 3 (December 2005): 394–96.

Glotzhober, Robert C., and Bradley T. Lepper. *Serpent Mound: Ohio's Enigmatic Effigy Mound.* Columbus: Ohio Historical Society, 1994.

Gonzalez, Ray, ed. *Without Discovery: A Native Response to Columbus.* Seattle: Broken Moon Press, 1992.

Grace, Patricia. *Potiki.* 1986. Reprint, Honolulu: University of Hawai'i Press, 1995.

———. *Baby No-Eyes.* Honolulu: University of Hawai'i Press, 1999.

Green, Joseph C. Review of *They Came Here First: The Epic of the American Indian,* by D'Arcy McNickle. *The American Historical Review* 55, no. 4 (July 1950): 947–48.

Greene, Candace S. "Changing Times, Changing Views: Silver Horn as a Bridge to Nineteenth- and Twentieth-Century Kiowa Art." In *Transforming Images: The Art of Silver Horn and His Successors,* by Robert G. Donnelley, 15–25. Chicago: University of Chicago Press, 2000.

———. *Silver Horn: Master Illustrator of the Kiowas.* Norman: University of Oklahoma Press, 2002.

———. "Calendars from Other Plains Tribes." In *The Year the Stars Fell: Lakota Winter Counts at the Smithsonian,* edited by Candace S. Greene and Russell Thornton, 299–316. Lincoln: University of Nebraska Press, 2007.

Greene, Candace S., and Russell Thornton, eds. *The Year the Stars Fell: Lakota Winter Counts at the Smithsonian.* Lincoln: University of Nebraska Press, 2007.

Gridley, Marion E., ed. and comp. *Indians of Today.* Chicago: Lakeside Press, 1936.

———. *Indians of Today.* 2nd ed. Chicago: Millar Publishing, 1947.

———. *Indians of Today.* 3rd ed. Chicago: Towertown Press, 1960.

———. *Indians of Today.* 4th ed. Chicago: I.C.F.P., 1971.

Griffin-Pierce, Trudy. *Earth Is My Mother, Sky Is My Father: Space, Time, and Astronomy in Navajo Sandpainting.* Albuquerque: University of New Mexico Press, 1992.

Guardian. "Australia's Apology in Full." February 12, 2008. http://www.guardian .co.uk/world/2008/feb/12/australia.aborigines.

Habib, Rowley (Rore Hapipi). "When I of Fish Eat." *Te Ao Hou* 40 (September 1962): 4.

———. *The Raw Men: Selected Poems 1954–2004.* Vol. 1. Taupo, New Zealand: O-A-Tia Publishers, 2006.

Harlan, Judith. *American Indians Today: Issues and Conflicts.* An Impact Book. New York: Franklin Watts, 1987.

Harris, Helen L. "The Bi-Centennial Celebration and the Native American." *Indian Historian* 7, no. 4 (Fall 1974): 5–8.

Hau'ofa, Epeli. "Our Sea of Islands." In *We Are the Ocean: Selected Works,* 27–40. Honolulu: University of Hawai'i Press, 2008.

Hedge Coke, Allison Adelle. *Blood Run: Free Verse Play.* Cambridge, UK: Salt Publishing, 2006.

Hedge Coke, Allison Adelle, ed. Introduction to *Sing: Poetry from the Indigenous Americas,* 1–19. Tucson: University of Arizona Press, 2011.

Heiss, Anita, and Peter Minter, eds. *Anthology of Australian Aboriginal Literature.* Montreal: McGill-Queen's University Press, 2008.

Henderson, Jennifer, and Pauline Wakeham, eds. "Aboriginal Redress." Special issue, *English Studies in Canada* 35, no. 1 (March 2009).

Holm, Bill. *Northwest Coast Indian Art: An Analysis of Form.* Seattle: University of Washington Press, 1965.

Holm, Bill, and William Reid. *Form and Freedom: A Dialogue on Northwest Coast Indian Art.* Houston, Tex.: Institute for the Arts, Rice University, 1975.

———. *Indian Art of the Northwest Coast: A Dialogue on Craftsmanship and Aesthetics.* Seattle: University of Washington Press, 1976.

Holt, John Dominis. *On Being Hawaiian.* Honolulu: Star-Bulletin Printing, 1964.

———. *On Being Hawaiian.* 2nd ed. With a new introduction. Honolulu: Topgallant Publishing, 1974.

Ho'omanawanui, Ku'ualoha. "He Lei Ho'oheno no nā Kau a Kau: Language, Performance, and Form in Hawaiian Poetry." *The Contemporary Pacific* 17, no. 1 (2005): 29–81.

Howe, Craig. "Keep Your Thoughts above the Trees: Ideas on Developing and Presenting Tribal Histories." In *Clearing a Path: Theorizing the Past in Native American Studies,* edited by Nancy Shoemaker, 161–79. New York: Routledge, 2002.

Howe, LeAnne. *Shell Shaker.* San Francisco: Aunt Lute Books, 2001.

———. *Miko Kings: An Indian Baseball Story.* San Francisco: Aunt Lute Books, 2007.

Huhndorf, Shari M. *Going Native: Indians in the American Cultural Imagination.* Ithaca, N.Y.: Cornell University Press, 2001.

Ihimaera, Witi. "The Whale." In *Pounamu, Pounamu,* 115–22. Auckland, New Zealand: Heinemann, 1972.

———. "Te Tohorā." In *Pounamu, Pounamu*, Māori edition, translated by Jean Wikiriwhi, 121–28. Auckland, New Zealand: Heinemann, 1986.

———. *The Whale Rider*. Illustrated by John Hovell. Auckland, New Zealand: Heinemann, 1987.

———. *Te Kaieke Tohorā*. Translated by Timoti Karetu. Illustrated by John Hovell. Auckland, New Zealand: Reed Publishing, 1995.

———. "The Whale." In *Pounamu, Pounamu*, thirtieth-anniversary edition, 152–62. Auckland, New Zealand: Heinemann, 2003.

———. *The Whale Rider*. Orlando, Fla.: Harcourt, 2003.

———. *The Whale Rider*. Twentieth-anniversary edition. Auckland, New Zealand: Reed Books, 2007.

———. "A One-Man Cultural Revolution?" Interview by Jehan Casinader. *Mana* 87 (April/May 2009): 70–71.

Jahnke, Robert. "Voices beyond the *Pae*." In *Double Vision: Art Histories and Colonial Histories in the Pacific*, edited by Nicholas Thomas and Diane Losche, 193–209. Cambridge: Cambridge University Press, 1999.

———. "Māori Art towards the Millennium." In *State of the Māori Nation: Twenty-first Century Issues in Aotearoa*, edited by Malcolm Mulholland and contributors, 41–51. Auckland, New Zealand: Reed, 2006.

Johansen, J. Prytz. *The Maori and His Religion in Its Non-ritualistic Aspects*. Copenhagen: Munksgaard, 1954.

Johnson, E. Pauline. *The Moccasin Maker*. 1913. Reprint, Tucson: University of Arizona Press, 1987.

Johnston, Tim. "Australia to Apologize to Aborigines for Past Mistreatment." *New York Times*, January 31, 2008.

Kelsey, Penelope Myrtle. *Tribal Theory in Native American Literature: Dakota and Haudenosaunee Writing and Indigenous Worldviews*. Lincoln: University of Nebraska Press, 2008.

Kent, Kate Peck. *The Story of Navaho Weaving*. Phoenix: Heard Museum, 1961.

King, Thomas. *Green Grass, Running Water*. New York: Bantam, 1993.

———. *The Truth About Stories: A Native Narrative*. Minneapolis: University of Minnesota Press, 2003.

Kirk, Ruth. *David, Young Chief of the Quileutes: An American Indian Today*. New York: Harcourt, Brace and World, 1967.

Krupat, Arnold. *All That Remains: Varieties of Indigenous Expression*. Lincoln: University of Nebraska Press, 2009.

Langton, Marcia. "Aboriginal Art and Film: The Politics of Representation." In *Blacklines: Contemporary Critical Writing by Indigenous Australians*, edited by Michelle Grossman, 109–24. Melbourne, Australia: Melbourne University Press, 2003.

Larsen, Dean L. *American Indians Today*. Provo, Utah: Division of Continuing Education, Brigham Young University, 1965.

Larson, Charles R. *American Indian Fiction*. Albuquerque: University of New Mexico Press, 1978.

León-Portilla, Miguel, ed. "Indians in the Hemisphere Today: Guide to the Indian

Population." Translated by Virginia B. García. In "Indianist Yearbook," no. 22, supplement, *America Indigena* (1962).

Lepper, Bradley T. "Tracking Ohio's Great Hopewell Road." *Archaeology*, November/ December 1995, 52–56.

———. *The Newark Earthworks: A Wonder of the Ancient World*. Columbus: Ohio Historical Society, 2002.

Levine, Stuart, and Nancy O. Lurie, eds. "The Indian Today." Special issue, *Midcontinent American Studies Journal* 6, no. 2 (Fall 1965).

———. *The American Indian Today*. Deland, Fla.: Everett Edwards, 1968. Reprint, Baltimore, Md.: Penguin Books, 1970, 1972.

Lewis, David. *We, the Navigators: The Ancient Art of Landfinding in the Pacific*. 2nd ed. Honolulu: University of Hawai'iPress, 1994. First published in 1972 by University of Hawai'iPress.

Lincoln, Kenneth. *Native American Renaissance*. Berkeley: University of California Press, 1983.

Linton, Ralph. Review of *The Coming of the Maori*, by Sir Peter Buck. *American Anthropologist* 52, no. 3 (July–September 1950): 397–98.

Lonetree, Amy. "Museums as Sites of Decolonization: Truth Telling in National and Tribal Museums." In *Contesting Knowledge: Museums and Indigenous Perspectives*, edited by Susan Sleeper-Smith, 322–37. Lincoln: University of Nebraska Press, 2009.

Lopenzina, Drew. "What to the American Indian Is the Fourth of July? Moving beyond Abolitionist Rhetoric in William Apess's *Eulogy on King Philip*." *American Literature* 82, no. 4 (December 2010): 673–99.

Loram, C. T., and T. F. McIlwraith, eds. *The North American Indian Today*. Toronto, Canada: University of Toronto Press, 1943.

Losch, Naomi. "Blood Quantum." In *Whetu Moana: Contemporary Polynesian Poems in English*, edited by Albert Wendt, Reina Whaitiri, and Robert Sullivan, 120. Auckland, New Zealand: Auckland University Press, 2003.

Leuthold, Steven. *Indigenous Aesthetics: Native Art, Media, and Identity*. Austin: University of Texas Press, 1998.

Marsden, Peter. H. "From Waka to Whakapapa, Or: Carving Your Own Canoe. The Verse of Robert Sullivan." New Zealand Electronic Poetry Centre. Last Modified May 11, 2001. www.nzepc.auckland.ac.nz/authors/Sullivan/marsden.asp.

Martinez, David. "Along the Horizon a World Appears: George Morrison and the Pursuit of an American Indian Esthetic." In *American Indian Thought: Philosophical Essays*, edited by Anne Waters, 256–62. Oxford, UK: Blackwell, 2004.

McLerran, Jennifer. "Textile as Cultural Text: Contemporary Navajo Weaving as Autoethnographic Practice." In *Weaving Is Life: Navajo Weavings from the Edwin L. & Ruth E. Kennedy Southwest Native American Collection*, edited by Jennifer McLerran, 8–33. Athens, Ohio: Kennedy Museum of Art, Ohio University/ Seattle: University of Washington Press, 2006.

M'Closkey, Kathy M. *Swept under the Rug: A Hidden History of Navajo Weaving*. Albuquerque: University of New Mexico Press, 2002.

McNickle, D'Arcy. "The American Indian Today." *Missouri Archaeologist* 5, no. 2 (September 1939): 1–10.

———. *They Came Here First: The Epic of the American Indian.* The Peoples of America Series. Philadelphia: J. B. Lippincott Company, 1949.

———. "The Indian Tests the Mainstream." *Nation,* September 26, 1966, 275–79.

———. *Native American Tribalism: Indian Survivals and Renewals.* Institute of Race Relations / New York: Oxford University Press, 1973.

———. *They Came Here First: The Epic of the American Indian.* Rev. ed. New York: Harper and Row, 1975.

Mead, Sidney Moko. "Nga Timunga Me Nga Paringa O Te Mana Maori: The Ebb and Flow of Mana Maori and the Changing Context of Maori Art." In *Te Maori: Maori Art from New Zealand Collections,* edited by Sidney Moko Mead, 20–36. New York: Abrams, 1984.

———. "Te Tupu Te Toi Whakairo Ki Aotearoa: Becoming Maori Art." In *Te Maori: Maori Art from New Zealand Collections,* edited by Sidney Moko Mead, 63–75. New York: Abrams, 1984.

Megill, William J. "Editor's Note-Book." *Canadian Geographical Journal* 67, no. 6 (December 1963): v.

Mignolo, Walter D. *Local Histories/Global Designs: Coloniality, Subaltern Knowledges, and Border Thinking.* Princeton, N.J.: Princeton University Press, 2000.

Mignolo, Walter D., and Freya Schiwy. "Double Translation: Transculturation and the Colonial Difference." In *Translation and Ethnography: The Anthropological Challenge of Intercultural Understanding,* edited by Trullio Maranhao and Bernhard Streck, 3–29. Tucson: University of Arizona Press, 2003.

Milliken, Robert. "Obituary: Burnum Burnum." *London Independent,* August 20, 1997.

Momaday, N. Scott. *House Made of Dawn.* New York: Harper and Row, 1968.

———. "The Man Made of Words." In *Indian Voices: The First Convocation of American Indian Scholars,* 49–84. San Francisco: Indian Historian Press, 1970.

———. "The Gourd Dancer." In *The Gourd Dancer,* 35–37. New York: Harper and Row, 1976.

———. *The Names: A Memoir.* New York: Harper and Row, 1976.

———. "Carnegie, Oklahoma, 1919." In *In the Presence of the Sun: Stories and Poems, 1961–1991,* 136. New York: St. Martin's, 1992.

———. Foreword to *Earth Is My Mother, Sky Is My Father: Space, Time and Astronomy in Navajo Sandpainting,* by Trudy Griffin-Pierce, xv–xvii. Albuquerque: University of New Mexico Press, 1992.

———. "Sacred Places." In *The Man Made of Words: Essays, Stories, Passages,* 113–117. New York: St. Martin's, 1997.

Morrissey, Philip. "Restoring a Future to a Past." *Kunapipi* 10, nos. 1–2 (1988): 10–15.

Mullard, Chris. *Aborigines in Australia Today.* Woden, ACT, Australia: National Aborigine Forum, 1974. Reprint, ACT: Australian National University, Centre for Continuing Education, 1976.

Naranjo-Morse, Nora. *Mud Woman: Poems from the Clay.* Tucson: University of Arizona Press, 1992.

Narogin, Mudrooroo (Colin Johnson). "Paperbark." In "Aboriginal Culture Today," edited by Anna Rutherford. Special issue, *Kunapipi* 10, nos. 1–2 (1988): 36–49.

Nasnaga (Roger Russell). *Indians' Summer.* New York: Harper and Row, 1975.

———. "Two Paths to Eternity." *Antaeus* 25/26 (Spring/Summer 1977): 83–92.

———. *Faces beneath the Grass.* Centerville, Ohio: n.e.i. productions, 1979.

———. *Warriors.* Dayton, Ohio: Nas'Naga Enterprises, 1979.

National Museum of the American Indian. *Essays on Native Modernism: Complexity and Contradiction in American Indian Art.* NMAI Editions. Washington, D.C.: Smithsonian, 2006.

Navajo Nation. "Navajo Nation Bids Farewell to Preeminent Educator Dr. Robert A. Roessel, Jr., First Diné College President." Press release. February 18, 2006. http://www.navajo-nsn.gov/images/pdf%20releases/George%20Hardeen/feb06/Navajo%20Nation%20loses%20renowned%20educator%20for%20Feb%20%2018.pdf.

Neihardt, John G. *Black Elk Speaks: Being the Life of a Holy Man of the Oglala Sioux.* 1932. Reprint, Lincoln: University of Nebraska Press, 1961.

Nelson, Anne. *Nga Waka Maori: Maori Canoes.* Auckland, New Zealand: MacMillan, 1991.

Ngata, H. M. *English–Maori Dictionary.* Wellington, New Zealand: Learning Media, 1993.

Nicholas, Darcy. "Introduction: Breath of the Land." In *Manawa—Pacific Heartbeat: A Celebration of Contemporary Maori and Northwest Coast Art,* edited by Nigel Reading and Gary Wyatt, 7–25. Seattle: University of Washington Press, 2006.

Nicolar, Joseph. *The Life and Traditions of the Red Man.* 1893. Modern edition, edited, annotated, and with an introduction by Annette Kolodny. Durham, N.C.: Duke University Press, 2007.

Norst, Marlene J. *Burnum Burnum: A Warrior for Peace.* East Roseville, Australia: Kangaroo Press, 1999.

O'Connor, Mark. "Aboriginal Literature Becomes a Force." In "Aboriginal Culture Today," edited by Anna Rutherford. Special issue, *Kunapipi* 10, nos. 1–2 (1988): 246–53.

Office of Native American Programs, American Revolution Bicentennial Administration. *Annual Report.* Denver, Colo.: Government Printer, 1975.

Orbell, Margaret. *The Illustrated Encyclopedia of Maori Myth and Legend.* Christchurch, New Zealand: Canterbury University Press, 1995.

———. *A Concise Encyclopedia of Māori Myth and Legend.* Christchurch, New Zealand: Canterbury University Press, 1998.

Ortiz, Simon J., ed. *Beyond the Reach of Time and Change: Native American Reflections on the Frank A. Rinehart Photograph Collection.* Tucson: University of Arizona Press, 2004.

Ortiz, Simon J. *from Sand Creek.* Tucson: University of Arizona Press, 1981.

Oskison, John Milton. *The Singing Bird: A Cherokee Novel.* Edited by Timothy B. Powell and Melinda Smith Mullikin. Norman: University of Oklahoma Press, 2007.

Owens, Louis. "N. Scott Momaday." In *Conversations with N. Scott Momaday,* edited by Matthias Schubnell, 178–91. Jackson: University of Mississippi Press, 1997.

———. *Other Destinies: Understanding the American Indian Novel.* Norman: University of Oklahoma Press, 1992.

Palmer, Gus, Jr. *Telling Stories the Kiowa Way.* Tucson: University of Arizona Press, 2003.

Parker, Dorothy R. *Singing an Indian Song: A Biography of D'Arcy McNickle*. Lincoln: University of Nebraska Press, 1992.

Parker, Robert Dale. *The Invention of Native American Literature*. Ithaca, N.Y.: Cornell University Press, 2003.

Parker, Robert Dale, ed. *Changing Is Not Vanishing: A Collection of American Indian Poetry to 1930*. Philadelphia: University of Pennsylvania Press, 2010.

Penney, David. "Native Art." In *American Indian Nations: Yesterday, Today, and Tomorrow*, edited by George Horse Capture, Duane Champagne, and Chandler C. Jackson, 51–58. Lanham, Md.: AltaMira Press, 2007.

Perez, Craig Santos. Review of *Star Waka*, by Robert Sullivan. *Octopus Magazine* 9. www.octopusmagazine.com/issue09/perez.htm.

Press, Robert M. Review of *Indians' Summer*, by Nasnaga. *Christian Science Monitor*, March 26, 1975.

Raymer, Robert G. Review of *They Came Here First: The Epic of the American Indian*, by D'Arcy McNickle. *The Pacific Historical Review* 19, no. 1 (February 1950): 59–60.

Reading, Nigel, and Gary Wyatt. *Manawa—Pacific Heartbeat: A Celebration of Contemporary Maori and Northwest Coast Art*. With an introduction by Darcy Nicholas. Seattle: University of Washington Press, 2006.

Reay, Marie, ed. *Aborigines Now: New Perspective in the Study of Aboriginal Communities*. Sydney, Australia: Angus and Robertson, 1964.

Reid, Bill. *Solitary Raven: The Selected Writings of Bill Reid*. Edited and with an introduction by Robert Bringhurst. Vancouver, Canada: Douglas & McIntyre / Seattle: University of Washington Press, 2000.

Revard, Carter. "Discovery of the New World." In *Voices of the Rainbow: Contemporary Poetry by American Indians*, edited by Kenneth Rosen, 99–101. New York: Viking Press, 1975.

———. "Discovery of the New World." In *Ponca War Dancers*, 43–44. Norman, Okla.: Point Riders Press, 1980.

———. "Herbs of Healing: American Values in American Indian Literature." In *Speak to Me Words: Essays on Contemporary American Indian Poetry*, edited by Dean Rader and Janice Gould, 173–92. Tucson: University of Arizona Press, 2003.

———. "Discovery of the New World." In *How the Songs Come Down: New and Selected Poems*, 97–98. Cambridge, UK: Salt Publishing, 2005.

Rickard, Jolene. "Sovereignty: A Line in the Sand." In "Strong Hearts: Native American Visions and Voices." Special issue, *Aperture* 139 (Summer 1995): 51–54.

Roemer, Kenneth M. "Ancient Children at Play—Lyric, Petroglyphic, and Ceremonial." In *Critical Perspectives on Native American Fiction*, edited by Richard F. Fleck, 99–113. Washington, D.C.: Three Continents Press, 1993.

Robinson, Dorothy F. *Navajo Indians Today*. San Antonio, Tex.: Naylor, 1966.

———. *Navajo Indians Today*. Revised and expanded edition. San Antonio, Tex.: Naylor, 1969.

Romain, William F. *Mysteries of the Hopewell: Astronomers, Geometers, and Magicians of the Eastern Woodlands*. Akron, Ohio: University of Akron Press, 2000.

Romain, William F., and Jarrod Burks. "LiDAR Assessment of the Newark Earthworks." Ohio Archaeological Council website. Last modified February 7, 2008.

http://www.ohioarchaeology.org/joomla/index.php?option=com_content&task=view&id=232&Itemid=32.

———. "LiDAR Analyses of Prehistoric Earthworks in Ross County, Ohio." Ohio Archaeological Council website. Last modified March 3, 2008. http://www.ohioarchaeology.org/joomla/index.php?option=com_content&task=view&id=233&Itemid=32.

Rosaldo, Renato. *Culture and Truth: The Remaking of Social Analysis.* Boston: Beacon Press, 1989.

Rose, Wendy. *Long Division: A Tribal History.* New York: Strawberry Press, 1976.

———. *Lost Copper.* Banning, Calif.: Malki Museum Press, 1980.

———. *The Halfbreed Chronicles & Other Poems.* Albuquerque, N.Mex.: West End Press, 1985.

Rosen, Kenneth, ed. *Voices of the Rainbow: Contemporary Poetry by American Indians.* New York: Viking Press, 1975.

Rudd, Kevin. "Apology to Australia's Indigenous Peoples." Australian Government website. February 13, 2008. http://australia.gov.au/about-australia/our-country/our-people/apology-to-australias-indigenous-peoples.

Ruppert, James. *Mediation in Contemporary Native American Fiction.* Norman: University of Oklahoma Press, 1995.

Rutherford, Anna, ed. "Aboriginal Culture Today." Special issue, *Kunapipi* 10, nos. 1–2 (1988).

Said, Edward W. *Orientalism.* New York: Vintage, 1978.

Salmond, Anne. "Nga Huarahi O Te Ao Maori: Pathways in the Maori World." In *Te Maori: Maori Art from New Zealand Collections,* edited by Sidney Moko Mead, 109–37. New York: Abrams, 1984.

Sarris, Greg. *Keeping Slug Woman Alive: A Holistic Approach to American Indian Texts.* Berkeley: University of California Press, 1993.

Scarberry-Garcia, Susan. *Landmarks of Healing: A Study of "House Made of Dawn."* Albuquerque: University of New Mexico Press, 1990.

Schubnell, Matthias. *N. Scott Momaday: The Cultural and Literary Background.* Norman: University of Oklahoma Press, 1985.

Schwimmer, Erik, ed. *The Maori People in the Nineteen-Sixties: A Symposium.* With the cooperation of John Forster, William Parker, and James E. Ritchie. Auckland, New Zealand: Blackwood and Janet Paul, 1968.

Sciascia, Piri. "Ka Pu Te Ruha, Ka Hao Te Rangatahi: As the Old Net Piles Up on Shore, the New Net Goes Fishing." In *Te Maori: Maori Art from New Zealand Collections,* edited by Sidney Moko Mead, 156–66. New York: Abrams, 1984.

Silko, Leslie Marmon. *Ceremony.* 1977. Reprint, New York: Penguin, 1986.

Simmen, Edward, ed. *Pain and Promise: The Chicano Today.* New York: New American Library, 1972.

Simmons, J. L., and Barry Winograd. *It's Happening: A Portrait of the Youth Scene Today.* Santa Barbara, Calif.: Marc-Laird Publications, 1966.

Simpson, George E., and J. Milton Yinger, eds. "American Indians and American Life." Special issue, *Annals of the American Academy of Political and Social Sciences,* no. 311 (May 1957).

Smith, Linda Tuhiwai. *Decolonizing Methodologies: Research and Indigenous Peoples.* Dunedin, New Zealand: University of Otago Press / New York: Zed Books, 1999.

Smith, Martin (Cruz). *The Indians Won.* New York: Belmont Books, 1970.

Smith, Paul Chaat, and Robert Allen Warrior. *Like a Hurricane: The Indian Movement from Alcatraz to Wounded Knee.* New York: New Press, 1996.

Sullivan, Robert. *Star Waka.* Auckland, New Zealand: Auckland University Press, 1999.

———. *Voice Carried My Family.* Auckland, New Zealand: Auckland University Press, 2005.

———. "A Poetics of Culture: Others' and Ours, Separate and Commingled." *Landfall*, no. 211 (April 2006): 9–18.

Szabo, Joyce M. "Native American Art History: Questions of the Canon." In *Essays on Native Modernism: Complexity and Contradiction in American Indian Art*, 69–87. Washington, D.C.: National Museum of the American Indian, 2006.

Tapsell, Paul. *Pukaki: A Comet Returns.* Auckland, New Zealand: Reed, 2000.

Tate, Charles. "The Bicentennial." *Indian Historian* 7, no. 4 (Fall 1974): 35.

Taylor, Apirana. "Sad Joke on a Marae." In *Eyes of the Ruru*, 15. Wellington, New Zealand: Voice, 1979.

Taylor, Diana. *The Archive and the Repertoire: Performing Cultural Memory in the Americas.* Durham, N.C.: Duke University Press, 2003.

Te Awekotuku, Ngahuia. *Mana Wahine Maori: Selected Writings on Maori Women's Art, Culture, and Politics.* Auckland, New Zealand: New Women's Press, 1991.

Te Punga Somerville, Alice. "The Lingering War Captain: Maori Texts, Indigenous Contexts." *Journal of New Zealand Literature* 24, no. 2 (2007): 20–43.

Teuton, Sean. *Red Land, Red Power: Grounding Knowledge in the American Indian Novel.* Durham, N.C.: Duke University Press, 2008.

Thomas, Wesley. "Shil Yool T'ool: Personification of Navajo Weaving." In *Woven by the Grandmothers*, edited by Eulalie H. Bonar, 33–42. Washington, D.C.: Smithsonian, 1996.

Thompson, Hildegard. *Getting to Know American Indians Today.* Illustrated by Shannon Stirnweis. New York: Coward-McCann, 1965.

Torrence, Gaylord. *The American Indian Parfleche: A Tradition of Abstract Painting.* Seattle: University of Washington Press, 1994.

Trask, Haunani-Kay. *From a Native Daughter: Colonialism and Sovereignty in Hawai'i.* Rev. ed. Honolulu: University of Hawai'iPress, 1999.

Tremblay, Gail. *Indian Singing in 20th Century America.* Corvallis, Ore.: Calyx Books, 1990.

———. "Speaking in a Language of Vital Signs." In *Joe Feddersen: Vital Signs*, 35–51. Seattle: University of Washington Press, 2008.

Turnbull, David. "Pacific Navigation: An Alternative Scientific Tradition." In *Masons, Tricksters and Cartographers: Comparative Studies in the Sociology of Scientific and Indigenous Knowledge*, 131–60. Amsterdam: Harwood Academic Publishers, 2000.

Underhill, Ruth M. Review of *They Came Here First*, by D'Arcy McNickle. *Western Folklore* 10, no. 2 (April 1951): 190–91.

Upper Hutt Posse. "Tangata Whenua." On *Movement in Demand*. Tangata Records, 1995, compact disc.

———. "Tangata Whenua." On *Te Reo Māori Remixes*. Kia Kaha, 2002, compact disc.

Valandra, Edward C. "National Coexistence Is Our Bull Durham: Revisiting 'The Indian Today.'" *American Studies* 46, nos. 3–4 (Fall/Winter 2005): 59–76.

Virginia Quarterly Review. Unsigned review of *Indians' Summer*, by Nasnaga. 51 (Summer 1975): 124.

Vizenor, Gerald. *Manifest Manners: Postindian Warriors of Survivance*. Hanover, Conn.: Wesleyan University Press, 1994.

———. *Fugitive Poses: Native American Indian Scenes of Absence and Presence*. Lincoln: University of Nebraska Press, 2000.

———. "Aesthetics of Survivance: Literary Theory and Practice." In *Survivance: Narratives of Native Presence*, edited by Gerald Vizenor, 1–23. Lincoln: University of Nebraska Press, 2008.

Walters, Harry. "The Navajo Concept of Art." In *Woven by the Grandmothers*, edited by Eulalie H. Bonar, 29–31. Washington, D.C.: Smithsonian, 1996.

Warren, Robert Penn. "The Negro Now." *Look*, March 23, 1965, 23–31.

———. *Who Speaks for the Negro?* New York: Random House, 1965.

Warrior, Robert Allen. *Tribal Secrets: Recovering American Indian Intellectual Traditions*. Minneapolis: University of Minnesota Press, 1995.

———. *The People and the Word: Reading Native Nonfiction*. Minneapolis: University of Minnesota Press, 2005.

———. "Organizing Native American and Indigenous Studies." *PMLA* 123, no. 5 (October 2008): 1683–91.

Welch, James. *Fools Crow*. New York: Penguin, 1986.

Wilson, Norma. "Nesting in the Ruins." In *English Postcoloniality: Literatures from around the World*, edited by Radhika Mohanram and Gita Rajan, 179–87. Westport, Conn.: Greenwood Press, 1996.

Wilson, Waziyatawin Angela, and Michael Yellowbird, eds. *For Indigenous Eyes Only: A Decolonization Handbook*. Santa Fe, N. Mex.: School of American Research Press, 2005.

Witherspoon, Gary. *Language and Art in the Navajo Universe*. Ann Arbor: University of Michigan Press, 1977.

———. "The Semiotical Geometry of Navajo Weaving." In *Art in Small-Scale Societies: Contemporary Readings*, edited by Richard L. Anderson and Karen L. Field, 317–31. Englewood Cliffs, N.J.: Prentice Hall, 1993.

———. "Cultural Motifs in Navajo Weaving." In *North American Indian Anthropology: Essays on Society and Culture*, edited by Raymond J. DeMallie and Alfonso Ortiz, 355–76. Norman: University of Oklahoma Press, 1994.

Witherspoon, Gary, and Glen Peterson. *Dynamic Symmetry and Holistic Asymmetry in Navajo and Western Art and Cosmology*. New York: Peter Lang, 1995.

Womack, Craig. *Red on Red: Native American Literary Separatism*. Minneapolis: University of Minnesota Press, 1999.

Wong, Hertha Dawn. *Sending My Heart Back across the Years: Tradition and Innovation in Native American Autobiography*. New York: Oxford University Press, 1992.

Worth, Sol, and John Adair. *Through Navajo Eyes: An Exploration in Film Communication and Anthropology.* 1972. Rev. ed, with foreword and afterword by Richard Chalfen. Albuquerque: University of New Mexico Press, 1997.

Wroe, Nicholas. "Crime Pays." *Guardian,* March 26, 2005. http://www.guardian .co.uk/books/2005/mar/26/featuresreviews.guardianreview15.

Yinger, J. Milton, and George Eaton Simpson, eds. "American Indians Today." Special issue, *Annals of the American Academy of Political and Social Sciences,* no. 436 (March 1978).

Yothu Yindi. "Treaty." On *Tribal Voice.* Mushroom Records, 1992, compact disc.

Index

Chadwick Allen is professor of English at The Ohio State University. He is the author of *Blood Narrative: Indigenous Identity in American Indian and Maori Literary and Activist Texts.*